UNDERSTANDING THE FIRST AMENDMENT

UNDERSTANDING THE FIRST AMENDMENT

Fifth Edition

Russell L. Weaver
Professor of Law & Distinguished University Scholar
University of Louisville Louis D. Brandeis School of Law

ISBN: 978-1-6304-3071-9
eBook ISBN: 978-1-6304-3072-6

Library of Congress Cataloging-in-Publication Data
Weaver, Russell L., 1952- author
    Understanding the First Amendment / Russell L. Weaver, Professor of Law and Distinguished University Scholar,
University of Louisville Louis D. Brandeis School of Law. -- Fifth Edition.
      pages cm.
    Includes index.
    ISBN 978-1-6304-3071-9
    1. United States. Constitution. 1st Amendment. 2. Freedom of expression--United States. I. Title.
    KF4770.W43 2014
    342.7308'5--dc23
  2014008779

NOTE TO USERS
To ensure that you are using the latest materials available in this area, please be sure to periodically check the LexisNexis Law School web site for downloadable updates and supplements at www.lexisnexis.com/lawschool.

Editorial Offices
121 Chanlon Rd., New Providence, NJ 07974 (908) 464-6800
201 Mission St., San Francisco, CA 94105-1831 (415) 908-3200
www.lexisnexis.com

MATTHEW◆BENDER

Dedication

To Ben, Kate, and Laurence with love, RLW

Table of Contents

Table of Contents

Table of Contents

Table of Contents

Table of Contents

Table of Contents

Chapter 1

THE ORIGINS AND NATURE OF THE FIRST AMENDMENT

FOCAL POINTS FOR CHAPTER 1

- Historical and philosophical influences upon the First Amendment.
- The colonial experience with speech and religion.
- The uncertainty regarding the original intent of the First Amendment.
- The suppression of dissent in early American history.
- The judiciary's role in developing the First Amendment's meaning.
- The values underlying the First Amendment.
- Primary methods of First Amendment analysis.
- Content-based and content-neutral regulation.
- Speech categorization and balancing.
- Basic Establishment Clause principles.
- Basic Free Exercise Clause principles.

---

§ 1.01 BACKDROP TO THE FIRST AMENDMENT

Expressive and religious freedoms are deeply rooted in the nation's origins and evolution. Enumeration of freedom of speech, freedom of the press, freedom of religion, and protection against official establishment of a religion, coupled with the prominent placement of these guarantees in the United States Constitution's first amendment, indicates an interest of particularly high magnitude. The history of the First Amendment demonstrates, however, that these liberties and safeguards are not indefeasible. For practical purposes, their meaning is determined by processes of judicial review which determine whether the enumerated guarantee must give way to some higher priority. The law of the First Amendment thus is an accumulation of case law that marks the boundaries between the aforementioned liberties and government action.

First Amendment doctrine, like law generally, is a function of experience. Concepts of expressive and religious freedom evolved in response to official efforts to secure conformity of thought, expression, and belief. Given the gravitational pull of self-interest, official efforts to control these processes tend to be more effective in achieving formal than functional compliance. The colonial American experience is a case in point. Revolutionary sentiment eventually overcame professions of loyalty and undid objectionable regulation. Modern testament to this reality is evidenced on a variety of fronts.

Despite its illegality, obscenity thrives particularly through on-line technology. The ability of totalitarian regimes to manage information flow is challenged by the advent of new communications methodologies that can bypass traditional methods of control. With respect to religion, the Establishment Clause represents a strong and persisting response to the smothering experience of an intertwined church and state. The speech, press, and religion clauses collectively represent a sentiment that expressive and spiritual matters are better consigned to processes of autonomous rather than authoritarian selection.

[A]　Pre-Colonial Developments

In the course of history, freedom of expression and religion are relatively new realities. Intolerance of expressive and religious diversity have much longer traditions. Prior to the late seventeenth century, concepts like freedom of expression and religion largely were alien to those societies in which American law is firmly rooted. Those societies were dominated by two institutions: church and state. In England, political and religious authority merged so that even political decisions had a divine cast to them. The state thus was authenticated by the church, and dissent was intolerable both on religious and secular grounds.

Many who emigrated to the American colonies were seeking to escape the suffocating relationship between church and state in England. Individuals were persecuted because their religious views differed from official dogma. In those colonies, despite their origins, all colonies were not models of religious tolerance. Over time, some began to argue for a separation between church and state. Illustrative is Virginia where the leadership of Thomas Jefferson and James Madison produced the metaphorical "wall" between church and state. This model was not universally embraced in the colonial context. Some states aligned themselves with a particular church and established an official religion. For these states, the guarantee against establishment of religion ensured that the federal government would not compete with them on matters of faith.

Even before the technology of movable type established a basis for mass communication, English law had strong disincentives for expressive liberty. As early as the thirteenth century, England imposed the crime of seditious libel. Seditious libel was premised on the notion that the head of state could do no wrong and thus could not be criticized. Under the English legal system, there was no need to prove any harm in order to gain the conviction. Moreover, truth was not a defense since mere criticism of the state was the basis for liability. Indeed, on the theory that criticisms might do more harm, truth increased the gravity of the punishment.

Introduction of the printing press in the late fifteenth century provided church and state with the means to communicate, and propagate their commands, more effectively and efficiently. However, the ability to mass produce and disseminate information created correlatively higher risks to settled norms and orders. In an attempt to minimize the risk that the printing press might be used for purposes at odds with the state's objectives, England chose to license printing presses. The licensing system made printing subject to the crown's authorization. Printers and printing presses alike were controlled both with respect to numbers and functions. This result was accomplished by the creation of an official company to which all printing tasks were assigned. Official management of information was augmented by harsh penalties for criticizing church or state, systems of taxation, and prepublication review and censorship.

These suppressive means and tendencies eventually were challenged by new philosophies of reason and liberation. The emergence of natural law, a primary wellspring for the Declaration of Independence, established expressive freedom as a primary doctrinal value. Among natural law's primary exponents was John Locke, whose writings during the seventeenth century laid the groundwork for the future. Locke's theory, that the state's legitimacy depends upon the consent of the governed, had major implications for expressive and religious freedom and what eventually became the American system of representative governance. Particularly foundational for a system of freedom of expression was his sense that expressive freedom was a critical facilitator for the discovery of truth.

Complementing Locke's sentiments were the thoughts of John Milton, who identified expressive liberty as the most important freedom and advocated discernment of truth through free competition of ideas rather than official selection. As he put it:

> the liberty to know, to utter, and to argue freely according to conscience, [is] above all liberties. . . . Though all the winds of doctrine were let loose to play upon the earth, so Truth be in the field, we do injuriously by licensing and prohibiting to misdoubt her strength. Let her and falsehood grapple; whoever knew Truth put to the worse in free and open encounter.[1]

Milton's writings sketched out a concept that First Amendment case law eventually would style as the marketplace of ideas. As Justice Holmes noted, in terms paralleling Milton's sentiments, "the ultimate good is better reached by free trade in ideas [and] the best test of truth is the power of thought to get itself accepted in the marketplace of ideas."[2]

Milton's argument that prior restraint undermines the interest of truth also prefaced William Blackstone's discernment that "liberty of the press is . . . essential to the nature of a free state, [and] consists in laying no previous restraints upon publications."[3] Blackstone noted, however, that an individual who "publishes what is improper, mischievous, or illegal [must] take the consequence of his own temerity."[4] This distinction between prior restraint and subsequent punishment was imported into seminal First Amendment jurisprudence.

As the United States Supreme Court noted in *Patterson v. Colorado*,[5] "the main purpose [is] 'to prevent all such *previous restraints* upon publications as had been practiced by other governments,' and they do not prevent the subsequent punishment of such as may be deemed contrary to the public welfare."[6] This distinction between prior restraint and subsequent punishment is a fixture of First Amendment case law. It is a point, moreover, that eventually caused Parliament to abandon

---

[1] AREOPAGITICA (1644).

[2] Abrams v. United States, 250 U.S. 616, 630 (1919) (Holmes, J., dissenting).

[3] Near v. Minnesota, 283 U.S. 697, 713 (1931) (quoting 4 W. Blackstone, COMMENTARIES ON THE LAWS OF ENGLAND 151–52 (2d ed. 1872)).

[4] *Id.*

[5] 205 U.S. 454 (1907).

[6] *Id.* at 462.

England's licensing laws by the end of the Seventeenth Century.

The end of licensing did not disarm the state of other powerful weapons of suppression. Seditious libel laws continued to exist as an effective deterrent to potential critics of church and state. Taxation of printers in the Eighteenth Century was a particular source of aggrievement in the American colonies. Ascending notions of liberty accounted for challenges to other constraints upon expression. Catalyzing and accelerating this evolution was the American colonial experience.

[B]   Colonial Developments

Economic opportunity and religious freedom were primary propellants of migration from England to the colonies. Perceptions with respect to the proper relationship between church and state, as noted previously, varied among the colonies. This condition has made interpretation of the Establishment Clause a vexing and competitive exercise. Much of the Court's Establishment Clause jurisprudence has been referenced to the Virginia model, which established a clear separation between church and state. Some members of the Court have challenged this model. In *Wallace v. Jaffree*,[7] for instance, Justice Rehnquist maintained that the Establishment Clause guards only against government creation of an official church or sectarian discrimination. Government aid to religion, which a wall between church and state precludes, is more readily achieved according to Justice Rehnquist's understanding.

Traditions of expressive freedom did not come naturally to the colonies. To the contrary, many of those fleeing to the colonies for religious reasons sought a social and political environment that was friendly to and supportive of their values. Tolerance for other points of view or beliefs was not necessarily part of the equation. Expressive freedom in the American colonies largely was coextensive with the scope of expressive freedom in England. With licensing having been abandoned in England in the late Seventeenth Century, prior restraint was not a significant factor in the colonies. The ability to criticize government officials, however, still was denied by the law of seditious libel.

A primary turning point in the evolution toward a tradition of expressive freedom was the trial of John Peter Zenger in 1735. Zenger was a printer who published articles, characterizing the royal governor of New York as greedy, corrupt, and imperial. These articles fueled public sentiment for a change in administration. A measure of the governor's unpopularity was illustrated by a grand jury's refusal to indict Zenger when presented with charges of seditious libel. The governor nonetheless had Zenger arrested and prosecuted for the crime. Technically, the government was only required to prove the fact of publication. Zenger's lawyers conceded this point, but urged the jury to consider truth as a defense to the charges. Contrary to the law, the jury returned a verdict in Zenger's favor. This outcome did not officially rewrite the law of seditious libel. Nor did it preclude the possibility of other prosecutions. It illuminated, however, a growing public sensitivity to the utility of expressive liberty. The Zenger experience also became a rallying point for the emerging influence of partisan editors whose

---

[7] 472 U.S. 38, 81 (1985) (Wallace, J., dissenting).

publications helped shape and advance the case for revolution.

As the colonies coursed toward independence, newspapers were the primary forum for debating the wisdom of independence. Anti-British publications identified colonial abuses and disseminated grievances against the governing order. They also mobilized revolutionary sentiment. The experience of pro-British publishers illuminated the tension that exists between principle in the abstract and in its application. Journalistic voices that criticized or opposed revolution, particularly those with overt British sympathies or loyalties, typically were silenced by vandalization and intimidation. This experience represents an early lesson with respect to the challenges confronting a system of express freedom. As Justice Holmes put it, the First Amendment accounts not for "free thought for those who agree with us, but freedom for the thought that we hate."[8] Traditions of suppression that predated and inspired revolution, as noted in Section 1.03, in some instances survived the political order's restructuring.

§ 1.02   ADOPTION OF THE FIRST AMENDMENT

The initial stage of post-colonial governance was a failure. Experience under the Articles of Confederation was characterized by sectional conflict, trade wars, and a nation that was largely dysfunctional. This situation led to an assembly in Philadelphia in 1787 that framed the United States Constitution. The primary purpose of the Constitutional Convention was to establish the bases and allocations of federal power. The Constitution, as originally ratified, distributed federal power among three branches of government and established the basic relationship between national and state authority. Missing from the document was any enumeration of rights and liberties.

This omission reflected an initial sense that fundamental rights and freedoms were self-evident and would be accounted for by the states and the representative process. The Framers believed that the federal government was bound by enumerated powers, and those powers did not include the authority to regulate expression. Many in the ratifying conventions disagreed. Consistent with fears regarding a strong central government, sentiment grew in favor of an explicit statement of rights and liberties, and threatened to derail the ratification process. To avoid this result, it was agreed that the first Congress would adopt the Bill of Rights. Heading the list of guarantees was the First Amendment, which provides that "Congress shall make no law . . . abridging the freedom of speech, or of the press."[9] Incorporation of most provisions of the Bill of Rights into the Fourteenth Amendment of the Constitution, over the course of the twentieth century, extended the First Amendment's reach to the states. Interpretation of the First Amendment was eventually expanded to cover administrative and judicial processes as well. Concepts of the press, for First Amendment purposes, have grown beyond the print model to include technologies that did not exist at the time of framing and ratification.

---

[8] United States v. Schwimmer, 279 U.S. 644, 654–55 (1937) (Holmes, J., dissenting).

[9] U.S. Const., amend. I.

§ 1.03　DEVELOPMENT OF THE FIRST AMENDMENT

The First Amendment, for practical purposes, is a work in progress. Attempts to discern the intentions of those who framed and ratified it have yielded no certain understanding. The repudiation of systems of prior restraint even prior to independence was part of the First Amendment's prelude. So too, however, was the intolerance toward those with anti-Revolutionary viewpoints. The intent of those who framed and ratified the First Amendment has been a long-standing source of debate. Indicative of the uncertainty that exists with respect to original understanding are the diverging positions of one of the nation's most prominent First Amendment scholars.

In 1960, Leonard Levy published a highly regarded book[10] that characterized the framers as having a narrow view and limited understanding of expressive freedom. Levy maintained that the preservation and utilization of seditious libel laws, even after the First Amendment was ratified, perpetuated rather than severed the English tradition of silencing dissent. One-quarter of a century later, Levy published a law review article[11] that challenged his original premise. Contrary to his original conclusion, Levy asserted that colonial experience was characterized by vigorous political debate and discourse that established the basis for a system that protected dissenting political voices. Regardless of which view is correct, modern understandings of the First Amendment has expanded beyond the political framework and interests that incubated the guarantee.

Development of the First Amendment's meaning largely has been the acquired responsibility of the judiciary which, in *Marbury v. Madison*,[12] established itself as the ultimate authority in interpreting the Constitution. Judicial review of the First Amendment, and consequent amplification of its meaning, is largely a Twentieth Century phenomenon. Particularly before the judiciary's power "to say what the law is"[13] was firmly established, the dimensions of expressive and religious liberty were configured largely by the political process.

[A]　An Early Tradition of Suppression

Even though the early Americans demanded speech protections, those protections were not consistently enforced. In the nation's formative years, debate over the nation's direction and governance was intense with ideological conflict between the Federalists and Jeffersonians. The intensity of this clash was illuminated early in President Adams' administration, when the Sedition Act was passed. This law made it a crime to:

> write, print, utter, or publish [any] false, scandalous and malicious writing or writings against the government of the United States, or either house of the Congress of the United States, or the President of the United States,

---

[10] Leonard Levy, Legacy of Suppression: Freedom of Speech and Press In Early American History (1960).

[11] Leonard W. Levy, *The Legacy Reexamined*, 37 Stan. L. Rev. 767 (1985).

[12] 5 U.S. 137 (1803).

[13] *Id.* at 177.

with intent to defame the said government, or either house of the said Congress, or the said President, or to bring them, or either of them, into contempt or disrepute, or to excite against them or either of them, the hatred of the good people of the United States, or to stir up sedition within the United States.[14]

As conceived and deployed, the Sedition Act provided the basis for punishing persons for their political beliefs and expressions, drawing upon the long-standing legal tradition of punishing seditious libel.

Even though the Sedition Act provided that truth was a defense, the law was used to prosecute, convict, and, incarcerate administration critics. The Act involved a calculated exercise in suppression by one political faction in an effort to silence its critics, and suggests an uncertain meaning of the First Amendment in its early existence. This approach contrasts with modern case law that establishes political speech as the most valued form of expression. The episode also reveals how freedom of expression is more readily achieved in theory rather than in fact. Notwithstanding their outrage over the law's application, Jeffersonians, when empowered, were quick to capitalize upon it for purposes of politically persecuting their own critics.

The Sedition Act eventually was abandoned by congressional action rather than through judicial review.[15] The experience, however, has not escaped the Court's attention or judgment. In *New York Times Co. v. Sullivan*,[16] the Court established First Amendment limits upon the reach of defamation law. The majority opinion used this opportunity to affirm that the Sedition Act, despite its operation, represented a wrong turn in the evolution toward a system of freedom of expression. As the Court put it:

> [a]lthough the Sedition Act was never tested in this Court, the attack upon its validity has carried the day in the court of history. Fines levied in this prosecution were repaid by Act of Congress on the ground that it was unconstitutional. Calhoun, reporting to the Senate . . . assumed that its invalidity was a matter "which no one now doubts." Jefferson, as President, pardoned those who had been convicted and sentenced under the Act and remitted their fines, stating: "[I] consider, that law to be a nullity, as absolute and as palpable as if Congress had ordered us to fall down and worship a golden image. [The] invalidity of the Act has been assumed by Justices of this Court. These views reflect a broad consensus that the Act, because of the restraint it imposed upon criticism of government and public officials, was inconsistent with the First Amendment.[17]

---

[14] New York Times Co. v. Sullivan, 376 U.S. 254, 273 (1964).

[15] In the United Kingdom, Section 73 of the Coroners and Justice Act of 2009 eliminated "the old common law offenses of sedition, seditious libel, obscene libel, and defamatory libel." According to Justice Minister Claire Ward, "Abolishing these offenses will allow the UK to take a lead in challenging similar laws in other countries, where they are used to suppress free speech." *Criminal libel and sedition offenses abolished*, PRESS GAZETTE (U.K.), January 13, 2010, http://www.pressgazette.co.uk/story.asp?storycode=44884.

[16] 376 U.S. 254 (1965).

[17] *Id.* at 276.

As this passage from the *Sullivan* decision indicates, the meaning of expressive liberty has been established on an evolutionary rather than a preordained basis. Over the course of the nineteenth century, expressive freedom remained an incident of political rather than judicial process. Abolitionist literature was banned from states that permitted slavery. Union organization was impaired by hostile legislation. The earliest interpretation of the First Amendment related to the Free Exercise Clause which the Court found did not protect polygamy.[18] Not until the second decade of the twentieth century did the Court begin to make meaningful inquiries into the First Amendment's meaning and application.

[B]   Judicial Review and the First Amendment

Judicial interpretation of the First Amendment began in earnest towards the end of World War I. Many of the cases that arose then involved individuals and organizations who dissented from official government policy. Through the late 1920s, judicial decisions generally were deferential toward government efforts to control dissent during wartime and to punish indications of subversive activities. Minority opinions by Justices Oliver Wendell Holmes, Jr. and Justice Louis Brandeis, during this period, framed the basis for doctrine that eventually became more protective of expressive liberty. By the 1930s and 1940s, the Court had developed a body of case law that established resistance to systems of prior restraint,[19] provided space for political dissent and organization by individuals and groups,[20] and established the concept of public forums.[21] Not until the mid-Twentieth Century, however, did the Court seriously begin to plumb the meaning of the religion clauses.[22] The civil rights movement became a primary propellant of case law concerning expressive freedom, as the Court strengthened protection for political dissidence,[23] narrowed the boundaries of defamation law,[24] established the right of association,[25] and fortified public forum doctrine.[26] This high growth period was paralleled by Establishment Clause case law that imposed new limitations upon interaction between church and state.[27] The Court during the 1960s and 1970s also broadened the range of protected speech interests[28] and began to account for the First Amendment interests of new media technologies.[29]

The Court's outputs in the final two decades of the Twentieth Century and early years of the Twenty-First Century have announced principles that have been both

---

[18] Reynolds v. United States, 98 U.S. 145 (1878).

[19] Near v. Minnesota, 283 U.S. 697 (1931).

[20] Herndon v. Lowry, 301 U.S. 242 (1937).

[21] Schneider v. State of New Jersey, 308 U.S. 147 (1939).

[22] Everson v. Board of Education, 330 U.S. 1 (1947).

[23] Brandenburg v. Ohio, 395 U.S. 444 (1969).

[24] New York Times Co. v. Sullivan, 376 U.S. 254 (1964).

[25] NAACP v. Alabama, 357 U.S. 449 (1958).

[26] Brown v. State of Louisiana, 383 U.S. 131 (1966).

[27] School District v. Schempp, 374 U.S. 203 (1963).

[28] Virginia State Board of Pharmacy v. Virginia Citizens Consumer Council, 425 U.S. 748 (1976).

[29] Red Lion Broadcasting Co. v. Federal Communications Commission, 395 U.S. 367 (1969).

expansive and restrictive some of these trends. Regulation that does not regulate speech directly, but nonetheless inhibits it on an incidental basis, increasingly has been accommodated.[30] Dissatisfaction with existing standards of review, among members of the Court itself, has been a defining aspect of Establishment Clause and source of future uncertainty.[31] Technology's demonstrated capacity to create new instrumentalities of communication and redefine existing models has presented significant and growing challenges to traditional constitutional premises.[32] Constructing principles that correlate to these evolutions are among the Court's primary looming tasks.

§ 1.04 FIRST AMENDMENT VALUES

The First Amendment, like any other constitutional provisions, represents an overarching statement of the people's will. Its textual placement and operation indicate the importance of its values. However, among constitutional theorists, significant variances exists with respect to the worth and utility of First Amendment liberties. Development of the value system that underlies these basic freedoms, as noted in Section 1.01, predates the framing of the First Amendment itself. Consistent with the rapid growth of First Amendment case law over the course of the twentieth century, courts and scholars alike have devoted extensive attention to the task of developing a theory of the First Amendment.

An inquiry into the value of expressive freedom confronts what is essentially a philosophical question. Among the most influential exponents of expressive liberty was John Stuart Mill who, in the mid-nineteenth century, promoted the vision of a marketplace of ideas.

> First, if any opinion is compelled to silence, that opinion for aught we can certainly know, be true. To deny this is to assume our own infallibility. Secondly, though this silenced opinion be in error, it may and very commonly does, contain a portion of the truth, and since the generally prevailing opinion of any subject is rarely or never the whole truth, it is only by the collision of adverse opinion that the remainder of the truth had any chance being supplied. Thirdly, even if the received opinion be not only true but the whole truth; unless it is suffered to be, and actually is vigorously amid earnestly contested, it will, by most of those who receive it, be held in the manner of a prejudice, with little comprehension or feeling of its natural grounds. And not only this, but fourthly, the meaning of the doctrine itself will be in danger of being lost or enfeebled.[33]

---

[30] Ward v. Rock Against Racism, 491 U.S. 781 (1989); City of Renton v. Playtime Theaters, Inc., 475 U.S. 41 (1986).

[31] *See, e.g.*, Lee v. Weisman, 505 U.S. 577, 644–46 (1992) (Scalia, J., dissenting, joined by Rehnquist, C.J., White, J., and Thomas, J.).

[32] Historically, the Court has operated on the premise that each medium is unique and thus subject to different First Amendment standards. *Red Lion Broadcasting Co. v. Federal Communications Commission*, 395 U.S. at 386. With modern media increasingly having interconnected and similar capabilities, this premise is being superseded by the phenomenon of convergence.

[33] JOHN STUART MILL, ON LIBERTY (1859).

Mill's observations represent a classic libertarian perspective upon expressive freedom as a means for discovering truth. It is an understanding that is at the core of modern First Amendment theory and the basis for a protective scope that has expanded beyond just political speech. For example, in holding that advertising is protected expression under the Free Speech Clause, the Court noted that it was "a matter of public interest that [private economic] decisions [be] intelligent and well-informed. To this end, the free flow of commercial information is indispensable."[34] Such language illustrates how the Court has embraced the First Amendment in terms framed by Mill and expanded it into a broad spectrum "instrument [toward] enlightened public decision-making in a democracy."[35]

The First Amendment has been described as "the matrix, the indispensable condition of nearly every other form of freedom."[36] Like the marketplace of ideas metaphor, this characterization is a grand abstraction that generates little disagreement. Efforts to construct a consensual theory of expressive freedom break down when discourse moves to a higher level of specificity. At this point, numerous theories vie with each other to establish the value of expressive liberty. Some theorists maintain that the liberty is important because it advances personal knowledge and facilitates self-development.[37] Others focus on expressive freedom's utility for purposes of promoting participatory decision-making,[38] checking the potential for official abuse,[39] or providing a social safety value for the discontented.[40]

Although none of these theories is without significant gravity, the Court has placed greater emphasis on some theories rather than others. The Court's First Amendment decisions have assigned the highest currency to the perspective of Alexander Meiklejohn, who maintained that expressive freedom's primary value is ensuring an informed electorate.[41] Pursuant to this premise, speech relating to informed self-government has the highest value and thus merits the most protection, especially against governmental attempts to regulate or control. From this departure point, a hierarchy of speech interests has evolved that gives political speech the highest status, provides lesser but not insignificant protection to commercial speech, and categorically devalues fighting words, and obscenity. A parallel ranking system exists for the media that is a function not of value but of each medium's unique characteristics, which determine regulatory susceptibility.[42]

The valuation of religious freedom has been no less of a competitive exercise. Efforts to glean the underlying values of the Establishment Clause, as noted in

---

[34] Virginia State Board of Pharmacy v. Virginia Citizens Consumer Council, 425 U.S. 748, 763 (1976).

[35] *Id.* at 765.

[36] Palko v. Connecticut, 302 U.S. 319, 327 (1937).

[37] *E.g.*, Martin Redish, Freedom of Expression: a Critical Analysis (1984).

[38] *E.g.*, Alexander Meiklejohn, *The First Amendment is an Absolute*, 1961 Sup. Ct. Rev. 245 (1961).

[39] *E.g.*, Vincent Blasi, *The Checking Value in First Amendment Theory*, 1977 A.B.A. Found. Res. J. 521 (1977).

[40] *E.g.*, Whitney v. California, 274 U.S. 357 (1927) (Whitney, J., concurring).

[41] *E.g.*, *New York Times Co.*, 376 U.S. at 254.

[42] *See* Chapter 9.

Section B, are complicated by competing perspectives regarding the Framers' intent. Given the divergent reasons that coalesced into support for the Establishment Clause, and led to its creation and ratification, the search for a singular purpose reasonably may prove elusive.

The high value assigned to First Amendment freedoms sometimes has been a source of rhetorical excess and misleading signals. Reference to freedom of speech and of the press as the "indispensable condition" for other basic rights and liberties has generated arguments that the First Amendment overrides other constitutional interests. Contributing to this premise is the Court's own observation that "freedom of press [and] freedom of speech [are] in a preferred position."[43] The notion of a preferred position was challenged as loose and dangerous terminology. Justice Frankfurter, in particular, warned against interpreting the First Amendment by reflex rather than reason. Insofar as the Court responded to content-based regulation of protected speech with heightened standards of review, and expanded its meaning by identifying penumbral guarantees,[44] the First Amendment has operated as a constitutional priority. The Court largely has not always prioritized the First Amendment over other constitutional provisions when conflicts arise. Description of the First Amendment as occupying a preferred position, therefore, is better understood as a term of art rather than one of precision.

The Court also has shied away from regarding the First Amendment as an absolute command. On its face, the speech, press, and religion clauses have little if any qualifying language. In this respect, the First Amendment contrasts with the conditioning terminology imposed on other constitutional guarantees such as the protection against "*unreasonable* searches and seizures,"[45] the requirement of "*just* compensation,"[46] or the prohibition against "[e]*xcessive* bail."[47] The foremost exponent of First Amendment absolutism was Justice Black, who wrote numerous opinions on this point often with the support of Justice Douglas. Black consistently maintained that "the First Amendment's unequivocal command that there shall be no abridgment of the rights of free speech [shows] the men who drafted the Bill of Rights did all the 'balancing' that was to be done."[48] The Court never has embraced this proposition. Responding to Justices Black and Douglas, Justice Harlan asserted that the First Amendment did not automatically trump regulation of speech or press, and he maintained that the scope of First Amendment protection could not be determined based solely on a literal reading of the provision. Justice Harlan's understanding has been reflected in principles of review that consider whether a given form of speech is within the protective ambit of the First Amendment and, if so, whether a competing interest is strong enough to override the constitutional guarantee. It also has engendered an understanding that the

---

[43] Murdock v. Pennsylvania, 319 U.S. 105, 115 (1943).

[44] Freedom of association, for instance, was established as a penumbra rather than textual provision of the First Amendment. National Association for the Advancement of Colored People v. Alabama, 357 U.S. 449 (1966).

[45] U.S. Const. amend. IV.

[46] *Id.* amend. V.

[47] *Id.* amend. VIII.

[48] Konigsberg v. State Bar of California, 366 U.S. 36, 56 (Black, J., dissenting).

First Amendment prohibits not regulation of expression itself, but freedom of expression — whatever the contours of that liberty may be.

§ 1.05 UNDERSTANDING AND APPLYING FIRST AMENDMENT STANDARDS OF REVIEW

On its face, the case for absolutism would appear to simplify the law of expressive freedom. Although instances of content regulation might be resolved on a bright line basis, there is more to First Amendment jurisprudence than a simple inquiry into official efforts to control speech on the basis of its message. Case law over the course of the twentieth century, among other things, has wrestled with distinctions between speech and conduct, developed rules for appropriate forums for expression, and drawn distinctions between regulations directed at speech itself and those having only an incidental or secondary effect upon expression.

[A] Speech

Freedom of speech analysis has two primary tracks. The first track of review focuses upon whether a given category of speech is entitled to First Amendment protection. The second track of review is concerned with whether regulation is content-based or content-neutral. Content-based regulation typically triggers closer judicial scrutiny than content-neutral regulation. This higher level of review follows, however, only for speech that qualifies for First Amendment protection. A basic premise of First Amendment jurisprudence is that some but not all categories of expression are deserving of constitutional protection.

The common denominator of categorically unprotected expression is a finding that it constitutes "no essential part of any exposition of ideas" and "has slight social value as a step to the truth."[49] The Court has placed obscenity, fighting words, and (at one point) defamation in the realm of unprotected expression. Pursuant to this designation, judicial review amounts to a rational basis inquiry. The extent of deference in this context is evidenced by the Court's observation that regulation of obscenity is permissible even on the basis of "unprovable assumptions."[50] It is important to note, however, that categorically unprotected speech is not "invisible"[51] to the First Amendment. To the extent that government discriminates on the basis of content or viewpoint, even with respect to unprotected speech, the Court will employ strict scrutiny.

For protected categories of speech, the standard of review varies with the type of expression and the value assigned to it. Political expression, for instance, is regarded as high value speech. Consistent with this estimation, exacting standards such as the clear and present danger test and strict scrutiny apply. For less valued forms of speech, protected but intermediate levels of scrutiny apply. Although the calibration of standards may vary with the subcategory of protected speech, the analytical process consists essentially of balancing the competing constitutional

---

[49] Chaplinsky v. New Hampshire, 315 U.S. 568, 572 (1942).

[50] Paris Adult Theatre I v. Slaton, 413 U.S. 49, 62 (1973).

[51] R.A.V. v. City of St. Paul, 505 U.S. 377, 383 (1992).

and regulatory interests. In each instance, the Court essentially asks whether the regulatory concern is strong enough to outweigh the interest in expressive freedom. The weighting of factors also may be affected by the medium that is used to disseminate expression. As noted in Chapter 9, and like speech, some media are afforded more First Amendment protection than others.

Close attention to content-based regulation reflects a well-established sense that first and foremost "the First Amendment means that government has no power to restrict expression because of its message, its ideas, its subject matter, or its content."[52] Quite often, government regulates on a content-neutral basis that nonetheless incidentally burdens expression. Examples of such content-neutral legislation range from regulation prohibiting the burning of draft cards[53] to zoning restrictions on adult entertainment enterprises.[54] The Court has found that these laws are aimed at interests unrelated to speech, such as ensuring the efficiencies of the military draft and protecting against neighborhood degradation. The incidental or secondary effects upon speech are not insignificant, and some would argue that the incidental or secondary designation is deceiving. When the burden on speech is found to be indirect, the Court will employ one of two tests — each of which is in the nature of intermediate review. When government regulation indirectly burdens speech, the Court will consider whether it advances an important state interest, whether that interest is unrelated to the suppression of speech, and whether the incidental burden is any greater than necessary to achieve the interest. In cases concerning regulation of secondary effects or time, place, and manner control, the Court's focus is upon whether the regulation accounts for an important or substantial interest and whether sufficient alternative channels of communication are left open.

A threshold question in many freedom of speech cases is whether a regulation is vague or overbroad. A law is vague if it is not written clearly enough to provide notice of the activity that is being prohibited. Overbreadth problems arise when a law sweeps so broadly that it burdens both protected and unprotected expression. A law found to be vague or overbroad typically cannot be applied to the individual who has challenged it. The doctrines of vagueness and overbreadth have a common purpose of ensuring that regulation does not chill or deter protected freedom. These concepts and the principles that limit their operation are discussed fully in Chapter 5.

[B] Press

The free press clause generally has been interpreted as having no significance independent of the speech clause. The importance of this understanding is amplified in Chapter 10, which notes that the press does not have any greater First Amendment rights or interests than the public. Although the Court has made no formal distinction between speech and the press, dissemination of expression through a medium may have a bearing upon First Amendment protection. This

---

[52] Police Dept. of Chicago v. Mosley, 408 U.S. 92, 95 (1972).

[53] United States v. O'Brien, 391 U.S. 367 (1968).

[54] *City of Renton*, 475 U.S. 41.

phenomenon is a function of standards of review that vary from medium to medium (a.k.a., "medium specific").

Traditionally, the print media has been the most protected, and broadcasting has been the least protected under the First Amendment. This variance in status is reflected in standards of review that are more exacting for regulation of print than broadcasting. Notwithstanding the facial similarities between broadcasting and cable, and the fact that most broadcast programming is delivered to viewers through cable systems, it appears that cable is regarded more like print for First Amendment purposes. The emergence of the Internet and social media have introduced new realities that blur traditional structural distinctions among media (and present new expressive opportunities and societal risks).

[C] Religion

[1] Establishment

Standards of review in the Establishment Clause context are disorderly and confusing. For nearly three decades, the Court's primary test focused on whether a law has a secular purpose, neither advances nor inhibits religion as its primary effect, and excessively entangles government in religion. This model of review has been criticized by several members of the Court including two, Justices Scalia and Thomas, who have sworn never again to employ it. When this tripartite formula is not used, the Court typically focuses upon whether a law involves an "endorsement" of religion (unconstitutional), or accommodates (constitutionally acceptable) (constitutionally unacceptable) religion. Given the considerable dissatisfaction with established principles, but the failure of the Court to unify in support of an alternative, Establishment Clause standards have a particularly uncertain future.

[2] Free Exercise

Standards of review in the Free Exercise Clause setting evolved from an initial distinction between religious beliefs (constitutionally protected) and religious conduct (not protected) to a consideration of whether a regulation imposes a direct or an indirect burden on the free exercise of religion. Recent free exercise case law focuses upon whether a regulation is one of general applicability or directed at a religion. The distinction that this standard requires is exemplified by *Employment Division, Department of Human Resources of Oregon v. Smith.*[55] In this case, the Court considered whether a ban on the use of controlled substances in religious ceremonies violated the Free Exercise Clause. Finding that the law was neutral and of general applicability, the Court deferred to legislative judgment prohibiting use of the drug. Laws of general applicability thus can be analogized to content neutral regulation in the freedom of speech context. When such enactments are challenged, and even if they impose a substantial burden upon free exercise interests, strict scrutiny is not triggered. Exacting review is reserved for those instances in which a law involves purposeful discrimination against religion. As is the case in determining whether a law is content-based or content-neutral, discerning whether

---

[55] 494 U.S. 872 (1990).

regulation is discriminatory or neutral toward religion is a treacherous exercise.

§ 1.06   A SAMPLE ANALYSIS

First Amendment standards vary with content and are medium specific. Complicating their application, in the free speech setting, is the muddled line that exists between protected and unprotected expression and content-based and content-neutral regulation. Even without these difficulties, analysis of First Amendment problems tends to be layered. To facilitate comprehension and competence in the selection and application of standards, the following problem and recommended points of inquiry are set forth. The problem is drawn from *Federal Communications Commission v. Pacifica Foundation.*[56] A suggested line of inquiry follows for purposes.

[A]   The Problem

The Federal Communications Commission (FCC) has taken regulatory action against a radio station that broadcasts an "indecent" program during the day. This action was taken pursuant to a congressional enactment providing that "[n]o person shall utter any obscene, indecent, or profane language by means of radio communication." The speech at issue was a monologue by a well-known social satirist who repeatedly used vulgar terminology to lampoon society's attitudes toward vulgarity. The FCC justifies the regulation on grounds that it must protect children who populate the listening audience during the middle of the day.

[B]   An Analytical Roadmap

- Is the speech within a category that is protected or unprotected by the First Amendment? Although obscene expression is not constitutionally protected, indecent expression is within the zone of constitutional protection.

- Is the regulation content-based or content neutral?

- If the regulation is content-based, it is necessary to classify the speech. Is it highly valued political speech, that requires searching review, or less valued speech at the margins of First Amendment protection.

- If the regulation is not content-based, does it account for an important interest unrelated to speech? Here, it may be argued that the regulation is designed to protect children and thus only indirectly or incidentally burdens speech.

- What is broadcasting's constitutional status? As indicated in Chapter 11, broadcasting has less constitutional protection than other media.

- Note threshold questions of whether the regulation is vague or overbroad, concepts that are discussed in Chapter 5.

---

[56] 438 U.S. 726 (1978).

§ 1.07   THE FIRST AMENDMENT IN SUMMARY

Although the First Amendment is stated in short and facially simple terms, it's meaning is complex and layered as interpreted by the courts. If reconstituted to account for judicial interpretations, the Amendment might read as follows:

> No branch of government, federal, state, or local, shall abridge freedom of speech or of the press except (1) when expression has only slight, or no, social value; (2) in intended to incite imminent lawless conduct, and is likely to produce such conduct; (3) defames a private person at least negligently and a public official or figure with actual malice; (4) invades privacy in an unacceptable way; (5) advertises a good or service that is illegal, or does so falsely or deceptively; (6) represents commercial speech that is outweighed by a substantial state interest and governed by regulation that is narrowly tailored to achieve its objective; and (7) is sexually explicit (albeit not obscene) or pandered or readily available to children. Freedom of speech and of the press does not prohibit government from managing speech in a content neutral way or regulating conduct or effects associated with speech. The level of speech protection may vary with the nature of the speech or the medium. The establishment clause generally guards against unacceptable levels of interaction between church and state. The free exercise clause prohibits government from abridging religion unless it can satisfy the demands of strict scrutiny.

Several exceptions to First Amendment protection thus exist. Although false speech is not protected in certain instances, as with false advertising or perjury, the Court has not carved out categorical protection for it. As a four justice plurality observed in *United States v. Alvarez*,[57] it never has determined that "false statements generally should constitute a new category of unprotected speech." The Court has been reluctant to broaden the range of exceptions to the First Amendment, In *United States v. Stevens*,[58] the Court rejected arguments that depictions of animal cruelty are categorically unprotected. In so doing, it noted that its "cases cannot be taken as establishing a freewheeling authority to declare new categories of speech outside the scope of the First Amendment."

Most First Amendment jurisprudence has focused upon the speech, press, or religion clauses. Less frequently litigated is the petition clause, which establishes "the right of the people . . . to petition the Government for a redress of grievances." This provision was at issue in the Court's decision, in *Borough of Duryea v. Guarnieri*,[59] limiting a government employee's ability to sue his employer. The Court, in a majority opinion authored by Justice Kennedy, determined that a public employee could bring an action pursuant to the petition clause only if his or her claim concerned a policy matter of public concern. It thus could not be used as the basis for a suit relating to an "ordinary workplace grievance."

---

[57] 132 S. Ct. 2537 (2012).

[58] 559 U.S. 460 (2010).

[59] 131 S. Ct. 2488 (2012).

This outcome is congruent with case law concerning the scope of the speech clause in the public employment setting. Consistent with this result, the Court noted the government has an "interest in managing its internal affairs [that] requires proper restraints on the invocation of rights by employees when the workplace or the government employer's responsibilities may be affected." The Court thus linked the utility of the petition clause to circumstances in which an issue may be of "interest to the community as a whole" (as opposed to a workplace matter).

Justice Thomas (concurring) and Justice Scalia (concurring in part and dissenting in part) doubted whether lawsuits constituted petitions under the First Amendment's original meeting. They also opposed importing the "public concern" standard into petition clause jurisprudence and would have distinguished between government in its role as employer and as sovereign. The First Amendment's prominent placement and associated rhetoric attest to its significance. The volume of litigation that it has generated indicates a high residual of indeterminacy with respect to the First Amendment's ultimate meaning. Against this backdrop, the following chapters will be devoted to facilitating understanding in a way that optimizes learning efficiency, comprehension, and retention.

POINTS TO REMEMBER

- The First Amendment is rooted in 17th Century philosophies of liberation and reason.

- The Framers' intent with respect to the First Amendment is more debated than certain.

- The nation's early experience included active suppression of political dissent pursuant to the law of seditious libel.

- The absolutist view of the First Amendment has never been embraced by the Court.

- Speech categorically excluded from the First Amendment's ambit may be freely regulated, provided that government does not discriminate on the basis of viewpoint.

- Protected speech is classified on the basis of the value it has to society and informed self-governance.

- Regulation of protected speech typically requires a balancing of constitutional and regulatory interests.

- Content-neutral regulation is reviewed pursuant to a standard that is less than strict but more than deferential.

- Establishment Clause review is in an unsettled state, but the dominant standard of review inquires into purpose, primary effect, and the potential for entanglement between church and state.

- Free Exercise Clause review limits strict scrutiny to instances in which religion is targeted by a regulatory burden.

Chapter 2

SPEECH ADVOCATING VIOLENT OR ILLEGAL ACTION

SYNOPSIS

§ 2.01   **FORMATIVE CASE LAW**

§ 2.02   **TOWARD A MORE SPEECH PROTECTIVE STANDARD**

§ 2.03   **DOCTRINAL UNCERTAINTY**

§ 2.04   **THE MODERN STANDARD OF REVIEW**

FOCAL POINTS OF CHAPTER 2

- The nature of and influences upon early standards relating to advocacy of violence or illegal action.

- The prelude to modern standards relating to advocacy of violence or illegal action, particularly the influence of Justices Brandeis and Holmes.

- Doctrinal uncertainty in the evolution of standards relating to advocacy of violence or illegal action.

- Modern standards relating to advocacy of violence or illegal action.

- Political and societal factors that may bear upon the protection afforded speech advocating violence of illegal action.

---

§ 2.01   FORMATIVE CASE LAW

Seminal jurisprudence relating to expressive freedom was generated in the context of wartime and its aftermath. The dominant cases in this category concern advocacy of opposition to World War I or political change through violent or illegal methods. Such expression borders upon or overlaps the type of speech that, because of its utility in facilitating an informed electorate, generates the highest level of constitutional protection. In the earliest free speech cases, antiwar protesters who challenged American participation in World War I or urged resistance to the draft were prosecuted under the federal Espionage Act of 1917. This law, among other things, prohibited interference with military recruiting and enlistment. Criminal penalties for violation of the Espionage Act ranged up to 20 years in prison. The law was enforced aggressively. Notable convictions included a major presidential candidate and notable socialist, Eugene Debs. He was sentenced to 10 years in prison for his antiwar sentiments. While imprisoned, Debs received nearly one million votes in the 1920 presidential election. Indicative of how freedom of speech doctrine would evolve in subsequent decades, one constitutional law scholar has noted that Deb's conviction was "somewhat as though George McGovern had been sent to prison for his criticism of the [Vietnam] war."[1]

The rise of Bolshevism in Russia, during and after World War I, heightened national attention to perceived internal security risks. In addition to the Espionage Act, Congress passed the Sedition Act of 1918 and many states passed criminal syndicalism laws. These enactments provided the basis for prosecuting individuals who advocated communism or espoused anarchic or revolutionary doctrine. They also presented the Court with its first serious exposure to the Free Speech Clause. Case law during wartime and its aftermath commenced a half century journey toward doctrine that eventually struck a settled balance between legitimate societal interests in thwarting subversion and providing the breathing room necessary for political dissent. Within this context of profound but competing concerns, the critical need is for a standard that enables government to account for self-preservation but without overreacting and unduly inhibiting the competing perspectives that facilitate informed self-governance.

The early freedom of speech decisions exhibit tendencies associated with cases of first impression. With no meaningful precedent to draw upon, they contain few citations to authority. They also speak in relatively broad terms and, consistent with the processes of learning and experience, do not yield immediately satisfactory results. The key issue, in the cases concerning advocacy of violence or unlawful action, is not whether government may forbid speech that incites these results. The primary question, which the Court struggled with for nearly half a century, is when. To the extent disruption or destruction of the political and economic system itself is being advocated, government has a strong interest in self-preservation. It also has a responsibility, however, to avoid action that abridges freedom of speech and of the press. Seminal case law commenced the process of reaching a satisfactory accommodation between these interests.

The first free speech case of real influence did not make it past the first level of appellate review. In *Masses Publishing Co. v. Patten*,[2] a federal district court enjoined a postmaster from excluding a revolutionary journal from the mail. Judge Learned Hand, who figured prominently in the debate over and development of First Amendment standards, determined that the Espionage Act only operated against speech that "counsel[ed] the violation of law" and did not extend to expression that merely "arouse[d] a seditious disposition." Judge Hand thus previewed what eventually would become an important distinction between mere advocacy and incitement. Unless free speech doctrine made this separation, Judge Hand believed that government could suppress any expression critical of the government. Although Judge Hand was reversed by the court of appeals, this

---

[1] Harry Kalven, Jr., *Professor Ernst Freund and* Debs v. United States, 40 U. Chi. L. Rev. 235, 237 (1973).

[2] 244 F. 535 (S.D.N.Y.), *rev'd*, 246 F.24 (2d Cir. 1917).

seminal distinction eventually would prevail as a significant element of modern First Amendment jurisprudence.

Two years after the *Masses Publishing Co.* decision, the Supreme Court generated its first significant freedom of speech outputs. In a trilogy of cases, the Court introduced a first generation version of the clear and present danger test and indicated a readiness to punish speech merely for a tendency to produce an illegal consequence. Each of these decisions affirmed conspiracy convictions under the Espionage Act. They emerged against a backdrop of national insecurity generated by the rapid rise of Bolshevism in Europe and violent activities by radical labor organizers. These developments begot intense law enforcement efforts to address what historians refer to as the Great Red Scare. During this period, law enforcement worked aggressively to identify, prosecute, and punish individuals who advocated or promoted subversive action.

In *Schenck v. United States,*[3] the Court upheld the conviction of protesters who had disseminated leaflets urging draft-eligible men to resist military service. Based upon these activities, the defendants were prosecuted for obstructing military recruiting in violation of the Espionage Act. The *Schenck* decision introduced the original version of the clear and present danger test. Writing for a unanimous Court, Justice Holmes noted that the question "is whether the words are used in such circumstances and are of such a nature as to create a clear and present danger that they will bring about the substantive degree of evils the Congress has a right to prevent." As framed in *Schenck*, the inquiry is merely into the "proximity and degree" of possible harm.

The *Schenck* decision established some primary premises for interpreting the speech and press clauses. It established that the First Amendment was not an indefeasible bar to regulating expression. This point was supported by the maxim that "[t]he most stringent protection of free speech would not protect a man in falsely shouting fire in a theater and causing a panic." The Court also noted the relevance of context, specifically that the outcome might have been different had the case arose during peacetime. This observation is consistent with the Court's general tendency to defer toward the political branches when national security is a significant factor. The clear and present danger test, as articulated in *Schenck*, indicated that the harm must be both identifiable and close at hand. The standard did not insist upon any likelihood of occurrence, a factor that would be accounted for four decades later.

In two companion cases, *Frohwerk v. United States*[4] and *Debs v. United States*,[5] the Court also upheld convictions of antiwar protesters under the Espionage Act. Instead of applying clear and present danger principles, however, the Court focused upon the speech and its "natural tendency and reasonably probable effect."[6] This development established the dominant reference point for freedom of speech decisions through the late 1930s. The focus upon bad tendency was the basis, in

---

[3] 249 U.S. 47 (1919).

[4] 249 U.S. 204 (1919).

[5] 249 U.S. 211 (1919).

[6] *Id.* at 216.

Abrams v. United States,[7] for upholding the Espionage Act convictions of several self-styled "rebels," "revolutionaries," and "anarchists."

The most significant consequence of the *Abrams* decision, for long-term purposes, was Justice Holmes' dissenting opinion. This dissent established much of the foundation upon which modern doctrine rests. Many historians attribute Justice Holmes' evolution toward a more First Amendment friendly position to the influence of Judge Hand, whom he corresponded extensively with on the subject of expressive freedom. As Justice Holmes put it in his dissent, speech should not be punished unless it "so imminently threaten[s] immediate interference with the lawful and pressing purpose of the law that an immediate check is required to save the country." Holmes' dissent also introduced the marketplace of ideas metaphor into First Amendment jurisprudence. He thus observed that "the ultimate good is better reached by free trade in ideas and that the best test of truth is the power of thought to get itself accepted in the competition of the market."

As Holmes laid the groundwork for future doctrine, the Court during the 1920s proceeded with the notion that government may regulate when speech manifests a "bad tendency." In *Gitlow v. New York,*[8] the Court upheld a conviction of persons who had printed and distributed a manifesto advocating class struggle and mass political strikes. These actions were prosecuted under the state's criminal anarchy statute, which prohibited advocacy of violent insurrection. The *Gitlow* Court determined that, in circumstances where the legislature specifically had identified the type of speech to be prohibited, there was no room for judicial inquiry. It thus consigned clear and present danger analysis to instances when the state prohibited an activity but made no reference to any expression that might be punishable. The *Gitlow* decision is noteworthy, not merely for perpetuating bad tendency analysis, but for incorporating the freedom of speech and press clauses into the Fourteenth Amendment.

It also provided an opportunity for Justices Holmes to press further for investment in clear and present danger principles. Pursuant to this formula, as they noted, there was no proximate risk that the manifesto would have incited insurrection. From their perspective, every idea could be viewed as an incitement, but government could intervene only when the risk of harm was imminent. Given this possibility, the Court in *Gitlow* believed that government should not have to assume the risk of belated action.

The Court continued on the same bad tendency track, in *Whitney v. California,*[9] when it affirmed a conviction for helping to organize a Marxist-oriented group in violation of a state criminal syndicalism statute. Criminal syndicalism, as defined by the law, included any doctrine that advocated, taught, or aided and abetted the commission of crime, sabotage; unlawful force and violence; or unlawful methods of terrorism as a means of effecting economic or political change. The defendant was a member of the Communist Labor Party who had signed a resolution at an organizing convention noting "the value of political action as a means of spreading

---

[7]　250 U.S. 616 (1919).

[8]　268 U.S. 652 (1925).

[9]　274 U.S. 357 (1927).

communist propaganda" and stressing the value of political power as a means of facilitating the liberation of workers. Although the organization supported violent methods of change, the defendant maintained that she advocated reform through the established political process and had opposed and protested activities that were illegal. She nonetheless was prosecuted on the basis of assisting in the organization of a group dedicated to political change by means of unlawful action.

§ 2.02   TOWARD A MORE SPEECH PROTECTIVE STANDARD

Consistent with other early First Amendment decisions, the *Whitney* Court's long-term contributions are not to be found in the majority opinion. In upholding her conviction, the Court emphasized that she belonged to and assisted an organization while knowing its illegal aim of overthrowing the government. Justice Brandeis, joined by Holmes, authored an opinion in *Whitney* that laid a foundation for modern case law. They began with an attack upon the *Gitlow* premise that precluded meaningful judicial review when the legislature prohibited a specified form of expression. Their initial point was that the defendant could challenge her conviction by maintaining that her actions did not present a clear and present danger of serious harm. Although the Brandeis and Holmes opinion has the tone of a dissent, it was styled as a concurrence because the defendant did not raise the lack of a clear and present danger as a basis for challenging her conviction.

Brandeis' and Holmes' opinion provided an amplified rationale for the clear and present danger test and a foundational discourse on the values underlying a system of freedom of expression. Drawing upon history, they maintained that the nation's founders valued liberty both as a means and an end. Original understanding, as Brandeis and Holmes perceived it, included a sense that "freedom to think as you will and to speak as you think are means indispensable to the discovery and spread of political truth."[10] Contrary to the majority's perspective, they argued that public order is secured by freedom rather than suppression of speech. As they put it, "fear breeds repression; repression breeds hate; that the path of safety lies in the opportunity to discuss freely supposed grievances and proposed remedies; and that the fitting remedy for evil counsels is good ones."[11] Advocacy of illegal action should not be abridged when it "falls short of incitement and there is nothing to indicate that the advocacy would be immediately acted on."[12] They advanced a clear and present danger standard that would have found mere advocacy of illegal action, no matter how morally objectionable, inadequate justification for denying free speech "where the advocacy falls short of incitement and there is nothing to indicate that the advocacy would be immediately acted upon. No danger flowing from speech can be deemed clear and present unless the incidence of evil apprehended is so imminent that it may befall before there is opportunity for full discussion."[13]

---

[10] *Id.* at 376–77 (Brandeis and Holmes, JJ. concurring).

[11] *Id.*

[12] *Id.* at 376 (Brandeis and Holmes, JJ. concurring).

[13] *Id.* at 377.

The Brandeis-Holmes model of analysis competed against a standard that allowed government to squelch expression at the first sign of possible risk. As the Court put it in *Gitlow*, "[a] single revolutionary spark may kindle a fire that, smouldering for a time, may burst into a sweeping and destructive conflagration."[14] Consistent with this perspective, government was not required to defer action until "revolutionary utterances lead to actual disturbances [or] destruction."[15] This orientation, somewhat more slowly than surely, eventually gave way to doctrine that reflected the perspective of Brandeis and Holmes.

The future, as inspired by Brandeis and Holmes, was previewed to some extent during the 1930s and 1940s. Clear and present danger principles were referenced in *DeJonge v. Oregon*,[16] at least in part, when the Court announced that freedom of speech, press, and assembly could not be abridged minus "incite[ment] to violence and crime." In *Herndon v. Lowrey*,[17] the Court reversed the conviction of a communist party organizer for inciting insurrection in violation of state law. The conviction was based upon the defendant's efforts to recruit party members and his possession of party literature. In finding the statute unconstitutionally vague, the Court determined that expression could not be punished merely because of its dangerous tendency. Such a standard required "pure speculation as to future thoughts and trends"[18] and thus essentially was standardless. The Court concluded that a conviction could not stand without "a reasonable apprehension of danger to organized government."

These applications of clear and present danger concepts proved to be more tentative than enduring. They emerged, however, against a backdrop of indications that the Court would review carefully official impositions upon enumerated rights. This message was communicated in *United States v. Carolene Products Co.*[19] The *Carolene Products* decision announced the end of substantive due process review as a basis for generating and protecting economic rights. This change of direction was coupled with a signal that the Court would be less deferential toward regulation that implicated "a specific prohibition of the Constitution, such as those of the first ten amendments."

A more vigorous application of clear and present danger principles was evidenced in the context of speech that criticized the judiciary and became the basis for a finding of contempt. In *Bridges v. California*,[20] the Court determined that a contempt citation could be upheld only if the speech would effect an "extremely serious" substantive evil and the imminence factor was "extremely high." Further development of clear and present danger standards as they related to political dissidents, however, was arrested by fallout from the Cold War and McCarthyism following World War II. Paralleling the response to national insecurities during and

---

[14] *Gitlow*, 268 U.S. at 669.

[15] *Id.*

[16] 299 U.S. 353 (1937).

[17] 301 U.S. 242 (1937).

[18] *Id.* at 263.

[19] 304 U.S. 144 (1938).

[20] 314 U.S. 252 (1941).

after World War I, free speech doctrine was characterized by heightened deference to the political process. Within the political context of strong anti-communist sentiment, the Court demonstrated a reinvigorated concern with bad tendency.

§ 2.03 DOCTRINAL UNCERTAINTY

Reversion toward standards that were less protective of speech interests was evidenced when the Court reviewed convictions under the Smith Act for conspiring to organize the Communist Party. In *Dennis v. United States*,[21] a plurality of the Court announced the clear and present danger test as its standard of review. The application of this standard, however, digressed from the formulation propounded by Brandeis and Holmes. The plurality considered "whether the gravity of the 'evil,' discounted by its improbability, justifies such invasion of free speech as is necessary to avoid the danger." This formulation represented a higher level of deference toward the legislature, which the plurality believed had a substantial interest in preventing violent insurrection. Reminiscent of thinking associated with 1920s case law, the plurality maintained that government need not "wait until the *putsch* is about to be executed, the plans have been laid and the signal is awaited" before acting.

As recast by the *Dennis* plurality, the clear and present danger test was substantially diluted. Under this formula, government could intervene even if the prospect for evil was remote rather than probable. The greater the gravity of the evil, the less incumbent it was upon government to demonstrate that the danger was clear or present. Reduced to its basic nature, the reconstituted clear and present danger test balanced the potential seriousness of harm against the interest in expressive freedom. Given the gravity of the evil (violent insurrection), official abridgment could be justified upon lesser indications of clarity and presence. As Justice Black noted in his dissent, the plurality's version of the clear and present danger test reduced judicial review to an inquiry into whether abridgment of speech was "reasonable." Justice Black also noted the standard's vulnerability to popular "pressures, passions, and fears."

Although viewed as a regression from more speech protective principles, the *Dennis* decision contained the seeds of more fortified free speech doctrine. Justice Douglas, in his dissenting opinion, urged a distinction between teaching of abstract doctrine and incitement of illegal action. Although agreeing that speech could lose its constitutional immunity, that moment did not arrive until it "fan[ned] such destructive flames that it must be halted in the interests of the safety of the Republic." For Douglas, free speech was the rule until it was demonstrated that conditions were so critical that there was no opportunity to avert the danger. This focus upon imminence was a missing link in the *Dennis* plurality version of clear and present danger. Post-*Dennis* case law moved gradually toward an understanding that recaptured this element.

For a decade after *Dennis*, prosecution for membership in the Communist Party provided the Court with a steady flow of free speech cases. In *Yates v. United*

---

[21] 341 U.S. 494 (1951) (plurality opinion).

States,[22] the Court qualified the reach of *Dennis*. The *Yates* case concerned the conviction of several Communist Party officials under the Smith Act. These defendants had been prosecuted for (1) advocating and teaching the necessity of violent overthrow of the government, and (2) organizing the Communist Party with the intent of causing violent overthrow of the government. The Court overturned the convictions on grounds the trial court had misinterpreted *Dennis*. As the Court put it, *Dennis* had not "obliterated the traditional dividing line between advocacy of abstract doctrine and advocacy of action." It thus distinguished *Dennis* as a case concerning "a conspiracy to advocate presently the taking of forcible action in the future."

The *Yates* decision did not draw a distinction between harm that was imminent or in the future. Constitutional protection thus was not extended to expression that advocated violent action, so long as it was reasonable to believe that the action would occur when conditions were ripe. This theme was central to the outcome in *Scales v. United States*,[23] when the Court upheld Smith Act convictions based upon membership in the Communist Party. The basis for the prosecution was that the defendants, through their active membership in the party, knew of its illegal aims and advocated violent overthrow of the government whenever "circumstances would permit." The Court distinguished this outcome from a case in which guilt was based merely upon association and sympathies. Again the Court embraced present advocacy of violence, without a requirement of immediate action, as the appropriate standard for conviction.

HARRY POTTER and
§ 2.04 THE MODERN STANDARD OF REVIEW

The modern rule governing speech advocating illegal action draws more heavily upon the Brandeis-Holmes model of analysis. The reclamation and enhancement of clear and present danger standards began in the 1960s. The distinction between teaching doctrine and inciting actual violence was reaffirmed in *Noto v. United States*.[24] The *Noto* Court, however, did not make a distinction between advocacy of immediate or future illegal action. Advocacy of actual action remained punishable, whether imminent or remote.

In *Bond v. Floyd*,[25] the Court reviewed the Georgia legislature's refusal to swear in and seat an elected representative. The legislature's determination was based upon his criticism of the Vietnam War and the draft, which house members viewed as advocating resistance to military service. The Court found that the antiwar statements could not be understood as an incitement.

A similar analysis governed *Watts v. United States*,[26] when the Court reviewed a conviction under a federal law prohibiting threats against the president's life. The defendant had been convicted for making a statement, during an antiwar protest,

---

[22] 354 U.S. 298 (1957).

[23] 367 U.S. 203 (1961).

[24] 367 U.S. 290 (1961).

[25] 385 U.S. 116 (1966).

[26] 394 U.S. 705 (1969) (per curiam).

that the first person he would aim his rifle at if drafted would be the president. The Court considered the context of the statement and determined that it was an instance of "political hyperbole" rather than an actual threat or incitement. Important too was the fact that the speech posed no imminent danger to the president. Consideration of this factor represented an important step toward a more speech protective model of review.

In *Brandenburg v. Ohio*,[27] the Court announced a standard of review that made no reference to the clear and present danger test but embraced principles reflecting an amplified and fortified version of what even Brandeis and Holmes contemplated. This case concerned the conviction of several Ku Klux Klan members who had been prosecuted under the state's criminal syndicalism law. The speech that triggered their prosecution related to the group's intention to march on Washington, D.C. and included a statement that, if the political process "continues to suppress the white, Caucasian race, it's possible that there might have to be some revengeance [*sic*] taken."

For practical purposes, the state law was indistinguishable from the statute providing the basis for conviction in *Whitney v. California* The *Brandenburg* Court, however, described *Whitney* as a "thoroughly discredited" decision and formally overruled it. In so doing, the Court abandoned standards correlated to general bad tendencies. The standard of review set forth in *Brandenburg* provides that government may not abridge advocacy of force or illegal action unless it "is directed to inciting or producing imminent lawless action and is likely to incite or produce such action." This principle reaffirmed the distinction between mere abstract teaching of the morality of force and violence and actual incitement of such consequences. It broadened the First Amendment's reach even further, however, by distinguishing between imminent and remote consequences and requiring a showing that they were likely.

The *Brandenburg* decision thus represents a triumph of marketplace theory. So long as time exists for the marketplace of ideas to counter speech with dangerous tendencies, official abridgment is impermissible. Within this framework, reasoned discourse is the preferred alternative to government action. Only to the extent that speech has the capacity to incite an immediate violent response can government take action to intercept the consequences. Judicial inquiry pursuant to *Brandenburg* thus must focus upon whether (1) the speaker intended to incite violence; (2) the speech was likely to produce unlawful action; (3) the risk of unlawful action was imminent; and (4) unlawful action was likely.

Justices Black and Douglas, although concurring in the result, expressed concern that the test could be distorted during peak periods of national insecurity. Despite the fortified standard of review, they maintained that any balancing test was subject to manipulation and subjective assessment of risks. Justice Douglas in particular challenged the distinction between advocacy of abstract doctrine and action. Quoting from Justice Holmes' dissent in *Abrams v. United States*, he noted that "[e]very idea is an incitement." From Justice Douglas' perspective, First Amendment interests and principled decision-making would be accounted for

---

[27] 395 U.S. 444 (1969).

better by standards that candidly acknowledged this reality.

The *Brandenburg* decision includes a peculiar reference to *Dennis* as precedent for discrediting *Whitney*. This notation is puzzling, because the *Dennis* plurality applied an analytical regimen associated with *Whitney* and other decisions that focuses upon bad tendencies. Despite this somewhat confusing reference, jurisprudence since *Brandenburg* has given no indication of reverting back toward less speech protective standards. Continuing fidelity to the *Brandenburg* formula was evidenced in *Hess v. Indiana*,[28] when the Court reversed a disorderly conduct conviction stemming from alleged threats of illegal action during an antiwar demonstration. A finding of incitement had been based upon the defendant's yelling out that "we'll take the fucking street later." The Court found that the defendant's statement was not aimed at any person or group and thus could not have produced an imminent unlawful response. Nor was there sufficient clarity that the speech constituted an incitement. This determination suggests that it is not merely the subjective expectations of the speaker that are relevant for purposes of factoring whether speech was intended to incite unlawful consequences. As the *Hess* decision indicates, the Court also will inquire into whether objectively the speech could be understood as inciting such results.

The *Brandenburg* decision ushered in an era of doctrinal stability. Notwithstanding the introduction of key terminology such as incitement, imminence, and likelihood, the fact remains that these standards have an elastic nature. Even if these standards had been in effect during the 1920s and 1950s, when the national insecurity index was high, it is conceivable that the outcomes in *Gitlow, Whitney*, and *Dennis* would have been the same. When fears and apprehensions are elevated, risks that otherwise may seem distant or improbable can be exaggerated with respect to proximity and likelihood. Particularly to the extent ideas are incitements, the degree of risk may be magnified by the influence of perceived vulnerability upon the faculties of reason. It should be anticipated, so long as protection of speech is not absolute, that context and state of mind always will loom as factors having the potential to spin analysis toward a different outcome than might be achieved in another setting or at another time.

In *Planned Parenthood of Columbia/Willamette, Inc. v. American Coalition of Life Activists*, 422 F.3d 949 (9th Cir. 2005), the court applied the so-called "true threat" doctrine (which applies when a reasonable observer would believe that he will be subjected to physical violence) to an attempt to intimidate physicians. Physicians who performed abortions sued alleging that the American Coalition of Life Activists (ACLA) engaged in "a campaign of terror and intimidation" by targeting them with three specific threats — the "Deadly Dozen GUILTY" poster (which identified Hern and the Newhalls among ten others;), the "Crist" poster (which contained Crist's name, addresses and photograph), and the "Nuremberg Files" (a compilation of those who the ACLA believed might be put on trial for crimes against humanity one day). The posters identifying these physicians were circulated in the wake of a series of "WANTED" and "unWANTED" posters that had identified other doctors who performed abortions and who were murdered after the "WANTED" and "unWANTED" posters were circulated. The suit alleged that

---

[28] 414 U.S. 105 (1973).

the ACLA had violated or conspired to violate the Freedom of Access to Clinic Entrances Act (FACE) and the Racketeer Influenced and Corrupt Organizations Act (RICO), 18 U.S.C. §§ 1961–1968. Plaintiffs were awarded both compensatory damages and punitive damages. However, the initial award of $108.5 million in punitive damages was remitted to $45,000 to $75,000 per defendant.

The Court did not apply the *Brandenburg* formula in a case concerning a federal law that prohibited "material support" to any group that the Secretary of State has designated as a "foreign *terrorist* organization."[29] Humanitarian organizations providing training in peaceful dispute resolution and other non-violent methods maintained that the law chilled their freedoms of speech and association. In *Holder v. Humanitarian Law Project*, the Court determined that the First Amendment did not preclude Congress from barring aid even if the activity had a speech component. In reaching this result, the Court employed strict scrutiny. Although there was no disagreement on whether combating terrorism was a compelling interest, the Court fractured over whether the regulatory means were narrowly tailored. The majority concluded that government reasonably could conclude that the assistance provided by the groups, even if designed to advance peaceful outcomes, likely would promote terrorist goals. The Court noted in this regard that providing aid for a group's humanitarian activities could free up resources for terrorist activities.

Justice Breyer, in a dissent joined by Justices Ginsburg and Sotomayor, commenced his opinion with a reference to *Brandenburg*, reiterating that "the First Amendment protects advocacy even of *unlawful* action so long as that advocacy is not 'directed to inciting or producing *imminent lawless action* and . . . *likely to incite or produce* such action.' " He noted that, in this instance, the groups sought to advocate peaceful, lawful action to secure political ends. The speech itself, Breyer observed, thus could not be prohibited as incitement under *Brandenburg*. He also contested the premise that aid in the form of promoting peaceful processes (as opposed to food, money, or computer training) would free up resources that could be used for sinister purposes.

The result has been criticized on grounds the Court did not require a strong showing of likely harm (which would have been necessitated under the *Brandenburg)* formula, and that it settled for a rationale that the law was "preventive" of potential harm (so that virtually any regulation on point would survive scrutiny). Detractors also have observed that the government's interest, in ensuring that listed groups are not legitimized in the public eye, reflects viewpoint discrimination. Although the Court historically has been highly intolerant of viewpoint discrimination, it did not address the matter in this case. It is noteworthy that the Court differentiated speech and advocacy coordinated with a foreign terrorist group (i.e., "material support" from independent speech or advocacy. In this regard, it noted that the plaintiffs were free to exercise their "pure political speech" rights.

---

[29] Holder v. Humanitarian Law Project, 130 S. Ct. 2705 (2010).

POINTS TO REMEMBER

- Seminal freedom of speech analysis focused upon the harmful tendencies of speech and was deferential toward government.

- The dissenting opinions of Justices Holmes and Brandeis laid much of the groundwork for modern analysis concerning speech advocating violent or illegal action.

- The mid-Twentieth Century was a period of doctrinal turmoil, when case law reverted to seminal principles.

- The modern statement of the law, concerning speech advocating violent or illegal action, requires an assessment of the degree, imminence, and likelihood that the expression will incite the result.

Chapter 3

CONTENT REGULATION

```
┌─────────────────────────────────────────────────────────────┐
```

FOCAL POINTS FOR CHAPTER 3

- The two primary models for reviewing content based regulation of speech.

- The categorical exclusion of speech that has slight if any value toward the discovery of truth.

- The various methods of balancing protected speech against regulatory interests.

- The actual malice standard in defamation and other torts as a First Amendment safeguard.

- The concept of public officials and public figures.

- The public interest factor in defamation law.

- The media's right to publish private information that is lawfully acquired and newsworthy.

- Parallels between defamation law and privacy law.

- The right of publicity.

- Obscenity as unprotected speech.

- The problem of defining obscenity and establishing workable standards of review.

- The debate over whether obscenity should have First Amendment status.

§ 3.01 BASIC CONCEPTS AND APPLICATIONS

Regulation of speech because of the message it communicates represents content-based control. The starting point for analysis of content regulation is the principle that the First Amendment, above all else, denies government the "power to restrict expression because of the message, ideas, its subject matter or its content."[1] Despite this basic premise, content regulation may be permissible under two sets of circumstances. To the extent that speech fits into a category of expression that is unprotected by the free speech clause, government may prohibit it. Examples of this type of expression are obscenity, fighting word, and child pornography. It should be noted, however, that discrimination on the basis of viewpoint is impermissible even when unprotected expression is the regulatory focal point. A municipal ordinance prohibiting fighting words that perpetuate stereotypical views regarding race, religion, and gender, is invalid even though the prohibited

---

[1] Police Dept. of Chicago v. Mosley, 408 U.S. 92, 95 (1972).

speech otherwise was beyond the purview of the First Amendment.[2]

Content regulation of expression fitting within a protected category also may be permissible in limited situations. Analysis in these circumstances typically requires a balancing of constitutional and regulatory interests. This balancing may take place in the form of a clear and present danger test, which applies to speech advocating illegal action or when criticism of the judiciary results in a contempt of court citation. Balancing also may be evidenced by strict scrutiny, which is triggered when government regulates political speech in its purest forms. It also is manifested by an intermediate standard review which operates in the context of commercial speech and indecent expression.

§ 3.02 FIGHTING WORDS

In *Chaplinsky v. New Hampshire*,[3] the Court held that so-called "fighting words" are not entitled to First Amendment protection. It defined "fighting words" as those words "which by their very utterance inflict injury or tend to incite an immediate breach of the peace." In *Chaplinsky*, a Jehovah's Witness was distributing literature on the streets of Rochester on a Saturday afternoon. In addition, he denounced all religion as a "racket." When members of the crowd complained, the police informed Chaplinsky that he was acting lawfully and that the crowd was getting restless. Eventually, when a disturbance occurred, they escorted Chaplinsky towards the police station, but did not inform Chaplinsky that he was being arrested or that he was under arrest. On the way to the station, they encountered the City Marshall who had been informed that a riot was under way (as a result of Chaplinsky's remarks) and was hurrying towards the scene. When Chaplinsky saw the Marshall, he stated that "You are a God damned racketeer" and "a damned Fascist and the whole government of Rochester are Fascists or agents of Fascists." Chaplinsky was found guilty of violating a New Hampshire law that prohibited anyone from addressing "any offensive, derisive or annoying word to any other person who is lawfully in any street or other public place" and also prohibited anyone from calling such person by any "offensive or derisive name."

In affirming Chaplinsky's conviction, the Court began by recognizing that the right to free speech is not absolute. The Court went on to hold that there are "certain well-defined and narrowly limited classes of speech, the prevention and punishment of which have never been thought to raise any Constitutional problem." The Court included within these categories, the lewd and obscene, the profane, the libelous, and insulting or "fighting" words. The Court defined "fighting words" as those words "which by their very utterance inflict injury or tend to incite an immediate breach of the peace." In the Court's view, such "utterances are no essential part of any exposition of ideas, and are of such slight social value as a step to truth that any benefit that may be derived from them is clearly outweighed by the social interest in order and morality.[4] Resort to epithets or personal abuse is not in any proper sense communication of information or opinion safeguarded by the

---

[2] R.A.V. v. City of St. Paul, 505 U.S. 377 (1992).

[3] 315 U.S. 568 (1942).

[4] Chafee, *op. cit.*, 150.

Constitution, and its punishment as a criminal act would raise no question under that instrument."

Of course, the Court was left with the problem of how to define the term "fighting words." The *Chaplinsky* Court concluded that the term included such words "as have a direct tendency to cause acts of violence by the person to whom, individually, the remark is addressed." "The test is what men of common intelligence would understand would be words likely to cause an average addressee to fight." The Court ultimately upheld the New Hampshire law because it did no more than "prohibit the face-to-face words plainly likely to cause a breach of the peace by the addressee, words whose speaking constitute a breach of the peace by the speaker — including 'classical fighting words,' words in current use less 'classical' but equally likely to cause violence, and other disorderly words, including profanity, obscenity and threats."

The Heckler's Veto. Some decisions suggest that the government can suppress speech when there is a hostile audience reaction (even though the speech may not officially rise to the level of "fighting words") which creates a substantial threat of public disorder.[5] These cases are disturbing because they allow the listener to dictate the scope of the speaker's free speech rights. As a general rule, government should protect the speaker, and prosecute the listener who tries to terminate the speech, rather than suppress the speech. For example, a few years ago, when the Cincinnati, Ohio, created a free speech forum, the Ku Klux Klan (KKK) decided to erect a cross. Objectors repeatedly tried to tear down the cross, and the police tried to protect it. However, at some point, if the listeners are sufficiently out of control, and pose a sufficient threat to public order, it might be appropriate to limit the speech.

In recent years, free speech has sometimes produced violent reactions around the world. In general, courts have tended to uphold the rights of individuals to engage in such speech notwithstanding the violent reactions. Three instances of such speech are detailed below.

The Danish Cartoons. In December 2005, a Danish newspaper, Jyllands-Posten, published caricatures of the Prophet Mohammed in order to raise questions about Muslim violence and suicide bombings. Muslims were outraged by the cartoon, not only because Muslim law prohibits publication of pictures of the Prophet, but also because the Prophet was portrayed as a terrorist (e.g., with a bomb in his turban). The publication led to Muslim protests around the world. Although some of the protests were peaceful, others were quite violent and involved property damage and deaths. Even though the U.S. government did not have the power to prohibit publication of the cartoons, virtually all U.S. media outlets decided not to publish or show the cartoons. The violent response raises interesting questions regarding a possible application of the "hostile audience" doctrine, and the question of whether the reactions of the listeners should dictate the scope of a speaker's right to express ideas. As a general rule, with some exceptions, U.S. courts have cut that balance in favor of the speaker rather than by allowing the audience's reaction to control the discourse.

---

[5] *See* Feiner v. New York, 340 U.S. 315 (1951).

The Minister and the Koran. In a similar vein, a pastor in Florida threatened to burn a copy of the Koran in commemoration of the 9/11 terrorist attacks. Governmental officials feared that the burning of the Koran would spark violence and anti-U.S. backlash around the world. Although the minister initially agreed not to follow through with the threat to burn the Korans, he eventually held a mock trial and did burn one. The minister's actions did not provoke violence in the U.S., but did provoke significant violence in countries such as Afghanistan. As with the Danish cartoons, officials tended to uphold the right of the minister to engage in this speech despite the violent reactions. They did, however, try to dissuade him from burning the Koran (to no avail).

Anti-Islamic Video Protests. In July 2012, a short video was uploaded to YouTube. The video appeared under two titles, "The Real Life of Muhammad" and the "Muhammad Movie Video." According to those involved, anti-Islamic content was added to the video after the filming was complete, and the content was also added in Arabic. When a blogger wrote about the video, and a short excerpt was aired on Egyptian television, violent demonstrations erupted that demanded that the video be removed from the Internet. Although the U. S. Embassy in Cairo issued a statement disavowing the video, protestors attacked the Embassy compound and destroyed a U.S. flag. The next day, protestors attacked the U.S. embassy in Yemen, prompting a police reaction that killed 4 protestors and injured 11 others. In the ensuing days, there were attacks on Multinational Force and Observers' compound in the Sinai Peninsula, the U.S. embassies in Tunis and Jakarta, the American Cooperative School in Tunisia, a U.S. consulate in India, a U.S. military camp (killing two Marines). The U.S. government ultimately asked YouTube and Google to review the video, and they blocked it in Egypt, Libya, Indonesia, Saudi Arabia, Malaysia, India, Singapore, Pakistan, and Jordan. Other countries blocked the YouTube website for failing to block the video. By this time, as many as 75 deaths had been attributed to protests of the video in various countries. *See* David D. Kirkpatrick, *Cultural Clash Fuels Muslim Raging at Film*, THE NEW YORK TIMES (Sept. 16, 2012); Madé Sentana & James Hookway, *Anti-U.S. Protests Flare Again*, THE WALL STREET JOURNAL, A-1 (SEPT. 18, 2012).

POINTS TO REMEMBER

- "Fighting words" are not protected under the First Amendment.
- "Fighting words" are words which, by their very utterance, "inflict injury or tend to incite an immediate breach of the peace."
- However, it is difficult to draft a valid "fighting words" ordinance.
- Most ordinances utilize language that is unconstitutonally vague or overbroad.

Although *Chaplinsky* held that fighting words are not protected under the First Amendment, many convictions under "fighting words" statutes are reversed on vagueness and overbreadth grounds. For example, in *Gooding v. Wilson*,[6] defendant

---

[6] 405 U.S. 518 (1972).

was convicted under a Georgia law that provided as follows: "Any person who shall, without provocation, use to or of another, and in his presence . . . opprobrious words or abusive language, tending to cause a breach of the peace . . . shall be guilty of a misdemeanor." The evidence showed that he stated to a police officer: "White son of a bitch, I'll kill you." "You son of a bitch, I'll choke you to death." Count 4 alleged that the defendant "did without provocation use to and of T.L. Raborn, and in his presence, the following abusive language and opprobrious words, tending to cause a breach of the peace: 'You son of a bitch, if you ever put your hands on me again, I'll cut you all to pieces.' " The Court concluded that the terms "opprobrious" and "abusive" were broader than the term "fighting" words and therefore were impermissibly imprecise.[7]

§ 3.03 DEFAMATION

The concept of defamation comprehends the torts of libel and slander, which speak to reputational injury that is caused respectively by written and spoken falsehoods. Until the middle of the Twentieth Century, defamation categorically was regarded as constitutionally unprotected expression. Under British colonial law, as noted in Chapter 1, truth was an aggravating rather than ameliorating factor with respect to defamation. Common law in the United States evolved a variety of defenses to defamation claims, including truth, fair comment, and certain types of privilege. Beginning in the 1960s, the First Amendment emerged as a source of protection for some types of defamatory expression. Constitutional limitations upon the law of defamation, as noted in the following sections, reflect the high value that has been assigned to speech facilitating informed self-governance.

[A] Traditional Doctrine and Seeds of Change

The intersection of First Amendment principles and defamation law grew out of the political and social ferment that catalyzed the civil rights movement. This phenomenon reflects the strong correlation, particularly during the Warren Court era, between the evolution of First Amendment principles and the struggle for racial justice.[8] A preview of this dynamic was evident in *Beauharnais v. Illinois*,[9] when the Court reviewed a group libel statute used to convict a person who had circulated literature that disparaged African-Americans. The law criminalized any publication portraying a racial or religious group in terms of "depravity, criminality, unchastity, or lack of virtue" and bringing "contempt, derision, [or] obloquy" or producing "breach of the peace or of riots."[10] The leaflets at issue, advocating resistance to neighborhood integration, urged white persons to preserve their racial identity and avoid "forced mongrelization."

---

[7] *See also* City of Houston v. Hill, 482 U.S. 451 (1987) (invalidating a Houston ordinance as unconstitutionally overbroad).

[8] *See* Harry Kalven, Jr., The Negro and the First Amendment (1965).

[9] 343 U.S. 250 (1952).

[10] *Id.* at 252.

Such expression, notwithstanding its offensive presentation, communicated a political point of view. By a 5-4 vote, and consistent with conventional understanding of defamation, the Court concluded that the expression was not a constitutionally protected form of speech. From the majority's perspective, group libel in particular deserved no shelter because it facilitated the deprivation of individual dignity and social opportunity. This premise is consistent with modern arguments for hate speech control which, to date, have not been well-received by the Court.[11] Although the *Beauharnais* decision has never been overruled formally, subsequent defamation case law and the Court's attitude toward hate speech control indicate that it has little, if any, vitality.

Today, the most significant aspect of *Beauharnais* is Justice Black's dissenting opinion which previews the future of defamation law. Black's underlying premise, consistent with his general theory of the First Amendment, was that government cannot abridge any type of speech. Although this view never has commanded a majority, Black's concern with respect to the potential risks of libel laws was prophetic. Responding to the majority's sense that racial minorities would benefit from laws that protected their reputation, he maintained that such regulation actually heightened their exposure to the risk of repression. Justice Black thus anticipated that defamation law could be turned against minorities who might challenge or criticize racial injustice. As he put it, "there may be minority groups who hail this holding as their, victory, [but] they might consider the possibility of this ancient remark: 'Another such victory and I am undone.' "[12]

[B]   Defamation as Protected Expression: The Actual Malice Requirement

[1]   Public Officials

Justice Black's warning accurately forecast the risks of defamation law for minorities seeking to challenge a repressive political system. The Court's next major defamation case concerned not just a garden variety libel claim, but a calculated effort to incapacitate the civil rights movement. These circumstances contributed to a heightened appreciation that defamation law, unless properly restrained, can be used to silence expression that is critical to informed and effective self-governance. With this understanding, the Court moved toward a reconstructed view of defamation law that included constitutional protection of such speech under certain circumstances.

This landmark decision was rendered in *New York Times Co. v. Sullivan*,[13] when the Court reversed a state court verdict and damages award to the police commissioner of Montgomery, Alabama. The case arose from an editorial advertisement published in the *New York Times* that criticized police handling of civil rights demonstrations in Montgomery, and other locations, and referenced the efforts of "southern violators" who responded to non-violent protests with intimi-

---

[11] R.A.V. v. City of St. Paul, 505 U.S. 377 (1992).

[12] *Id.* at 275 (Black, J., dissenting).

[13] 376 U.S. 254 (1964).

dation and violence. The advertisement contained some inaccuracies that largely were minor and immaterial. Although not specifically named in the advertisement, the police commissioner maintained that it created the impression that his office condoned lawless action. A jury agreed that he had been defamed and awarded him one-half million dollars in damages based upon state law that enabled the jury to presume damages rather than compute them on the basis of some demonstrated showing of loss.

The trial jury's verdict and damages award were upheld by the state supreme court. Based upon traditional defamation law, the opinion was airtight. The immediate consequence was that the *New York Times* stopped distribution in Alabama and was faced with the possibility of debilitating financial burdens if other civil rights opponents followed suit. Under these circumstances, the potential for chilling important political discourses was manifest. The result was indistinguishable from what traditionally had been achieved by seditious libel laws. To avoid these results, the Court concluded that it was necessary to reconfigure the traditional understanding and operation of defamation law, and turned to the First Amendment as a basis for recasting defamation law.

The *Sullivan* decision examined defamation against what it characterized as a "profound national commitment to the principle that debate on public Issues should be uninhibited, robust, and wide-open, and that it may well include vehement, caustic, and sometimes unpleasantly sharp attacks on government and public officials."[14] The facts of the *Sullivan* case provided ample proof that defamation law could be applied in a fashion that was inimical to this policy. Traditional defenses, such as truth, provided inadequate protection to defamation when the law was used as an instrument for achieving political results. The plaintiff could rely on minor and inconsequential inaccuracies to construct a defamation case. Although the newspaper might have been negligent in publishing the inaccuracies, without independently checking the facts, the cost and consequences of liability in these circumstances seemed disproportionate. The *Sullivan* decision reflected a sensitivity to these factors and attempted to create more breathing space for First Amendment interests

Central to the *Sullivan* decision was a new standard for defamation actions brought by public officials that imposed a higher barrier to recovery. The Court emphasized that public officials occupy a position at the center of government activity and policy, and their actions and decisions should be subject to scrutiny by the electorate they represent. As the agents of the people, they should be subject to public approval or criticism. Since public officials are immune from liability for defamatory statements they make in the course of their official duties,[15] it followed as a matter of congruity that critics of public officials should have expanded room to critique the performance of those officials. Criticism is a critical aspect of informed self-governance. As a result, the Court decreed that a public official cannot recover for defamation without showing, by clear and convincing evidence, that the

---

[14] *Id.* at 270.

[15] Barr v. Matteo, 360 U.S. 564 (1959).

statement was made with "actual malice."[16] By creating this qualified privilege, the Court conferred constitutional protection upon a speech that defamed public officials.

The term "actual malice" is a term of art. It is not synonymous with mean-spiritedness or ill will. Rather, it relates to the state of mind that produced the defamatory statement. In other words, a public official could only recover for defamation when the defendant made the defamatory statement with "knowledge that [the statement] was false or [in] reckless disregard of whether it was true or false."[17] In other words, public officials could not recover defamation damages based on strict liability or negligence principles. The meaning of the term "reckless disregard" was not precisely defined. In the Court's own words, reckless disregard "cannot be fully encompassed in one infallible definition."[18] Indications of reckless disregard, however, are a defendant's "high degree of awareness of probable falsity" or "entertain[ing] serious doubts as to the truth truth of his publication."[19] When a person has the opportunity to check the truthfulness of information, but bypasses, he or she technically may not have the requisite state of mind for actual malice.[20] Whether "actual malice" exists is treated as a constitutional question and thus will be reviewed independently by appellate courts.[21]

For a public official plaintiff, it is not easy to prove that actual malice exists. It is not enough to show that the defendant was in error. On the contrary, the plaintiff must probe the editorial process in an effort to show that the publisher had the requisite mental state. In recognition of this need, the Court has rejected arguments for an editorial privilege against discovery.[22]

The *Sullivan* decision candidly reflected concern that the tort of defamation could be used to silence public criticism and undermine the purpose of the First Amendment. A primary problem presented by the public official designation is determining who qualifies for such status. A "public official" has been defined as a person empowered with significant responsibility and discretion in managing public affairs.[23] Candidates for public office,[24] and former office holders to the extent comments relate to their performance of official duties,[25] are included in the concept. When a defamation relates to private aspects of a public official's life, the actual malice standard may apply because the official's private actions may bear upon the official's fitness to hold public office. Given the range of responsibilities performed by public employees, the characterization creates the potential for difficult line-drawing. The Court has not articulated precise standards for deter-

---

[16] *New York Times Co.*, 376 U.S. at 279–80.

[17] *Id.* at 280.

[18] St. Amant v. Thompson, 390 U.S. 727, 730 (1968).

[19] *Id.* at 731.

[20] Harte-Hanks Communications, Inc. v. Connaughton, 491 U.S. 657 (1989).

[21] Bose Corporation v. Consumers Union, 466 U.S. 485 (1984).

[22] Herbert v. Lando, 441 U.S. 553 (1979).

[23] Rosenblatt v. Baer, 383 U.S. 75, 85 (1966).

[24] Monitor Patriot Co. v. Roy, 401 U.S. 265, 271 (1971).

[25] Curtis Publishing Co. v. Butts, 388 U.S. 130, 164 (1967).

mining who does and does not qualify for public official status.

[2] Public Figures

Public officials are a significant but not exclusive source of influence upon public discourse. Once Sullivan recognized that speech that is material to informed self-governance should be protected, questions inevitably arose regarding whether other categories of individuals should be subject to higher defamation standards such as individuals who, because of their stature, fame, credibility, or personality, command the public's attention and therefore wield influence. The boundaries of constitutionally protected defamation soon expanded beyond public officials to include persons who, although not holding public office, nonetheless had a significant public presence. In *Curtis Publishing Co. v. Butts*,[26] the Court extended the actual malice standard to so-called "public Figures." In doing so, the Court recognized that public figures, like public officials, can be "intimately involved in the resolution of important public questions or, by reason of their fame, shape events in areas of concern to society at large."[27]

A common denominator of the *Sullivan* and *Butts* decisions was that expression, even if defamatory, merits First Amendment protection if it implicates public issues material to effective self-governance. This premise might suggest that First Amendment standards in the defamation context should correlate to the nature of the speech rather than to the status of the defendant. A plurality of the Court embraced this proposition in *Rosenbloom v. Metromedia, Inc.*[28] when it decreed that the actual malice standard should extend to defamatory statements concerning matters of general or public interest. Under this approach, any defamed person whose experience intersected a matter of public concern could be held to the actual malice standard whether or not the individual was a public official or a public figure. This plurality view ultimately failed to command a majority of justices then or over the long run, but did assume importance in the Court's treatment of defamation actions by private individuals. The actual malice standard has remained correlated to the public status of the defamed individual.

[a] The Outer Limits of the Actual Malice Standard

Although falling short of Justice Black's absolutist position that defamation was protected fully by the free speech clause, the *Rosenbloom* plurality marked the potential outer limits of the actual malice standard. As the Warren Court increasingly transitioned into the Burger Court, a majority coalesced against shifting the focus of actual malice from persons to issues. In *Gertz v. Robert Welch, Inc.*,[29] the Court held that the actual malice standard applied only to public officials and public figures. The Court's decision reflected a sense that the balance between constitutional policy and tort law, as calibrated by the *Rosenbloom* plurality, undervalued legitimate reputational interests.

---

[26] 388 U.S. 130 (1967).

[27] *Id.* at 164.

[28] 403 U.S. 29 (1971).

[29] 418 U.S. 323 (1974).

Gertz involved a defamation action by an attorney who had represented a family in a wrongful death action against a police officer. A magazine had described the lawyer as a "Communist fronter" and stated that his efforts were part of a "Communist campaign against the police" and "frame-up" of the particular officer. The Court was forced to decide whether the attorney should be treated as a public official or public figure since, in addition to being an attorney, and thus an officer of the court, the plaintiff had served on various government boards and commissions. Rejecting the notion that the plaintiff was a public official or public figure, the Court focused upon the standards that should apply to a defamation action brought by a private individual.

The Court determined that, when private individuals sue for defamation, the actual malice standard exacts too high a price. Unlike public officials or figures, they do not invite public attention or warrant an assumption that they voluntarily have exposed themselves to a higher risk of reputational harm. Nor do they command access to the media and possess an ability to undo or mitigate reputational injury. Based upon these premises, the Court concluded that lower burden of proof requirements should apply to a defamation action by a private individual. So long as a state does not impose strict liability, therefore, it may apply a burden of proof that is less rigorous than the actual malice standard. In other words, the standard could vary from state-to-state. And, in fact, states do apply different standards with some applying the actual malice standard, and others applying a negligence or public interest standard.

In addition to limiting the application of the actual malice standard, *Gertz* provided guidance regarding the definition of the term "public figure." The Court suggested that public figures are individuals who "have assumed roles of especial prominence in the affairs of society." They fall into two main categories: those who "occupy positions of such pervasive power and influence that they are deemed public figures for all purposes,"[30] and those who "have thrust themselves to the forefront of particular public controversies in order to influence the resolution of the issues involved."[31] The common denominator of individuals assigned to either of these classifications is that they have invited attention or comment. The Court acknowledged, at least hypothetically, the possibility of an "involuntary public figure" who achieves this status unwillingly. It noted, however, that such a person would be rare.

Melania Trump?

Applying these standards to Gertz, the Court found that he did not have widespread fame in the community and thus did not fit into the first category of public figures. To the extent Gertz took on a relatively high profile case, however, the argument could be made that he thrust himself into the controversy with an intent (and even obligation) to influence the outcome. The Court, however, refused to draw trial lawyers into the actual malice web. Ultimately, the *Gertz* decision limited the Court's expansion of the categories of individuals to which the actual malice standard applied.

Gertz also granted states permission to apply a lower burden of proof to actions

---

[30] *Curtis Publishing Co.*, 388 U.S. at 162.

[31] *Id.* at 16.

by defamation actions brought by private individuals. Provided they did not impose strict liability, and they limited a plaintiff's recovery to actual damages, the states were free to impose liability based on a negligence standard. Presumed and punitive damages remained possible for instances when the private plaintiff could prove that the defendant acted with actual malice. Post-*Gertz* case law leaves open the question of whether the same protections apply to defamatory statements by non-media defendants.

While the *Gertz* approach may not be entirely consistent with the principles of informed self-governance articulated in *Sullivan*, they reveal the Court's willingness to balance complex competing interests in this context. It should, perhaps, have been foreseen that there would come a point when the balance between speech and reputation would require speech principles to give way. Private individuals typically have less access to the media than public officials or public figures, so are less able to secure remedies for reputational damage through self-help. They also do not thrust themselves into public controversies. These considerations helped convince the Court that the status of the plaintiff, rather than the content of the speech, was the logical basis for a dividing line between constitutionally protected and less protected defamatory speech.

As the Internet has spawned new forms of communication, defamation principles are being applied in new contexts involving non-media professionals. For example, in a number of instances, individual bloggers have been sued for defamation. *See* Caryn Rousseau, *Bloggers Learn to Deal with Media Pitfalls: Citizen Journalists Get Training*, THE COURIER-JOURNAL (Louisville, KY), A-6, c. 1-3 (June 15, 2008). While some bloggers are journalists who work for traditional newspapers, others are individuals who choose to comment on social, political or economic issues. *See* id. Similar issues have arisen regarding websites. See David L. Hudson, Jr., Taming the Gossipmongers: Websites That Dish Dirt May Soon Get Their Publishers' Hands Muddy, A.B.A.J. 19 (July, 2008).

[b]   The Public Figure Concept Refined

Subsequent case law has narrowed the concept of a public figure. In *Time, Inc. v. Firestone*,[32] the Court determined that a well-known socialite was not a public figure. This finding was made in the context of a divorce proceeding that, because of the lurid testimony it generated, drew extensive public attention. At the trial's conclusion, a national news magazine published a brief report that the husband was granted a divorce on the basis of his wife's adultery and extreme cruelty. The characterization of adultery as a basis for the divorce decree technically was inaccurate.

Two factors were critical to the outcome in *Firestone* and hence material to understanding the concept of a public figure. First, the plaintiff's prominent stature in elite social circles was not sufficient for placement in the category of a public figure. Nor had she voluntarily injected herself into a public controversy for purposes of influencing its outcome. This determination was made even though she had conducted news conferences, retained a public relations expert to present her

---

[32] 424 U.S. 448 (1976).

story to the public, and maintained a clipping service. Second, the Court found that a divorce proceeding was not the type of controversy that rose to the level of a public concern. Although the public might have an interest in such matters, and a divorce trial can implicate the process of governance, the impact of such proceedings upon the public are relatively more remote. The Court effectively limited public figure status, therefore, to contexts where serious issues of public policy clearly are present.

The public figure configuration was detailed further in *Proxmire v. Hutchinson*[33] and *Wolston v. Reader's Digest Association, Inc.*[34] In *Proxmire*, the Court reviewed a United States Senator's comments characterizing a researcher's federally subsidized research as worthless and a waste of taxpayer money. The senator's comments were well-publicized, but these remarks by themselves could not be the basis for making the plaintiff a public figure. Because the plaintiff possessed neither pervasive fame nor notoriety and had not pursued the limelight, the Court reversed a lower court finding that he was a public figure.

The *Wolston* case concerned publication of a book identifying the plaintiff as a Soviet agent. Although having been subpoenaed in the past to testify in an investigation, and having been held in contempt for failing to comply, he denied any Soviet relationship. As in *Proxmire*, the Court found that the plaintiff had not sought public attention. Mere involvement in a criminal matter did not provide a sufficient basis for achieving public figure status. Coupled with *Firestone and Proxmire*, the *Wolston* decision evidenced reticence toward defining the concept of limited public figures expansively or animating the notion of an involuntary public figure.

[3] The Not Entirely Irrelevant Public Concern Factor

Among the reasons that the public interest standard of *Rosenbloom* never captured majority support was a sense that it would require the Court to make *ad hoc* judgments about what type of issues would qualify as involving the "public interest." Although this difficulty was evident in *Gertz*, the Court's self-proclaimed reticence and lack of expertise did not stop it from identifying a "real" public controversy for purposes of defining a public figure in *Firestone*. Whether a statement related to a matter of public concern also is relevant in other defamation contexts. In *Philadelphia Newspapers, Inc. v. Hepps*,[35] the Court determined that a private plaintiff suing a media defendant need not prove actual falsehood if the statement does not touch a matter of public concern.

Despite its stated reluctance to be drawn into processes of treacherous line-drawing, for purposes of applying the actual malice standard, the Court adopted a similar framework for purposes of framing the scope and availability of damages. The *Gertz* Court announced, in a case concerning a media defendant, that presumed or punitive damages must be conditioned upon a showing of actual malice. Minus such proof, a plaintiff's compensation is limited to "actual damages." These include

---

[33] 443 U.S. 157 (1979).

[34] 443 U.S. 111 (1979).

[35] 475 U.S. 767 (1986).

"out-of-pocket loss" and "impairment of reputation and standing in the community, personal humiliation, and mental anguish and suffering."[36] This standard thus factors into actual damages at least some of the considerations that traditionally have been referenced in connection with presumed damages. What was left unclear in *Gertz*, however, was whether presumed and punitive damages could be recovered in a case that implicated only purely private interests.

This question presented itself in *Dun & Bradstreet, Inc. v. Greenmoss Builders, Inc.*,[37] a case concerning a credit reporting agency's dissemination of an inaccurate credit report. Instead of focusing upon the status of the defendant for purposes of damages, a plurality looked to whether the defamatory statement related to a matter of public interest. Pursuant to this model, the actual malice standard governs presumed or punitive damages only when the defamation implicates a matter of public concern.

[4]   Second Thoughts on the Actual Malice Standard

The *Dun & Bradstreet* decision is notable for some second thoughts with respect to the actual malice standard itself. Justice White, who embraced the standard in *Sullivan*, had become convinced that the Court had struck an "improvident balance" with respect to freedom of speech and reputational interests. From his standpoint, the actual malice standard "countenances two evils: first, the stream of information about public officials is polluted and often remains polluted by false information; and second, the reputation and professional life of the defeated plaintiff may be destroyed by falsehoods that might have been avoided with a reasonable effort to investigate the facts."[38] Despite criticism by Justice White and others, the actual malice standard as defined by *Sullivan* and *Gertz* remains intact.

Because of the *New York Times* standard, the United States is very much an outlier in the defamation area.[39] The rules applied (at the time of the decision) in Commonwealth countries were very pro-plaintiff, and struck the balance between speech and reputation decisively in favor of reputation lest[40] "good men fall prey to foul rumor."[41] In the last couple of decades, defamation rules in some Common-wealth countries (e.g., Australia[42] and England[43]) have become more pro-defendant, but those countries still do not provide the level of protection provided under the

---

[36] *Gertz*, 418 U.S. at 350.

[37] 472 U.S. 749 (1985).

[38] *Id.* at 769 (White, J., concurring).

[39] *See* RUSSELL L. WEAVER, ANDREW T. KENYON, DAVID F. PARTLETT & CLIVE P. WALKER, THE RIGHT TO SPEAK ILL: DEFAMATION, REPUTATION AND FREE SPEECH 131–150 (2006) [hereafter THE RIGHT TO SPEAK ILL].

[40] *See* THE RIGHT TO SPEAK ILL, *supra* note 39, at 17.

[41] Norman L. Rosenberg, PROTECTING THE BEST MEN: AN INTERPRETIVE HISTORY OF THE LAW OF LIBEL 17, 251 (1986).

[42] *See* Lange v. Australian Broadcasting Corp. (1997) 182 C.L.R. 104 (Austl.) (extending common law qualified privilege).

[43] *See* Reynolds v. Times Newspapers Ltd., 3 W.L.R. [2001] 2 A.C. 127 (HL) (extending common law qualified privilege).

New York Times standard.[44]

In clashes between the *New York Times* liability standards, and the standards applied in other countries, the United States has tended to adhere to the *New York Times* standards. Indeed, U.S. courts have refused to enforce foreign free speech (or defamation) judgments that are not consistent with U.S defamation liability standards.[45] Since no other nation applies the *New York Times* actual malice standard, the effect is that foreign defamation liability judgments are not enforceable in the United States.

[C] Fact and Opinion

Most constitutional case law concerning defamation relates to the boundaries and operation of the actual malice standard. In framing the criterion's contours in *Gertz*, the Court observed that "there is no such thing as a false idea" under the First Amendment.[46] It further noted that society depends upon the marketplace of ideas, rather than on the judicial process, to correct opinions that may be pernicious. This premise reflects John Stuart Mill's theory of expressive freedom, which assigns utility to false ideas for purposes of keeping minds active, achieving informed judgment, and strengthening the processes of autonomous judgment. It also suggests the possibility that unlike false statements of fact, opinions are beyond the pale of defamation law. The Court repudiated this distinction in *Milkovich v. Lorain Journal*,[47] when it refused to find a privilege for expressions of opinion. Insofar as opinions can be understood to relate or imply falsehood, they are as actionable as a statement of fact. Although this ruling may be perceived as unfriendly toward First Amendment interests, defendants may argue that a particular fact should not be inferred from a given opinion, and a number of courts have so held. They also retain the common law privilege of fair comment.

[D] False Speech

The Court, in *New York Times v. Sullivan*, provided "breathing space" for false speech. This protection, however, is not unlimited. False advertising and perjury are examples of speech that would not be protected. In *United States v. Alvarez*,[48] the Court invalidated a law that prohibited persons from falsely claiming they had received a military decoration or medal. A plurality of four justices, in an opinion by Justice Kennedy, declined the government's invitation to make "false statements [a] new category of unprotected speech." It thus determined that falsity by itself was an insufficient basis for removing speech from the First Amendment's protection. The plurality, using strict scrutiny, concluded there was an insufficient linkage between the government's interest in securing the military honors system's integrity and the restriction on false claims. It further noted that "counter speech"

---

[44] *See* THE RIGHT TO SPEAK ILL, *supra* note 39, at 201–292.

[45] *See* Investorshub.com v. Mina Mar Group Inc., 39 Media. L. Rptr. 2078 (N.D. Fla. 2011); Sarl Louis Feraud International v. Viewfinder, Inc., 406 F. Supp. 2d 274 (S.D.N.Y. 2005).

[46] *Gertz* at 418.

[47] 497 U.S. 1 (1990).

[48] 132 S. Ct. 2537 (2012).

provided an adequate and less constitutionally invasive solution to the problem. Justice Breyer (joined by Justice Kagan) maintained that, although false statements are entitled to some protection, the enactment was valid because its objective could have been achieved in less restrictive ways. Their inquiry was grounded not in strict scrutiny but in asking "whether the statute works speech-related harm that is out of proportion to its justifications."

POINTS TO REMEMBER

- Defamation historically has been unprotected under the First Amendment.

- Defamatory expression may include speech that is facilitative of informed self-government and thus worthy of First Amendment protection.

- Public officials and public figures may not recover for defamation unless they establish actual malice.

- A public figure is someone who occupies a position of such pervasive power and influence as to be a public figure for all purposes, or who has thrust himself or herself into the forefront of a particular public controversy in order to influence the resolution of the issues involved.

- Presumed or punitive damages generally may not be recovered absent a showing of actual malice.

- If a defamatory statement does not implicate a matter of public concern, presumed or punitive damages may be recovered without a showing of actual malice.

- The Court has not privileged statements of opinion from a defamation claim.

---

§ 3.04 INTENTIONAL INFLICTION OF EMOTIONAL DISTRESS

Does the Constitution also provide special protection in "emotional distress" cases? Or, to state the converse, do the states have greater authority to define the tort of intentional infliction of mental distress than they do the tort of defamation?

The leading case is *Hustler Magazine v. Falwell*,[49] which significantly restricted recovery in emotional distress cases. That case involved the Reverend Jerry Falwell, "a nationally known minister who [was] active as a commentator on politics and public affairs." Falwell sued *Hustler Magazine* over a "parody" of a Campari Liqueur advertisement that contained Falwell's name and picture and was entitled "Jerry Falwell talks about his first time." The parody was based on actual Campari ads that involved actual interviews with celebrities about their "first times." Although the ads focused on the "first time" the celebrities tried Campari, the ads

---

[49] 485 U.S. 46 (1988).

were suggestive of sexual "first times." The Falwell ads depicted an "interview" with Falwell in which he stated that his "first time" involved "a drunken incestuous rendezvous with his mother in an outhouse." The ad portrayed respondent and his mother as drunk and immoral, and suggested that respondent was a hypocrite who preached only while drunk. The ad contained a disclaimer, "ad parody — not to be taken seriously," that was set forth in small print at the bottom of the page, and the magazine's table of contents listed the ad as "Fiction; Ad and Personality Parody."

Because of the disclaimer, Falwell could not sue Hustler for defamation. Defamation requires a misstatement of a material fact, and the disclaimer made it clear that the ad involved satire rather than a misstatement of fact. Accordingly, Falwell sued Hustler for intentional infliction of mental distress, and a jury awarded him $100,000 in compensatory damages and $50,000 in punitive damages. Before the United States Supreme Court, Falwell argued that the state interest in protecting public figures from emotional distress was sufficient to deny Hustler's parody First Amendment protection. Falwell further argued that the speech was patently offensive and intended to inflict emotional injury.

The Court began by noting that one who intentionally inflicts emotional distress is not entitled to "much solicitude," and noted that virtually all jurisdictions have imposed liability when the infliction is "sufficiently 'outrageous.' " Nevertheless, the Court held that Hustler's parody was entitled to First Amendment protection. The Court expressed concern that the imposition of liability could inhibit speech "if the speaker must run the risk that it will be proved in court that he spoke out of hatred."[50] In addition, the Court recognized that even hateful utterances can "contribute to the free interchange of ideas and the ascertainment of truth" when honestly believed.[51]

The Court was particularly concerned about the fact that, if Falwell's "patently offensive" standard were to be adopted, political cartoonists and satirists might be subject to liability. Indeed, the:

> appeal of the political cartoon or caricature is often based on exploitation of unfortunate physical traits or politically embarrassing events — an exploitation often calculated to injure the feelings of the subject of the portrayal. The art of the cartoonist is often not reasoned or even-handed, but slashing and one-sided. One cartoonist expressed the nature of the art in these words: "The political cartoon is a weapon of attack, of scorn and ridicule and satire; it is least effective when it tries to pat some politician on the back. It is usually as welcome as a bee sting and is always controversial in some quarters." Long, The Political Cartoon: Journalism's Strongest Weapon, The Quill 56, 57 (Nov. 1962). Several famous examples of this type of intentionally injurious speech were drawn by Thomas Nast, probably the greatest American cartoonist to date, who was associated for many years during the post-Civil War era with Harper's Weekly. In the pages of that publication Nast conducted a graphic vendetta against William M. "Boss" Tweed and his corrupt associates in New York City's "Tweed Ring." It has

---

[50] *Id.* at 51.

[51] *Id.*

been described by one historian of the subject as "a sustained attack which in its passion and effectiveness stands alone in the history of American graphic art." M. Keller, THE ART AND POLITICS OF THOMAS NAST 177 (1968). . . .

Despite their sometimes caustic nature, from the early cartoon portraying George Washington as an ass down to the present day, graphic depictions and satirical cartoons have played a prominent role in public and political debate. Nast's castigation of the Tweed Ring, Walt McDougall's characterization of Presidential candidate James G. Blaine's banquet with the millionaires at Delmonico's as "The Royal Feast of Belshazzar," and numerous other efforts have undoubtedly had an effect on the course and outcome of contemporaneous debate. . . . [O]ur political discourse would have been considerably poorer without them.[52]

In an attempt to distinguish his case from traditional political cartoons, Falwell argued that the Hustler parody was "outrageous." Although the Court agreed, viewing Hustler's cartoon as "at best a distant cousin of" political cartoons, the Court doubted whether it could draw a "principled standard" separating the Hustler cartoon from political cartoons. The Court specifically rejected the "outrageousness" standard because of its "inherent subjectiveness." The Court feared that this standard would "allow a jury to impose liability on the basis of the jurors' tastes or views, or perhaps on the basis of their dislike of a particular expression." So, in the final analysis, the Court concluded that an "outrageousness" standard "runs afoul of our longstanding refusal to allow damages to be awarded because the speech in question may have an adverse emotional impact on the audience."[53]

In its holding, the Court reaffirmed its earlier precedent stating that "speech that is vulgar, offensive, and shocking is not entitled to absolute constitutional protection under all circumstances," and that "a State could lawfully punish an individual for the use of insulting fighting words — those which by their very utterance inflict injury or tend to incite an immediate breach of the peace." But the Court found that the Hustler parody did not fit within either of those precedents.

The Court held that Falwell was required to satisfy the *New York Times* "actual malice" standard in order to recover. In other words, he (like other public figures and public officials in defamation actions) could only recover for the tort of intentional infliction of emotional distress if he could show that the publication contained a false statement of fact which was made with " 'actual malice,' *i.e.*, with knowledge that the statement was false or with reckless disregard as to whether or not it was true." The Court concluded that the "actual malice" standard was necessary to provide "adequate 'breathing space' to the freedoms protected by the First Amendment." The Court readily concluded that Falwell was a "public figure," and that he could not satisfy the "actual malice" standard.

---

[52] *Id.* at 55.

[53] *Id.*

In the same year that *Falwell* was decided, the Ninth Circuit decided *Dworkin v. Hustler Magazine, Inc.*,[54] That case involved facts similar to *Falwell*. Andrea Dworkin, the plaintiff, was an outspoken feminist author and activist, a vocal advocate for the prohibition of pornography, and a drafter of an (unconstitutional) ordinance prohibiting pornography enacted by the city of Indianapolis. In the case, she admitted that she was a public figure. "Dworkin's beliefs and Hustler's editorial viewpoint were inimical to one another."[55] In several editions, Hustler published features mentioning Dworkin's name in a derogatory fashion. One was a cartoon which "depict[ed] two women engaged in a lesbian act of oral sex with the caption, 'You remind me so much of Andrea Dworkin, Edna. It's a dog-eat-dog world.' " A later issue of the magazine contained a ten page pictorial consisting of photographs of women engaged in, among other things, acts of lesbianism or masturbation. One photograph, supposedly of a Jewish male, had a caption which stated: "While I'm teaching this little shiksa the joys of Yiddish, the Andrea Dworkin Fan Club begins some really serious suck-'n'-squat. Ready to give up the holy wafers for matzoh, yet, guys?" Another issue had a feature in the "Porn from the Past" section of the magazine which depicted a man performing oral sex on an obese woman while he masturbates. A portion of the caption stated: "We don't believe it for a minute, but one of our editors swears that this woman in the throes of ecstacy is the mother of radical feminist Andrea Dworkin." In her suit, Dworkin claimed that Hustler should be denied First Amendment protection except for what she referred to as "high-minded" discourse, and she claimed that the ads were not "high-minded." The Ninth Circuit disagreed concluding that First Amendment protections are not limited to "high minded discourse."

The Court's most recent intentional infliction of emotional distress decision was rendered in *Snyder v. Phelps*.[56] That case involved the Westboro Baptist Church (and its pastor Fred Phelps) which believes that God hates and punishes the United States for its tolerance of homosexuality, particularly in America's military. In an effort to publicize its views, the church frequently pickets at military funerals, and has picketed at nearly 600 funerals over the last twenty years. After Marine Lance Corporal Matthew Snyder was killed in Iraq in the line of duty, six Westboro parishoners decided to protest his funeral. They did so on public land adjacent to public streets near the Maryland State House, the United States Naval Academy, and Matthew Snyder's funeral, and carried signs with messages such as "God Hates the USA/Thank God for 9/11," "America is Doomed," "Don't Pray for the USA," "Thank God for IEDs," "Thank God for Dead Soldiers," "Pope in Hell," "Priests Rape Boys," "God Hates Fags," "You're Going to Hell," and "God Hates You." The Westboro picketers displayed their signs for about 30 minutes prior to the funeral, and they also sang hymns and recited Bible verses. However, the picketers did not enter church property or go to the cemetery.

Although Snyder's father could not read the signs, despite the fact that the funeral procession passed within 200 to 300 feet of the picket site, he could see the tops of picket signs. He did see the signs later that evening while watching a news

---

[54] 867 F.2d 1188 (9th Cir. 1988).

[55] *Id.* at 1190.

[56] 131 S.Ct. 1207 (2011).

broadcast. In addition, while doing an Internet search, he came across a Web posting (referred to by the Court as the "epic") that was posted several weeks after the funeral which contained religiously oriented denunciations of the Snyders interspersed among lengthy Bible quotations. Snyder filed suit against Phelps, his daughters, and the Westboro Baptist Church, alleging five state tort law claims: defamation, publicity given to private life, intentional infliction of emotional distress, intrusion upon seclusion, and civil conspiracy. Although the trial court rendered judgment against Snyder on the defamation and publicity claims, the remaining claims went to trial where Snyder testified that he was "unable to separate the thought of his dead son from his thoughts of Westboro's picketing, and that he often becomes tearful, angry, and physically ill when he thinks about it." Expert witnesses testified that Snyder had suffered "emotional anguish" and "severe depression" which exacerbated his pre-existing health conditions. Snyder prevailed in the trial court on the intentional infliction of emotional distress, intrusion upon seclusion, and civil conspiracy claims, and obtained judgments against Westboro liable for $2.9 million in compensatory damages and $8 million in punitive damages. However, the punitive damages were remitted to $2.1 million.

The United States Supreme Court reversed the judgment. The Court refused to consider the epic because it was not submitted to the jury and was not mentioned in Snyder's petition for certiorari. The Court emphasized that the picketing related to a matter of public concern (Westboro's views regarding the U.S. positions on homosexuality), rather than to matters of purely private concern, and therefore was entitled to First Amendment protection because "speech concerning public affairs is more than self-expression; it is the essence of self-government."[57] For that reason, the Court held that "speech on public issues occupies the highest rung of the hierarchy of First Amendment values, and is entitled to special protection."[58]

The Court did suggest that states might have greater leeway to impose liability for the tort of intentional infliction of emotional distress when speech relates to "matters of purely private significance" (as in the *Dun & Bradstreet* case which involved a private credit report). The Court concluded that, when private speech is involved, there "is no threat to the free and robust debate of public issues; there is no potential interference with a meaningful dialogue of ideas"; and the "threat of liability" does not pose the risk of "a reaction of self-censorship" on matters of public import.[59] The dividing line between the two types of speech focuses on whether the speech relates to matters of "political, social, or other concern to the community," as well as whether it involves "a subject of legitimate news interest; that is, a subject of general interest and of value and concern to the public." The mere fact that the method or style of speech is inappropriate does not deprive it of First Amendment protection when a matter of public interest is involved.

Despite the offensiveness of the signs, the Court viewed the signs as conveying messages related to matters of public interest because they highlighted "the political and moral conduct of the United States and its citizens, the fate of our

---

[57] *Id.* at 1215 (quoting Garrison v. Louisiana, 379 U.S. 64, 74–75 (1964)).

[58] *Id.* (quoting Connick v. Myers, 461 U.S. 138, 145 (1983)).

[59] *Id.* (quoting Dun & Bradstreet, Inc. v. Greenmoss Builders, Inc., 472 U.S. 749, 760 (1985)).

Nation, homosexuality in the military, and scandals involving the Catholic clergy."
In addition, by focusing on military funerals, Westboro was trying to reach a
broader audience. Even though a few of the signs focused on Matthew Snyder
himself (e.g., signs which stated that "You're Going to Hell" and "God Hates You"),
the overall thrust of the picketing was on American policy rather than on Snyder
himself. The Court noted that "Westboro had been actively engaged in speaking on
the subjects addressed in its picketing long before it became aware of Matthew
Snyder, and there can be no serious claim that Westboro's picketing did not
represent its 'honestly believed' views on public issues."[60] In addition, since there
was no pre-existing relationship or conflict between Westboro and Snyder, there
was no indication that Westboro's speech was a thinly veiled attempt to attack
Snyder. Moreover, even though Westboro chose to use Snyder's funeral as a way to
communicate its views, a platform that was particularly hurtful to Snyder's father,
that fact did not deprive the protest of First Amendment protection." The Court
emphasized that the protest was held in a public place, and that such places occupy
"special position in terms of First Amendment protection."

The Court went on to note that it has "repeatedly referred to public streets as
the archetype of a traditional public forum," and concluded that " '[t]ime out of
mind' public streets and sidewalks have been used for public assembly and debate.'
Frisby v. Schultz, 487 U. S. 474, 480 (1988)."[61] Of course, the state was free to
impose reasonable time, place and manner restrictions on the protests. However,
the distress caused by the picketing did not relate to the time, place and manner of
the demonstration, but rather to the content and the viewpoint. The Court
emphasized that: "If there is a bedrock principle underlying the First Amendment,
it is that the government may not prohibit the expression of an idea simply because
society finds the idea itself offensive or disagreeable."[62] The Court rejected the trial
court's conclusion that Westboro could be held liable simply because the jury viewed
the picketing as "outrageous" which might allow a juror to punish statements that
they dislike. The Court worried that such a standard might pose "a real danger of
becoming an instrument for the suppression [of] 'vehement, caustic, and sometimes
unpleasan[t]' expression. *Bose Corp. [v. Consumers Union of United States, Inc.]*,
466 U. S. [485], 510 (quoting *New York Times [Co. v. Sullivan]*, 376 U.S. [254] at
270)."[63] The Court held that, instead, " 'in public debate [we] must tolerate insulting,
and even outrageous, speech in order to provide adequate 'breathing space' to the
freedoms protected by the First Amendment.' *Boos v. Barry*, 485 U.S. 312, 322
(1988)."[64]

The Court also rejected the trial court's holding that Westboro could be held
liable for intrusion upon seclusion and civil conspiracy on the basis that Snyder was
an unwilling listener or viewer of the protests: "the Constitution does not permit the
government to decide which types of otherwise protected speech are sufficiently
offensive to require protection for the unwilling listener or viewer. Rather, [the]

---

[60] *Id.* at 1217.

[61] *Id.* at 1218.

[62] *Id.* at 1219 (quoting Texas v. Johnson, 491 U.S. 397, 414 (1989)).

[63] *Id.* at 1219.

[64] *Id.*

burden normally falls upon the viewer to avoid further bombardment of [his] sensibilities simply by averting [his] eyes."[65] Since Westboro stayed away from the memorial service, and Snyder could see no more than the tops of the signs, "there is no indication that the picketing in any way interfered with the funeral service itself." As a result, the Court refused to extend the captive audience doctrine to this case, emphasizing that "Westboro addressed matters of public import on public property, in a peaceful manner, in full compliance with the guidance of local officials. The speech was indeed planned to coincide with Matthew Snyder's funeral, but did not itself disrupt that funeral, and Westboro's choice to conduct its picketing at that time and place did not alter the nature of its speech."

Justice Alito, the lone dissenter in the case, argued that the nation's "profound national commitment to free and open debate is not a license for the vicious verbal assault that occurred in this case." He also argued that Snyder was entitled to "bury his son in peace," but was deprived of that right because of a "malevolent verbal attack on Matthew and his family at a time of acute emotional vulnerability" that caused the father "severe and lasting emotional injury." He concluded that Westboro had no "right to brutalize Mr. Snyder."

The *Phelps* decision is broadly consistent with U.S. First Amendment jurisprudence. While the views of Westboro Baptist Church, as well its tactics, may be offensive to many (most?) people, the Westboro protestors have a constitutional right to express those views. In some respects, Westboro Baptist Church is no different than other dissident or minority views that have received constitutional protection. During the Civil Rights Era, might Southern officials have regarded the demands of African-American protestors for equal rights as "extremist"? Likewise, at the turn of the last century, when women demanded the right to vote might some officials have regarded those views as "extremist" as well. Nevertheless, these views were entitled to constitutional protection.

POINTS TO REMEMBER

- The actual malice standard governs other tort claims for intentional infliction of emotional distress brought by public officials or figures.

- When the plaintiff is a private person, the Court has focused upon whether the speech pertains to a matter of public or private concern.

---

§ 3.05 PRIVACY

Privacy as a legal interest has dimensions that are protected by and compete against constitutional principles. The right of privacy, insofar as it secures the liberty to make personal choices in certain settings, is an incident of liberty protected by the Due Process Clause of the Fifth and Fourteenth Amendment. The Fourth Amendment protects persons against unreasonable searches and seizures. The "right to be let alone," although not specifically enumerated by the Constitu-

---

[65] *Id.* at 1220 (quoting Erznoznik v. Jacksonville, 422 U. S. 205, 210–11 (1975)).

tion, has been described in transcendent terms. Justice Brandeis thus described this guarantee as "the most comprehensive of rights and the right most valued by civilized men."[66] Strands of First Amendment jurisprudence secure associational rights and freedom of conscience. Privacy interests, particularly those associated with the home, have been the basis for restricting the state's ability to regulate obscenity — a form of expression that otherwise is beyond the First Amendment's protective cast.[67]

The multifaceted constitutional aspects of privacy indicate that it is a societal interest of significant gravity. Further reflecting the value assigned to privacy are the many and diverse laws that protect it. Privacy protective regulation governs public and private record-keeping and disclosure practices and a wide variety of technology applications. Extensive as the legal system's interest in privacy may be, the history of laws protecting privacy is relatively short. Unlike the law of defamation, privacy torts are not rooted in the Anglican legal system. To this day, there is no privacy tort in British law.

The wellspring for privacy torts is a law review article, authored by Samuel D. Warren and Louis D. Brandeis, who viewed the advent of photojournalism and newspaper sensationalism with alarm and disdain. Warren and Brandeis were disturbed by what they regarded as growing media curiosity and probing into "the sacred precincts of private and domestic," editorial practices that overstepped the boundaries of decency and propriety, and unauthorized circulation of private portraits. These pathologies, driven by a then intensely competitive newspaper industry, necessitated a legal remedy. Over the course of the Twentieth Century, privacy torts became a statutory or common law fixture in every state. Some of these torts, most notably publication of private or confidential information, the right of publicity, and false light privacy, have the potential to cut against interests in expressive freedom. As is the case with defamation law, the Court has developed First Amendment principles that limit the application of laws designed to protect these privacy interests.

[A]   Publication of Personal Information

The typical invasion of privacy case concerns a media report that accurately discloses personal, embarrassing, or intimate details about an individual. The most obvious question presented in this type of action is whether truth establishes a full defense. The case for a First Amendment privilege on grounds of truthfulness has been presented to the Court more than once. In each instance, the Court has refused to embrace the proposition fully. In *Cox Broadcasting Corp. v. Cohn*,[68] the Court reviewed a finding of liability based upon a state law prohibiting publication of a rape victim's name. The Court determined, because the victim's identity had been obtained legally from a public record, the privacy claim and verdict could not stand. This outcome thus depended not just upon the truth of the report but upon the public nature of the record.

---

[66] 277 U.S. 438 (1928).

[67] Stanley v. Georgia, 394 U.S. 557 (1969).

[68] 420 U.S. 469 (1975).

The question of a First Amendment privilege resurfaced in *Landmark Communications, Inc. v. Virginia.*[69] At issue was a newspaper report concerning a confidential judicial disciplinary proceeding. Finding that the information not only was truthful but lawfully obtained, the Court sided with the newspaper. For similar and other reasons, the First Amendment prevailed over privacy concerns in *Smith v. Daily Mail Publishing Co.*[70] That case concerned a newspaper's publication of a child murderer's name that had been obtained legally. Although the Court refused to establish an absolute privilege for disclosure of truthful private information, it held that liability for publishing accurate information on an issue of "public significance" could not be established minus "a state interest of the highest order."[71] The reference to issues of public significance reserves the possibility that truth may be insufficient to shield a plaintiff from liability. What constitutes a matter of public significance potentially presents the same challenge to principled line-drawing that has confronted definition of public figures and public controversies in the defamation context.

This factor also was a significant consideration in *The Florida Star v. B.J.F.*[72] Like *Cohn*, that case concerned a newspaper's publication of a rape victim's identity in violation of state law. The fact pattern differed, however, insofar as law enforcement officials inadvertently had provided the victim's name to the newspaper. The newspaper itself had a policy against publishing the name's of sex offense victims, but editors did not catch the violation before the story was published. Another distinguishing circumstance was that the victim was still alive and allegedly received threatening calls from the perpetrator after the story was published.

Notwithstanding the newspaper's negligence and other circumstantial differences, the Court restated the proposition set forth in the *Smith* decision. Because the information had been lawfully obtained, liability for breach of privacy required narrowly tailored means of achieving a state interest of the highest order. Because the law did not distinguish between inadvertent and intentional publications, the Court found that the narrowly tailored requirement was not satisfied. In a dissenting opinion, Justice White maintained that the decision effectively swallowed the tort. He would have found the law defective because it applied only to the mass media.

To date, the Court has consistently trumped public disclosure tort law with First Amendment principle. It has stopped short, however, of declaring that truthfulness of information by itself is an absolute defense. Truthfulness has proved to be an important factor. Pivotal too has been whether the sensitive information was procured in a lawful manner and related to a matter of public importance. Even when private information is obtained illegally, the newsworthiness factor by itself may be a sufficient defense to liability. This possibility was established in *Bartnicki*

---

[69] 435 U.S. 829 (1978).

[70] 443 U.S. 97 (1979).

[71] *Id.* at 103.

[72] 491 U.S. 524 (1989).

v. Vopper,[73] a case that concerned an intercepted cellular telephone conversation that was aired on a radio show in violation of state and federal law. The intercepted conversation included a teacher's union president's real or rhetorical threats of physical harm to management in the course of a discussion with his chief negotiator. The Court acknowledged that privacy is an important interest, and fear of public disclosure of private communications might chill private speech. These privacy concerns were out-weighed, however, by the conversation's newsworthiness. The Court found the statutes unconstitutional as applied to a case where the defendants played no role in the illegal procural of the material, access to the conversation was obtained lawfully, and the conversation related to a public issue. The important message of *Bartnicki*, therefore, is that the state cannot impose liability upon "the publication of truthful information of public concern." The Court refused to decide, however, whether protection would extend to disclosure of trade secrets, domestic gossip, or other matters of purely private concern.

[B]　False Light Privacy

The law of false light privacy actions overlaps in important respects with defamation law. Both arise from false statements that are a source of personal injury. Unlike defamation's concern with harm to reputation, the invasion of privacy itself is the basis for harm in a false light privacy case. Falsehoods that do not rise to the level of defamation thus may be sufficient to support a false light privacy claim. Given the significant commonality of the torts, it is not surprising that the First Amendment concerns that apply to defamation been have extended to false light privacy cases.

The seminal application of First Amendment principles to the law of false light privacy was *Time, Inc. v. Hill*.[74] That case concerned a magazine's misrepresentation of a family's hostage experience. The action was based upon a state law that permitted false light privacy claims even if the subject was newsworthy. The Court imported the actual malice standard from defamation law and applied it to false light privacy. Unless the publisher made the statements with knowledge of falsehood or reckless disregard of the truth, liability could not be established. A claim also could not be pressed successfully if the story, although false, was newsworthy. In *Cantrell v. Forest City Publishing Co.*,[75] a case concerning a newspaper's mischaracterization of a family's living conditions, the actual malice standard was applied and satisfied. The Court suggested the possibility that, consistent with defamation law, actual malice might not be constitutionally required for private plaintiffs. To the extent that a negligence standard applied in such circumstances, it is conceivable that the *Hill* decision itself would be decided differently.

---

[73]　532 U.S. 514 (2002).

[74]　385 U.S. 374 (1967).

[75]　419 U.S. 245 (1974).

[C] Right of Publicity

The right of publicity protects an individual's economic interest in the use of name, image, and talent. It is an interest that is of special concern to athletes, entertainers, and performers. Protection of name, image, and likeness also imposes restrictions on newsgathering and thus implicates First Amendment interests. In *Zacchini v. Scripps-Howard Broadcasting Co.*,[76] the Court confronted the conflict between the right of publicity and the First Amendment. At issue was a television station's broadcast of a human cannonball's performance from blast-off to landing. Although there was debate over what constituted the entire act, the key moments were captured and broadcast to the television audience. The Court found that the right of publicity accounted for two significant concerns, the right of an entertainer to trade upon his or her talents to make a living and society's interest in the facilitation of creative energy. Although recognizing newsgathering as an important media function, the Court concluded that an accounting for the plaintiff's publicity interests would not impose a significant burden on the press. Persons interested in viewing the act had ready access to it, provided they were willing to pay the admission price. Minus the opportunity to earn money for the spectacle, incentive to deliver the performance and opportunities to view it would diminish or vanish.

POINTS TO REMEMBER

- Information from public records, concerning a matter of public significance, may be published barring a state interest of the "highest order."

- Truth has not been established as an absolute defense to a privacy action based upon publication of information taken from public records.

- Newsworthiness will be a defense in cases concerning disclosure of private information, provided that the information was lawfully acquired and truthful.

- False light privacy claims are governed by the actual malice standard and newsworthiness considerations.

- The right of publicity is violated when a performer's entire act is broadcast without permission.

---

§ 3.06 OBSCENITY

Obscenity constitutes a category of expression that is constitutionally unprotected. Not all forms of sexually explicit expression are obscene. The rationale for obscenity's unprotected status is that it has "no essential part of any exposition of ideas, and [has] such slight social value as a step to the truth."[77] Because of obscenity's unprotected nature, government regulation of it is subject to minimal

---

[76] 433 U.S. 562 (1977).

[77] Chaplinsky v. New Hampshire, 315 U.S. 568, 572 (1942).

review. The primary challenge presented by obscenity is defining it. Much of the case law concerning obscenity is devoted to this task.

[A] The Definitional Challenge

Even though obscenity is unprotected, the Court has encountered great difficulty defining the term. *Roth v. United States*,[78] the case that established that obscenity is unprotected speech, was decided against a backdrop of First Amendment theory and dicta that largely preordained the Court's decision. Regulation of obscenity had a long history that post-dated framing and ratification of the First Amendment. Congress enacted legislation prohibiting obscenity during the latter half of the Nineteenth Century. Through the middle of the Twentieth Century, judicial decisions suggested that obscenity was not protected speech under the First Amendment. These sentiments were communicated in decisions concerning prior restraints,[79] fighting words,[80] and defamation.[81] Although these decisions involved other forms of speech, they repeatedly expressed the view that obscenity was among those forms of expression that had slight if any value toward the discovery of truth. The basis for this assessment was not amplified.

In *Roth*, the Court referenced this jurisprudential heritage in support of the proposition that obscenity is not protected under the Free Speech Clause. Although prior case law had not articulated a rationale on this point, and despite a relatively limited regulatory tradition, the Court tied obscenity's unprotected status to a historical understandings of the First Amendment and attitudes toward such expression. For the Court, it was well-established that obscenity was "utterly without redeeming social importance."[82] Because obscenity thus is beyond the First Amendment's range of concern, judicial review of its regulation should be highly deferential toward the legislative judgment. Absent constitutional protection, the Court would apply rational basis review in reviewing an obscenity statute. Although some have argued that obscenity regulations should only be upheld when the publication creates a clear and present danger of harm, the Court has not requiried the state to prove that obscenity causes antisocial conduct or some other injury in order to regulate it.

Roth acknowledged that sex and obscenity are not synonymous terms. On the contrary, it concluded that not all sexual speech is obscene, and that obscenity involves speech that "deals with sex in a manner appealing to the prurient interest."[83] In developing standards for other types of expression, the Court has demonstrated the ability to generate an objective and understandable definition of the speech at issue. Such competence was not evident in *Roth*. Instead of formulating an all-purpose definition, the Court announced a standard a case-by-case standard, requiring inquiry into whether "the average person, applying

---

[78] 354 U.S. 476 (1957).

[79] Near v. Minnesota, 283 U.S. 697 (1931).

[80] Chaplinsky v. New Hampshire, 315 U.S. 568 (1942).

[81] Beauharnais v. Illinois, 343 U.S. 250 (1952).

[82] Roth v. United States, 354 U.S. at 484.

[83] *Id.* at 489.

contemporary community standards, [would find that] the dominant theme of the material taken as a whole appeals to prurient interest."[84] This standard aimed to avoid a finding of obscenity based upon a particularly sensitive group's response to sexually explicit expression, and to avert the possibility that material could be declared obscene on the basis of an isolated passage.

The *Roth* formulation placed the Court on a path that turned out to be long and tortured. Under that test, the Court focused on the question of prurience which the Court associated with the "tendency to excite lustful thoughts."[85] Amplification of the term's meaning by reference to the dictionary illuminated rather than resolved the definitional problem. Perceptions of prurience predictably vary with culture, context, orientation, and understanding. Both Justice Black and Douglas criticized the majority for operating on the basis of assumption rather than fact with respect to the value of or harms associated with obscenity. They maintained that punishment for what the state perceived as an *"undesirable* impact on thoughts"[86] represented a radical separation departure from First Amendment norms. Because the Court's assessments were based upon assumptions rather than empirical data, the door was left open for debate and research on the relationship, if any, between obscenity and pathological behavior. Scholars, commentators, and presidential commissions have reached divergent results. As the obscenity debate has raged on, the basic premise of *Roth* largely remains unchanged.

Roth plunged the Court into a jurisprudential morass. Through the 1960s and early 1970s, the Court struggled to establish a viable definition of obscenity. The Court's task was complicated by the broad spectrum of factual circumstances that presented themselves in obscenity cases. Epitomizing the concept's elusiveness was Justice Potter Stewart's observation, in *Jacobellis v. Ohio*,[87] that the Court was engaged in a process of "trying to define the undefinable."[88] Even if he could not describe it, Justice Stewart maintained that "I know it when I see it."[89] The Court in *Jacobellis* announced that, because constitutional rights were implicated, it must assess independently whether material in fact was obscene. Without a clear working definition of obscenity, the Court effectively became a book and film review board that judged works on the basis of individualized standards of acceptability.

[B] Doctrinal Chaos

Post-*Roth* cases demonstrated the risks and burdens that the Court's approach to obscenity had assumed. In *A Book Named "John Cleland's Memoirs of a Woman of Pleasure," v. Attorney General of Massachusetts*,[90] the Court reversed an obscenity conviction based upon dissemination of a book (Fanny Hill) that many regarded as a literary classic. A three justice plurality decided to modify the *Roth*

---

[84] *Id.*

[85] *Id.* at 487 n.20.

[86] *Id.* at 509 (Douglas, J., dissenting).

[87] 378 U.S. 184 (1964).

[88] *Id.* at 197 (Stewart, J., concurring).

[89] *Id.*

[90] 383 U.S. 413 (1966).

three-part test in the following way: First, the material must appeal to the prurient interest. Second, it must be found offensive pursuant to contemporary community standards. Third, it must be utterly lacking in redeeming social value. This final factor was critical for purposes of avoiding a finding of obscenity. Even if material appealed to the prurient interest, and might be found offensive in some communities, it could not be deemed obscene if some redeeming social value was identified. Social utility could be offset, however, by marketing that touts the sexually provocative aspect of the material. The Court, in *Ginzburg v. United States*,[91] thus bypassed an inquiry into a sexually explicit magazine's social value. Promotion of a magazine that pandered to the prurient interest was sufficient in itself to establish obscenity. This premise was established before the recasting of *Roth* and has survived that reformulation.

Through the 1960s and early 1970s, there was little progress toward developing an obscenity standard that comanded majority support. Review of obscenity convictions during this period devolved into a series of *per curiam* opinions that reflected bottom line results, notwithstanding the diverging standards of individual justices. Periodically, as the *Ginzburg* decision illustrated, a majority would coalesce in support of a proposition unrelated to a definition or understanding of obscenity itself. Another example of this phenomenon was the Court's determination, in *Mishkin v. New York*,[92] that obscenity standards may be a function of the publisher's or distributor's target audience. For groups whose tastes are outside the sexual mainstream, therefore, the prurient appeal test is correlated to idiosyncratic rather than conventional interests. The definition of obscenity also may vary with the age of the audience. Consistent with this variable, the Court in *Ginsberg v. New York*[93] upheld the conviction of a defendant who sold a sexually explicit magazine to a minor. Although finding that the publication was not obscene for adults, the Court found the purchaser's age relevant to whether it was obscene under the circumstances. Another variable was introduced, in *Stanley v. Georgia*,[94] when the Court established the home as a safe harbor for possession of obscene materials. That decision, as discussed in Section D, neither recast the definition of obscenity nor departed from the premise that obscenity is valueless.

Although the Court's rulings of the late 1960s represented significant developments, the Court remained stalled in its ability to develop satisfactory standards for determining obscenity. Movement toward a majority position was attributable in significant part to extensive personnel turnover that transformed the Warren Court into the Burger Court. In *Miller v. California*,[95] the Court building upon the central thesis of *Roth*, tweaked and recast some of its reference points, and synthesized a new criterion for obscenity. This decision established no dictionary definition for obscenity. Rather, it created a multi-tier analytical structure for juries to use in identifying it.

---

[91] 383 U.S. 463 (1966).

[92] 383 U.S. 502 (1966).

[93] 390 U.S. 629 (1968).

[94] 394 U.S. 557 (1969).

[95] 413 U.S. 15 (1973).

Pursuant to the *Miller* formula, the focal points for discerning obscenity are:

(1) whether the average person applying contemporary community standards would find that the work, taken as a whole, appeals to the prurient interest,

(2) whether it depicts or describes, in a patently offensive way, sexual conduct specifically defined by the applicable state law, and

(3) whether the work taken as a whole, lacks serious literary, artistic, political, or scientific value.[96]

These check points operate in the conjunctive rather than the disjunctive. The three-part test candidly was prefaced with an acknowledgment of the dangers "inherent" in managing any form of expression and that laws designed to regulate obscenity must be "carefully limited." It was framed, however, as a means of resolving conclusively the "intractable obscenity problem." This resolution was anticipated through utilization of local standards that presumably would minimize the Court's function as an obscenity review board.

[C] *Miller* Amplifications and Applications

The *Miller* decision represented a step forward at least insofar as it commanded majority support. It has not removed the Court entirely from the process of deciding what is obscene. Nor has it quelled debate over whether obscenity should be categorically unprotected or silenced critics who are dissatisfied with how the definition problem was resolved. The primary post- *Miller* focal points have related to the nature of community standards, specificity of prohibition, and whether material has value sufficient to avoid being characterized as obscene. Case law has addressed loose ends on each of these fronts.

[1] Prurient Interest and Community Standards

Although *Miller* imported the prurient interest factor from *Roth*, that decision layered this factor with a new understanding. Until *Miller*, it was an open question whether the community standards for measuring appeal to the prurient interest were to be national standards or local standards. The *Miller* Court rejected the proposition that the standard to be applied was necessarily national. Although the Court noted that tolerance levels for sexually explicit materials may vary according to location, the dimensions of the relevant community are not necessarily manifest. The Court held that trial may use a national standard.[97] If a trial court opts for community standards, moreover, it is not obligated to provide any geographical reference.[98] Minus any such guidance, individual jurors may supply the necessary meaning on their own. Under these circumstances, significant variances may exist on the basis of class, culture, and neighborhood. The Court also held that a state cannot define through legislation the community standards that apply in determin-

---

[96] *Id.* at 24.

[97] Hamling v. United States, 418 U.S. 87 (1974).

[98] *Id.*

ing prurient interest or patent offensiveness.[99] Although community standards cannot reference the particularly sensitive, such persons need not be excluded from the matrix of individuals that determine whether material is obscene.[100]

Of course, by allowing the use of "contemporary community standards," the Court created a risk that the applied standards might be so extreme as to ensare mainstream material may be ensnared by a local jury's obscenity findings. This possibility prompted the Court in *Jenkins v. Georgia*,[101] to hold that appellate courts retain the power independently to review obscenity determinations. In *Jenkins*, the Court reversed a jury's finding that a mainstream R-rated movie was obscene. The Court stressed that, although the question of pruriency and patent offensiveness are jury questions, an obscenity verdict cannot stand unless there is a depiction of "patently offensive 'hard Core" sexual conduct."[102] *Jenkins* affirmed that, although a jury must determine whether material violates contemporary community standards, the Court reserves to itself the power to identify constitutional deficiencies and review obscenity determinations.

[2] Patent Offensiveness Specified

Given the historical difficulty of defining obscenity, it is not surprising that overbreadth and vagueness principles have been commonly used to challenge obscenity laws. *Miller* emphasized that obscenity prosecutions must be limited to materials that "depict, or describe patently offensive 'hard core' sexual conduct specifically defined by the regulating state law, as written or construed."[103] To help legislatures minimize the risk of overbroad or vague regulation, *Miller* provided an example of legislation that would survive constitutional review. The specificity requirement thus is satisfied by a statute that reaches:

(a) [p]atently offensive representations or descriptions of ultimate sexual acts, normal or perverted, actual or simulated.

(b) [p]atently offensive representations or descriptions of masturbation, excretory functions, and lewd exhibition of genitals.[104]

Despite the creation of this safe harbor, many states have crafted obscenity law in their own terms. Case law supports their authority to construct laws with different phraseology and emphasis. The Court has approved these differences by noting that the suggested terminology in *Miller* involved "examples" of obscenity rather than an "exhaustive" listing.[105] Although *Miller* made clear that obscenity is not coextensive with sex and nudity, a statute that overreaches conceptually will not necessarily be invalidated. For example, a law that equated prurient interest with

---

[99] Smith v. United States, 431 U.S. 291 (1977).

[100] Pinkus v. United States, 436 U.S. 293 (1978).

[101] 418 U.S. 153.

[102] *Id.* at 160.

[103] *Miller*, 413 U.S. at 24.

[104] *Id.* at 25.

[105] Ward v. Illinois, 431 U.S. 767, 771 (1977).

lust was found to be overbroad in *Brockett v. Spokane Arcades, Inc.*[106] The overbreadth was cured by review that deleted the term "lust" from an otherwise valid statute.

[3] Speech Value

The sense that obscenity is without any value in the search for truth explains obscenity's categorical exclusion from the First Amendment's zone of interest. The *Miller* Court recast the value inquiry from a consideration of whether material "utterly" lacks social value to whether there is an absence of "serious" literary, artistic, political, or scientific value. Of course, the Court could have treated the right to view obscene materials as a "liberty" or "self-fulfillment" interest, but the Court has tended to focus on social value. Moreover, the shift from "utterly" without redeeming value to a lacking "serious" value resulted in a softer standard that increased the potential for an obscenity determination. Unlike the reference points for assessing prurient interest and patent offensiveness, contemporary community standards are not the criteria for determining whether material lacks the required value. Rather, as noted in *Pope v. Illinois*,[107] the inquiry is whether a "reasonable person" would find the material so lacking.

[D] Obscenity's Safe Harbor

Even if obscenity does not possess sufficient value to justify protection under the First Amendment, other factors may operate to give it constitutional shelter. In *Stanley v. Georgia*,[108] the Court found that conviction for possessing obscene material in one's own home violated a homeowner's right of privacy. The Court determined that the privacy concern, which is not grounded in the First Amendment, outweighed the state's interest in controlling the dissemination of obscenity. Consistent with this premise, the Court noted that the privacy interest extended only to possession in the home and not to sale or purchase. The *Stanley* Court stressed the state's retention of "broad power" to prohibit and punish obscenity.

Subsequent case law has established that a homeowner's privacy interest does not outweigh the state's interest in punishing possession of child pornography.[109] In *Osborne*, the Court distinguished *Stanley* on grounds the regulation was directed at concerns beyond the user. The child pornography law specifically was aimed at eliminating demand for a product that is dependent upon the abuse and exploitation of children. This result was consistent with the Court's determination, in *New York v. Ferber*,[110] that a more deferential standard operates for purposes of determining whether child pornography is obscene. Protecting children from predatory conduct also was the basis for this ruling. Although impact upon or exploitation of children may be the basis for a relaxed standard of review, the

---

[106] 472 U.S. 491 (1985).

[107] 481 U.S. 497 (1987).

[108] 394 U.S. 557 (1969).

[109] Osborne v. Ohio, 495 U.S. 103 (1990).

[110] 458 U.S. 747 (1982).

general public's access to sexually explicit materials cannot be denied merely because they may have an adverse impact upon children. As the Court put it in *Butler v. Michigan*,[111] such a rule would limit adult exposure to only what is fit for children.

The *Stanley* Court's distinction between possession and distribution was based in part upon the different risks of obscene materials falling into the hands of children or persons who might be exposed to them unwillingly. Justice Brennan, who authored the majority opinion in *Roth*, believed that experience undermined the wisdom of the Court's obscenity doctrine. In *Paris Adult Theatre I v. Slaton*,[112] he would have extended the logic of *Stanley* to adult movie theaters that posted content warnings and refused admission to children. That case involved an adult movie theater that limited entry to informed and consenting adults. Despite these safeguards, the Court declined to consider their efficacy and relied upon the traditional premise that obscenity is without First Amendment value and protection. In so doing, the Court elaborated on the legitimate reasons for obscenity regulation. These justifications included not only the risk of exposure to unconsenting adults and minors but quality of life and neighborhoods, the tone of urban commerce, and perhaps public safety. Although none of the harms could be demonstrated conclusively or empirically, rational basis review does not require the Court to achieve such certainty. Consistent with this premise, obscenity regulation remains hinged to "unprovable assumptions."[113]

POINTS TO REMEMBER

- Obscenity is unprotected under the First Amendment.

- Historically, the primary problem presented by obscenity cases has been defining the term.

- The modern approach to obscenity is set forth by the three-part *Miller* standard.

- Although contemporary community standards are the basis for determining whether material is obscene, courts may review a jury's finding on this point.

- A homeowner's right of privacy shields him or her against punishment for possession of obscenity, except for child pornography.

- Safeguards that effectively deny access to children or unwanted exposure to obscenity are not a factor in determining whether obscenity is protected outside a person's home.

---

[111] 353 U.S. 380 (1957).

[112] 413 U.S. 49 (1973).

[113] *Id.* at 62.

Chapter 4

CONTENT REGULATION: OTHER CANDIDATES FOR CATEGORICAL EXCLUSION OR LIMITED PROTECTION

FOCAL POINTS FOR CHAPTER 4

- Offensive speech as protected speech.
- The status of child pornography under the First Amendment.
- Government's right to prohibit "virtual" child pornography.
- Government's right to suppress offensive views about women.
- Commercial speech as protected speech under the First Amendment.
- The unsettled nature of standards governing commercial speech.

---

§ 4.01 "OFFENSIVE" SPEECH

Does the government have any special powers over "offensive" or "indecent" speech? Or, to ask the question from another perspective, does the First Amendment give citizens the right to speak "offensive" ideas?

Perhaps the most famous "offensive" speech case is *Cohen v. California.*[1] Paul Cohen was convicted in Los Angeles Municipal Court of violating California Penal Code § 415 which prohibited "maliciously and willfully disturb[ing] the peace or quiet of any neighborhood or person [by] offensive conduct," and given 30 days' imprisonment. The prosecution was based on the fact that he wore a jacket bearing the words "Fuck the Draft" in the Los Angeles County Courthouse while women and children were present. At his trial, Cohen testified that he wore the jacket as a means of protesting the Vietnam War and the draft. Cohen did not engage in or threaten to engage in violence, and no one responded violently to his actions.

The court of appeals held that Cohen's behavior could be prohibited as "offensive conduct," which the court defined as "behavior which has a tendency to provoke others to acts of violence or to in turn disturb the peace." The court went on to hold that "[i]t was certainly reasonably foreseeable that such conduct might cause others to rise up to commit a violent act against the person of the defendant or attempt to forcibly remove his jacket." The United States Supreme Court disagreed and reversed Cohen's conviction.

In considering the case, the Supreme Court began by noting that the words on the jacket constituted "pure speech" rather than "conduct" because the conviction was based upon the "offensiveness" of the words and the content of the message. The only "conduct" involved in the case was the "fact of communication." Since the state could not show that Cohen intended to "incite disobedience to or disruption of the draft," the Court concluded that Cohen could not be punished for using the chosen words.

The Court recognized that, although Cohen's jacket used the "F" word, it did not fit within any of the categories of unprotected speech. For example, the jacket was not obscene because it was not erotic and was not intended to be erotic. In addition, the Court concluded that the jacket's wording could not be construed as "fighting words" because they did not involve "personally abusive epithets" likely to provoke violent reaction. While Cohen's words could have been employed in a "personally provocative fashion," the Court found that no one present at the time could have regarded the words as a direct personal insult. The Court also rejected the idea that Cohen's jacket could be prohibited in an effort to prevent a hostile crowd reaction. The Court found that no one reacted hostilely to the jacket.

So, the Court came to the final question: whether Cohen could be prosecuted for the distasteful nature of his expression and the fact that it was thrust upon unwilling views. The Court answered both of these questions in the negative. While the State may prohibit a speaker from imposing "unwelcome views" into the privacy of another person's home, the Court found that "we are often 'captives' outside the sanctuary of the home and subject to objectionable speech." Such dialogue could be

---

[1] 403 U.S. 15, 16–17 (1971).

shut off only on a showing that "substantial privacy interests" had been invaded in an "essentially intolerable manner." The Court viewed a courthouse as different than a home, and noted that those offended by Cohen's jacket could simply avert their eyes. The Court also rejected the idea that speech could be banned based on an "undifferentiated fear or apprehension of disturbance."

Of course, Cohen could have made his point in less objectionable language. The Court held that the courts could not control the content of public discourse:

> To many, the immediate consequence of this freedom may often appear to be only verbal tumult, discord, and even offensive utterance. These are, however, within established limits, in truth necessary side effects of the broader enduring values which the process of open debate permits us to achieve. That the air may at times seem filled with verbal cacophony is, in this sense not a sign of weakness but of strength. . . . Surely the State has no right to cleanse public debate to the point where it is grammatically palatable to the most squeamish among us. Yet no readily ascertainable general principle exists for stopping short of that result were we to affirm the judgment below. For, while the particular four-letter word being litigated here is perhaps more distasteful than most others of its genre, it is nevertheless often true that one man's vulgarity is another's lyric. Indeed, we think it is largely because governmental officials cannot make principled distinctions in this area that the Constitution leaves matters of taste and style so largely to the individual.

Indeed, "distasteful" language may be chosen because of its emotional impact on the listener: "much linguistic expression serves a dual communicative function: it conveys not only ideas capable of relatively precise, detached explication, but otherwise inexpressible emotions as well. In fact, words are often chosen as much for their emotive as their cognitive force." Accordingly, the Court held that it could not control the form of words without running the risk of suppressing ideas.

While *Cohen* specifically addressed the "offensive speech" issue, most such cases are decided on "vagueness" or "overbreadth" grounds. In several leading cases — *Gooding v. Wilson*,[2] *Lewis v. City of New Orleans*,[3] and *Hess v. Indiana*[4] — the Court struck down ordinances using vagueness and overbreadth principles. In *Gooding*, defendant said to a policeman, "you son of a bitch. I'll choke you to death." In *Lewis*, defendant had said "you gaddamn motherfucking police." In *Hess*, defendant had said "We'll take the fucking streets later." In *Cohen*, the Court expressed similar concerns about vagueness. The statute sought to "preserve an appropriately decorous atmosphere in the courthouse where Cohen was arrested," and the Court concluded that the statute failed to put Cohen on notice that his conduct was not permissible: "No fair reading of the phrase 'offensive conduct' can be said sufficiently to inform the ordinary person that distinctions between certain locations are thereby created." Interestingly enough, when Cohen entered the building, he removed his jacket and stood with it folded over his arm. A policeman

---

[2] 405 U.S. 518 (1974).

[3] 415 U.S. 130 (1974).

[4] 414 U.S. 105 (1973).

nonetheless asked the judge to hold Cohen in contempt of court. When the judge refused, the officer arrested Cohen as he left the courtroom.

Of course, a number of recent cases have involved "offensive speech" issues. *Snyder v. Phelps, supra* Chapter 3, involved a claim that the Westboro Baptist Church's funeral protests were not only offensive, but also outrageous. Likewise, in April 2009, a jury held that Professor Ward Churchill was wrongfully dismissed from his post at the University of Colorado. Churchill was a tenured ethnic studies professor who referred to some of the 9/11 terrorist attack victims as "little Eichmanns." The jury concluded that Churchill's views were a substantial or motivating factor in his dismissal, and that he otherwise would not have been dismissed (despite claims of plagiarism and falsification of research). Although the jury awarded Churchill only $1 in damages (because damages were not requested), the court deliberated regarding whether to order reinstatement.

Pacifica *and* Broadcast Zoning. *Cohen* was followed by the holding in *FCC v. Pacifica Foundation.*[5] *Pacifica* involved an FCC proceeding relating to a broadcaster's decision to air George Carlin's monologue entitled "Filthy Words" which contained a multitude of expletives. Carlin began by referring to "the words you couldn't say on the public, ah, airwaves, um, the ones you definitely wouldn't say, ever." He then proceeded to list those words and repeat them over and over again in a variety of colloquialisms. The radio station aired the monologue as part of a program on contemporary attitudes towards speech.

The Federal Communications Commission issued a declaratory order which concluded that Pacifica could have been the subject of administrative sanctions for the broadcast. In its order, the Commission characterized the language of the Carlin monologue as "patently offensive," though not necessarily obscene, and expressed the opinion that it is subject to regulation by channeling it to times of the day when "children most likely would not be exposed to it." The United States Supreme Court upheld the order because of the special attributes of broadcast technology:

> [Broadcasting] has received the most limited First Amendment protection. [T]he broadcast media have established a uniquely pervasive presence in the lives of all Americans. Patently offensive, indecent material presented over the airwaves confronts the citizen, not only in public, but also in the privacy of the home, where the individual's right to be left alone plainly outweighs the First Amendment rights of an intruder. Because the broadcast audience is constantly tuning in and out, prior warnings cannot completely protect the listener or viewer from unexpected program content. [Also,] broadcasting is uniquely accessible to children, even those too young to read.

The Court emphasized that the FCC did not try to ban the speech altogether, but simply to channel it to late night hours when children were less likely to be listening.

---

[5] 438 U.S. 726 (1978).

"Offensiveness" and the National Endowment for the Arts. *National Endowment for the Arts v. Finley,*[6] involved a congressional requirement that the National Endowment for the Arts consider "general standards of decency and respect for the diverse beliefs and values of the American public" in making awards. The Court upheld the restriction noting that the statute only required the NEA merely to take "decency and respect" into consideration, and therefore there was no assurance that the provision would be used to engage in "invidious viewpoint discrimination."

"Offensiveness" and Drive-In Movie Theaters. *Erznoznik v. City of Jacksonville,*[7] involved a facial challenge to a Jacksonville, Florida, ordinance that prohibited the showing of films containing nudity by a drive-in movie theater when its screen was visible from a public street. Although the films in question were not "obscene," under the standards articulated by the Supreme Court in *Miller v. California,* the state argued that it could protect its citizens against unwilling exposure to materials that may be offensive. The Court rejected the argument:

> The plain, if at times disquieting, truth is that in our pluralistic society, constantly proliferating new and ingenious forms of expression, "we are inescapably captive audiences for many purposes." Much that we encounter offends our esthetic, if not our political and moral, sensibilities. Nevertheless, the Constitution does not permit government to decide which types of otherwise protected speech are sufficiently offensive to require protection for the unwilling listener or viewer. Rather, absent the narrow circumstances described above, the burden normally falls upon the viewer to "avoid further bombardment of [his] sensibilities simply by averting [his] eyes." *Cohen.* [T]he screen of a drive-in theater is not "so obtrusive as to make it impossible for an unwilling individual to avoid exposure to it."

The Court also found that the ordinance was "broader than permissible":

> The ordinance is not directed against sexually explicit nudity, nor is it otherwise limited. Rather, it sweepingly forbids display of all films containing *any* uncovered buttocks or breasts, irrespective of context or pervasiveness. Thus it would bar a film containing a picture of a baby's buttocks, the nude body of a war victim, or scenes from a culture in which nudity is indigenous. The ordinance also might prohibit newsreel scenes of the opening of an art exhibit. . . . Clearly all nudity cannot be deemed obscene even as to minors. Nor can such a broad restriction be justified by any other governmental interest pertaining to minors. Speech that is neither obscene as to youths nor subject to some other legitimate proscription cannot be suppressed solely to protect the young from ideas or images that a legislative body thinks unsuitable for them. In most circumstances, the values protected by the First Amendment are no less applicable when government seeks to control the flow of information to minors. Thus, if Jacksonville's ordinance is intended to regulate expression accessible to minors it is overbroad in its proscription.

---

[6] 524 U.S. 569 (1998).

[7] 422 U.S. 205 (1975).

The Court rejected the state's attempt to justify the ordinance as a "traffic regulation" because nudity on a drive-in movie screen could distract passin g motorists.. The Court found that the law was underinclusive because a variety of other movie scenes could be equally distracting to passing motorists.

Chief Justice Burger, joined by Justice Rehnquist, dissenting argued that a motion picture screen is "highly intrusive and distracting." As a result, public lawmakers had a legitimate interest in regulating such displays, especially when they involve nudity.

Nazi Marches. *Collin v. Smith*,[8] involved an attempt by the American Nazi party to hold a march in Skokie, Illinois despite the presence of several thousand survivors of the Nazi holocaust. The marchers intended to carry Nazi flags and display swastikas. Although one lower court enjoined the march, higher courts ultimately held that the march could go forward despite its "offensiveness" to many. The American Nazi party ultimately decided to march elsewhere.

The Danish Cartoons. A controversy arose in 2005 when a Danish newspaper, *Jyllands-Posten*, published caricatures of the Prophet Mohammed. The point of the caricatures was to raise questions about Muslim violence and suicide bombings. Muslims were outraged because Muslim law prohibits depictions of the Prophet, as well as because the Prophet was portrayed as a terrorist (*e.g.*, with a bomb in his turban). The publication produced Muslim protests. Although some of the protests were peaceful, others were violent, involving property damage and deaths. Interestingly, although the United States government did not attempt to suppress publication of the cartoons, most media outlets discussed but did not show them. The cartoons were republished in various foreign countries (*e.g.*, France).

The Pussy Riot Case. Different countries take different approaches to so-called "offensive" speech. A couple of years ago, Pussy Riot (a rock band) decided to conduct a protest in Moscow's main Russian Orthodox cathedral. The Cathedral was chosen as the site for the demonstration in order to protest Vladimir Putin' political alliance with the church hierarchy. The women wore colorful balaclavas, and danced in front of the Holy Doors leading to the altar, dancing, chanting, and lip-synching for what became a profane video beseeching the Virgin Mary to rid Russia of Putin. The women were convicted of hooliganism inspired by religious hatred and sentenced to two years in a labor camp. *See* David M. Herszenhorn, *Anti-Putin Stunt Earns Punk Band Two Years in Jail*, THE NEW YORK TIMES (Aug.20, 2012); Kathy Lally & Monica Hesse, *Pussy Riot Generates Outrage in Russia, Acclaim in the West*, THE WASHINGTON POST (June 9, 2013).

POINTS TO REMEMBER

- Even "offensive" speech is protected under the First Amendment.
- Government may have greater authority to limit or prohibit "offensive" or "indecent" speech in broadcast mediums.

---

[8] 578 F.2d 1197 (7th Cir. 1978).

§ 4.02   CHILD PORNOGRAPHY

Starting in the 1970s, states began to pass laws aimed at combating child pornography. Many of these laws targeted not only "obscene," but non-obscene depictions of child sexuality. The United States Supreme Court confronted the constitutionality of these laws in *New York v. Ferber.*[9] That case involved a New York criminal statute prohibiting persons from knowingly distributing depictions of sexual performances by children under the age of 16. By the time the case reached the United States Supreme Court, 47 states and the federal government had passed child pornography laws, and 35 states had laws prohibiting the distribution of child pornography. Many of these laws prohibited child pornography without regard to whether the material was legally obscene.

In *Ferber*, the law before the Court was Article 263 of the New York Penal Law which created a class D felony: "A person is guilty of promoting a sexual performance by a child when, knowing the character and content thereof, he produces, directs or promotes any performance which includes sexual conduct by a child less than sixteen years of age." The law defined "sexual performance" as "any performance or part thereof which includes sexual conduct by a child less than sixteen years of age." "Sexual conduct" was defined as "actual or simulated sexual intercourse, deviate sexual intercourse, sexual bestiality, masturbation, sado-masochistic abuse, or lewd exhibition of the genitals." A performance was defined as "any play, motion picture, photograph or dance" or "any other visual representation exhibited before an audience." "Promote" was defined as conduct designed to "procure, manufacture, issue, sell, give, provide, lend, mail, deliver, transfer, transmute, publish, distribute, circulate, disseminate, present, exhibit or advertise, or to offer or agree to do the same." Article 263.10 banned the knowing dissemination of obscene material.

The case arose when Ferber, the proprietor of a Manhattan bookstore specializing in sexually oriented products, sold two films to an undercover police officer. The films were devoted almost exclusively to depictions of young boys masturbating. A jury acquitted Ferber on two counts of promoting an obscene sexual performance, but found him guilty of two counts under § 263.15. There was no proof that the material was legally obscene under *Miller v. California.*[10]

In upholding the law, the Court began by considering whether the State has broader power to ban works portraying sexual acts or lewd exhibitions of genitalia by children. Although the Court expressed concern about whether laws directed at child pornography present the risk of suppressing protected expression, the Court upheld the law. In deciding the case, the Court specifically rejected the argument that the *Miller* obscenity test should apply to the distribution of child pornography. The Court found that, although individual states were free to apply the *Miller* test to child pornography, States have a "particular and more compelling interest" in prosecuting those who sexually exploit children. Thus, even though a work may not be obscene under *Miller*, a child may have been sexually exploited and may have suffered physical or psychological harm in the production.

---

[9] 458 U.S. 747 (1982).

[10] 413 U.S. 15 (1973).

The Court offered several justifications for giving states more freedom to ban child pornography. First, the Court found that New York had a "compelling" interest in "safeguarding the physical and psychological well-being" of minors, and the Court was unwilling to "second-guess" the legislature on its conclusion that suppression of child pornography was necessary to achieve this objective. Second, the Court found that the distribution of photograph s and films depicting sexual activity by juveniles was intrinsically related to the sexual abuse of children. The materials constitute a permanent record of the children's participation and the harm is reinforced by circulation. In addition, the Court found that the most effective means of law enforcement was to "dry up the market" through the imposition of severe criminal penalties on those who sell, advertise or promote the product. Third, the advertising and selling of child pornography provided an "economic motive" for the production of such materials. Fourth, the Court emphasized that the value of this material was "exceedingly modest, if not de minimis." Indeed, the Court expressed doubt about whether "visual depictions of children performing sexual acts or lewdly exhibiting their genitals would often constitute an important and necessary part of a literary performance or scientific or educational work."[11] Fifth, the Court emphasized that First Amendment protections often depended on the content of the speech. Because the New York law was so closely related to the welfare of children, the Court found that "the balance of competing interests" was "clearly struck" so that these materials could be denied First Amendment protection.

The Court placed few limits on the scope of state authority. The Court held that the statute must adequately define the prohibited conduct. That standard was met in *Ferber* because New York limited the offense to works that visually depict sexual conduct by children below a specified age. In addition, the statute must particularly describe the "sexual conduct" being prohibited.

Sexting. In recent years, there has been much controversy regarding whether prosecutors should criminally prosecute teens who send text messages depicting nude or revealing photos of themselves or other minors to friends.[12] In some cases, prosecutors have charged the teenagers who sent the text messages, as well as the teens who received the text message photos but did not delete them from their phones. Apparently, students have a variety of motivations for sending these images. In some instances, when they text photos of themselves, they are engaging in a high tech method of flirting. In other instances, students send text message photos of others to harass or embarrass them (*e.g.*, after a high school boy and girl break up, one sends nude pictures of the others to friends out of spite). Technically, all of these images fit within the ban on the dissemination or possession of child pornography, but there are legitimate questions about whether officials should handle these problems through prosecution rather than education. Of course, adults who distribute pictures of children, including teenagers, are subject to prosecution.

Cable Operators and Child Pornography. In July 2008, the United States' largest cable operators agreed to block child pornography websites identified by the

---

[11] *Id.* at 762.

[12] *See* Chana Joffe-Walt, *"Sexting": A Disturbing New Teen Trend?*, National Public Radio broadcast (Mar. 12, 2009), http://www.npr.org/templates/story/story.php?storyId=101735230.

National Center for Missing and Exploited Children. Since most cable operators also provide broadband service, the agreement provides some protection against child pornography sites.

Child Pornography in the Home. *Ferber* was followed by the holding in *Osborne v. Ohio.*[13] That case involved an Ohio law, Ohio Rev. Code Ann. § 2907.323(A)(3), which made it illegal to possess child pornography.[14] Clyde Osborne was convicted of violating the statute and sentenced to six months in prison, after the Columbus, Ohio, police found four photographs in Osborne's home during an otherwise valid search (conducted pursuant to a warrant). Each photograph depicted a nude male adolescent posed in a sexually explicit position. The Ohio Supreme Court read § 2907.323(A)(3) as only applying to depictions of nudity involving a lewd exhibition or graphic focus on a minor's genitals.

In an opinion by Justice White, the Court upheld the law. The Court distinguished its prior holding in *Stanley v. Georgia,*[15] in which the Court struck down a Georgia law prohibiting the private possession of obscene material on the basis that the state could not override Stanley's right to receive information in the privacy of his home. In *Osborne*, the Court reaffirmed *Ferber's* conclusion that the "value of permitting child pornography has been characterized as 'exceedingly modest, if not de minimis.'" The Court then held that "the interests underlying child pornography prohibitions" are far more important than the interests involved in *Stanley*. In *Stanley*, Georgia was concerned that pornography might "poison the minds of its viewers" and the Court held that Georgia did not have the right to control "a person's private thoughts." In *Osborne*, the Court found that the state interest was more compelling because the state was trying to destroy the "market for the exploitative use of children" and it was "surely reasonable for the State to conclude that it will decrease the production of child pornography if it penalizes those who possess and view the product, thereby decreasing demand" — even if they do so in the security of their homes. The Court concluded that Ohio could try to "stamp out this vice at all levels in the distribution chain." Relying on *Ferber*, the Court noted that child pornography "permanently record[s] the victim's abuse" and "causes the child victims continuing harm by haunting the children in years to come." As a result, a ban on possession and viewing encourages the possessors of these materials to destroy them. Moreover, the Court found that the State could encourage destruction of such materials "because pedophiles might use child pornography to seduce other children into sexual activity."

---

[13] 495 U.S. 103 (1990).

[14] The law provided in pertinent part:

(A) No person shall do any of the following: . . .

(3) Possess or view any material or performance that shows a minor who is not the person's child or ward in a state of nudity, unless one of the following applies: (a) The material or performance is [disseminated or possessed] for a bona fide artistic, medical, scientific, educational, religious, governmental, judicial, or other proper purpose, by or to a physician, psychologist, sociologist, scientist, teacher, person pursuing bona fide studies or research, librarian, clergyman, prosecutor, judge, or other person having a proper interest in the material or performance. (b) The person knows that the parents, guardian, or custodian has consented in writing to the photographing or use of the minor in a state of nudity and to the manner in which the material or performance is used or transferred.

[15] 394 U.S. 557 (1969).

Justice Brennan dissenting, joined by justices Marshall and Stevens, agreed that child sexual exploitation is a serious problem, but argued that the States have other means to combat such abuse including enacting laws prohibiting the creation, sale, and distribution of child pornography and obscenity involving minors. In addition, Justice Brennan would have applied *Stanley's* holding to child pornography.

Virtual Child Pornography. *Ferber* and *Osborne* were followed by the holding in *Ashcroft v. The Free Speech Coalition*,[16] a case dealing with the question of whether the State could prohibit "virtual" child pornography. The Child Pornography Prevention Act of 1996 (CPPA), 18 U.S.C. § 2251 et seq., extended child pornography prohibitions to so-called "virtual child pornography" which it defined as "any visual depiction, including any photograph, film, video, picture, or computer or computer-generated image or picture" that "is, or appears to be, of a minor engaging in sexually explicit conduct." The prohibition applied whether or not the image was created with real children. In enacting the law, Congress recognized that it was possible to use computer images to create what appear to be realistic images of children engaged in sexual activity. Another provision of the law, Section 2256(8)(C), prohibited a more common and lower tech means of creating virtual images, known as "computer morphing" in which innocent pictures of real children are altered to make it appear that they are engaged in sexual activity.

The Free Speech Coalition, a trade association for the adult entertainment industry, challenged the CPPA. The Coalition argued that *Ferber's* analysis did not extend to virtual child pornography because that case focused on "the State's interest in protecting the children exploited by the production process," and no children were exploited in the production of virtual child pornography. The Coalition did not challenge the "computer morphing" provisions.

In an opinion by Justice Kennedy, the Court struck down the law. The Court began by recognizing that the age of children involved in sex, whether real or virtual children, could be relevant to whether a work was obscene under *Miller.* However, the Court noted that the CPPA was not directed at obscenity, and reached even depictions having "redeeming social value." In addition, the Court refused to embrace the notion that "virtual child pornography should be regarded as an additional category of unprotected speech." The Court noted that the law applied even to pictures in psychology manuals depicting the horrors of child sexual abuse. Moreover, the law applied even to images that were not "patently offensive," that did not "contravene community standards," and that had "serious literary, artistic, political, or scientific value." The Court found that the statute proscribed "the visual depiction of an idea — that of teenagers engaging in sexual activity" that has been a theme of art and literature "throughout the ages." The Court noted that the law imposed an age limit that was higher than the legal age for marriage in most states, and higher than the age at which persons could consent to sexual relations. The Court noted that the "themes — teenage sexual activity and the sexual abuse of children — have inspired countless literary works" including Romeo and Juliet (in which one of the lovers was only 13 years old). The Court also noted that "many contemporary movies involve similar themes including the movie *Traffic*, nominated for Best Picture, which portrayed a 16-year-old, addicted to drugs, who trades sex

---

[16] 535 U.S. 234 (2002).

(with an older man) for drugs. In addition, the film contains a scene in which a man believes he is watching a teenage boy perform a sexual act on an older man." Finally, the Court recognized that the law could not be upheld as a prohibition against obscenity because the law was inconsistent with *Miller* which required that redeeming value be judged by considering the work as a whole and with reference to community standards.

In deciding the case, the Court refused to extend *Ferber* to virtual pornography. The Court viewed *Ferber* as applying to instances of child sexual abuse and as holding that records of such abuse could be prohibited whether or not they depicted works of value. "The production of the work, not its content, was the target of the statute." By contrast, the CPPA did not involve speech that recorded a crime or created victims by its production. Even though virtual child pornography could lead to the actual abuse of children, the Court found that the causal link was "contingent and indirect" because the harm did not flow from the speech itself (or its production), but on some "unquantified potential for subsequent criminal acts." The Court also rejected the idea that *Ferber* had held that child pornography lacks speech value viewing that decision as focusing on how child pornography was made.

The Court also rejected the argument that specific harms could flow from virtual child pornography. For example, although pedophiles could use virtual child pornography to seduce children, the Court noted that many "innocent" things can be abused — including cartoons, video games, and candy — but such items cannot be prohibited merely "because they can be misused." The Court found that, rather than prohibiting child pornography, the government could respond to this problem by punishing adults who provide unsuitable materials to children, and by enforcing criminal penalties for unlawful solicitation. The Court also found inadequate the argument that virtual child pornography "whets the appetites of pedophiles and encourages them to engage in illegal conduct." The "mere tendency of speech to encourage unlawful acts is not a sufficient reason for banning it." Ultimately, the Court applied the *Brandenburg* test which held that advocacy of illegal conduct could only be prohibited when it is "directed to inciting or producing imminent lawless action and is likely to incite or produce such action. *Brandenburg v. Ohio*, 395 U.S. 444, 447 (1969) (per curiam)." The Court found that there was "no attempt, incitement, solicitation, or conspiracy" and that there was "no more than a remote connection between speech that might encourage thoughts or impulses and any resulting child abuse."

The Court also rejected the argument that virtual child pornography could be prohibited on the basis that a prohibition on virtual images would help eliminate the market for pornography that uses real children. The Government had argued that virtual images are indistinguishable from real ones, are part of the same market and are often exchanged. "In this way, it is said, virtual images promote the trafficking in works produced through the exploitation of real children." The Court found the argument "implausible" noting that pornographers would shift to virtual images rather than risk prosecution for creating images with real children.

One argument raised by the government was that the existence of virtual child pornography could make it difficult to prosecute those who produce pornography using real children. The government argued advancing technology might make it difficult to determine whether a particular picture was made using real children or by using computer imaging. The Court concluded that the government could not suppress lawful speech as the means of suppressing unlawful speech.

Justice Thomas concurring argued that technology may evolve to the point that those who possess and distribute pornographic images of real children can "escape conviction by claiming that the images are computer-generated, thereby raising a reasonable doubt as to their guilt." If that happens, then Justice Thomas felt that the Government may well have a compelling interest in prohibiting virtual child pornography. Justice O'Connor, joined by Chief Justice Rehnquist and Justice Scalia, concurred in part and dissented in part. She would have upheld the statute to the extent that it was construed to apply only to images that were "virtually indistinguishable from actual children." She would have found that such a construction was narrowly tailored and avoided vagueness problems.

Chief Justice Rehnquist, joined in part by Justice Scalia, dissented arguing that Congress has a compelling interest in its ability to enforce prohibitions against actual child pornography, and Congress could reasonably have concluded that "rapidly advancing technology" would soon make it virtually impossible to enforce such laws. While he agreed that "[s]erious First Amendment concerns would arise were the Government ever to prosecute someone for simple distribution or possession of a film with literary or artistic value, such as 'Traffic' or 'American Beauty,' " he found that the Act "need not be construed to reach such materials." He would have applied the statute to computer generated images that are virtually indistinguishable from real children engaged in sexually explicitly conduct.

In *United States v. Williams*,[17] the Court upheld portions of the Prosecutorial Remedies and Other Tools to end the Exploitation of Children Today Act of 2003, § 2252A(a)(3)(B) of Title 18, United States Code, which criminalized the pandering or solicitation of child pornography. The interesting aspect of the statute was that an individual could be convicted of soliciting or pandering the sale of child pornography even if the material being sold did not constitute child pornography. The plaintiffs raised overbreadth and vagueness challenges which are discussed *infra*.

Civil Remedy for Victims of Child Pornography Crimes. In 2003, Congress enacted 18 U.S.C § 2252B, a companion statute to § 2252A (the federal version of the child pornography crime), which provided a civil remedy for child pornography. The law provided as follows:

> Any person who, while a minor, was a victim of a violation of § 2252A, and who suffers personal injury as a result of such violation, regardless of whether the injury occurred while such person was a minor, may sue in any appropriate U. S. District Court and shall recover the actual damages such person sustains and the cost of the suit, including a reasonable attorney's fee. Any person as described in the preceding sentence shall be deemed to have sustained damages of no less than $150,000 in value.

Under the statute, parents may sue, on behalf of their minor children, those who

---

[17] 128 S. Ct. 1830 (2008).

engage in conduct such as possession of images of their children in violation of the child pornography statute.

POINTS TO REMEMBER

- Government has greater authority to prohibit child pornography (so-called "kiddie porn").

- There is a compelling governmental interest in protecting children against exploitation and abuse.

- The government may not prohibit the production or distribution of so-called "virtual child pornography" (simulated pornography produced through computer technology without the use of real children).

- Virtual pornography is different than "kiddie porn" because real children are not exploited or abused in its production.

- If technology improves to the point that it is no longer possible to distinguish between virtual child porn and kiddie porn and impossible therefore to prosecute those who create kiddie porn, government may have a compelling interest in prohibiting virtual child porn.

---

§ 4.03 PORNOGRAPHY AS DISCRIMINATION AGAINST WOMEN

Professors Catherine MacKinnon and Andrea Dworkin have argued that pornography, even non-obscene pornography, is subject to regulation because of the messages that it sends about women. *See* Catherine MacKinnon, *Pornography, Civil Rights and Speech*, 20 HARV. C.R.-C.L. L. REV. 1 (1985); Andrea Dworkin, *Against the Male Flood: Censorship, Pornography and Equality*, 8 HARV. WOMEN'S L.J. 1 (1985). In 1983, the City of Indianapolis adopted MacKinnon and Dworkin's model ordinance which prohibited "pornography" as a practice that discriminates against women, and defined it as "the graphic sexually explicit subordination of women, whether in pictures or in words, that also includes one or more of the following:

(1) Women are presented as sexual objects who enjoy pain or humiliation; or

(2) Women are presented as sexual objects who experience sexual pleasure in being raped; or

(3) Women are presented as sexual objects tied up or cut up or mutilated or bruised or physically hurt, or as dismembered or truncated or fragmented or severed into body parts; or

(4) Women are presented as being penetrated by objects or animals; or

(5) Women are presented in scenarios of degradation, injury, abasement, torture, shown as filthy or inferior, bleeding, bruised, or hurt in a context that makes these conditions sexual; or

(6) Women are presented as sexual objects for domination, conquest, violation, exploitation, possession, or use, or through postures or positions of servility or submission or display.

Indianapolis Code § 16-3(q). The statute provided that the "use of men, children, or transsexuals in the place of women in paragraphs (1) through (6) above shall also constitute pornography under this section."

The ordinance applied to both obscene and non-obscene pornography even though the ordinance did not satisfy the obscenity test articulated in *Miller* because the ordinance did not refer to the prurient interest, to patently offensive sexual conduct, or to the standards of the community, "because it did not focus the entire work and did not consider whether the work had literary, artistic, political, or scientific value." The City defended the ordinance on the basis that "pornography influences attitudes" and that "the statute [was] a way to alter the socialization of men and women rather than to vindicate community standards of offensiveness." A drafter of the statute argued "if a woman is subjected, why should it matter that the work has other value?" It was also argued that the ordinance would "play an important role in reducing the tendency of men to view women as sexual objects, a tendency that leads to both unacceptable attitudes and discrimination in the workplace and violence away from it."

In *American Booksellers Association, Inc. v. Hudnut*,[18] in an opinion by Judge Easterbrook, the Seventh Circuit struck down the law because it involved "content discrimination." "Speech treating women in the approved way — in sexual encounters 'premised on equality' — is lawful no matter how sexually explicit. Speech treating women in the disapproved way — as submissive in matters sexual or as enjoying humiliation — is unlawful no matter how significant the literary, artistic, or political qualities of the work taken as a whole." The state "may not ordain preferred viewpoints" and may not "declare one perspective right and silence opponents."[19] Judge Easterbrook went on to note that: "If there is any fixed star in our constitutional constellation, it is that no official, high or petty, can prescribe what shall be orthodox in politics, nationalism, religion, or other matters of opinion or force citizens to confess by word or act their faith therein." Judge Easterbrook concluded that the law was content discriminatory:

Under the ordinance graphic sexually explicit speech is "pornography" or not depending on the perspective the author adopts. Speech that "subordinates" women and also, for example, presents women as enjoying pain, humiliation, or rape, or even simply presents women in "positions of servility or submission or display" is forbidden, no matter how great the literary or political value of the work taken as a whole. Speech that portrays women in positions of equality is lawful, no matter how graphic the sexual content. This is thought control. It establishes an "approved" view of women, of how they may r eact to sexual encounters, of how the sexes may relate to each other. Those who espouse the approved view may use sexual images; those who do not, may not.

---

[18] 771 F.2d 323 (7th Cir. 1985).

[19] *Id.*

Indianapolis justifies the ordinance on the ground that pornography affects thoughts. Men who see women depicted as subordinate are more likely to treat them so. Pornography is an aspect of dominance. It does not persuade people so much as change them. It works by socializing, by establishing the expected and the permissible. In this view pornography is not an idea; pornography is the injury.

There is much to this perspective. Beliefs are also facts. People often act in accordance with the images and patterns they find around them. . . . Therefore we accept the premises of this legislation. Depictions of subordination tend to perpetuate subordination. The subordinate status of women in turn leads to affront and lower pay at work, insult and injury at home, battery and rape on the streets. . . . Yet this simply demonstrates the power of pornography as speech. All of these unhappy effects depend on mental intermediation. Pornography affects how people see the world, their fellows, and social relations. . . . Racial bigotry, anti-semitism, violence on television, reporters' biases — these and many more influence the culture and shape our socialization. None is directly answerable by more speech, unless that speech too finds its place in the popular culture. Yet all is protected as speech, however insidious. Any other answer leaves the government in control of all of the institutions of culture, the great censor and director of which thoughts are good for us. . . .

Defenders of the ordinance argued that some pornographers depict "sexual torture, penetration of women by red-hot irons and the like." In addition, they noted that some pornographers use fraud, trickery, or force to compel women to perform. But Judge Easterbrook rejected these arguments as a permissible basis for regulation noting that the state is free to prohibit such conduct, and that it can do so without prohibiting the ideas conveyed by the pornographers. He went on:

Much of Indianapolis's argument rests on the belief that when speech is "unanswerable," and the metaphor that there is a "marketplace of ideas" does not apply, the First Amendment does not apply either. The metaphor is honored; Milton's AEROPAGITICA and John Stewart Mill's ON LIBERTY defend freedom of speech on the ground that the truth will prevail, and many of the most important cases under the First Amendment recite this position. The Framers undoubtedly believed it. As a general matter it is true. But the Constitution does not make the dominance of truth a necessary condition of freedom of speech. To say that it does would be to confuse an outcome of free speech with a necessary condition for the application of the amendment.

A power to limit speech on the ground that truth has not yet prevailed and is not likely to prevail implies the power to declare truth. At some point the government must be able to say (as Indianapolis has said): "We know what the truth is, yet a free exchange of speech has not driven out falsity, so that we must now prohibit falsity." If the government may declare the truth, why wait for the failure of speech? Under the First Amendment, however, there is no such thing as a false idea so the government may not restrict speech on the ground that in a free exchange truth is not yet dominant.

Judge Easterbrook also rejected the argument that pornography is "low value" speech. He noted that, even with lower value speech, the government is not allowed to choose among viewpoints. Moreover, he questioned whether pornography is low value speech:

> Indianapolis seeks to prohibit certain speech because it believes this speech influences social relations and politics on a grand scale, that it controls attitudes at home and in the· legislature. This precludes a characterization of the speech as low value. True, pornography and obscenity have sex in common. But Indianapolis left out of its definition any reference to literary, artistic, political, or scientific value. The ordinance applies to graphic sexually explicit subordination in works great and small. The Court sometimes balances the value of speech against the costs of its restriction, but it does this by category of speech and not by the content of particular works. Indianapolis has created an approved point of view and so loses the support of these cases.

> Any rationale we could imagine in support of this ordinance could not be limited to sex discrimination. Free speech has been on balance an ally of those seeking change. Governments that want stasis start by restricting speech. Culture is a powerful force of continuity; Indianapolis paints pornography as part of the culture of power. Change in any complex system ultimately depends on the ability of outsiders to challenge accepted views and the reigning institutions. Without a strong guarantee of freedom of speech, there is no effective right to challenge what is. . . .

Judge Easterbrook did hold that the state could impose liability on a pornographer if it were shown that a woman suffered physical attack and she could show that the attack was "directly caused by specific pornography." Of course, the constitutionality of such a provision would depend on how it was construed.

In the wake of the *Hudnut* decision, Professor Naden Strossen, in her article *A Feminist Critique of "the" Feminist Critique of Pornography*, 79 VA. L. REV. 1099 (1993), argued that prohibitions on soft pornography are undesirable. She questions whether such provisions could be effective. In her view, censorship schemes are likely to push pornography underground where it may have more impact. She also questioned the alleged causal link between "exposure to 'pornography' and misogynistic discrimination or violence." As a result, she concluded that the "speculative benefits" of censorship are outweighed by the "demonstrable costs" of censorship on women's rights. She argued that such censorship has historically been used to "stifle women's sexuality, women's expression, and women's full and equal participation in our society." As a result, women have a strong interest in preserving free expression, and should use that expression to turn society against pornography.

POINTS TO REMEMBER

- Government may not prohibit non-obscene pornography merely because it dislikes the view of women that it portrays.

- Such prohibitions involve content-based and viewpoint-based discrimination against speech.

---

§ 4.04 CRUSH VIDEOS

There has also been litigation regarding whether the Court should create a new category of excluded speech for so-called "crush videos."[20] *United States v. Stevens* involved a federal law that imposed criminal penalties on anyone who knowingly "creates, sells, or possesses a depiction of animal cruelty," if done "for commercial gain" in interstate or foreign commerce. 18 U.S.C. § 48(a). The law defined "animal cruelty" as a depiction "in which a living animal is intentionally maimed, mutilated, tortured, wounded, or killed," if that conduct violates federal or state law where "the creation, sale, or possession takes place." The law created an exception for any depiction "that has serious religious, political, scientific, educational, journalistic, historical, or artistic value."

In enacting the law, Congress expressed concern regarding the interstate market for "crush videos." Such videos feature the torture and killing of helpless animals, including cats, dogs, monkeys, mice, and hamsters by women who slowly crush the animals to death "with their bare feet or while wearing high heeled shoes." In some of the videos, the women are shown "talking to the animals in a kind of dominatrix patter" which is heard above "[t]he cries and squeals of the animals, who are obviously in great pain." Such videos are purchased by individuals with a sexual fetish for such activities. The particular acts in question are prohibited by the animal cruelty laws of all 50 states and the District of Columbia. In most instances, the crush videos do not disclose the participants' identities, thereby making it difficult for the government to prosecute the underlying conduct.

The law was challenged by Stevens who was indicted for selling videos depicting fights between dogs and other animals. Among other things, the government argued that depictions of animal cruelty are not entitled to First Amendment protection. The Court disagreed. Noting that government may not "restrict expression because of its message, its ideas, its subject matter, or its content," the Court rejected the law because it explicitly regulated content: "The statute restricts 'visual [and] auditory depiction[s],' such as photographs, videos, or sound recordings, depending on whether they depict conduct in which a living animal is intentionally harmed." As a result, the Court held that the law was subject to strict scrutiny, meaning that it would be regarded as "presumptively invalid" and that the government would bear the burden of proving constitutionality. In other words, the Court declined to create a new category of speech that was beyond the scope of First Amendment protection.

---

[20] *United States v. Stevens*, 130 S. Ct. 1577 (2010).

It preferred to limit excepted speech to areas that had traditionally been excepted.

The Court also rejected the argument that crush video depictions have such "minimal redeeming value" as to deprive them of First Amendment protection. The Court concluded that the First Amendment includes the idea that "the benefits of its restrictions on the Government outweigh the costs." Even though most First Amendment exceptions involve balancing, in the sense that the speech involves "such slight social value as a step to truth that any benefit that may be derived from them is clearly outweighed by the social interest in order and morality," the Court rejected the idea that speech was subject to a simple cost-benefit analysis, and suggested that even recent exceptions (*e.g.*, child pornography) were based on a showing of a compelling governmental interest (in the case of child pornography, that interest involved the protection of children against abuse) and the speech had *de minimis* value. In addition, the Court was concerned about the fact that the statute suffered from overbreadth.

Justice Alito dissented, arguing that the statute was focused on "horrific acts of animal cruelty — in particular, the creation and commercial exploitation of 'crush videos,' a form of depraved entertainment that has no social value." Noting that it is difficult to prosecute those involved in the making of such videos, because their faces are shielded from public view, he pointed out that Congress had chosen to suppress the sale of such videos in order to suppress the market. Moreover, such videos depict the portrayal of criminal acts. Thus, he regarded the statute as within the tradition of child pornography statutes upheld in *Ferber.* Finally, he argued that "the harm caused by the underlying crimes vastly outweighs any minimal value that the depictions might conceivably be thought to possess," especially because the "animals used in crush videos are living creatures that experience excruciating pain." As a result, he concluded that the videos have "no appreciable social value" and "the suffering lasts for years rather than minutes."

§ 4.05 VIOLENT VIDEOS

The Court also rejected the idea that violent videos are not entitled to First Amendment protection even when they are purchased by children. In *Brown v. Entertainment Merchants Association*, 131 S. Ct. 2729 (2011), the Court struck down a California statute that prohibited the sale or rental of "violent video games" to minors, and that required that their packaging be labeled "18." The Act applied to games which allow a player to engage in "killing, maiming, dismembering, or sexually assaulting an image of a human being, if those acts are depicted" in a manner that "[a] reasonable person, considering the game as a whole, would find appeals to a deviant or morbid interest of minors," that is "patently offensive to prevailing standards in the community as to what is suitable for minors," and that "causes the game, as a whole, to lack serious literary, artistic, political, or scientific value for minors." § 1746(d)(1)(A). The statute was enforceable by civil fines of up to $1,000.

In response to a challenge by video-game and software industry companies, the Court struck the law down concluding that the "Free Speech Clause exists principally to protect discourse on public matters," but "that it is difficult to distinguish politics from entertainment, and dangerous to try." The Court concluded that video games "communicate ideas — and even social messages — through many familiar literary devices (such as characters, dialogue, plot, and music) and through features distinctive to the medium (such as the player's interaction with the virtual world)." As a result, the Court concluded that video games are entitled to First Amendment protection, and it went on to affirm the idea that government may not "restrict expression because of its message, its ideas, its subject matter, or its content" unless speech fits within one of the categories of excepted speech (*e.g.*, fighting words, obscenity, child pornography). However, the Court regarded those exceptions as "well-defined and narrowly limited classes of speech, the prevention and punishment of which have never been thought to raise any Constitutional problem." .

The California statute was interesting because it tracked the Court's obscenity jurisprudence as reflected in *Ginsberg v. New York*, 390 U.S. 629 (1968). Under that jurisprudence, states could prohibit the sale to minors of *sexual* material that would be obscene from the perspective of a child, and therefore harmful to children. Following this approach, the California statute made it illegal to sell videos that might be harmful to children. Nevertheless, the Court rejected the analogy: "No doubt a State possesses legitimate power to protect children from harm, but that does not include a free-floating power to restrict the ideas to which children may be exposed." In other words, when speech is not obscene as to children, Congress cannot suppress it merely "from ideas or images that a legislative body thinks unsuitable for them." Moreover, the Court noted that the nation had rarely taken steps to insulate children from depictions of violence:

> Certainly the *books* we give children to read — or read to them when they are younger — contain no shortage of gore. Grimm's Fairy Tales, for example, are grim indeed. As her just deserts for trying to poison Snow White, the wicked queen is made to dance in red hot slippers "till she fell dead on the floor, a sad example of envy and jealousy." THE COMPLETE BROTHERS GRIMM FAIRY TALES 198 (2006 ed.). Cinderella's evil stepsisters have their eyes pecked out by doves. And Hansel and Gretel (children!) kill their captor by baking her in an oven.

The Court also rejected California's claim that video games present are "of special concern because they are 'interactive,' in that the player participates in the violent action on screen and determines its outcome." The Court noted that interactive games had existed since 1969, and that the current games are different only as "a matter of degree than of kind." Even if the games contain disgusting levels of violence, or violence directed at particular ethnic groups, the Court concluded that "disgust is not a valid basis for restricting expression" and government's objection to particular messages cannot provide the basis for repression. Because the statute was content-based, the Court concluded that the statute could only be upheld if it could survive strict scrutiny in the sense that "it is justified by a compelling government interest and is narrowly drawn to serve that interest." The Court concluded that California could not satisfy this standard because it could not "show a direct causal link between violent video games and harm to minors." Although California submitted various psychological studies, in an attempt to show the casual link, the Court found that the state's evidence was not compelling, noting that the studies were "rejected by every court to consider them," and do not "prove that violent video games *cause* minors to *act* aggressively (which would at least be a beginning)." The Court found "significant, admitted flaws in methodology." Even if the studies showed "some effect on children's feelings of aggression," the Court concluded that "those effects are both small and indistinguishable from effects produced by other media."

The Court also held that the California statute was underinclusive as well as overinclusive. It was underinclusive because it failed to restrict other depictions of violence to children. As a result, the Court raised questions about whether the government's asserted justification for the video game ban was its true justification: "California has singled out the purveyors of video games for disfavored treatment — at least when compared to booksellers, cartoonists, and movie producers — and has given no persuasive reason why." In any event, parents could use the industry's voluntary rating system to control their children's use of inappropriate video games if they chose to do so. The statute was overinclusive because the statute prohibited children from purchasing video games on their own even when the children did not object.

The decision produced a couple of dissents. Justice Thomas argued that the "founding generation believed parents had absolute authority over their minor children and expected parents to use that authority to direct the proper development of their children," and this law only prohibited purchases by minors when the parents were not involved. Justice Breyer argued that the state has special power to control the conduct of children, and that the regulation of communications to children were not subject to the First Amendment. He also concluded that the law was not vague. Finally, he would have placed much greater emphasis on psychological studies as showing that there was a casual link suggesting that playing violent video games causes harm to youth: "Longitudinal studies, which measure changes over time, have found that increased exposure to violent video games causes an increase in aggression over the same period," and "[e]xperimental studies in laboratories have found that subjects randomly assigned to play a violent video game subsequently displayed more characteristics of aggression than those who played nonviolent games." He went on to note that: " 'meta-analyses,' *i.e.*, studies of all the studies, have concluded that exposure to violent video games 'was positively associated with aggressive behavior, aggressive cognition, and aggressive affect,' and that 'playing violent video games is a *causal* risk factor for long-term harmful outcomes.' " He concluded that there was sufficient evidence so that the Court should accord the California legislature "some degree of deference in respect to legislative facts of this kind, particularly when they involve technical matters that are beyond our competence, and even in First Amendment cases."

§ 4.06   SUPPORT FOR TERRORIST ORGANIZATIONS

The Court did carve out a First Amendment exception in *Holder v. Humanitarian Law Project*, 130 S.Ct. 2705 (2010), for individuals who provide "material support or resources" to certain foreign organizations that engage in terrorist activity. A federal statute imposed that prohibition after Congress found that certain specified organizations "are so tainted by their criminal conduct that any contribution to such an organization facilitates that conduct." The law was challenged by individuals who sought to support the lawful, nonviolent purposes of the prohibited groups, and who contended that the law violated their rights to freedom of speech and association.

The Court rejected the plaintiffs' claims that the provision of such support involved pure political speech (and not conduct), as well as the government's claim that the support involved only conduct. The Court applied strict scrutiny because it viewed the prohibition as a content-based restriction on speech. Importantly, the law did not prohibit all communication with the prohibited groups. Communication was permissible if it involved the conveyance of only general or unspecialized knowledge., but was prohibited if it involved the communication of a "specific skill" or communication of advice derived from "specialized knowledge" (*e.g.*, training on the use of international law or advice on petitioning the United Nations). In upholding the prohibition, the Court held that the government's interest in combating terrorism "is an urgent objective of the highest order," and the Court rejected plaintiff's argument that a prohibition on material support was necessary to achieve that objective. The Court expressed doubt about whether foreign terrorist organizations "meaningfully segregate support of their legitimate activities from support of terrorism" so that support for one part of an organization's activities, even a non-violent part, can free up resources that can be put to violent ends. Moreover, the Court concluded that foreign aid provides legitimacy to terrorist groups. Finally, the Court noted that the statute did not prohibit all association with foreign groups. On the contrary, it only prohibited "material support coordinated with or under the direction of a designated foreign terrorist organization. Independent advocacy that might be viewed as promoting the group's legitimacy is not covered."

The Court went on to note that it saw no reason to doubt Congress's finding that "international cooperation is required for an effective response to terrorism," or Congress' conclusion that a prohibition on material-support furthers this objective "by prohibiting aid for foreign terrorist groups that harm the United States' partners abroad[.]" While the Court was unwilling to suggest that it was precluded from reviewing congressional judgments on foreign policy issues, it was reluctant to do so: "Given the sensitive interests in national security and foreign affairs at stake, the political branches have adequately substantiated their determination that, to serve the Government's interest in preventing terrorism, it was necessary to prohibit providing material support in the form of training, expert advice, personnel, and services to foreign terrorist groups, even if the supporters meant to promote only the groups' nonviolent ends."

The Court sustained the prohibitions even though plaintiffs wished to pursue only peaceful objectives: 1) to train members of the prohibited groups how to use humanitarian and international law to peacefully resolve disputes; 2) to teach members of the prohibited groups how to petition various representative bodies such as the Untied Nations for relief." The Court concluded that the prohibited groups might use these skills to promote terrorism. In addition, to the extent that plaintiffs wished to provide money for humanitarian purposes, that money would allow the prohibited groups to redirect more funds to terrorism.

Justice Breyer, joined by justices Ginsburg, and Sotomayor, dissented, arguing that the government could not preclude the prohibited groups from pursuing lawful political objectives. Although he viewed the government's interest in protecting the United States against terrorist threats as compelling, he doubted that the government could show a link between the statute's prohibition and the alleged security interest. He doubted that the support was fungible in the sense that it could readily be transferred from peaceful to violent means. He would have analogized to the Court's incitement of illegal advocacy cases in which "pure advocacy of even the most unlawful activity" is permissible so long as it "directed to inciting or producing imminent lawless action [and] likely to incite or produce such action."

§ 4.07   LIES REGARDING THE CONGRESSIONAL MEDAL OF HONOR

The Court declined to create yet another category of excepted speech in *United States v. Alvarez*.[21] That case involved Xavier Alvarez, a man who lied in claiming to have won the Congressional Medal of Honor (at a district water board meeting), and was criminally charged with violating the Stolen Valor Act of 2005.[22] Since the Act imposed a content-based restriction on speech, the Court applied strict scrutiny. Again, the Court emphasized that, as "a general matter, the First Amendment means that government has no power to restrict expression because of its message, its ideas, its subject matter, or its content." The Court also rejected the idea that speech could be restricted based simply on a "free-floating test" for First Amendment coverage involving "an ad hoc balancing of relative social costs and benefits," noting that content-based restrictions on speech are allowed only when they involve one of a few "historic and traditional categories of expression long familiar to the bar" (e.g., advocacy intended, and likely, to incite imminent lawless action, speech integral to criminal conduct, so-called "fighting words," child pornography, fraud, true threats, and speech presenting some grave and imminent threat the government has the power to prevent). The Court concluded that these categories of speech "have a historical foundation in the Court's free speech tradition," but do not unduly intrude upon the "vast realm of free speech and thought always protected in our tradition."

In particular, the Court refused to recognize any general exception to the First Amendment for false speech. Relying on *New York Times v. Sullivan*, the Court emphasized "that some false statements are inevitable if there is to be an open and vigorous expression of views in public and private conversation, expression the First Amendment seeks to guarantee."[23] While there have been some limitations on false speech in cases involving "defamation, fraud, or some other legally cognizable harm associated with a false statement, such as an invasion of privacy or the costs of vexatious litigation, in those decisions the falsity of the speech at issue was not irrelevant to the Court's analysis, "but neither was it determinative." Of course, as the Court recognized, there have been instances when the government can prohibit

---

[21]   132 S. Ct. 2537 (2012).

[22]   18 U.S.C. § 704.

[23]   See *Sullivan, supra,* at 271.

lies: "first, the criminal prohibition of a false statement made to a Government official, 18 U.S.C. § 1001; second, laws punishing perjury; and third, prohibitions on the false representation that one is speaking as a Government official or on behalf of the Government, see, *e.g.*, § 912; § 709." However, the Court did not view these exceptions as creating "a principle that all proscriptions of false statements are exempt from exacting First Amendment scrutiny." Rather, the Court viewed these as more limited prohibitions relating to the functioning of government. For example, the Court viewed prejury as "at war with justice" because perjury "undermines the function and province of the law and threatens the integrity of judgments that are the basis of the legal system." Likewise, "Statutes that prohibit falsely representing that one is speaking on behalf of the Government, or that prohibit impersonating a Government officer, also protect the integrity of Government processes, quite apart from merely restricting false speech."

Turning specifically to the Stolen Valor Act, while the Court emphasized that the First Amendment stands against any "freewheeling authority to declare new categories of speech outside the scope of the First Amendment," the Court recognized that there may exist "some categories of speech that have been historically unprotected [but] have not yet been specifically identified or discussed [in] our case law." The Court indicated that it would not recognize a new category of exempted speech without being presented with "persuasive evidence that a novel restriction on content is part of a long (if heretofore unrecognized) tradition of proscription." The Court concluded that there was insufficient evidence that "false statements generally should constitute a new category of unprotected speech on this basis." The Court emphasized that the Act could have been applied to "personal, whispered conversations within a home," and that it seeks to control and suppress false statements of this type "in almost limitless times and settings." Moreover, the Court expressed concern that, if the government were allowed to prohibit this lie, there might emerge a general principle suggesting a general governmental authority "to compile a list of subjects about which false statements are punishable." The Court rejected this idea, noting that, were "this law to be sustained, there could be an endless list of subjects the National Government or the States could single out." The court did recognize that false claims can be restricted when they are designed to "effect a fraud or secure moneys or other valuable considerations." But the Court viewed the Act as creating a "broad censorial power unprecedented in this Court's cases or in our constitutional tradition," and that would create "a chill, a chill the First Amendment cannot permit if free speech, thought, and discourse are to remain a foundation of our freedom."

Since the Act imposed a content-based restriction on speech, the Court emphasized that it was required to apply the "most exacting scrutiny." Although the Court agreed that military medals "serve the important public function of recognizing and expressing gratitude for acts of heroism and sacrifice in military service," and admitted that the "Government's interest in protecting the integrity of the Medal of Honor is beyond question," the Court held that the law could not survive strict scrutiny" which requires that the Act be "actually necessary" to achieve that interest. In particular, the Court found that "the dynamics of free speech, of counterspeech, of refutation, can overcome the lie. Respondent lied at a public meeting." Indeed, after Alvarez's lie was exposed, he "was ridiculed online, his actions were reported in the press, and a fellow board member called for his resignation." "It is a fair assumption that any true holders of the Medal who had heard of Alvarez's false claims would have been fully vindicated by the community's expression of outrage, showing as it did the Nation's high regard for the Medal." The government argued that counterspeech will not necessarily be effective because some military records have been lost or are unverifiable. The Court rejected this argument, noting that "in cases where public refutation will not serve the Government's interest, the Act will not either." In addition, the Court concluded that the Act is not the "least restrictive means among available, effective alternatives." In particular, Government could create a database of Congressional Medal of Honor Award winners.

Justice Alito, joined by justices Scalia and Thomas, dissented. He argued that "Only the bravest of the brave are awarded the Congressional Medal of Honor, but the Court today holds that every American has a constitutional right to claim to have received this singular award," and argued that these "lies have no value in and of themselves, and proscribing them does not chill any valuable speech." He also argued that the law imposes substantial harm, and that alternative approaches would not be adequate. In particular, the government could not create an effective list of award recipients because the government does not have sufficient information regarding prior winners. Finally, he argued that "false factual statements possess no intrinsic First Amendment value."

Of course, Alvarez raises questions regarding the government's authority to declare "truth" For example, the French courts have upheld the French Gayssot Law which makes it illegal to deny that the Holocaust occurred, and also prohibits individuals from contesting the rulings of the Nuremburg War Crimes Tribunal.[24] It is hard to believe that such a law would be constitutional in the United States. In addition, a law passed by France's Senate would have made it a crime to deny that the Ottoman Empire had committed genocide against the Armenians with penalties that included fines up to €45,000 and up to a year in prison. Some believe that 1.5 million Armenians were killed in the genocide. Turkey argues that no more than 500,000 people died, and that many of these individuals died from starvation or exposure rather than as a result of deliberate killings. The law created a potential conflict with a Turkish law (that makes it a crime to insult Turkishness), and then French President Nicholas Sarkozy was prohibited from signing the law until the French Constitutional Court could rule on its constitutionality. On February 28, 2012, the Constitutional Court struck the French law down.[25]

§ 4.08   REPARATIVE THERAPY

Working its way through the courts are challenges to a California law that prohibits mental health providers from engaging in sexual orientation change efforts (SOCE) with minors. The law provides that "[a]ny sexual orientation change

---

[24] *See* Russell L. Weaver, Nicolas Delpierre & Laurence Boissier, *Holocaust Denial and Governmentally Declared "Truth"; French and American Perspectives*, 41 TEXAS TECH L. REV. 495 (2009).

[25] *See* Scott Sayare, *French Council Strikes Down Bill on Armenian Genocide Law*, INTERNATIONAL HERALD TRIBUNE, Feb. 29, 2012, A6.

efforts attempted on a patient under 18 years of age by a mental health provider shall be considered unprofessional conduct and shall subject a mental health provider to discipline by the licensing entity for that mental health provider." The law defines "sexual orientation change efforts" as "any practice by mental health providers that seek to change an individual's sexual orientation, and includes efforts to change behaviors or gender expressions, or to eliminate or reduce sexual or romantic attractions or feelings toward individuals of the same sex." The law excludes "psychotherapies that provide acceptance, support, and understanding of clients or the facilitation of clients' coping, social support, and identity exploration and development, including sexual orientation-neutral interventions to prevent or address unlawful conduct or unsafe sexual practices; and do not seek to change sexual orientation." The bill defines "mental health provider" as "a physician or surgeon specializing in the practice of psychiatry, a psychologist, a psychological assistant, intern, or trainee, a licensed marriage and family therapist, a registered marriage and family therapist, intern, or trainee, a licensed educational psychologist, a credentialed school psychologist, a licensed clinical social worker, an associate clinical social worker, a licensed professional clinical counselor, a registered clinical counselor, intern, or trainee, or any other person designated as a mental health professional under California law or regulation." The law has been challenged by a licensed marriage and family therapist, an ordained minister, who operates a non-profit professional counseling center. He believes that "human sexuality is to be expressed only in a monogamous lifelong relationship between one man and one woman within the framework of marriage." As a result, he has historically provided treatment that qualifies as SOCE under the law.[26]

§ 4.09 COMMERCIAL SPEECH

Commercial expression has been described as speech that "propose[s] an economic transaction"[27] or that pertains "solely to the economic interests of the speaker and audience."[28] Commercial speech in its most common form consists of advertising. The most common form of expression meeting these definitional guidelines is advertising. Like defamation, fighting words, and obscenity, commercial speech traditionally was viewed as categorically unprotected. Its history is similar to obscenity's insofar as this exclusion from First Amendment protection typically was assumed rather than explained. This parallel ended in the 1970s when the Court more carefully examined the value of commercial expression and concluded that it merited First Amendment attention.

[A]   The Backdrop to Modern Commercial Speech Doctrine

Commercial speech historically was not protected by the First Amendment. This premise traces back to *Valentine v. Chrestensen*.[29] In this case, the Court reviewed a city ordinance that prohibited the distribution of commercial leaflets in

---

[26] *See Welch v. Brown*, 907 F. Supp.2d 1102 (E.D. Cal. 2012).

[27] Virginia State Board of Pharmacy v. Virginia Citizens Consumer Council, Inc., 425 U.S. 748 (1976).

[28] Central Hudson Gas & Electric Co. v. Public Service Commission, 447 U.S. 557 (1980).

[29] 316 U.S. 52 (1942).

the street. The distributor attempted to evade the ordinance by publishing a political message on the back of the handbill, which advertised the public exhibition of a submarine. Despite the exhibitor's creativity, the Court focused upon the advertiser's primary purpose which was to attract customers. It concluded that the city's interest in controlling litter provided adequate support for the ordinance. Minus any elaboration, the Court also observed that "purely commercial advertising" was not protected by the First Amendment.

For nearly a quarter of a century, it generally was understood that commercial speech occupied the same pariah status under the First Amendment as defamation, fighting words, and obscenity. Some critics maintained that commercial speech actually has significant value in a society that was grounded in free enterprise and consumer autonomy. Justice Douglas challenged the perception that commercial expression was valueless. He authored a concurring opinion, in *Cammarano v. United States*,[30] characterizing the *Valentine v. Chrestensen* decision as "casual, almost offhand" and not having "survived reflection." In *New York Times Co. v. Sullivan*,[31] the Court refused to view a politically motivated but paid advertisement as commercial. At least through the early 1970s, however, commercial speech continued to exist in the constitutional wilderness.

Movement toward First Amendment status began in *Pittsburgh Press Company v. Pittsburgh Commission on Human Relations*.[32] This case concerned a city ordinance that prohibited newspapers from segregating help-wanted classified advertisements on the basis of gender. The Court noted that discrimination not only was commercial activity but illegal commercial activity. To the extent that any activity is unlawful, the Court reasoned, the state may prohibit promotion of it. Implicit in this observation was the possibility that, if an activity was legal, the state might not be able to ban advertising of it.

In *Bigelow v. Virginia*,[33] this point was made more explicitly. The *Bigelow* case concerned a state law that prohibited advertising of abortion services. In reviewing the statute, the Court questioned the underlying premise of *Valentine v. Chresentensen* and characterized it as a public forum case. It also noted that the decision was not intended to place all laws regulating commercial advertising beyond constitutional challenge. Most importantly, the Court forthrightly announced that a state could not prohibit advertising of a lawful activity.

[B]   Commercial Speech as Protected Expression

The value of commercial speech was recognized, and its First Amendment status established accordingly, in *Virginia State Board of Pharmacy v. Virginia Citizens Consumer Council*.[34] At issue was a state law that banned the advertisement of prescription drugs. The rationale for the enactment was that advertising would

---

[30] 358 U.S. 498 (1959) (Douglas, J., concurring).

[31] 376 U.S. (1964).

[32] 413 U.S. 376 (1973).

[33] 421 U.S. 809 (1975).

[34] 425 U.S. 748 (1976).

lead to price competition, which would cause pharmacists to cut corners, rush their work, and endanger consumer health. Viewing the regulation as an incident of protectionism, the Court observed that competition was a positive factor facilitated by advertising. Contrary to traditional understanding that commercial speech had no value, the Court stressed its utility. It thus observed that the public interest is served when private economic decisions, concerning allocation of resources, are intelligent and informed. Particularly within the context of a free enterprise economy, commercial expression provides information that is "indispensable." Commercial speech doctrine thus was correlated to traditional virtues associated with free trade in the marketplace of ideas.

Although noting that a consumer's interest in freely flowing commercial information may be as keen as his or her interest in political matters, the Court intimated that commercial speech would not be afforded the same level of protection given political speech. It noted, for instance, that commercial speech could be subjected more readily to prior restraint and disclaimer, disclosure, or warning requirements. This disparity in protection owes to what the Court viewed as "commonsense differences," specifically a sense that commercial speech is hardier and its accuracy is easier to verify. These propositions at least are debatable. It is questionable, for instance, whether the motivation for selling a product or service is less intense than the desire to be elected or change a policy. Speech promoting commercial and political agendas alike share the powerful propellant of self-interest. Political speech also may present daunting challenges to verification. Pledges not to raise taxes, spend more money, or engage in foreign conflict are among the types of representations political candidates have made and, when elected, have broken. Despite acknowledging the value of commercial speech, and the debatable premises for distinction, the Court has given it a reduced level of protection.

[C] The Standard of Review

A standard of review governing commercial speech cases was set forth in *Central Hudson Gas & Electric Co. v. Public Service Commission.*[35] The Court in this case struck down a rule that banned promotion of electricity by public utilities. This regulation had been adopted as an energy conservation measure and reflected the sense that advertising stimulated demand. Consistent with the premise that commercial speech is protected by the First Amendment, but has qualities that disqualify it from the highest level of protection, review is less exacting than strict scrutiny but more demanding than rational basis inquiry. Commercial speech regulation is evaluated pursuant to a four-part test. The first question is whether the speech is misleading or related to an unlawful activity. If such a finding is made, the inquiry ends in favor of the state. This result preserves the categorically unprotected status of commercial speech on a narrowed basis. As evidenced by the actual malice standard in the defamation context, the First Amendment creates breathing room for political speech that may be false or misleading. No similar tolerance exists for commercial speech.

---

[35] 447 U.S. 557 (1980).

Assuming the expression is neither misleading nor connected with an unlawful activity, the second question under *Central Hudson* focuses upon whether the regulation is supported by a substantial government interest. The third question asks whether the regulation directly advances this interest. The fourth question factors whether the interest could be achieved by a less burdensome restriction on commercial speech. This final part of the analytical equation has been superseded by *Board of Trustees of State University of New York v. Fox*,[36] which establishes a less demanding narrowly tailored requirement. In this case, the Court considered whether regulation of on-campus merchandising parties burdened substantially more speech than necessary to advance its interest in maintaining an educational environment. The Court upheld the rule notwithstanding arguments that there were alternatives less burdensome to free speech interests. Although these less restrictive means may be relevant, they are not dispositive.[37] The final prong of the *Central Hudson* test can be satisfied by a rule that is tailored to its objective, even if it is not the least restrictive means of achievement. Satisfaction of this standard, however, requires the state to demonstrate that it has carefully factored the regulatory costs and benefits.

The Court's decision, in *Posadas de Puerto Rico Associates v. Tourism Co. of Puerto Rico*,[38] appeared to depart from the *Central Hudson* test. This case concerned a law that prohibited casino advertising except to the extent it was aimed at tourists. The regulation balanced the commonwealth's interest in promoting tourism and deterring local demand for gambling. The Court, in upholding the law, determined that the commonwealth had a substantial health, safety, and welfare interest and that restrictions on advertising would advance this concern directly. It also concluded that the fit between regulatory means and ends was sufficiently tight. This result overlooked less restrictive options, noted in Justice Brennan's dissenting opinion, such as education, counter advertising, vigorous law enforcement, and oversight of casino operations. Justice Brennan also criticized the majority for undue deference toward the legislature. In support of this point, he noted the Court's readiness to speculate on the gravity of harms rather than having the legislature prove that they are real and substantial.

Perceptions that the Court was devaluing commercial speech were heightened by a finding that the greater power to prohibit gambling established the lesser power to ban the advertising of it. Critics noted the risk that this proposition could justify the prohibition of any constitutionally protected subordinate activity, so long as it was within the scope of government power over the general activity. The premise was discounted in *Rubin v. Coors Brewing Co.*,[39] when the Court struck down a law prohibiting the display of alcohol content on beer labels. The regulation aimed toward controlling industry competition on the basis of a beer's alcohol volume. Although rejecting the greater includes the lesser premise, the Court observed that states have more latitude to regulate speech promoting socially harmful activities than other types of expression.

---

[36] 492 U.S. 469 (1989).

[37] City of Cincinnati v. Discovery Network, Inc., 507 U.S. 410 (1993).

[38] 478 U.S. 328 (1986).

[39] 514 U.S. 476 (1995).

In *United States v. Edge Broadcasting Co.*,[40] the government was urged to apply the greater includes the lesser premise in reviewing a federal law banning broadcast of lottery information in certain instances. The law applies to broadcasters in states that prohibit lotteries. It does not prohibit broadcasters in other states, whose signals reach the anti-lottery state, from transmitting such information. The Court declined the opportunity to apply the greater includes the lesser standard. It also upheld the law on grounds the enactment directly advanced government's substantial interest in balancing the states' competing policy concerns and constituted a reasonable fit.

Case law since the 1970s has reaffirmed that commercial speech was protected under the First Amendment. At the same time, the level of that protection was uncertain. So too was the ultimate analytical structure of commercial speech doctrine. Decisions during the final years of the Twentieth Century and early years of the Twenty-First Century revealed disunity among the justices with respect to standards of review and adaptability of a single criterion to all commercial speech contexts. In *44 Liquormart, Inc. v. Rhode Island*,[41] the Court's reviewed a law that banned retail liquor advertising except at the point of sale. The Court was unanimous in concluding that the restriction was unconsitutional, however there was no majority opinion. A plurality of four justices, in an opinion authored by Justice Stevens, advocated a "rigorous" standard of review for total bans on "truthful nonmisleading commercial messages for reasons unrelated to the preservation of a fair bargaining process." The Stevens plurality expressed misgiving with advertising bans that "keep people in the dark," because they rarely protect consumers from harm, rest on the "offensive" assumption that people will respond irrationally to the truth, and impede debate over important public policy issues. Justice Thomas expressed a like concern and would have found all attempts to keep citizens ignorant of their legal choices to be "impermissible." Another group of four justices, in an opinion authored by Justice O'Connor, maintained that the *Central Hudson* test provided the appropriate standard of review. The O'Connor plurality determined the liquor advertising ban could not survive this analysis, because it burdened speech too heavily. This group of justices also acknowledged that the *Posadas de Puerto Rico* decision had been too lax in assessing the state's objective and the consequent burden on speech interests. Because subsequent case law had been more vigorous in applying the fourth prong of the *Central Hudson* test, the O'Connor plurality saw no need for further doctrinal revision.

The O'Connor view evolved into a majority perspective in two subsequent commercial speech cases. In *Lorillard Tobacco Co. v. Reilly*,[42] the Court struck down a comprehensive regulatory scheme that restricted outdoor advertising, point-of-sale advertising, retail sales and mail transactions, promotions, sampling, and labeling of tobacco products. The law primarily represented an effort to address cigarette smoking and smokeless tobacco use by underage consumers. Cigar labeling requirements were imposed as a means of informing the public of

---

[40] 506 U.S. 1032.

[41] 517 U.S. 484 (1996).

[42] 533 U.S. 525 (2002).

health risks and dispelling false perceptions that cigars are a safe alternative to cigarettes. Restrictions of retail outlet sales practices included making it an unfair or deceptive act to use self-service displays for tobacco products or shelve them in a way that was physically reachable by consumers. The law also restricted outdoor and in-store tobacco advertising within 1,000 feet of a public playground, playground area in a park, or elementary or secondary school. Despite the diverging opinions in *44 Liquormart* and the petitioners' urging of strict scrutiny, the Court found that the *Central Hudson* standard as applied in recent cases afforded "an adequate basis for decision." Focusing upon the final two prongs of this test, the Court emphasized the need for a showing that "the speech restriction directly and materially advanc[e] the asserted government interest." The Court noted that this burden can be discharged, not by speculation or conjecture, but by evidence that the harms are "real" and regulation will address them "to a material degree." The Court found ample evidence to support the state's premise that product advertising stimulates demand, and suppression of advertising has the opposite effect.

Characterizing the final step of the *Central Hudson* test as the "critical inquiry in this case," the Court found that the "broad sweep" of the regulations indicated that the state had not "carefully calculate[d] the costs and benefits" attributable to the burden on speech. Among other things, the Court determined that the 1,000 foot restriction in some areas would have operated as a complete ban on communication of truthful information to adults. Because the burden upon protected speech would vary depending upon whether the location is rural, suburban, or urban, the Court observed that the "uniformly broad sweep of the geographical limitation demonstrates a lack of tailoring." The Court also found that the spectrum of communications restricted was unduly broad. The law, for instance, made no distinction between an outdoor billboard and oral communication within 1,000 feet of a restricted use. Nor did height restrictions take into account the unique security concerns of convenience stores that favor full visibility of the store from outside. A key factor in the Court's analysis, despite the state's characterization of prohibited tobacco sales and advertising practices as deceptive, was the fact that the sale of tobacco products to and use by adults is legal. The Court concluded that the advertising restrictions unduly burdened the legitimate interests of sellers and consumers in receiving truthful information about a lawful product.

Justice Thomas, in a concurring opinion, restated his position that there is no historical or philosophical basis for analyzing commercial speech as having lesser value than noncommercial expression. From his perspective, "all attempts to dissuade legal choices by citizens by keeping them ignorant, are impermissible." He thus advocated abandonment of the *Central Hudson* test, at least when the state's interest is to be served by keeping persons "in the dark." He would extended the First Amendment's full protection regardless of whether the speech was political or commercial.

Justice Stevens, in a dissenting opinion embraced also by Justices Ginsburg and Breyer, maintained that the narrowly tailored issue had not been fully developed and should have been remanded for further proceedings. The "crucial question," in determining whether the location restriction imposed excessive burdens upon adult speech, was whether the regulation leaves open adequate alternative channels of communication.

The invigorated *Central Hudson* formula carried over to another commercial speech case, *Thompson v. Western States Medical Center.*[43] This case concerned a federal law that prohibited manufacturers of compounded drugs from advertising or promoting a particular drug or class of type of drug. Compounded drugs are those which are tailored to the need of a particular patient who, for instance, might be allergic to a mass-produced product. The Court invalidated the law because government had failed to demonstrate that the speech restrictions were no more extensive than necessary to achieve its interests. After identifying several potentially less burdensome options, and finding "no hint" that government had considered any of them, the Court stressed that "[i]f the First Amendment means anything, it means that regulating speech is a last — not first — resort."

Although the *Central Hudson* test commanded majority support in this instance, commercial speech doctrine still evidenced significant ferment. Justice Thomas reiterated his opposition to the *Central Hudson* standard and support for a test that did not differentiate between commercial and noncommercial speech. Four dissenting justices, in an opinion authored by Justice Breyer, maintained that the Court's commercial speech doctrine is too strict and too rigid. From Breyer's perspective, commercial speech regulation typically does not suppress self-expression, rarely interferes with the functioning of the democratic political process, and often reflects a democratically determined decision to regulate an enterprise, product, or service to protect the consumer, public health, personal safety, or the environment. Breyer argued that using the First Amendment to prevent the legislature from enacting necessary protections assumes the risk of replicating the mistakes of early substantive due process review and producing "a tragic constitutional misunderstanding."

In *Tennessee Secondary School Athletic Association v. Brentwood Academy*, 551 U.S. 291 (2007), the Court held that a state athletic association could limit a high school football coach's recruitment of prospective athletes without infringing the First Amendment. The Court relied heavily on its prior decisions in *Ohralik v. Ohio State Bar*[44] and *Bates v. State Bar of Arizona*[45] discussed in Section [D] below.

The Court reaffirmed the vitality of the *Central Hudson* standard in *Sorrell v. IMS Health.*[46] At issue was a state law prohibiting the sale or use of pharmacy records, showing physician prescription practices, for marketing purposes. Such information was used by pharmaceutical companies for purposes of marketing their products to physicians. The state maintained that the law was necessary to protect physicians' privacy and minimize health care costs.

---

[43] 535 U.S. 357 (2002).

[44] 436 U.S. 447 (1978).

[45] 433 U.S. 350 (1977).

[46] 131 S. Ct. 2653 (2011).

The Court viewed the law as a content-based restriction on speech and applied heightened scrutiny. The Court viewed the law as content-based because it prohibited the sale of such information based on the content of a purchaser's speech. In other words, those who sought the information for "educational communications" were allowed to purchase it, but those who wished to obtain it for marketing purposes (specifically pharmaceutical manufacturers) were prohibited from purchasing it. Likewise, pharmaceutical detailers were prohibited from using the information. The Court concluded that heightened scrutiny is required whenever the government imposes "a regulation of speech because of disagreement with the message it conveys." The Court rejected the idea that heightened judicial scrutiny should not apply because the law involved "a mere commercial regulation." "While the burdened speech results from an economic motive, so too does a great deal of vital expression. Vermont's law does not simply have an effect on speech, but is directed at certain content and is aimed at particular speakers." The Court also rejected the idea that the Act did not involve "speech," but rather "access to information." The Court noted that an "individual's right to speak is implicated when information he or she possesses is subjected to "restraints on the way in which the information might be used" or disseminated.

Although the Court concluded that stricter scrutiny should be applied, the Court applied the lower commercial speech standard: "To sustain the targeted, content-based burden § 4631(d) imposes on protected expression, the State must show at least that the statute directly advances a substantial governmental interest and that the measure is drawn to achieve that interest." In other words, there must be a "fit between the legislature's ends and the means chosen to accomplish those ends." The State asserted various interests in support of the Act: an interest in protecting medical privacy, including physician confidentiality, avoidance of harassment, and the integrity of the doctor-patient relationship; and improved public health and reduced healthcare costs. The Court rejected these interests as sufficient. The problem with the first justification is that Vermont made prescriber-identifying information available to an almost limitless audience except pharmaceutical manufacturers. In regard to the possibility for harassment, the Court suggested that the State failed to explain "why remedies other than content-based rules would be inadequate. Physicians can, and often do, simply decline to meet with detailers, including detailers who use prescriber-identifying information." As for the interests in lowering the costs of medical services and promoting public health, the Court rejected the idea that those arguments were sufficient to justify the restriction. The "fear that people would make bad decisions if given truthful information" cannot justify content-based burdens on speech, and the Court concluded that many doctors find find detailing "very helpful" because it allows detailers to shape their messages to each doctor. "[P]eople will perceive their own best interests if only they are well enough informed, and that the best means to that end is to open the channels of communication rather than to close them." The choice "between the dangers of suppressing information, and the dangers of its misuse if it is freely available" is one that the Court concluded that "the First Amendment makes for us."

Justice Breyer authored a dissenting opinion, joined by Justices Ginsburg and Kagan, suggesting that the question should be whether the harm to First

Amendment interests "is disproportionate to their furtherance of legitimate regulatory objectives." He again raised concern that commercial speech doctrine raised the potential for neo-Lochnerism. The *Sorrell* decision, although referencing *Central Hudson* only briefly, nonetheless applied its standard of review and represents evolution toward a more cohesive position on commercial speech.

Craigslist and Prostitution Advertisements. Since prostitution is illegal in most jurisdictions, the state has the power to prohibit commercial advertising by prostitutes. In recent years, some prostitutes have tried to advertise their wares on Craigslist. Recently, an Illinois sheriff sued Craigslist to require it to monitor sex advertisements or to shut the list down.[47]

[D] Special Circumstances: Lawyer Advertising

Advertising for professional services has been a primary source of First Amendment case law with respect to commercial speech. Lawyer advertising traditionally was prohibited by state regulations that adopted or paralleled disciplinary provisions of the American Bar Association Code of Professional Responsibility. A common basis for these rules was that advertising undermined the dignity of the profession. As the legal profession's population expanded during the second half of the Twentieth Century, and new forms of legal services evolved, interest in marketing increased. With much of the population being underserved by the legal profession, because of costs, advertising also represented an opportunity for lower-price service providers to capture a market niche.

One year after its decision in *Virginia State Board of Pharmacy v. Virginia Citizens Consumer Council*, the Court heard arguments that a state's prohibition of lawyer advertising violated the First Amendment. At issue, in *Bates v. State Bar of Arizona*,[48] was a newspaper advertisement that listed a law clinic's services and fees. No representations of quality or result were made. Consistent with the tone of its *Virginia State Board of Pharmacy* ruling, the Court stressed·the public's interest in receiving truthful information that facilitated informed consumer decisions.

Critical to the ˙outcome in *Bates* was the law's operation as a total prohibition. Left open was the possibility that more narrowly tailored regulation, protecting against unique risks of lawyer advertising, would survive. Among these perils are predatory behavior that can be particularly objectionable when persons are in a vulnerable condition due to the stresses or tragedies that often require a lawyer's assistance. In *Ohralik v. Ohio State Bar Association*, the Court indicated particular awareness of the potential for "fraud, undue influence, intimidation, overreaching, and other forms of 'vexatious conduct' " in the solicitation context.[49] It also acknowledged the state's interest in protecting against these harms. The Court, in *In re Primus*,[50] distinguished solicitation by not-for-profit organizations

---

[47] *See Illinois Sheriff Sues Craiglist Over Advertisement*, Associate Press wire report (Mar. 9, 2009), *available at* http://www.firstamendmentcenter.org/ill-sheriff-sues-craigslist-over-sex-ads.

[48] 433 U.S. 350 (1977).

[49] 436 U.S. 447 (1978).

[50] 436 U.S. 412 (1978).

that litigate to promote political or social agendas rather than for purposes of pecuniary gain. Given the orientation of such groups, the Court found a diminished risk of abuse or overreaching. The Court, in *Edelman v. Fane*,[51] observed that this risk is a function of unique advocacy and persuasive skills of lawyers. It thus struck down a state law banning personal solicitation of clients by accountants.

Many states, in an effort to curb puffing of qualifications, have adopted restrictions on how an attorney can depict his or her competence. In cases concerning these limitations, the Court again has focused upon whether the content was misleading. In *In re R.M.J.*,[52] the Court reviewed the case of an attorney disciplined for referencing specific areas of practice and qualifications beyond what the state's rules allowed. Because the advertisement was not deceptive, and the state offered no substantial interest in support of limiting the content, the Court struck down the rule. A similar result was achieved in *Peel v. Attorney Registration and Disciplinary Commission of Illinois*.[53] In *Peel*, the Court reviewed a rule that prohibited attorneys from representing themselves as "certified" or "specialists." Although the state supreme court found such designations misleading, and upheld the rule, the Court reversed. In a plurality opinion, Justice Stevens noted that each of the representations stated objective facts.

The risk of deception has been a pivotal factor in evaluating various methods of targeted advertising. In *Zauderer v. Office of Disciplinary Counsel*,[54] the Court struck down a restriction on self-touting and illustrations. The case concerned a newspaper advertisement directed at women who had suffered injuries from an inter-uterine contraceptive device. In addition to noting the lawyer's availability, the advertisement indicated that services would be provided without a legal fee unless damages were recovered. The Court noted that any restriction on advertising, aimed at avoiding consumer deception, should be no greater than necessary to prevent this harm. Because the advertisement did not mention the possibility of court charges, the Court upheld a finding that the statement pertaining to no legal fees was deceptive.

In *Shapero v. Kentucky Bar Association*,[55] the Court reviewed a state ban on direct mail solicitations that targeted potential clients with truthful information relating to specific legal problems. The Court found the risks associated with in-person solicitation, to be diminished in the direct mail context. In addition to finding that the perils of overreaching, invasion of privacy, undue influence, and fraud were reduced, the Court noted that direct mail solicitations could be more effectively monitored than in-person solicitations. Noting the privacy interests and vulnerability of accident victims and their families, in *Florida Bar v. Went for It, Inc.*,[56] the Court upheld a 30-day ban on targeted direct mail by personal injury

---

[51] Edenfield v. Fane, 507 U.S. 761 (1993).

[52] 455 U.S. 191 (1982).

[53] 496 U.S. 91 (1991).

[54] 471 U.S. 626 (1981).

[55] 486 U.S. 466 (1988).

[56] 515 U.S. 618 (1995).

lawyers.

POINTS TO REMEMBER

- Commercial speech, although originally unprotected, has achieved First Amendment status.

- Commercial speech has significant social value, given the interest of consumers in a free enterprise economy.

- Commercial speech is less protected than political speech on grounds it is hardier and its accuracy is easier to verify.

- The constitutionality of restrictions on commercial speech is assessed pursuant to the four-part *Central Hudson* test.

- The future of the *Central Hudson* test is somewhat unsettled, but a majority of the Court appears to favor a relatively vigorous application of it.

- Professional imperatives, such as guarding against lawyer overreaching, may justify unique burdens on commercial speech.

- Review of lawyer advertising restrictions typically focuses upon the interest in protecting the public from deception or abusive practices.

Chapter 5

OVERBREADTH, VAGUENESS, AND PRIOR RESTRAINTS

FOCAL POINTS FOR CHAPTER 5

- "Vagueness" and "overbreadth" doctrines as limitations on government ability to regulate speech.
- Prior restraints: historical practices that led to the presumption of invalidity.
- Injunctions against newspapers and for national security purposes.
- Enjoining abortion protests.

In deciding First Amendment cases, the Court often relies on various "non-substantive" doctrines including vagueness, overbreadth, and the prohibition against prior restraints. This chapter examines these doctrines.

§ 5.01 OVERBREADTH AND VAGUENESS

Two frequently invoked concepts are "overbreadth" and "vagueness." In "vagueness" cases, plaintiff argues that a law suffers from such "vagueness" that it should not be enforceable. In "overbreadth" cases, plaintiff argues that a law prohibits conduct that the government has the right to prohibit, as well as conduct that the government does not have the right to prohibit, and therefore is "overbroad."

Vagueness and overbreadth challenges can involve either a "facial" challenge to a law — a claim that the law is facially unconstitutional and should be struck down in its entirety — or an "as applied" challenge. The "facial" challenge is controversial because the party before the court may not be arguing that a particular law is "vague" or "overbroad" as to him (or his conduct), but may ask the court to strike down the law because it is overbroad or vague as applied to others. In other words, the party may be seeking to raise the rights of others not before the court.

As you should be aware from other courses, courts are generally reluctant to let individuals assert the rights of others. When constitutional rights are involved, the courts have generally required plaintiffs to establish "standing." In other words, they must show that their own rights are being or may be violated. In non-constitutional cases (*i.e.*, tort cases), courts generally require a plaintiff to establish that he is the "real party-in-interest." So, vagueness and overbreadth claims represent an exception to the ordinary rules requiring "standing" and establishment of "real party-in-interest" status.

In the First Amendment area, the courts have sometimes been willing to consider facial challenges, but even here are "reluctant" to create exceptions. For example, in *New York v. Ferber* (the child pornography case discussed in the prior chapter), the Courts referred to the "traditional rule" which prohibits litigants from raising the rights of others. The Court noted that this rule means "that a person to whom a statute may constitutionally be applied may not challenge [a] statute on the ground that it may conceivably be applied unconstitutionally to others in situations not before the Court." Likewise, in *Gooding v. Wilson*,[1] the Court referred to facial challenges as "strong medicine."

The Court has offered at least two reasons for its reluctance to sustain facial challenges. In general, the Court prefers to deal with the case before it, not with some hypothetical case that the parties might construct. As the Court noted in *Broadrick v. Oklahoma*,[2] it is better to work from a developed record with the "facts needed for an informed judgment." By using this approach, the Court has a better opportunity to decide whether a law can be narrowly construed to avoid constitutional infirmities. Despite the Court's reluctance, it sometimes permits facial challenges in the First Amendment area. As we shall see, when a law is so vague or overbroad that it tends to "chill" free expression, the court will sometimes allow a litigant to raise the rights of others. In general, such challenges are only permitted

---

[1] 405 U.S. 518 (1972).

[2] 413 U.S. 601, 610 (1973).

when a case involves protected expression.

[A] Overbreadth

In overbreadth cases, the fear is that an overbroad law will "chill" expression by causing "persons whose expression is constitutionally protected [to] refrain from exercising their rights for fear of criminal sanctions by a statute susceptible of application to protected expression."[3] As a result, the Court has allowed individuals to attack overbroad laws, even though their conduct is clearly unprotected and even though their conduct could have been proscribed by a narrowly drawn law.

The Court has applied the overbreadth doctrine "with hesitation" and "only as a last resort." As a result, the Court generally requires that the overbreadth be "substantial" before a law will be invalidated on its face. If the effect of a law is "too attenuated," "there comes a point where [the law's] effect — at best a prediction — cannot, with confidence, justify invalidating a statute on its face and so prohibiting a State from enforcing the statute against conduct that is admittedly within its power to proscribe."[4] This is particularly true where a statute affects "conduct" and not "merely speech." In such a situation, the overbreadth "must not only be real, but substantial as well, judged in relation to the statute's plainly legitimate sweep."

Broadrick provides a good example of the overbreadth doctrine. That case involved restrictions on political campaign activity. The Court noted that it had "never held that a statute should be held invalid on its face merely because it is possible to conceive of a single impermissible application, and in that sense a requirement of substantial overbreadth is already implicit in the doctrine."[5] In *Ferber*, the Court concluded that New York's child pornography law was not "substantially overbroad" concluding that the law's legitimate applications far exceeded its impermissible applications. The Court found that the law was directed at "the hard core of child pornography," but could reach some "protected expression" ranging from medical textbooks to pictorials in the National Geographic.[6]

In *Board of Airport Commissioners v. Jews for Jesus, Inc.*,[7] the Court invoked the overbreadth doctrine. That case involved a Los Angeles International Airport (LAX) resolution banning all First Amendment activities in the Central Terminal of the airport and subsequently asked Jews for Jesus, Inc. to leave the airport while distributing religious literature. The Court held that the restriction was substantially overbroad because it prohibited all expressive activity thereby creating what the Court referred to as a " First Amendment Free Zone." The ordinance was so broad that it seemed to prohibit even relatively minor acts such as talking, reading, or the wearing of campaign buttons or symbolic clothing. The

---

[3] *Gooding*, 405 U.S. at 521.

[4] *Broadrick*, 413 U.S. at 615.

[5] *Id.* at 630.

[6] *Ferber*, 458 U.S. 747, 773.

[7] 482 U.S. 569 (1987).

Court concluded that the ban was overbroad because it found that no governmental interest could justify such an absolute prohibition of speech.

Sometimes, in the face of an overbreadth claim, the Court will adopt a limiting construction that saves the law. For example, in *Board of Airport Commissioners*, the airport argued that the resolution was "intended to reach only expressive activity unrelated to airport-related purposes." The Court rejected even this construction noting that the limiting construction was itself vague. The Court expressed concern that the limitation would give airport officials broad power to decide whether a given activity was "airport related," and therefore carried with it the potential for abuse.

In *United States v. Williams*,[8] the Court upheld portions of the Prosecutorial Remedies and Other Tools to end the Exploitation of Children Today Act of 2003, § 2252A(a)(3)(B) of Title 18, United States Code, which criminalized, in certain specified circumstances, the pandering or solicitation of child pornography. That Act added a new anti-pandering and solicitation provision which read as follows:

(a) Any person who —

(3) knowingly . . . .

(B) advertises, promotes, presents, distributes, or solicits through the mails, or in interstate or foreign commerce by any means, including by computer, any material or purported material in a manner that reflects the belief, or that is intended to cause another to believe, that the material or purported material is, or contains —

(i)   an obscene visual depiction of a minor engaging in sexually explicit conduct; or

(ii) a visual depiction of an actual minor engaging in sexually explicit conduct, . . .

shall be punished as provided in subsection (b). 2252A(a)(3)(B) (2000 ed., Supp. V).

Section 2256(2)(A) defines "sexually explicit conduct" as

actual or simulated — (i) sexual intercourse, including genital-genital, oral-genital, anal-genital, or oral-anal, whether between persons of the same or opposite sex; (ii) bestiality; (iii) masturbation; (iv) sadistic or masochistic abuse; or (v) lascivious exhibition of the genitals or pubic area of any person.

Violation of § 2252A(a)(3)(B) incurs a minimum sentence of 5 years imprisonment and a maximum of 20 years. 18 U. S. C. § 2252A(b)(1). The statute prohibited offers to provide and requests to obtain child pornography, but does not require the actual existence of child pornography.

---

[8]   553 U.S. 285 (2008).

In enacting the statute, Congress was concerned that limiting the child-pornography prohibition to material that could be *proved* to feature actual children, as the Court's decision in *Free Speech Coalition* required, would enable many child pornographers to evade conviction. In particular, Congress was concerned that the "emergence of new technology and the repeated retransmission of picture files over the Internet could make it nearly impossible to prove that a particular image was produced using real children. . . ."

In rejecting the overbreadth challenge, the Court reaffirmed prior precedent in suggesting that invalidation for overbreadth is "strong medicine" that is not to be "casually employed." As a result, invalidation will only occur when a statute's overbreadth is "*substantial*, not only in an absolute sense, but also relative to the statute's plainly legitimate sweep." In upholding the statute, the Court emphasized that it contained a scienter requirement mandating that any violation be committed "knowingly" which the Court held applied to the provisions in their entirety. In addition, the Court noted that the statute contained a string of operative verbs (*e.g.*, "advertises, promotes, presents, distributes, or solicits") that must be shown in relation to a transfer of child pornography, and that a conviction require a "belief" that the pornography involve actual children, and that there be proof of "sexually explicit conduct." Finally, the Court noted that the terms "sexually *explicit* conduct" which involves an "actual depiction of the sex act rather than merely the suggestion that it is occurring."

[B] Vagueness

Closely related to overbreadth is the "vagueness" doctrine which finds its roots in the Due Process Clause. As the Court stated in *Connally v. General Construction Co.*,[9] "a statute which either forbids or requires the doing of an act in terms so vague that men of common intelligence must necessarily guess at its meaning and differ as to its application violates the first essential of due process of law."

In *Grayned v. City of Rockford*,[10] the Court stated the policy considerations that underlie the vagueness doctrine: "First, [vague laws] may trap the innocent by not providing fair warning. Second, if arbitrary and discriminatory enforcement is to be prevented, laws must provide explicit standards for those who apply them. A vague law impermissibly delegates basic policy matters to policemen, judges, and juries for resolution on an ad hoc and subjective basis, with the attendant dangers of arbitrary and discriminatory application."

As with overbreadth, the Court is particularly inclined to apply the vagueness doctrine when free speech is implicated. As the Court noted in *Grayned*, "[u]ncertain meanings inevitably lead citizens to steer far wider of the unlawful zone than if the boundaries of the forbidden areas were clearly marked." This so-called "chilling effect" is particularly objectionable when citizen's speech rights are implicated.

---

[9] 269 U.S. 385, 391 (1926).

[10] 408 U.S. 104 (1972).

Two illustrative "vagueness" cases are *Cox v. Louisiana*[11] and *Coates v. Cincinnati*.[12] In *Cox*, a state court construed a "breach of the peace ordinance" to mean "to agitate, to arouse from a state of repose, to molest, to interrupt, to hinder, to disquiet." The Court struck the law down on vagueness grounds because it could be used to punish individuals merely for "expressing unpopular views." In *Coates*, an ordinance punished the sidewalk assembly of three or more persons who "conduct themselves in a manner annoying to persons passing [by]." The Court struck the ordinance down as "impermissibly vague" because enforcement depended on the "completely subjective standard of 'annoyance.'"

In *United States v. Williams*,[13] discussed *supra*, the Court also rejected a vagueness challenge to the Prosecutorial Remedies and Other Tools to end the Exploitation of Children Today Act of 2003, § 2252A(a)(3)(B) of Title 18, United States Code. Consistently with prior precedent, the Court stated that a statute fails to comply with due process requirements if it "fails to provide a person of ordinary intelligence fair notice of what is prohibited, or is so standardless that it authorizes or encourages seriously discriminatory enforcement," but that "perfect clarity and precise guidance have never been required even of regulations that restrict expressive activity." In rejecting the vagueness challenge, the Court noted that the focus must be on whether the statute is so vague and standardless as to what may not be said that the public is left with no objective measure to which behavior can be conformed. Thus, the Court has struck down statutes that tied criminal culpability to whether the defendant's conduct was "annoying" or "indecent" which the Court described as "wholly subjective judgments without statutory definitions, narrowing context, or settled legal meanings." The Court found no such indeterminacy in the statute under consideration because the law required that defendant hold, "and make a statement that reflects, the belief that the material is child pornography; or that he communicate in a manner intended to cause another so to believe. Those are clear questions of fact."

During its 2010-2011 term, the Court continued to employ vagueness principles in First Amendment cases.[14]

POINTS TO REMEMBER

- When laws implicate speech or expressive interests, they can be scrutinized for vagueness or overbreadth.

- Courts are reluctant to entertain facial challenges to laws when the alleged vagueness or overbreadth does not affect the parties before them.

- Nevertheless, facial challenges are permitted in limited situations.

---

[11] 379 U.S. 536 (1965).

[12] 402 U.S. 611 (1971).

[13] 553 U.S. 285 (2008).

[14] *See, e.g.*, Brown v. Entertainment Merchants Association, 131 S. Ct. 2729 (2011).

§ 5.02   PRIOR RESTRAINTS

A "prior restraint" is a restriction on speech that is imposed prior to the dissemination of a communication. In common law England, prior restraints were common and included licensing. In this country, as the Court recognized in *Bantam Books, Inc. v. Sullivan*,[15] prior restraints are assumed to be invalid. They are particularly objectionable because they prevent ideas from reaching the public.

[A]   Licensing

[1]   Overview

With the invention of the printing press, people could communicate ideas more effectively and more widely. Previously, people had been able to communicate only by word of mouth or handwritten documents. By these methods, although information could be widely disseminated, the process required time and a great deal of effort. Because the printing press allowed ideas to be more easily circulated, it was regarded as more threatening and more dangerous. Accordingly, the English Crown imposed licensing schemes that required printers to submit manuscripts to government censors prior to publication. A license could be denied, or it could be granted on condition that certain objectionable information be deleted or altered.

In this country, perhaps the most famous licensing case is *Lovell v. City of Griffin*.[16] The City of Griffin, Georgia, passed a criminal ordinance that prohibited the distribution of circulars, handbooks, advertising, or literature within the city limits "without first obtaining permission from the City Manager of the City of Griffin." Anyone who distributed literature without obtaining the required permission could be fined $50 or sentenced to up to fifty days in jail. Lovell was prosecuted for distributing a pamphlet and magazine setting forth the gospel of the "Kingdom of Jehovah." Lovell did not apply for a permit because she believed that she had been sent "by Jehovah to do His work" and she regarded the application as "an act of disobedience to His commandment."

The Court concluded that the ordinance was "invalid on its face." In striking the law down, the Court stated a broad principle suggesting the invalidity of licensing schemes: "The struggle for the freedom of the press was primarily directed against the power of the licensor. It was against that power that John Milton directed his assault by his 'Appeal for the Liberty of Unlicensed Printing.' And the liberty of the press became initially a right to publish 'without a license what formerly could be published only with one.' " He goes on to note that "freedom from previous restraint upon publication" was one of the leading purposes of those who advocated adoption of the First Amendment. The Court concluded that the Georgia ordinance "would restore the system of license and censorship in its baldest form." The Court noted that freedom of the press is not limited to newspapers, but extends to "pamphlets and leaflets" which it described as "historic weapons in the defense of liberty, as the pamphlets of Thomas Paine and others in our own history abundantly attest." In

---

[15] 372 U.S. 58, 70 (1962).

[16] 303 U.S. 444 (1938).

other words, the term "press" includes "every sort of publication which affords a vehicle of information and opinion." The Court concluded that no distinction could be made between "distribution" and "publication" with the latter being deemed as essential as the former. Since the ordinance was "void on its face," the Court held that Lovell was not required to seek a permit under it.

[2] Motion Picture Licensing

Kingsley International Pictures Corp. v. Regents,[17] involved a New York statute that allowed censors to refuse to license any film that contained material that was "obscene, indecent, immoral, inhuman, sacrilegious, or [was] of such a character that its exhibition would tend to corrupt morals or incite to [crime]." Appellant was denied a license to distribute *Lady Chatterley's Lover* on the basis that the film was immoral because it presented "adultery as a desirable, acceptable and proper pattern of behavior." The Court held that the licensing authority had acted improperly by preventing exhibition of a picture because it advocates the idea that adultery may be proper behavior under certain circumstances. The Court found that the licensing scheme ran afoul of the "basic guarantee" of the "freedom to advocate ideas." Mr. Justice Douglas concurred arguing that he could find no room in the First Amendment for a censor — "whether he is scanning an editorial, reading a news broadcast, editing a novel or a play, or previewing a movie."

Despite *Kingsley's* holding, the Court has upheld motion picture licensing schemes. In *Times Film Corp. v. City of Chicago,*[18] the City of Chicago required that all motion pictures be licensed before they could be shown. Licensing could only occur after submission and review. The Times Film Corp., an exhibitor of films, challenged the law claiming that "the requirement of submission without more amounted to a constitutionally prohibited prior restraint" and that the "constitutional protection includes complete and absolute freedom to exhibit, at least once, any and every kind of motion picture [even] if this film contains the basest type of pornography, or incitement to riot, or forceful overthrow of orderly [government]." The Court disagreed and upheld the licensing scheme against a facial challenge finding that "[t]he protection even as to previous restraint is not absolutely unlimited."

Times Film Corp. was followed by *Freedman v. Maryland.*[19] Freedman, who wanted to challenge the constitutionality of Maryland's motion picture censorship statute, exhibited the film *Revenge at Daybreak* at his Baltimore theater without first submitting the picture to the State Board of Censors as required by statute. Although the State of Maryland admitted that the movie did not violate the statutory standards, and that Freedman would have been granted a license to show the film had he applied for one, it charged Freedman with violating the statute for refusing to submit the movie. Freedman was convicted.

The United States Supreme Court struck down the law expressing concern about delays and the lack of prompt judicial participation. While the Court recognized that

---

[17] 354 U.S. 436 (1957).

[18] 365 U.S. 43 (1961).

[19] 380 U.S. 51 (1965).

motion pictures are not "necessarily subject to the precise rules governing any other particular method of expression," the Court reiterated the presumption against prior restraints and recognized that any "censorship system for motion pictures presents peculiar dangers to constitutionally protected speech." The Court expressed concern about any censorship scheme that places the initial burden on the exhibitor or distributor. "Because the censor's business is to censor, there inheres the danger that he may well be less responsive than a court — part of an independent branch of government — to the constitutionally protected interests in free expression. And if it is made unduly onerous, by reason of delay or otherwise, to seek judicial review, the censor's determination may in practice be final." The Court struck down the law noting that there was no statutory provision for judicial participation in the process or any procedure for prompt judicial review.

The Court also articulated standards governing licensing systems. Although a law can require submission of a film to a censorship authority, the process is valid only it is accompanied by "procedural safeguards designed to obviate the dangers of a censorship system." These include the following requirements: 1) the burden of proving that the film is unprotected expression must rest on the censor; 2) even though the State may require advance submission of all films, the "requirement cannot be administered in a manner which would lend an effect of finality to the censor's determination whether a film constitutes protected expression." As a result, the censor must, "within a specified brief period, either issue a license or go to court to restrain showing the film." In imposing this requirement, the Court emphasized that "an administrative refusal to license, signifying the censor's view that the film is unprotected, may have a discouraging effect on the exhibitor." As a result, the procedure must be designed to "assure a prompt final judicial decision, to minimize the deterrent effect of an interim and possibly erroneous denial of a license." The Court concluded that, without these safeguards, a distributor might find it too burdensome to seek judicial review of a censor's determination: "An exhibitor's stake in a given picture may be insufficient to justify the expensive onerous course of litigation, particularly when the censor can freely distribute the film elsewhere."

The Court then approvingly referred to a New York law dealing with a procedure designed to prevent the sale of obscene books. In *Kingsley Books, Inc. v. Brown*, 354 U.S. 436, the Court upheld New York injunctive procedure that postponed all prior restraints against sale until a judicial determination of obscenity was made following notice and an adversary hearing. The statute provided for a hearing one day after joinder of the issue, and the judge was required to hand down a decision within two days after termination of the hearing. The New York procedure functioned without prior submission to a censor, a factor that the Court suggested would provide "all the more reason for expeditious determination of the question whether a particular film is constitutionally protected."

In *FW/PBS, Inc. v. Dallas*,[20] the Court considered the applicability of the *Freedman* standards to a municipal ordinance requiring a license for the operation of a sexually oriented business. Although the Court held that the Dallas licensing scheme did not provide the procedural safeguards required by its prior precedents, there was no majority opinion on the principal issues in the case. A majority agreed

---

[20] 493 U.S. 215 (1990).

that the first two *Freedman* safeguards are essential even in this context. In other words, the licensor must make the decision to issue the license within a specified and reasonable time period (during which there is a right to distribute and exhibit), and there must be a process for prompt judicial review if the license is denied. A different majority held that the third *Freedman* requirement did not apply.

[3]   Non-Licensing Notifications

What happens if, instead of using a licensing scheme, a state sends out "notifications" regarding objectionable material? Do such notifications constitute "prior restraints?" In *Bantam Books, Inc. v. Sullivan*,[21] the Rhode Island Legislature created the "Rhode Island Commission to Encourage Morality in Youth," and gave it "[the duty] to educate the public concerning any book, picture, pamphlet, ballad, printed paper or other thing containing obscene, indecent or impure language, or manifestly tending to the corruption of the [youth], and to investigate and recommend the prosecution of all violations of said [sections]." The Commission's practice was to notify distributors on official Commission stationery that certain designated books or magazines distributed by them had been reviewed by the Commission and had been declared by a majority of its members to be objectionable for sale, distribution, or display to youths under 18 years of age. The notice reminded distributors of the Commission's obligation to recommend to the Attorney General prosecution of purveyors of obscenity.

The Court struck the law down construing the blacklists as involving, not merely "legal advice," but as a system of prior administrative restraint. Reiterating the presumption against prior restraints, the Court found that the Rhode Island law lacked adequate safeguards. In particular, the law failed to provide for an immediate judicial determination regarding the validity of any determination. Justice Harlan dissented, arguing that "the Commission is constitutionally entitled (1) to express its views on the character of any published reading or other material; (2) to endeavor to enlist the support of law enforcement authorities, or the cooperation of publishers and distributors, with respect to any material the Commission deems obscene; and (3) to notify publishers, distributors, and members of the public with respect to its activities in these regards; but that it must take care to refrain from the kind of overbearing utterances already referred to and others that might tend to give any person an erroneous impression as to either the extent of the Commission's authority or the consequences of a failure to heed its warnings."

[4]   Parade Permits

Despite the presumption of invalidity that attaches to licensing schemes, courts have upheld content neutral time, place, and manner restrictions on parades and other public events.[22] Such restrictions are deemed essential to "prevent confusion by overlapping parades or processions, to secure convenient use of the streets by other travelers, and to minimize the risk of disorder." These permit requirements are discussed in Chapter 6.

---

[21]   372 U.S. 58 (1963).

[22]   *See* Cox v. New Hampshire, 312 U.S. 569 (1941).

[5] Licensing Fundraisers

Riley v. National Federation of the Blind[23] involved a North Carolina act that governed charitable contribution solicitations. The Act provided that professional fundraisers could not solicit without an approved license even though volunteer fundraisers were allowed to do so. The Court struck down the law, concluding that fundraisers were "speakers" even though they were paid by others to speak, and that "speakers need not obtain a license to speak." At most, North Carolina could impose reasonable time, place, and manner restrictions. Chief Justice Rehnquist, joined by Justice O'Connor, dissented arguing that the law did not prohibit fundraisers from engaging in protected speech, but simply limited their ability to engage in the profession of "solicitation" without a license.

[6] Newsrack Licensing

City of Lakewood v. Plain Dealer Publishing Co.[24] involved ordinances that permitted the placement of structures (including newspaper racks) on public property, but only under certain conditions. One ordinance specifically concerned newsracks, and gave the mayor the authority to grant or deny applications for annual newsrack permits. If the mayor denied an application, he was required to "stat[e] the reasons for such denial." When the mayor granted an application, the city issued an annual permit subject to several terms and conditions including (1) approval of the newsrack design by the city's Architectural Board of Review; (2) an agreement by the newsrack owner to indemnify the city against any liability arising from the newsrack, guaranteed by a $100,000 insurance policy; and (3) any "other terms and conditions deemed necessary and reasonable by the Mayor."

The Court sustained a facial challenge to the ordinance expressing concern about whether the law vested "unbridled discretion" in a government official over whether to permit or deny expressive activity. The Court found that the mere existence of censorial discretion, joined with the possibility of prior restraint, encourages parties to censor their own speech. In addition, the Court found that the absence of express standards made it difficult to distinguish between legitimate and illegitimate abuses of power noting that the law required newspapers to apply for licenses each year. Given the absence of standards, it was impossible to show that a denial was "unconstitutionally motivated" and therefore newspapers will be coerced to conform their speech to the censor's preferences.

The Court specifically rejected the dissent's suggestion that newspaper racks should be treated like machines selling soft drinks: "Newspapers are in the business of expression, while soda vendors are in the business of selling soft drinks." The Court expressed concern that city officials might engage in content discrimination against controversial newspapers, and therefore newspaper racks were more analogous to newspapers and leaflets.

---

[23] 487 U.S. 781 (1988).

[24] 486 U.S. 750 (1988).

[B]   Injunctions

[1]   Overview

Are restraints on speech more palatable when imposed by a court instead of a bureaucrat? In other words, may the courts impose prior restraints that other governmental officials could not impose? The landmark decision is *Near v. State of Minnesota*.[25] Chapter 285 of the Session Laws of Minnesota for the year 1925 provided for the abatement, as a public nuisance, of any "malicious, scandalous and defamatory newspaper, magazine or other periodical." Under this statute, the county attorney of Hennepin county brought suit to enjoin the publication of what he described as a "malicious, scandalous and defamatory newspaper, magazine or other periodical," known as *The Saturday Press* published by the defendants in the city of Minneapolis. The complaint alleged that the defendants, on September 24, 1927, and on eight subsequent dates, published and circulated editions with material that was "malicious, scandalous and defamatory." The trial court granted and continued an injunction that the appellate courts sustained.

The articles claimed that a Jewish gangster was in control of gambling, bootlegging, and racketeering in Minneapolis, and that law enforcement officials were "not energetically performing their duties." The articles charged the chief of police with "gross neglect of duty, illicit relations with gangsters, and with participation in graft," that the county attorney was aware of "existing conditions and with failure to take adequate measures to remedy them," and that a member of the grand jury was in sympathy with the gangsters. The Court concluded that "the articles made serious accusations against the public officers named and others in connection with the prevalence of crimes and the failure to expose and punish them."

In overturning the injunction, the Court reiterated the rule against prior restraints, and noted that appellants could resort to libel laws to protect their interests. The Court was troubled by the fact that the Minnesota law did not provide for punishment, but for suppression and restraint upon publication. The Court found that some "degree of abuse is inseparable from the proper use of everything, and in no instance is this more true than in that of the press. It has accordingly been decided by the practice of the States, that it is better to leave a few of its noxious branches to their luxuriant growth, than, by pruning them away, to injure the vigour of those yielding the proper fruits." As a result, the Court struck the Minnesota law down:

> "The fact that for approximately one hundred and fifty years there has
> been almost an entire absence of attempts to impose previous restraints
> upon publications relating to the malfeasance of public officers is significant
> of the deep-seated conviction that such restraints would violate constitu-
> tional right."

The Court concluded that public officers, "whose character and conduct remain open to debate and free discussion in the press," must "find their remedies for false

---

[25] 283 U.S. 697 (1931).

accusations in actions under libel laws providing for redress and punishment, and not in proceedings to restrain the publication of newspapers and periodicals." The Court emphasized the importance of the prohibition against prior restraints, and the Court held that the prohibition does not give way when there are allegations of defamation: "[The] fact that the liberty of the press may be abused by miscreant purveyors of scandal does not make any the less necessary the immunity of the press from previous restraint in dealing with official misconduct." The Court held that it makes "no difference that the press had charged the plaintiffs with "derelictions which constitute crimes."

The Court also rejected the argument that the law should be upheld because it allowed the publisher to show, prior to issuance of an injunction, that the matter published was true and was published with good motives and for justifiable ends. The Court found that the freedom to publish does not depend on proof of truth. The Court also rejected the argument that the statute was designed to prevent the circulation of "scandal which tends to disturb the public peace and to provoke assaults and the commission of crime." While the Court admitted that such charges might create "scandal," the Court found that a more serious evil resulted from the denial of publication.

Mr. Justice Butler dissented, arguing that defendants' "regular business" involved "the publication of malicious, scandalous, and defamatory articles" concerning public officials, many private persons, and Jews. He also found that the articles showed "malice" and concluded that it "is of the greatest importance that the states shall be untrammeled and free to employ all just and appropriate measures to prevent abuses of the liberty of the press." In addition, he rejected the idea that the Minnesota law operated as a prior restraint because it simply prevented the paper from printing allegations that had already been found to constitute a nuisance. Finally, he found that existing libel laws were inadequate to suppress evils of this nature.

Even though *Near* made it difficult for public officials to obtain injunctions prohibiting defamatory statements, there is less certainty regarding the ability of private individuals and public figures to obtain injunctions. In *Tory v. Cochran*,[26] Johnnie Cochran brought a state-law defamation action against petitioner Ulysses Tory. The state trial court determined that Tory had engaged in unlawful defamatory activity because Tory claimed, without foundation, that Cochran owed him money, engaged in a continuous pattern of libelous and slanderous activity, and had used false and defamatory speech to "coerce" Cochran into paying "amounts of money to which Tory was not entitled" as a "tribute" or a "premium" for "desisting" from this libelous and slanderous activity. Since Tory indicated that he would continue to engage in this activity, the court granted a permanent injunction restraining him from "picketing," from "displaying signs, placards or other written or printed material," and from "orally uttering statements" about Johnnie L. Cochran, Jr., and about Cochran's law firm in "any public forum." While the matter was on appeal, Cochran died and his widow was substituted as the plaintiff in the case. The Court concluded that the case was not moot, but concluded that it need not deal with the question of whether the First Amendment forbids the issuance of

---

[26] 544 U.S. 734 (2005).

a permanent injunction in a defamation case when the plaintiff is a public figure, and whether the injunction that was entered was not properly tailored and consequently violated the First Amendment. The latter issues were moot because Tory could not hope that further picketing would coerce Cochran into making a monetary payment. As a result, the Court concluded that the "injunction, as written, now amounts to an overly broad prior restraint upon speech, lacking plausible justification."

[2] Prior Restraints and National Security

Should the prohibition against prior restraints be loosened when a publication implicates national security interests? In *New York Times Co. v. United States*,[27] also known as the "Pentagon Papers" case, the United States sought to prohibit newspapers from publishing classified documents (the *Pentagon Papers*) entitled "History of U.S. Decision-Making Process on Viet Nam Policy." Although the trial courts refused to issue injunctions, the Second Circuit (the *New York Times* case) did issue an injunction. The District of Columbia (the *Washington Post* case) refused to issue an injunction. The cases then went to the United States Supreme Court with the *New York Times* arguing that the injunction constituted a "prior restraint" against speech.

In a *per curiam* opinion, the United States Supreme Court vacated the injunction. The Court began by reiterating the traditional rule that prior restraints come with a "heavy presumption" against their "constitutional validity" so that the Government "carries a heavy burden of showing justification for the imposition of such a restraint." The Court concluded that the government failed to meet the required burden and therefore vacated the injunction.

Even though a majority of the Court agreed that the injunction should be vacated, the justices held widely divergent views. Justice Black concurred arguing that the case should have been dismissed and the injunction should have been vacated without oral argument. He took a strong anti-prior restraint position: "Both the history and language of the First Amendment support the view that the press must be left free to publish news, whatever the source, without censorship, injunctions, or prior restraints." Justice Black's position was founded on his view of the press as a protector of the public and as an exposer of deception in government. He concluded:

> In my view, far from deserving condemnation for their courageous reporting, the *New York Times*, the *Washington Post*, and other newspapers should be commended for serving the purpose that the Founding Fathers saw so clearly. In revealing the workings of government that led to the Vietnam war, the newspapers nobly did precisely that which the Founders hoped and trusted they would do.

Justice Douglas concurred also relying on a broad and absolutist view of the First Amendment: "[T]he First Amendment [leaves] no room for governmental restraint on the press." Justice Douglas emphasized the history of the First Amendment

---

[27] 403 U.S. 713 (1971).

(which he viewed as prohibiting governmental suppression of embarrassing information).

Justice Brennan also concurred, taking a strong position in favor of disclosure. He viewed the First Amendment as imposing an "absolute bar" against prior restraints and as preventing "any injunctive relief whatsoever, interim or otherwise." The government must meet a high burden to justify a prior restraint, and the government could not meet that burden in this case, especially since it was claiming only that disclosure might harm national security. In his view, prior restraints were permissible only in limited situations: "Our cases [have] indicated that there is a single, extremely narrow class of cases in which the First Amendment's ban on prior judicial restraint may be overridden. [S]uch cases may arise only when the Nation "is at war" during which times "[n]o one would question but that a government might prevent actual obstruction to its recruiting service or the publication of the sailing dates of transports or the number and location of troops." He would have vacated the injunction because he found that the government had not shown that publication would precipitate problems of that magnitude.

Justice Stewart, concurring, also emphasized the importance of the press in a free society:

> [T]he only effective restraint upon executive policy and power in the areas of national defense and international affairs may lie in an enlightened citizenry — in an informed and critical public opinion which alone can here protect the values of democratic government. For this reason, it is perhaps here that a press that is alert, aware, and free most vitally serves the basic purpose of the First Amendment. For without an informed and free press there cannot be an enlightened people.

But Justice Stewart was also concerned about the government's need for secrecy, noting that the "successful conduct of international diplomacy and the maintenance of an effective national defense require both confidentiality and secrecy. Other nations can hardly deal with this Nation in an atmosphere of mutual trust unless they can be assured that their confidences will be kept." In his view, the Executive Branch possesses ultimate power over these issues. He would have dismissed because the government failed to show "direct, immediate, and irreparable damage to our Nation or its people."

Justice White, also concurred, emphasizing the presumption against prior restraints and the government's failure to meet the "very heavy burden" imposed in this case. He also expressed concern that the injunction created a standardless restraint. The government proposed a standard of "grave and irreparable danger." But the case would provide little precedent because "the material at issue here would not be available from the Court's opinion or from public records, nor would it be published by the press." Justice Marshall also concurred.

Chief Justice Burger dissented arguing that the matter was rushed to decision, but that he generally agreed with the dissents of justices Harlan and Blackmun. Justice Harlan dissented complaining about the "frenzied train of events" noting that both circuit courts of appeal rendered judgment on June 23rd, but that the case was briefed and argued before the United States Supreme Court only three days later. He felt that the Court should have approached the case more deliberately. "Forced" to reach the merits, he dissented noting that the judiciary may not "redetermine for itself the probable impact of disclosure on the national security" He would have vacated and remanded for further proceedings. Justice Blackmun dissented noting that the First Amendment is only one part of the Constitution. He noted that Article II gives the Executive Branch power over foreign affairs, and that the case required a weighing of the broad right of the press to publish against the government's right to suppress. As a result, he would have remanded the cases for further development.

The *Pentagon Papers* case was followed by *United States v. Progressive, Inc.*[28] In that case, the United States government sought to enjoin the Progressive, Inc., from publishing an article entitled "The H-Bomb Secret: How We Got It, Why We're Telling It." The article provided readers with information about how to build a hydrogen bomb. The government invoked a federal law, 42 U.S.C. §§ 2274(b) and 2280, which authorized relief against one who discloses restricted data "with reason to believe such data will be utilized to injure the United States or to secure an advantage to any foreign [nation]." The magazine responded that it wanted to publish the article to demonstrate laxness in the government's security system.

The government argued that much of the article's information was not in the public domain, and that some of the information had never before been published. The magazine claimed that the article was based on publicly available information. While disagreeing, the government contended that, whether or not the information is publicly available, others could not replicate the author's feat — the preparation of an article on the technical processes of thermonuclear weapons. The government emphasized that the article was dangerous because it exposed concepts never heretofore disclosed in conjunction with one another and that it could help a medium-sized nation build the H-bomb. The trial court entered the injunction, but ultimately lifted it later when it became clear that another magazine had published the information.

In *Snepp v. United States*,[29] the Court reviewed a case concerning unauthorized publication of classified information by a former Central Intelligence Agency employee. While working for the CIA, he agreed not to disclose classified information without the agency's consent. Snepp also agreed to submit all writings about the agency for prepublication review. After leaving the agency, Snepp published a book about CIA activities in South Vietnam without submitting the book to the CIA for prepublication review. The Court enforced the agreement and imposed a constructive trust on proceeds from the book.

[3] Injunctions Against Abortion Protests

In *Madsen v. Women's Health Center, Inc.*,[30] petitioners (antiabortion protestors) challenged the constitutionality of an injunction entered by a Florida state court that imposed various restrictions on their protest activities. The

---

[28] 467 F. Supp. 990 (W.D. Wis. 1979).

[29] 444 U.S. 507 (1980).

[30] 512 U.S. 753 (1994).

injunction imposed a 36-foot buffer zone around the clinic, prohibited the protestors from "singing, chanting, whistling, shouting, yelling, use of bullhorns, auto horns, sound amplification equipment or other sounds or images observable to or within earshot of the patients inside the [c]linic" during the hours of 7:30 a.m. through noon on Mondays through Saturdays," a prohibition on "images observable" from within the clinic, a requirement that petitioners refrain from physically approaching any person seeking services of the clinic "unless such person indicates a desire to communicate" in an area within 300 feet of the clinic. The state court was attempting to prevent clinic patients and staff from being "stalked" or "shadowed" by the petitioners as they approached the clinic, and a prohibition against picketing, demonstrating, or using sound amplification equipment within 300 feet of the residences of clinic staff.

In an opinion by Justice Rehnquist, the Court upheld the 36-foot buffer zone, but struck down a number of the other restrictions. In deciding the case, the Court was forced to grapple with whether the injunction involved either "content based" or "viewpoint based" restrictions on speech. If so, the Court would apply strict scrutiny. If not, the Court would apply a lesser standard of review. The Court concluded that an injunction should not necessarily be regarded as a "content based" or "viewpoint based" restriction on speech even though it is directed at particular speech:

> To accept petitioners' claim would be to classify virtually every injunction as content or viewpoint based. An injunction, by its very nature, applies only to a particular group (or individuals) and regulates the activities, and perhaps the speech, of that group. It does so, however, because of the group's past actions in the context of a specific dispute between real parties. The parties seeking the injunction assert a violation of their rights; the court hearing the action is charged with fashioning a remedy for a specific deprivation, not with the drafting of a statute addressed to the general public.

The Court found that this injunction was content neutral because court imposed restrictions on petitioners antiabortion message as a result of repeated violations of the court's original order.

The Court also rejected the argument that the injunction was "viewpoint based" because it restricted only abortion protestors and not those who protested in favor of abortion. The Court found that the injunction focused on viewpoint only because of "lack of any similar demonstrations by those in favor of abortion, and of any consequent request that their demonstrations be regulated by injunction." Moreover, the Court found no basis for concluding that the Florida courts would "not equally restrain similar conduct directed at a target having nothing to do with abortion." As a result, "none of the restrictions imposed by the court were directed at the contents of petitioner's message." As a result, the mere fact that the injunction applied to speakers with a particular viewpoint did not "render the injunction content or viewpoint based" and the Court refused to apply a heightened level of scrutiny.

The Court distinguished injunctions from ordinances noting that, had this case involved an ordinance imposing a time, place and manner restriction on the use of a "traditional public forum," the Court would have scrutinized the ordinance more carefully. More particularly, the Court would have asked whether the regulations were "narrowly tailored to serve a significant governmental interest." Nevertheless, the Court concluded that it was still necessary to apply a "some-what more stringent application of general First Amendment principles" to injunctions. The Court rejected a standard which would have asked whether an "injunction was no broader than necessary to achieve its desired goals" in favor of an emphasis on a "fit between the objectives of an injunction and the restrictions it imposes on speech" so that the relief is "no more burdensome to the defendants than necessary to provide complete relief to the plaintiffs." As a result, the Court decided to inquire "whether the challenged provisions of the injunction burden no more speech than necessary to serve a significant government interest."

In applying the "significant government interest" test, the Court upheld a 36-foot buffer zone around the clinic. The Court made a distinction between "the type of focused picketing banned from the buffer zone" and activities such as handbilling and solicitation. The Court viewed the buffer zone as a means of "protecting the entrances to the clinic and the parking lot is a means of protecting unfettered ingress to and egress from the clinic, and ensuring that petitioners do not block [traffic]." In addition, the Court found that the state court had few other options to protect access given the narrow confines around the clinic. Although the Court questioned whether a complete buffer zone was really necessary, it decided to defer to the trial court on this issue. However, the Court struck down the buffer zone as it applied to private property on the back and side of the clinic. The Court noted that the purpose of the buffer zone (to protect access to the clinic and to facilitate the orderly flow of traffic) need not extend to include private property.

The Court upheld that part of the injunction that restrained petitioners from "singing, chanting, whistling, shouting, yelling, use of bullhorns, auto horns, sound amplification equipment or other sounds or images observable to or within earshot of the patients inside the [c]linic" during the hours of 7:30 a.m. through noon on Mondays through Saturdays. The Court emphasized that "place" is important in determining whether restrictions burden more speech than necessary. Finding that noise control is important around hospitals and medical facilities during surgery and recovery periods, the Court upheld the noise restrictions.

The Court struck down the "images observable" provision. Although the Court found that the trial court could prohibit "threats or veiled threats," it held that the "images observable" provision burdened more speech than necessary to achieve the purpose of limiting threats. In addition, the Court found that, if the ban on "images observable" was designed "to reduce the level of anxiety and hypertension suffered by the patients inside the clinic," it would still be struck down. The Court concluded that, if patients were distressed by the anti-abortion message, it could deal with the problem by pulling the curtains.

The Court also struck down the prohibition on physically approaching any person seeking services of the clinic "unless such person indicates a desire to communicate" in an area within 300 feet of the clinic. The Court began by noting that the approaches could not be prohibited as "fighting words," and that the trial court's objective was to prevent clinic patients and staff from being "stalked" or "shadowed" by the petitioners as they approached the clinic. Nevertheless, the Court found that the restriction burdened more speech than necessary to ensure access to the clinic and prevent intimidation. The Court noted that citizens must "tolerate insulting, and even outrageous, speech in order to provide adequate breathing space to the freedoms protected by the First Amendment."

The Court also struck down the prohibition against picketing, demonstrating, or using sound amplification equipment within 300 feet of the residences of clinic staff and the prohibition against impeding access to streets that provide the sole access to streets on which those residences are located. The Court found that the problem of sound amplification equipment could be dealt with by requiring petitioners to turn down the volume if the protests overwhelmed the neighborhood. While the Court was sympathetic to the need to ban targeted residential picketing, viewing the privacy of the home as an interest "of the highest order in a free and civilized society," the Court concluded that the 300-foot zone around the residences was too large. The 300-foot zone would effectively ban marching through residential neighborhoods or walking in front of a block of houses. The Court found insufficient justification for such a broad ban, and held "that a limitation on the time, duration of picketing, and number of pickets outside a smaller zone could have accomplished the desired result."

Justice Stevens concurred in part and dissented in part. He argued that injunctive relief should be evaluated under a more lenient standard than legislation since ordinances apply to a whole community while "injunctions apply solely to an individual or a limited group of individuals who, by engaging in illegal conduct, have been judicially deprived of some liberty — the normal consequence of illegal activity." As a result, although he would have struck down a statute prohibiting demonstrations within 36 feet of an abortion clinic, he would be more likely to uphold an injunction directed at a limited group of persons who have engaged in unlawful conduct near the same clinic. In his view, an the injunction should be no more burdensome than necessary to provide complete relief. In addition, because of circumstances, an injunction may place appropriate restraints on future activities to prevent a reoccurrence and eliminate adverse consequences.

Justice Scalia, joined by justices Kennedy and Thomas, concurred in part and dissented in part arguing that the Court should apply strict scrutiny to injunctions whether they are content based or content neutral. He offered several reasons. He noted that the injunctions can be designed and used to suppress ideas. Indeed, he argued that it was more likely that an injunction would be used in that manner than an ordinance, and in this case the injunction was sought by a "single-issue advocacy group by persons and organizations with a business or social interest" in suppressing this particular view. He also argued that strict scrutiny should be applied because speech-restricting injunctions are issued by judges, individuals whose prior orders have been violated, and he questioned whether control over speech should "lightly be placed within the control of a single man or woman." He also noted that an injunction is more objectionable because, in a contempt proceeding, only limited defenses can be raised. More to the point, a defendant cannot argue that the injunction was unconstitutional. As a result, he felt that courts should apply the "strictest standard" for such orders. Finally, he concluded that the injunction in this case was content and viewpoint based because all who espoused similar views would be deemed to be acting in concert or participation with them. He concluded that an "injunction against speech is the very prototype of the greatest threat to First Amendment values, the prior restraint. [A] prior restraint on expression comes to this Court with a 'heavy presumption' against its constitutional validity."

[4]   Prior Restraints on Commercial Speech

Pittsburgh Press Co. v. Pittsburgh Commission on Human Relations,[31] concerned a Pittsburgh ordinance that prohibited newspapers from carrying "help wanted" advertisements in sex-designated columns except where the employer or advertiser was free to make hiring or employment referral decisions on the basis of sex. The Court concluded that the ads constituted commercial speech and upheld the ordinance because they involved want ad s proposing illegal transactions (*i.e.*, for the sale of narcotics or soliciting prostitutes). Chief Justice Burger dissented arguing that the First Amendment gives a paper the right to arrange its content including not only its news items and editorials, but its advertising. Justice Douglas also dissented arguing that the state cannot censor newspapers including their want ads or other commercial space.

In *Lowe v. Securities and Exchange Commission*,[32] the Securities and Exchange Commission (SEC) sought to permanently enjoin the publication of nonpersonalized investment advice and commentary in securities newsletters by individuals not registered as investment advisers under § 203(c) of the Investment Advisers Act of 1940 (Act). The injunction was challenged as a prior restraint. The Court avoided the First Amendment issue by holding Congress did not intend to apply the Act to such newsletters.

POINTS TO REMEMBER

- Prior restraints are presumptively invalid.
- There is a strong presumption against the constitutional validity of a prior restraint.
- Government has a heavy burden of justifying a system of prior restraint.
- Licensing schemes constitute the quintessential prior restraint, and therefore are likely to be invalidated except in regard to motion pictures.
- Injunctions against speech are carefully scrutinized.
- Careful scrutiny is particularly appropriate, even when national security interests are implicated, unless there is a showing of immediate and irreparable injury.

---

[31] 413 U.S. 376 (1973).

[32] 472 U.S. 181 (1985).

Chapter 6

CONTENT NEUTRALITY

FOCAL POINTS FOR CHAPTER 6

- Content-neutral regulation and First Amendment interests.
- Regulation of conduct mixed with speech.
- Regulation of secondary effects.
- The evolution of public forum doctrine.
- Traditional public forums.
- Designated or limited public forums.
- Reserved or nonpublic forums.
- Time, place, and manner regulation within public forums.
- Private property as a public forum.

Government regulation directed at the content of speech typically generates one of two responses depending upon whether the expression is classified as protected or unprotected under the First Amendment. Regulation of expression that is categorically excluded from the First Amendment, barring evidence of viewpoint discrimination, receives rational basis review. Whether constitutionally protected speech can be regulated depends upon how the balance is struck between the value of the expression and weight of the regulatory interest. Regulation on the basis of content is a primary but not exclusive means of controlling speech. Beyond content control is a range of other regulatory methodologies that do not necessarily target expression directly but nonetheless impact it. Primary examples of such governance include regulation of (1) activities with combined speech and nonspeech elements, (2) secondary effects, and (3) the time, place, or manner of speech in a public forum.

When speech is burdened by content-neutral regulation, the standard of review typically is less rigorous than for content-based regulation. Two primary models of analysis operate for purposes of reviewing content-neutral regulation under the First Amendment. When speech and conduct are mixed, and government targets an objective unrelated to expression, the Court looks for an important interest, determines whether that interest is unrelated to suppression of speech, and considers whether the regulation is narrowly tailored. In reviewing laws aimed at the secondary effects of speech, or establishing time, place, or manner restrictions, the Court examines whether the law actually is content-neutral, the regulation is supported by an important interest, the regulatory means are narrowly tailored toward their ends, and reasonably ample channels of communication are left open. These tests largely ask the same questions. The primary difference is that, when reviewing regulation purporting to regulate secondary effects or time, place, or manner, the Court inquires into the availability of alternative communication channels. This difference is explainable on grounds that the inquiry is relevant only when government is redistributing speaking opportunities, as it does in regulating secondary effects or time, place, or manner. Regulation of conduct mixed with speech prohibits expression altogether, so review of such laws need not be concerned with alternative outlets.

§ 6.01 SPEECH INTERTWINED WITH CONDUCT

Government in a variety of settings may seek to regulate activity that has a speech component. If the expression itself is targeted, First Amendment review follows the pertinent rule for content regulation. Insofar as government's regulatory focus is unrelated to the speech factor, a content neutral standard of review operates. In *United States v. O'Brien*,[1] the Court reviewed a conviction based upon a federal law that prohibited knowing destruction of a draft card. The Court acknowledged that the defendant's action had a communicative element, but also refused to accept the principle that any conduct expressing an idea must be evaluated as speech. It thus concluded that, when speech and nonspeech elements coalesce, incidental restrictions on First Amendment freedoms can be justified by an important enough interest in regulating the non-speech factor.

Against this backdrop, the Court fashioned a four-part test for use in reviewing laws that incidentally burden speech in the course of regulation associated conduct. When such a law is challenged, the questions are whether (1) government has the power to regulate in the field; (2) the regulation advances a substantial or important government interest; (3) the interest is unrelated to suppressing freedom of expression; and (4) the incidental burden on speech is no more than necessary to achieve the interest. In applying these standards, the Court found that the federal government is empowered to raise and support armies, the smooth and efficient operation of the military draft represents an important interest, this concern is

---

[1] 391 U.S. 367 (1968).

unrelated to suppression of speech, and the law was framed narrowly to account for operational smoothness and efficiency. The impact upon expression, although incidental, was not insignificant. Burning a draft card in front of a courthouse makes a strong political statement. Regulation targeted at the expression itself would have to meet a higher standard of review. For many readers of *O'Brien*, it is not evident how destruction of a draft card would impair management of the selective service system. The risk of overpredicting harm increases, however, when it is unnecessary to ask whether the regulatory methodology necessarily achieves the regulatory objective.

The *O'Brien* decision indicates that, when government burdens speech incident to managing an interest unrelated to expression, the Court will balance the competing constitutional and regulatory concerns. The standard of review will be less rigorous than when government regulates content of speech that is highly valued. It may roughly parallel, however, the criteria that apply when lower valued speech is subject to content regulation. As in cases concerning commercial speech or indecent expression, there is a focus upon the importance or substantiality rather than compelling nature of the regulatory concern and upon whether the law is narrowly tailored enough.

The *O'Brien* standard was framed in the context of a case concerning symbolic expression. Symbolic speech consists of conduct that has communicative utility. Examples include sit-ins, vigils, armbands, and a multitude of ways for expression by means of symbols, actions, or images. When symbolic speech is at issue, a twofold analysis is used. The first question is whether the conduct communicates a message. This determination is made by the actor's intent and audience's understanding. If the conduct is found to be expressive, the second question is what standard of review applies. For regulation directed at an interest unrelated to speech, the *O'Brien* formula operates. When government targets symbolic speech on the basis of its content, and unless the expression has low value, scrutiny is rigorous. Federal and state laws prohibiting desecration of the American flag thus were strictly scrutinized and struck down in *United States v. Eichman*[2] and *Texas v. Johnson*.[3] The regulations in these cases were perceived as content-based, because they conditioned the permissibility of flag destruction on the basis of whether it was respectful or not. None of the reasons for banning flag desecration, from the Court's perspective, rose to the level of a compelling state interest.

Following the decision in *Texas v. Johnson*, there have been numerous attempts to amend the United States Constitution to allow the government to prohibit flag burning. Supporters of an amendment view the flag as an important national symbol that government has the right to protect. Some opponents claim that the flag symbolizes free speech, including the right to dissent, and as a result, they argue that the United States should not attempt to prohibit flag burning. The most recent attempt to amend the Constitution failed in June, 2006. The proposed amendment passed in the United States House of Representatives, but failed by one vote in the United States Senate.

---

[2] 496 U.S. 310 (1990).

[3] 491 U.S. 397 (1989).

Although the *O'Brien* decision responded to a case of symbolic speech, the analytical model applies in any setting where regulation is on a content-neutral basis. In *Barnes v. Glen Theater, Inc.*,[4] a plurality used the *O'Brien* test upholding an ordinance banning nude dancing in establishments serving liquor. Because the law applied generally to public nudity, the plurality was satisfied that speech was not being singled out. It also determined that the ordinance was narrowly tailored to achieve government's important interest in public morality.

The *O'Brien* model's utility is evidenced further by the Court's decision in *Turner Broadcasting System, Inc. v. Federal Communications Commission.*[5] The *Turner* case concerned Federal Communications Commission rules that require cable operators to carry the signals of local broadcasters. These rules were challenged on grounds they curbed the editorial freedom of cable operators and were content-based. In support of this characterization, cable operators character-ized the must-carriage requirement as a redistribution of speaking opportunities that limited their ability to control programming. The Court, however, concluded that the rules were designed to protect the economic vitality of the broadcasting industry and the public's interest in accessing free television programming.

Because the must-carry provisions were characterized as content-neutral, the *O'Brien* formula was invoked as the proper standard of review. Applying it to the facts of the case, the Court determined that the federal government had the power to regulate telecommunications and had an important interest in preserving the benefits of free television. To the extent that cable operators refused to carry a broadcaster's signal, his or her advertising base would erode and market viability would be imperiled. The risk that cable operators would drop broadcasters from their systems became the basis for remand that was intended to elicit more evidence regarding the seriousness of this possibility. In a follow-up case, *Turner Broadcasting System, Inc. v. Federal Communications Commission,*[6] the Court determined that the risk was serious enough to justify the must carry requirement. Because the rules affected such a small number of channels, the Court also found that they burdened no more speech than necessary.

Turner illuminates the difficulty in drawing a clear and principled line between content-based and content-neutral regulation. Must-carry rules limit the range of a cable operator's editorial discretion. Redistribution of speaking opportunities in the context of print media have been viewed as content-based. A state law giving political candidates the right to reply in a newspaper that editorially attacked them, therefore, was struck down on grounds it abridged the editorial freedom guaran-teed by the First Amendment. To the extent cable operators must carry local broadcasting signals, they are put in a position similar to newspaper editors who must sacrifice space so that they can publish what the state requires.[7] These differing results, under similar circumstances, indicate the uncertainty of what triggers the *O'Brien* standard. Unpredictability owes in particular to the difficulty

---

[4] 501 U.S. 560 (1991).

[5] 512 U.S. 622 (1994).

[6] 520 U.S. 180 (1997).

[7] Miami Herald Publishing Co. v. Tornillo, 418 U.S. 241 (1973).

in discerning whether a law is directed toward speech regulation or some other purpose. It is legitimate to wonder whether the government sought to punish O'Brien for his views, particularly because a destroyed draft card has no impact upon the government's records pertaining to its holder or ability to locate or classify him or her. Different outcomes for laws that similarly redistribute media access opportunities may evoke further questions about consistent and principled application of standards. Determination of whether a regulation is content-based or content-neutral, particularly when high value speech is at stake, has serious implications for the relative intensity of First Amendment accounting. Case law indicates that drawing the line between content-based and content-neutral regulation at least is an imprecise art.

§ 6.02   SECONDARY EFFECTS

Regulation that burdens speech may be content-neutral, as the *O'Brien* line of cases indicates, if a court can identify a regulatory interest unrelated to the suppression of expression. In these circumstances of content-neutral regulation, expression may be prohibited altogether. A closely related but doctrinally distinct set of principles applies to regulation that is aimed not at the content of speech but the secondary effects of the means by which it is communicated. Attention to secondary effects was discernible in *Los Angeles City Council v. Taxpayers for Vincent.*[8] In this case, the Court upheld a city ordinance banning signs on public property. Included in this prohibition were political campaign signs, which posted information with core First Amendment value. The Court determined that the city had an important interest in maintaining community aesthetics, and that the regulation was narrowly tailored toward this end. The decision thus reflects an understanding that the ordinance was aimed not at speech but at the unattractive clutter that the particular method of expression created. It is noteworthy, moreover, that political candidates had other means for communicating their message to the public.

Secondary effects also were a determining factor in *Clark v. Community for Creative Non-Violence.*[9] This case concerned a National Park Service regulation that banned camping and sleeping in a District of Columbia park and on the mall. It was challenged by an organization that used these methods to draw attention to the problem of homelessness. Although acknowledging that camping and sleeping in the park were communicative, the Court found that the park service's regulatory purpose was unrelated to speech. Rather, it was aimed at preserving the areas for their intended use by the public. This objective was identified as an important government interest. Restrictions on camping and sleeping were found to be a narrowly tailored means of accounting for the interest. Significant also was the existence of reasonable alternative channels of communication for the demonstrators.

Secondary effects doctrine is particularly well-amplified in cases concerning zoning laws that restrict the location of adult entertainment enterprises. In *City of*

---

[8] 466 U.S. 789 (1984).

[9] 468 U.S. 288 (1984).

Renton v. Playtime Theatres, Inc.,[10] the Court examined a city ordinance regulating the placement of such businesses. The law prohibited adult movie theaters from operating within 1,000 feet of any residential zone, church, park, or school, and thus excluded them from approximately 94% of the land in the community. The Court acknowledged that the ordinance considered the content of the speech associated with adult movie theaters. The determinative factor, however, was that the city's "predominate intent" was unrelated to expression. The city's primary concern, in the Court's view, was with the secondary effects of crime and neighborhood decline.

Given these circumstances, the Court determined that a content-based standard of review should not operate. Instead, it looked to whether the regulation "serve[d] a substantial governmental interest [unrelated to speech] and allows for reasonable alternative channels of communication." The Court concluded that the secondary effects of adult movie theaters represented a substantial interest. Despite arguments that the law left practically no commercially viable land for an adult theater site, because of the limited land space and a tight real estate market, the Court determined that the respondents had to fend for themselves like any other prospective land buyer. It thus found that the reasonable alternative channels of communication criterion satisfied. The *Clark* decision indicated that alternative channels need not necessarily provide the speaker with the efficacy of his or her preferred forum. The *Playtime Theatres* ruling suggests that the alternatives need not be extensive.

The outcome in *Playtime Theatres* is consistent with the result in *Young v. American Minitheatres, Inc.*[11] This case concerned a Detroit zoning plan that prohibited adult enterprises within a designated range of certain properties and uses, such as churches and schools. The *American Mini Theatres* decision, although resolved on grounds the ordinance was a reasonable place regulation, hinged upon a determination that the law was content-neutral. Like the *Playtime Theatres* case, however, *the American Mini Theatres* decision is influenced strongly by the content of the speech. In both instances, speech was blamed for adverse social and economic consequences. The anti-content rhetoric in the *American Mini Theatres* opinion was particularly strident. Justice Stewart, who authored the majority opinion, observed that "few of us would send our sons and daughters off to war to preserve the citizen's right to see [sexually explicit expression] in the theaters of our choice."

The same secondary interests in neighborhood quality and crime abatement provided support for a city ordinance prohibiting knowing or intentional public nudity. In *City of Erie v. Pap's A.M.*,[12] a four-justice plurality determined that attention to these secondary effects represented a sufficient basis for establishing content neutrality.

Inherent in secondary effects doctrine is the possibility that content will be a primary rather than subordinate consideration in support of regulatory initiative. This peril exists to the extent that government identifies facially satisfactory reasons, other than content, as a basis for regulation. The problem in discerning the

---

[10] 475 U.S. 41 (1986).

[11] 427 U.S. 50 (1976).

[12] 528 U.S. 962 (2000).

real regulatory concern is not unlike the difficult challenge confronting courts in identifying racial discrimination when a racially neutral regulatory justification is advanced. Responding to this possibility, the Court in *Renton* indicated that government has the burden of proving a link between concentrated adult theaters and a substantial and independent government interest. In demonstrating a connection between speech and a secondary regulatory concern, the state may rely on any evidence that it "reasonably believe[s] to be relevant."[13] This standard was amplified, in *City of Los Angeles v. Alameda Books, Inc.*,[14] when the Court upheld an ordinance that imposed density limits on adult establishments. Noting that a municipality cannot rely on "shoddy data or reasoning," the Court maintained that secondary effects regulation "must fairly support" the rationale for the law.

In a concurring opinion, Justice Kennedy noted the risks of secondary effects analysis. He characterized the content neutrality denomination as a "fiction" that is "more confusing than helpful." Because the laws in the aforementioned cases are referenced to content, Justice Kennedy maintained that they should be acknowledged candidly as content-based. He would apply the same standard of review, however, rather than the stricter scrutiny that might be associated with content-based regulation. His rationale for a reduced level of review was based upon the unique nature of zoning laws. As Justice Kennedy saw it, their legitimate purpose of protecting against negative land use limits the risk that they will operate as an instrumentality of content discrimination.

The Court, in *City of Littleton v. Z.J. Gifts D-4, L.L.C.*,[15] considered whether enhanced procedural safeguards were required to ensure that permitting processes were not used in a manner that arbitrarily denied adult enterprises the opportunity to operate. In particular, it assessed whether the procedures for prompt action by and judicial review of film censors applied to the permitting of adult businesses. The Court determined that the risk of harm was different in the context of locating adult enterprises than it was with respect to movie censorship. It observed that the motion picture censorship scheme reviewed in *Freedman v. Maryland*[16] was based upon subjective standards. In *City of Littleton*, however, the Court found the permit standards to be objective. It thus concluded the state's ordinary judicial review procedures were sufficient provided that courts were sensitive to First Amendment risks.

§ 6.03   PUBLIC FORA

The most prolific source of content-neutral doctrine has related to official management of public forums. The threshold issue in public forum cases is definitional. When property is privately owned, and barring any basis for state action,[17] the First Amendment is not implicated. If the venue is public, it is necessary to determine whether the property is compatible with expressive activity.

---

[13] City of Renton v. Playtime Theatres, Inc., 475 U.S. at 51.

[14] 529 U.S. 277 (2000).

[15] 541 U.S. 774 (2004).

[16] 380 U.S. 51 (1965).

[17] Marsh v. Alabama, 326 U.S. 501 (1946).

This compatibility may be established either by tradition or designation. Traditional public forums are those that historically have been dedicated to assembly and debate. Primary examples are streets, sidewalks, and parks. Designated public forums are those that, although not traditionally open for expressive activity, the state specifically has opened for speech and assembly. A school auditorium that is opened to public organizations, or a university activity fund designed to support the publications of student groups, are examples of a designated forum. A nonpublic forum is a place that, although government owned, is closed to expressive activity. Jails and teacher mailboxes are among the sites that have been identified as nonpublic forums.

When government regulates speech in the public forum on the basis of content, review is driven by standards governing the particular category of expression. Public forum regulation has the potential to be a covering device for content control. This risk was illuminated during the 1960s, when civil rights protesters faced official impediments designed to limit or deny access to public forums. As was the case with the development of First Amendment principles that redefined the law of defamation, the civil rights era was a primary incubator of principles that shaped public forum doctrine.

Legitimate public forum management accounts for interests that are unrelated to speech content. These concerns include protection of property, management of competing uses, efficient traffic flow, public safety, and other similarly content-neutral considerations. Laws or policies that account for these interests typically relate to the time, place, or manner of expression. Time controls on parades, for instance, may reflect concern with traffic disruption. Place restrictions may take into account disruptive consequences on other uses, for instance, nearby schools when in session. A primary example of manner governance is a noise restriction that may protect environmental and privacy interests. Although such regulation is content-neutral, it imposes limits upon speech or assembly. Standards of review for time, place, or manner regulation accordingly reflect an appreciation that First Amendment interests are implicated in these circumstances. The intensity of judicial review, and corresponding level of constitutional protection, are determined largely by the nature of the forum. How a forum is depicted, therefore, is a particularly critical analytical factor.

The extent of First Amendment protection in a given case depends upon how the public forum is characterized. In *Pleasant Grove City v. Summum*,[18] the Court provided a succinct description of forum types and standards of review. As a starting point, the Court noted that it "long ago recognized that members of the public retain strong free speech rights when they venture into public streets and parks, 'which "have immemorially been held in trust for the use of the public and, time out of mind, have been used for purposes of assembly, communicating thoughts between citizens, and discussing public questions." ' " With respect to these "traditional public fora," the Court observed that government is strictly limited in its ability to regulate private speech. Reasonable time, place, and manner restrictions are permitted, but content-based regulation "must satisfy strict scrutiny, that is, the restriction must be narrowly tailored to serve a compelling government

---

[18] 555 U.S. 460 (2009).

interest, and restrictions based on viewpoint are prohibited."

Beyond streets and parks, the Court has recognized free speech rights on government property and in programs "that share essential attributes of a traditional public forum." In this regard, a government entity may create "a *designated public forum*" if government property that has not traditionally been regarded as a public forum is intentionally opened up for that purpose." The strict scrutiny standard of review, applicable in traditional public forums, applies to designated public forums.

The Court also has recognized a *limited forum* that is characterized by restricted access (i.e., reserved for use by certain groups or dedicated solely to the discussion of certain subjects). Regulation of a limited forum must be reasonable and viewpoint neutral.

Pleasant Grove concerned a city's denial of a religious group's request to place a monument in a city park, which already housed the monument to the Ten Commandments. The Court determined that this monument was a form of government speech and thus not subject to review under the First Amendment.

[A]   Traditional Public Forum

Primary examples of a traditional public forum are public streets, sidewalks, and parks. The understanding of these venues as traditional public forums actually has a relatively short tradition. The Court's seminal assessment of public parks and highways reflected an entirely different tradition with respect to their use for expressive purposes and the state's ability to limit speech in them. In *Davis v. Massachusetts*,[19] the Court upheld state and city policies that prohibited public speaking in a park or on a highway. Specifically rejecting the premise that parks "from time immemorial" had been open to public speaking, the Court determined that the legislature could limit use to the extent it deemed advisable. In support of this legislative discretion, the Court found that the foreclosure of public speaking in a highway or public park was no more of an infringement than for a homeowner to prohibit it in his or her house.

The modern concept of a public forum began to take shape in the late 1930s, as the Court recharacterized the utility of parks and highways for speech and assembly. Justice Roberts' concurring opinion in *Hague v. C.I.O.*[20] marked this redirection with the observation that

> "[w]herever the title of streets and parks may rest, they have been immemorially been held in trust for the use of the public and, time out of mind, have been used for purposes of assembly, communicating thoughts between citizens, and discussing public questions. Such use of the streets and public places has, from ancient time, been a part of the privileges, immunities, rights, and liberties of citizens."

---

[19]   167 U.S. 43 (1897).

[20]   307 U.S. 496 (1939).

As author of the majority opinion in *Schneider v. State*,[21] Justice Roberts also noted that government has legitimate interests unrelated to speech that may be a basis for regulation. With respect to public streets, for instance, the Court noted that their primary purpose is to carry traffic. A person thus could not exercise his or her liberty of expression by violating traffic regulations. The *Schneider* case concerned a regulation that prohibited distribution of handbills on public streets. The city had justified the ordinance as an anti-litter measure. The Court found it to be an overly burdensome imposition upon freedom of speech. It was unconvinced in particular that litter control provided a sufficient reason to justify the restriction on expression.

Early case law concerning traditional public forum etched general doctrinal perimeters. Among the early issues were licensing and permit schemes, which are a common way for government to manage otherwise competing uses in a public forum. These processes create the potential for First Amendment problems insofar as denial of a license or permit may mask an underlying hostility toward content. To minimize this risk, the Court has insisted upon procedures that limit an administrator's discretion and prohibit discrimination on the basis of content. In *Saia v. New York*,[22] the Court thus struck down a municipal ordinance that prohibited sound trucks unless authorized by the police chief. The primary defect in the law was that the police chief's discretion was unbridled.

Official efforts to deter organized protests in places historically associated with speech and assembly, as noted previously, were a common response to the civil rights movement during the 1960s. In *Edwards v. South Carolina*,[23] the Court determined that a state capitol grounds was a traditional public forum. The Court in *Edwards* reversed a breach of peace conviction based upon the refusal of civil rights protesters to cease their demonstration upon police command. A similar result was achieved in *Cox v. Louisiana*,[24] when the Court reversed the conviction of civil rights protesters who had picketed and demonstrated on public sidewalks. Even as the Court rendered decisions that preserved space and opportunity for expression, public forum doctrine suffered from lack of clarity and direction. In *Brown v. Louisiana*,[25] the Court reversed the breach of peace conviction of several defendants who had staged a silent civil rights protest in a public library. The Court determined that the orderly nature of the demonstration was not compatible with a library's primary purpose. A public library, however, is difficult to view as a place that since "ancient time" has been dedicated to speech and assembly. To the contrary, public libraries "immemorially" have been unfriendly to activity that disrupts the ability to read and think without distraction.

As public forum doctrine evolved later in the Twentieth Century, standards of review became better articulated and more precise. The Court, in *Perry Education*

---

[21] 308 U.S. 147 (1939).

[22] 334 U.S. 558 (1948).

[23] 372 U.S. 229 (1963).

[24] 379 U.S. 559 (1965).

[25] 383 U.S. 131 (1966).

Association v. Perry Local Educators' Association,[26] referred to traditional public forums as "quintessential public forums [where] government may not prohibit all communicative activity." Content-based regulation in this setting is permissible only when the state demonstrates a compelling interest and the law is narrowly framed to achieve this end. Content-neutral regulation may be allowed to the extent it is narrowly tailored to serve a significant government interest and ample alternative channels of communication are left open.

Restrictions on picketing in the public forum have been a primary source of content-based regulation. In *Police Department of Chicago v. Mosley*,[27] the Court reviewed a city ordinance that prohibited all public picketing except by labor organizations within a designated distance from schools and during specific hours. Although styled as a regulation of time and place, the ordinance discriminated on the basis of content. Minus a compelling reason for distinguishing one type of picketing from another, the rule violated a cardinal principle of public forum law. As the Court put it, "[o]nce a forum is opened to assembly or speaking by some groups, government may not prohibit others from assembling or speaking on the basis of what they intend to say."

The same rationale generated a like outcome in *Carey v. Brown*,[28] when the Court struck down a law that prohibited picketing of dwellings but excepted places of employment implicated in a labor dispute. The Court has upheld, however, a restriction on residential picketing directed toward a particular household. In *Frisby v. Schultz*,[29] the Court determined that the "well-being, tranquility, and privacy of the home" were interests of the "highest order." Relevant too was the state's interest in protecting "the unwilling listener," whose interests are heightened in "their own homes." Because the law did not ban all picketing in a neighborhood, but only focused picketing aimed at the household and not the public, the Court also found it narrowly tailored. The Court left open the possibility that focused picketing might be permissible in the event that it was directed toward a house being used as a place of business or for a public meeting.

The *Mosley, Carey*, and *Frisby* cases each concerned regulation that, because it singled out a form of picketing for exclusion or protection, was content-based. In *United States v. Grace*,[30] the Court reviewed a federal law that banned all picketing on public sidewalks adjacent to the United States Supreme Court. Although the enactment was content-neutral, the Court determined that it was not reasonable or supported by a significant government interest. The Court, in *Clark v. Community for Creative Non-Violence*,[31] found a limit on overnight usage of a public park to be a valid content-neutral regulation. The regulation was applied to demonstrators who had established a tent city in a Washington, D.C. park to draw public attention to homelessness. The Court determined that government had a substantial interest in

[26] 460 U.S. 37 (1983).

[27] 408 U.S. 92 (1972).

[28] 447 U.S. 455 (1993).

[29] 487 U.S. 474 (1988).

[30] 461 U.S. 171 (1983).

[31] 468 U.S. 288 (1984).

maintaining the park for its intended public uses. Because opportunities existed for protest during hours when the park was open, it was satisfied that the regulation left open sufficient alternative channels for communication.

In *Ward v. Rock Against Racism*,[32] the Court provided a significant elaboration of the narrowly-tailored requirement. The *Ward* case concerned a noise control rule governing the use of a bandshell in New York City's Central Park. The regulation, which required performers to use sound equipment and technicians provided by the city, was intended to balance the need for sound amplification against the interests of other park users and adjacent residences. The Court rejected the argument that, by interfering with artistic judgment, the city was regulating on the basis of content. Rather, it viewed the regulation as a means to account for a substantial interest in protecting citizens from unwelcome noise. The court of appeals had struck down the regulation on grounds there were less restrictive means of achieving the city's goals. On this point, the Court reversed and announced that the narrowly-tailored requirement is not coextensive with a least burdensome alternative standard. The Court thus reaffirmed the narrowly-tailored standard with an amplified understanding that regulation need only promote the government's interest more effectively than would be achieved without the law. With this key clarification, the resulting focus of narrowly-tailored inquiry is upon whether the regulatory means are substantially broader than necessary to achieve the government's interest. A law will not be struck down merely because a court can identify a less restrictive alternative means of accounting.

A city's effort to control sidewalk clutter, by limiting the number of new-stands, represented a manner restriction which the Court found to be content-based. In *City of Cincinnati v. Discovery Network, Inc.*,[33] the Court examined a city ordinance that prohibited advertising publications from using sidewalk newsracks. The law did not reach conventional newspapers. The Court determined that the type of publication had no bearing on the aesthetic or safety risk presented by newsracks. The ordinance thus was content-based. Because the expression at issue was classified as commercial speech, the Court did not inquire into whether the regulation was justified by a compelling interest. The focus instead was upon the substantiality of the regulatory concern.

In *Berger v. Seattle*,[34] the court struck down restrictions on street performers in city parks. In particular, the ordinance in question imposed permit and badge requirements, and prohibited street performers from actively soliciting donations as well as engaging in speech activities within 30 feet of patrons standing in food or ticket lines. The court concluded that the restrictions were not narrowly tailored to serve significant governmental interests.

Nationwide Protests by Occupy Movement. The Occupy Wall Street movement which began in New York on September 17, 2011, and took up residence in Zuccotti Park in New York City, raised public forum issues. The Occupy movement consisted of a diverse group of individuals, often from the left side of the political spectrum,

---

[32] 491 U.S. 781 (1989).

[33] 507 U.S. 410 (1993).

[34] 569 F.3d 1029 (9th Cir. 2009).

many of whom were unemployed. The movement purported to represent what they claimed was the 99% of the population that is disadvantaged by the current political and economic system. Occupy Wall Street did not have an organized plan of action, or demands. Indeed, given its anarchic roots, the Occupy movement was simply reluctant to embrace leaders or specific policy positions. The Occupy movement had an aversion to hierarchy, and to formal leaders, but a strong commitment to democratic principles. Participants in the movement seemed to share a level of anger regarding wealth disparities, special interests and the political system. Other issues bubbled to the surface in other protests, including unemployment and high levels of student debt.

Occupy protestors occupied certain public places such as public squares, parks and city property. Often, Occupy protestors literally lived at these sites, bringing in camping gear, tents, and cook stoves. Protests spread quickly to Madrid, London, Berlin, and across Asia, Europe, and to the Americas, and these protests involved thousands of people. In the United States, some 1,500 people turned up for an Occupy Orlando protest, and the protests spread to many other U.S. cities, including Phoenix, Portland, Louisville, Los Angeles, Chicago, Tucson, Boston, Atlanta, Oakland, Philadelphia, Albany, Berkeley, New Orleans, Fresno, Fort Myers, Oklahoma City, Nashville, Tampa, St. Petersburg, Augusta (Maine), the District of Columbia, Salt Lake City, Honolulu, Raleigh, Trenton, Wilmington, Lynchburg, and Bloomington. The protests of the Occupy Movement resulted in much litigation.[35]

Attorneys Fees for Plaintiffs Who Obtain Injunctions. In *Lefemine v. Wideman*,[36] the Court held that the plaintiff was entitled to attorneys fees under 42 U.S.C. § 1988 as the "prevailing party" in a § 1983 suit when plaintiff obtained an injunction on First Amendment grounds. The plaintiff abandoned his first sidewalk demonstration "to protest the availability of abortions" when police officers ordered him to stop using told him that he would receive citation arrest for disorderly conduct if he did not discard the graphic "pictures of aborted fetuses" that he was using as part of the demonstration. Later when the plaintiff informed the sheriff that he planned to conduct another demonstration using the images, he was informed that the same police response would occur at any such future demonstrations. The federal district court granted summary judgment to the plaintiff on the grounds that the police defendants violated his First Amendment rights, and permanently enjoyed the defendants "from engaging in content-based restrictions on [plaintiff's] display of graphic signs under similar circumstances." The Supreme Court found that plaintiffs are entitled as a "prevailing party" to receive attorneys fees when they obtain "actual relief on the merits" of a claim that "materially alters the legal relationship between the parties by modifying the defendant's behavior in a way that directly benefits the plaintiff." The Court noted that, "we have repeatedly

---

[35] *See, e.g., Isbell v. City of Oklahoma City*, 2012 U.S. Dist. LEXIS 107390 (W.D. Okla. Dec. 12, 2011); *Occupy Columbia v. Haley*, 866 F. Supp. 2d 545 (D.S.C. 2011); *Occupy Columbia v. Haley*, 2011 U.S. Dist. LEXIS 147630 (D. S.C. Dec. 22, 2011); *Occupy Minneapolis v. County of Hennepin*, 866 F. Supp. 2d 1062 (D. Minn. 2011); *Freeman v. Morris*, 2011 U.S. Dist. LEXIS 141930 (D. Me. Dec. 9, 2011) (Occupy Augusta, Maine); *Occupy Fort Myers v. City of Fort Myers*, 882 F. Supp. 2d 1320 (M.D. Fla. 2011); *Occupy Fresno v. County of Fresno*, 835 F. Supp.2d 849 (E.D. Ca. 2011).

[36] 133 S.Ct. 9 (2012).

held that an injunction or declaratory judgment, like a damages award, will usually satisfy that test."

[B] Designated Public Forums

Streets, sidewalks, and parks have well-established identities as venues for free speech and assembly. When confronted with a site that did not fit neatly into one of these conventional categories, the Court's inquiry historically has focused upon whether speech and assembly were compatible with a property's main use. Modern standards tend to be more simplified and focused upon what intent, if any, government had to create a forum. From this line of analysis has emerged a second category of public forums. Even if public property may not be dedicated to speech and assembly as a function of tradition, it may be a public forum by designation. A designated public forum is established when the state opens public property "for use by the public as a place for expressive activity."[37] The state is not required to create the forum or maintain it indefinitely. To the extent it keeps the forum open, however, the state is bound by the same rules that govern traditional forums. Content-based control in a designated public forum thus must be supported by a compelling state interest and must be narrowly drawn to achieve the objective. Time, place, and manner regulation is permissible to the extent it is content-neutral, is narrowly tailored to achieve a significant government interest, and leaves open ample alternative channels of communication.

The nature of a designated forum and analysis governing content-neutral speech control therein is illustrated by *Heffron v. International Society for Krishna Consciousness*.[38] *The Heffron* decision predates the Court's development of clear distinctions among forum types. It previews, however, the direction of the Court's thinking with respect to designated forums. The case concerned a state fair policy that restricted all sellers, vendors, and distributors to booths that could be rented on a first-come, first-served basis and to fixed locations on the fairgrounds. The regulation had been adopted as a crowd control measure. Having determined that the regulation was content-neutral, the Court found that it advanced the state's significant interest in maintaining order and access. Because the Court was convinced that no other regulatory means would have advanced the state's interest as effectively, the narrowly tailored requirement was satisfied. The ability to communicate from a fixed position, and the ability to interact off-property, indicated the availability of adequate alternative channels of communication.

The collision of free speech and Establishment Clause interests has been a significant source of designated public forum law. The starting point for this line of cases is *Widmar v. Vincent*. This case concerned a university policy that gave student groups access to campus facilities. Excluded from this policy, were student groups that would have used the facilities for religious purposes. The university had made this exception to avoid Establishment Clause problems. It ended up with a free speech problem in the form of a content-based regulation. Although avoidance of an Establishment Clause violation represented a compelling state

---

[37] Perry Education Association v. Perry Local Educators' Association, 460 U.S. 37, 45 (1983).

[38] 452 U.S. 640 (1981).

interest, the Court determined that the regulatory means failed the institution's ends. The Court determined that an equal access policy would have a secular purpose, not have the primary effect of advancing religion, and not incur a risk of entangling church and state. Minus a real Establishment Clause risk, the policy overreached and failed to meet the narrowly drawn standard.

Even if the university was not obligated to adopt an access policy, therefore, it was obligated to implement the provision on a non-discriminatory basis barring a compelling reason for exclusion. It also retained the option, not available for a traditional public forum, to close the forum to all student groups.

A school board's denial of access to school facilities for religious uses, despite a policy allowing public utilization for other purposes, was invalidated *in Lamb's Chapel v. Center Moriches Union Free School District.*[39] Given the Court's decision in *Widmar*, concern with an Establishment Clause violation could not rise to the level of a compelling government interest. The exclusionary policy thus represented an unconstitutional exercise in viewpoint discrimination.

The Court, in *Rosenberger v. Rector and Visitors of the University of Virginia*,[40] reviewed a university policy that funded the publications of registered student organizations except for religious groups.[41] The policy reflected official concern that funding of a religious publication would violate the Establishment Clause. Justice Kennedy, in authoring the majority opinion, identified "a forum more in a metaphysical than in a spatial or geographic sense, [to which] the same rules are applicable." Further elaboration of its nature was unnecessary, insofar as the policy was found to be a function of viewpoint discrimination. Exclusion on the basis of viewpoint is impermissible in any public forum, unless supported by a compelling government interest. From the Court's perspective, the inclusion of student religious groups would not have violated the Establishment Clause. Consequently, it found no basis for a compelling state interest.

In *United States v. American Library Association*,[42] the Court rejected the likening of Internet terminals in public libraries to the public forum identified in *Rosenberger.* The key basis for differentiation was that public libraries do not provide Internet access to create a public forum for expression. Rather, like other library resources, it is offered to facilitate research, learning, and recreational usage. The Court thus found the Internet simply to be a technological extension of a book stack. Because the Internet was a relatively new phenomenon, and thus not held in trust immemorially for the public, the Court also determined that it did not qualify as a traditional public forum.

In recent years, members of the Westboro Baptist Church of Topeka, Kansas, have been protesting at military funerals. The protestors believe that soldiers deaths are a "sign" of God's wrath for America's tolerance of homosexuality. The protests have extended to military funerals in Kentucky and elsewhere. In

---

[39] 508 U.S. 384 (1993).

[40] 515 U.S. 819 (1995).

[41] *Id.*

[42] 539 U.S. 194 (2003).

response to the protests, Kentucky passed the following statute:[43]

§ 525.155. Interference with a funeral.

(1) A person is guilty of interference with a funeral when he or she at any time on any day:

(a) Blocks, impedes, inhibits, or in any other manner obstructs or interferes with access into or from any building or parking lot of a building in which a funeral, wake, memorial service, or burial is being conducted, or any burial plot or the parking lot of the cemetery in which a funeral, wake, memorial service, or burial is being conducted;

(b) Congregates, pickets, patrols, demonstrates, or enters on that portion of a public right-of-way or private property that is within three hundred (300) feet of an event specified in paragraph (a) of this subsection; or

(c) Without authorization from the family of the deceased or person conducting the service, during a funeral, wake, memorial service, or burial:

1. Sings, chants, whistles, shouts, yells, or uses a bullhorn, auto horn, sound amplification equipment, or other sounds or images observable to or within earshot of participants in the funeral, wake, memorial service, or burial; or

2. Distributes literature or any other item.

(2) Interference with a funeral is a Class B misdemeanor.

Members of the legislature stated that "people should be allowed to attend funerals without outside stress from protesters" and that "virtually every civilized society today holds sacred the right to peacefully bury their dead." It is not clear that the Kentucky statute is constitutional because it may place impermissible restrictions on public forum protests. It might be possible to limit certain types of interferences with funerals (*e.g.*, obstructions), but it might be difficult to draft a statute that is free of vagueness or ambiguity.

[C]   Reserved Forums

Unless it is public by tradition or designation, government property for speech and assembly purposes is a reserved or nonpublic forum. Government ownership or control of property by itself does not establish a First Amendment right of access. Like a private owner of property, the state has an interest in using the property under its control for the use to which it was lawfully dedicated. The state may reserve such a forum for its intended purposes, communicative or otherwise, so long as the regulation on speech is reasonable and not designed to suppress expression on the basis of viewpoint.

---

[43] Ken. Rev. Stat. Ann. § 525.155 (2006).

Traditional public forums are well-established in their identity and thus readily discernible. Some reserved forums also are relatively easy to identify. Among the relatively easy cases are those that have identified jails[44] and military bases[45] as nonpublic forums. Distinguishing designated forums and traditional forums typically is not a difficult task. The dividing line between a designated forum and reserved forum is more challenging. The identification process is complicated because, in either case, the forum may be used for speech and association. Communication of information is the primary reason, for instance, why a school system would provide teachers with mailboxes. The question that must be resolved, however, is whether the school system has assumed the responsibility of providing equal access or may restrict their use. The answer depends upon whether the medium is characterized as a designated or reserved forum.

In *Perry Education Association v. Perry Local Educators Association*,[46] the Court reviewed a collective bargaining agreement provision that gave the teachers' elected bargaining agent a right of access to teacher mailboxes. Although certain community groups also could use the mail system, the contract denied a rival union access to them. The Court determined that the mailboxes were not public forums by tradition or designation. It differentiated between a policy that creates general access and a provision for specific access that's consistent with the institution's operational needs. Critical to this distinction is the government's intended purpose. If the objective is to open a facility for general access, the property should be classified as a designated forum. If government policy provides for selective access, the property will be characterized as a reserved or nonpublic forum.

Public forum doctrine over the past two decades has been increasingly friendly to the concept of reserved use. This category of nonpublic forums includes postal service mail boxes, utility poles, federal charity drives, airport terminals, and political candidate debates on public television. With respect to mail boxes, the Court in *United States Postal Service v. Council of Greenburgh Civic Associations*,[47] determined that unlimited public access to them would disrupt the postal service's ability to operate an efficient mail system. The Court in *Members of the City Council of Los Angeles v. Vincent*,[48] found insufficient evidence to support the proposition that utility poles were either traditional or designated forums. The posting of signs on utility poles, even when ordinances forbid it, provides at least arguable support for a tradition of communicative use. The Court found, in *Cornelius v. NAACP Legal Defense Fund*,[49] that exclusion of political and legal advocacy groups from a federal charity campaign was a reasonable decision. From the Court's perspective, a selective roster of recipient groups minimized the potential for disruption in the workplace and a negative impact on fund-raising. Insofar as groups were excluded because of their controversial nature, however, the argument could be made that viewpoint was a factor. The Court nonetheless

---

[44] Adderley v. Florida, 385 U.S. 39 (1966).

[45] Greer v. Spock, 424 U.S. 828 (1976).

[46] 460 U.S. 37 (1983).

[47] 453 U.S. 114 (1981).

[48] 466 U.S. 789 (1984).

[49] 473 U.S. 788 (1985).

concluded that exclusion of groups, because they could disrupt program aims or the workplace, did not amount to viewpoint discrimination.

Because airports have not been in existence since time "immemorial," and are dedicated primarily to travel rather than speech and assembly, the Court in *International Society for Krishna Consciousness, Inc. v. Lee,*[50] found that they lacked the attributes of a traditional public forum. A competing perspective is that airports predate the Court's conceptualization of a traditional public forum in the late 1930s, and that most airports are multi-use facilities that are adapted to speech and assembly.

Insofar as a public television station did not provide general access to the airwaves, but established eligibility requirements for a congressional candidates debate, the policy of selective access established a reserved forum. In *Arkansas Educational Television Commission v. Forbes,*[51] a third-party candidate argued that his exclusion was a function of viewpoint discrimination. This contention was trumped by evidence that his exclusion was based upon eligibility standards that required a minimum level of public support.

The inquiry with respect to nonpublic forums is threefold. The first question relates to whether the forum actually has been reserved for a specific use. The second question focuses upon whether restriction of access is reasonable. The final question looks to whether the limitation or exclusion is viewpoint neutral. Put another way, restricted access to a nonpublic forum will be upheld if the policy of exclusion is reasonable and viewpoint-neutral.

Pleasant Grove City, Utah v. Sumum,[52] involved a dispute regarding the right of a city to refuse to place a permanent monument (offered by a private religious group) in a city park. The park in question (a 2.5 acre public park, located in the Historic District of Pleasant Grove City, Utah) contained 15 permanent displays, 11 of which were donated by private groups or individuals, and one of which involved a Ten Commandments monument donated by the Fraternal Order of Eagles. The case arose when Summum, a religious organization, requested permission to erect a "stone monument," that contained "the Seven Aphorisms of SUMMUM," on the property. The monument was similar in size and nature to the Ten Commandments monument. The City denied the request on the basis that the city would only accept monuments that "either (1) directly relate to the history of Pleasant Grove, or (2) were donated by groups with longstanding ties to the Pleasant Grove community." The policy also mentioned other criteria, such as safety and esthetics. Although the Sumum's requested permission to erect a monument, they did not describe its historical significance or its connection to the community.

In upholding the denial, the Court construed the park monuments as "government speech" and noted that government "is entitled to say what it wishes," and to select the views that it wants to express. There are limits to the

---

[50] 505 U.S. 672 (1992).

[51] 523 U.S. 666 (1998).

[52] 555 U.S. 460 (2009).

governmental speech doctrine in the sense that governmental speech must be consistent with the Establishment Clause of the First Amendment, as well as with public forum doctrine. In addition, governments are prohibited from discriminating against speech based on its content.

The Court recognized that governments "have long used monuments to speak to the public," even when the monuments are donated by private entities, and governments are entitled to exercise selectivity in their choice of monuments, and can engage in both viewpoint and content discrimination. Moreover, the Court viewed permanent monuments as fundamentally different from other more transitory speech (such as marches, speeches or demonstrations) because of their permanence. Whereas parks can host many different types of transitory speech, they can accommodate only a limited number of permanent monuments. Moreover, there is no long history of allowing individuals to construct permanent monuments on public property.

The decision produced a number of concurring opinions. Justice Stevens, joined by Justice Ginsburg, argued that "the city's refusal would have been equally valid if its acceptance of the monument, instead of being characterized as 'government speech,' had merely been deemed an implicit endorsement of the donor's message." Justice Breyer would have required proof that the governmental decision to refuse the monument "burdens speech disproportionately in light of the action's tendency to further a legitimate government objective." He would have found no disproportionate restriction on speech because the city did not close off its parks to speech, and did not prevent the Summum from engaging in other more transitory speech.

§ 6.04   PRIVATE PROPERTY

Public forum doctrine by definition generally does not apply to private property. This proposition is consistent with the premise that state action is necessary for a First Amendment violation. State action doctrine establishes the possibility that under certain circumstances, private enterprise may be regarded as state action. Illustrative of this circumstance is the Court's determination, in *Marsh v. Alabama*,[53] that a company town exercised a public function. The case concerned the trespass conviction of a Jehovah's Witness who had been arrested for disseminating literature on the street. Because the city exercised all of the powers of a traditional municipality, the street effectively was regarded as a public forum.

The *Marsh* decision begot a series of cases that addressed the question of whether shopping centers also were state actors. *In Amalgamated Food Employees Union Local 590 v. Logan Valley Plaza, Inc.*,[54] the Court analogized a privately owned shopping center to public property. From the Court's perspective, shopping centers performed the same public function as a municipal shopping district. This understanding was overruled in *Hudgens v. National Labor Relations Board*,[55]

---

[53] 326 U.S. 501 (1946).

[54] 391 U.S. 308 (1968).

[55] 424 U.S. 507 (1976).

when the Court determined that a shopping center owner could exclude speech and assembly without First Amendment implications. Although the *Hudgens* decision did not overrule *Marsh*, it appears to have limited public function-based state action to instances where private use of property replicates all aspects of public control. In *PruneYard Shopping Center v. Robins*,[56] the Court reserved the possibility that public access to private property could be reserved by state law.

---

[56] 447 U.S. 74 (1980).

POINTS TO REMEMBER

- Content-neutral regulation may implicate First Amendment interests.

- Content-neutral standards of review apply to laws targeting conduct that is coupled with speech, secondary effects of speech, and time, place, and manner regulation in public forums.

- When regulation is directed at conduct associated with speech, a court must ask whether the law advances a substantial or important government interest, the interest is unrelated to suppressing freedom of expression, and the incidental burden on speech is no more than necessary to achieve the interest.

- When government regulates secondary effects, the inquiry is whether the law is supported by an important government interest, narrowly tailored to account for that interest, and leaves open ample alternative channels of communication.

- Public property (*e.g.*, streets, sidewalks, and parks) that has been used since time immemorial for speech and assembly is a traditional public forum.

- Public property that has been designated generally for uses of speech and assembly is a designated (or limited) public forum.

- Public property that has been set aside for its primary purpose, and by neither tradition nor designation is dedicated to speech and assembly, is a nonpublic forum.

- Content-based regulation in a traditional or designated public forum must be justified by a compelling state interest and must be narrowly tailored to achieve that interest.

- Content-neutral regulation in a traditional or designated public forum may be allowed to the extent it is narrowly tailored to serve a significant government interest and ample alternative channels of communication are left open.

- Government is not obligated to create a designated forum and reserves the power to close it altogether.

- Regulation of expression in a nonpublic forum is permissible provided it is reasonable and does not discriminate on the basis of viewpoint.

- Designated forums and nonpublic forums are differentiated primarily on the basis of whether government intends to provide general access or specific access.

- Private property is not subject to public forum analysis unless a basis exists for finding state action.

Chapter 7

TESTING THE BOUNDARIES OF DOCTRINE

FOCAL POINTS FOR CHAPTER 7

- Religious speech as protected speech.
- Establishment Clause concerns with religious speech.
- Religious groups and access to public facilities.
- "Hate speech" as protected speech.
- The validity of campus speech codes.
- Campaign finance laws as restrictions on speech.
- Governmental power to limit contributions to, or expenditures by, political campaigns.

---

§ 7.01 RELIGIOUS SPEECH

The Court has struggled to apply the First Amendment to religious speech. Although the First Amendment's speech clause gives all citizens the right to free expression, that Amendment also prohibits the government from "establishing" an official religion. These fundamental principles collide when religious groups seek to use governmental facilities or seek governmental funding for their speech.

In this context, the Court has been reluctant to allow the government to discriminate against religious speech in public forums. An important recent decision is *Lamb's Chapel v. Center Moriches Union Free School Dist.*,[1] in which a public school allowed outside groups to use school facilities after-hours for "social, civic or recreational use," but prohibited use "by any group for religious purposes." The school excluded a church that wanted to present films teaching family values from a Christian perspective. The Court overturned the exclusion holding that, because the films "dealt with a subject otherwise permissible" (the teaching of family values), the district's exclusion of the church constituted unconstitutional viewpoint discrimination.

Lamb's Chapel was followed and extended by the holding in *Rosenberger v. Rector and Visitors of University of Virginia.*[2] In *Rosenberger*, the University of Virginia authorized payment to outside contractors from its Student Activities Fund ("SAF") for the costs of printing a variety of student publications. In order to qualify for funding, a student organization was required to register as a Contracted Independent Organization (CIO), but CIO status was available to any group the majority of whose members were students, whose managing officers were full-time students, and that complied with stated procedural requirements. University guidelines provided that funding was available for a variety of purposes including "student news, information, opinion, entertainment, or academic communications media groups." Under the guidelines. Wide Awake Publications ("WAP"), a CIO, was denied funding because its student paper "primarily promotes or manifests a particular belief in or about a deity or an ultimate reality." The paper wrote about "philosophical and religious expression" offering "a Christian perspective on both personal and community issues, especially those relevant to college students at the University of Virginia."

In an opinion by Justice Kennedy, the Court concluded that WAP was entitled to funding on an equal basis with other student publications. The Court began by reaffirming the basic principle that once a government has opened a limited public forum, the government must abide by the rules it has established for that forum, and may not discriminate against speech based on its viewpoint. Content discrimination is only permitted to the extent that it serves the purposes of the limited forum.

After reiterating these basic principles, the Court recognized that although the SAF was a forum "more in a metaphysical than in a spatial or geographic sense" the Court concluded that the same principles apply. The Court easily found viewpoint discrimination because, although the University did not exclude religion as an acceptable subject, it singled out for "disfavored treatment" journalistic efforts with religious editorial viewpoints. The Court held that such "viewpoint discrimination" is unconstitutional:

---

[1] 508 U.S. 384 (1993).

[2] 515 U.S. 819 (1995).

Vital First Amendment speech principles are at stake here. The first danger to liberty lies in granting the State the power to examine publications to determine whether or not they are based on some ultimate idea and, if so, for the State to classify them. The second, and corollary, danger is to speech from the chilling of individual thought and expression. That danger is especially real in the University setting . . . . For the University, by regulation, to cast disapproval on particular viewpoints of its students risks the suppression of free speech and creative inquiry in one of the vital centers for the Nation's intellectual life, its college and university campuses.[3]

The Court rejected the University's argument that its actions were compelled by the Establishment Clause, and expressed concern that the regulations required public officials to review publications for their religious theory and belief, and created the risk of bias or hostility towards religion.

Justice Souter, joined by justices Stevens, Ginsburg and Breyer, dissented arguing that, if the University of Virginia gave funding to the WAF, it would run afoul of the Establishment Clause. In addition, he argued that the University did not engage in "viewpoint discrimination" because the Guidelines applied to other faiths as well as to agnostics, atheists and theists. "[A] university's decision to fund a magazine about racism, and not to fund publications aimed at urging repentance before God does not skew the debate either about racism or the desirability of religious conversion."[4]

Rosenberger was followed by the holding in *Good News Club v. Milford Central School.*[5] A New York law authorized local school boards to adopt regulations governing the use of their school facilities by outside groups. The Milford Central School (Milford School) enacted a "community use" policy which, inter alia, allowed buildings to be used for a number of purposes including the following: "First, district residents may use the school for 'instruction in any branch of education, learning or the arts.' Second, the school is available for 'social, civic and recreational meetings and entertainment events, and other uses pertaining to the welfare of the community, provided that such uses shall be nonexclusive and shall be opened to the general public.' "

The directors of the Good News Club (the Fourniers) lived in the Milford School district and were entitled to use the school's facilities provided their proposed use fell within the guidelines. They requested permission to hold meetings of the "Good News Club," a private Christian organization for children ages 6 to 12, in the school cafeteria. The Club described its activities as follows:

The Club opens its session with Ms. Fournier taking attendance. As she calls a child's name, if the child recites a Bible verse the child receives a treat. After attendance, the Club sings songs. Next Club members engage in games that involve, *inter alia*, learning Bible verses. Ms. Fournier then

---

[3] *Id.* at 835.

[4] *Id.* at 898.

[5] 533 U.S. 98 (2001).

relates a Bible story and explains how it applies to Club members' lives. The Club closes with prayer. Finally, Ms. Fournier distributes treats and the Bible verses for memorization.[6]

Milford officials concluded that "the kinds of activities proposed to be engaged in by the Good News Club were not a discussion of secular subjects such as child rearing, development of character and development of morals from a religious perspective, but were in fact the equivalent of religious instruction itself."[7] As a result, the Board rejected the Club's request to use Milford's facilities on the basis that permission would have violated the Establishment Clause.

In an opinion by Justice Thomas, the Court held that the Good News Club was entitled to use school facilities. The Court began by noting that different standards of review apply to different types of forums, that the Milford School had created a "limited public forum" and that the State may place restrictions on the use of the forum provided that it does not engage in "viewpoint" discrimination and provided that the restriction is "reasonable in light of the purpose served by the forum." Relying on *Lamb's Chapel* and *Rosenberger*, the Court found that the Milford School had engaged in viewpoint discrimination, noting that Milford had opened its facilities to a variety of purposes related to the welfare of the community including discussions of a variety of subjects such as child rearing and the development of character and morals. Although the Good News Club also taught morals and character development to children, it was precluded from teaching because it did so from a religious perspective. The Court held that Milford had engaged in viewpoint discrimination, and concluded that the District had illegally excluded the Club because of its religious viewpoint. The Court rejected the District's claim that it would be violating the Establishment Clause if it allowed the Club to use its facilities.

Justice Stevens dissented. Although he agreed that Milford School could not censor speech about an authorized topic based on the point of view expressed by the speaker, he argued that the School has "broad discretion to 'preserve the property under its control for the use to which it is lawfully dedicated.' "[8] He noted that the School prohibited the use of its facilities for "religious purposes" which meant that it "did not intend to exclude all speech from a religious point of view. Instead, it sought to exclude proselytizing religious speech.

Justice Souter, joined by Justice Ginsburg, also dissented, noting that the Good News Club was engaged in evangelical worship. "While Good News's program utilizes songs and games, the heart of the meeting is the 'challenge' and 'invitation,' [during which] 'saved' children who 'already believe in the Lord Jesus as their Savior' are challenged to 'stop and ask God for the strength and the 'want'. . . to obey Him.' "[9] The teacher also "invites" "unsaved" children " 'to trust the Lord Jesus to be your Savior from sin,' " and " 'receive [him] as your Savior from sin.' "[10]

---

[6] *Id.* at 103.

[7] *Id.* at 108.

[8] *Id.* at 131.

[9] *Id.* at 137–38.

[10] *Id.* at 138.

The children are then instructed that "if you believe what God's Word says about your sin and how Jesus died and rose again for you, you can have His forever life today. Please bow your heads and close your eyes. If you have never believed on the Lord Jesus as your Savior and would like to do that, please show me by raising your hand. If you raised your hand to show me you want to believe on the Lord Jesus, please meet me so I can show you from God's Word how you can receive His everlasting life."[11]

Justice Scalia disagreed with Justice Souter. "[W]e have previously rejected the attempt to distinguish worship from other religious speech, saying that "the distinction has [no] intelligible content," and further, no "*relevance*" to the constitutional issue. [If] the distinction did have content, it would be beyond the courts' competence to administer. And if courts (and other government officials) were competent, applying the distinction would require state monitoring of private, religious speech with a degree of pervasiveness that we have previously found unacceptable."[12]

Other cases have dealt with these issues in other context. For example, in in *Adams v. City of Alexandria*,[13] a federal district court struck down a municipal ordinance making it "unlawful for any person to engage in the business or practice of palmistry, card reading, astrology, fortune-telling, phrenology, mediums or activities of a similar nature within the city, regardless of whether a fee is charged." The plaintiff, a psychic, maintained that she had the ability to "understand and appreciate Tarot cards, telling of futures, psychic abilities and palmistry." The court found that the law was not supported by a compelling interest and thus invalidated it. In so doing, it observed that:

> The danger of the government deciding what is true and not true, real and unreal, should be obvious. For example, some might say that a belief in God or in a particular religion, for example, or in the "Book of Revelations" is not supported by demonstrable facts. Books that repeat the predictions of Nostradamus and the daily newspaper horoscope could be banned under the City's reasoning.

POINTS TO REMEMBER

- Government may not discriminate against religious speech.
- Despite Establishment Clause concerns, when the government opens a limited public forum, religious speakers are entitled to use that fo-rum in a manner consistent with the purposes of that forum.

---

[11] *Id.*

[12] *Id.* at 127.

[13] 2012 U.S. Dist. Lexis 97042 (W.D. La. 2012).

§ 7.02   "HATE" SPEECH

While the label "hate speech" is very imprecise, the term refers to expression that targets individuals or groups by reason of their race, ethnicity, sex, or sexual preference. Some prefer to refer to this speech as "bias" speech or "discriminatory" speech. No label is completely satisfactory.

[A]   Early Precedent

Beauharnais v. Illinois,[14] previously discussed in Chapter 3, was one of the United States Supreme Court's earliest discussions of the issue. § 224a of Division 1 of the Illinois Criminal Code provided that:

> It shall be unlawful for any person, firm or corporation to manufacture, sell, or offer for sale, advertise or publish, present or exhibit in any public place in this state any lithograph, moving picture, play, drama or sketch, which publication or exhibition portrays depravity, criminality, unchastity, or lack of virtue of a class of citizens, of any race, color, creed or religion which said publication or exhibition exposes the citizens of any race, color, creed or religion to contempt, derision, or obloquy or which is productive of breach of the peace or riots.

Petitioner was convicted under the law and fined $200 for distributing leaflets setting forth a petition calling on the Mayor and City Council of Chicago "to halt the further encroachment, harassment and invasion of white people, their property, neighborhoods and persons, by the [Negro]." The leaflet also called on "One million self respecting white people in Chicago to unite." adding that "If persuasion and the need to prevent the white race from becoming mongrelized by the negro will not unite us, then the aggressions [rapes,] robberies, knives, guns and marijuana of the negro, surely will." The leaflet concluded with an application for membership in the White Circle League of America, Inc.

In an opinion by Justice Frankfurter, the Court upheld the conviction. He viewed the law as anti-libel and noted that every jurisdiction punishes libels directed at individuals. He concluded that it is "libelous falsely to charge another with being a rapist, robber, carrier of knives and guns, and user of marijuana."

Justice Frankfurter then focused on whether the First Amendment prevented the state from punishing libels of this nature when made against a group, and quickly answered this question in the negative. The opinion applied a rational basis standard, and concluded that the State of Illinois had a valid basis for regulation: "wilful purveyors of falsehood concerning racial and religious groups promote strife and tend powerfully to obstruct the manifold adjustments required for free, ordered life in a metropolitan, polyglot community."[15] The opinion was deferential: "it would be out of bounds for the judiciary to deny the legislature a choice of policy, provided it is not unrelated to the problem and not forbidden by some explicit limitation on

---

[14] 343 U.S. 250 (1952).

[15] *Id.* at 259.

the State's power."[16] Although the power could be abused, the opinion concluded that this was an inadequate basis for striking down the law.

Beauharnais' holding has been subject to much criticism, and is probably not good law. In dissent, Justice Black argued that Beauharnais was making a "genuine effort" to petition his representatives. In addition, he questioned whether the petition should be regarded as "libel" because it was directed at a group rather than an individual: libel "has provided for punishment of false, malicious, scurrilous charges against individuals, not against huge [groups]."[17] Justice Douglas dissented with a similar argument: "[Today] a white man stands convicted for protesting in unseemly language against our decisions invalidating restrictive covenants. Tomorrow a Negro will be hailed before a court for denouncing lynch law in heated [terms]."[18] Justice Jackson also dissented noting that the case involved mere words: "Punishment of printed words, based on their *tendency* either to cause breach of the peace or injury to persons or groups, in my opinion, is justifiable only if the prosecution survives the "clear and present danger" test. Justice Reed dissented arguing that the words "virtue," "derision" and "obloquy" were unconstitutionally vague.

[B] *R.A.V.*

R.A.V. v. City of St. Paul[19] is the Court's most important pronouncement on hate speech. In that case, R.A.V. a minor, allegedly burned a crudely-made cross inside the fenced yard of a black family. Although R.A.V.'s action might have violated various laws (Minn. Stat. § 609.713(1) (1987) (terroristic threatening), § 609.563 (arson), § 609.595 (Supp.1992) (criminal damage to property)), he was charged, *inter alia*, with violating St. Paul's Bias-Motivated Crime Ordinance which provided as follows:

> Whoever places on public or private property a symbol, object, appellation, characterization or graffiti, including, but not limited to, a burning cross or Nazi swastika, which one knows or has reasonable grounds to know arouses anger, alarm or resentment in others on the basis of race, color, creed, religion or gender commits disorderly conduct and shall be guilty of a misdemeanor.

The Minnesota Supreme Court construed the law as applying only to fighting words.

In an opinion by Justice Scalia, the Court overturned the conviction. The opinion noted that content based and viewpoint based restrictions on speech are generally invalid, and have only been upheld "in a few limited areas, which are 'of such slight social value as a step to truth that any benefit that may be derived from them is clearly outweighed by the social interest in order and morality.' "[20] Justice Scalia

---

[16] *Id.* at 262.

[17] *Id.* at 271–72.

[18] *Id.* at 286.

[19] 505 U.S. 377 (1992).

[20] *Id.* at 385.

pointed specifically to such categories as libel, child pornography and fighting words, and noted "a particular instance of speech can be proscribable on the basis of one feature (*e.g.*, obscenity) but not on the basis of another (*e.g.*, opposition to the city government)" was "commonplace and has found application in many contexts."[21] "[B]urning a flag in violation of an ordinance against outdoor fires could be punishable, whereas burning a flag in violation of an ordinance against dishonoring the flag is not."[22] In other words, government may not regulate speech based on hostility — or favoritism — towards the underlying message.

R.A.V. held that the Minnesota ordinance was facially unconstitutional. Although the ordinance had been limited to fighting words, there was content-based discrimination. A speaker's words could contain "invective, no matter how vicious or severe," unless "they are addressed to one of the specified disfavored topics."[23] The Court held that the First Amendment did not permit "St. Paul to impose special prohibitions on those speakers who express views on disfavored subjects."[24]

The opinion also expressed concern that the ordinance went "beyond mere content discrimination, to actual viewpoint discrimination":

> Displays containing some words — odious racial epithets, for example — would be prohibited to proponents of all views. But "fighting words" that do not themselves invoke race, color, creed, religion, or gender — aspersions upon a person's mother, for example — would seemingly be usable *ad libitum* in the placards of those arguing *in favor* of racial, color, etc., tolerance and equality, but could not be used by those speakers' opponents. One could hold up a sign saying, for example, that all "anti-Catholic bigots" are misbegotten; but not that all "papists" are, for that would insult and provoke violence "on the basis of religion." St. Paul has no such authority to license one side of a debate to fight freestyle, while requiring the other to follow Marquis of Queensberry rules.[25]

The Court concluded that the state cannot silence speech based on its content.

The opinion also rejected the notion that R.A.V.'s speech could be regulated because of its "secondary effects." The City argued that the law was justified because it was designed to "protect against the victimization of a person or persons who are particularly vulnerable because of their membership in a group that historically has been discriminated against.' "[26] But the Court found that the ordinance could not be justified under its "secondary effects" precedent.

Finally, the Court rejected the argument that the ordinance was "narrowly tailored to serve compelling state interests." The City of St. Paul had argued that "the ordinance helps to ensure the basic human rights of members of groups that have historically been subjected to discrimination, including the right of such group

---

[21] *Id.*

[22] *Id.*

[23] *Id.* at 391.

[24] *Id.*

[25] *Id.* at 392.

[26] *Id.* at 394.

members to live in peace where they wish." While the Court agreed that these interests are "compelling," the Court held that "the 'danger of censorship' presented by a facially content-based statute requires that that weapon be employed only where it is *'necessary* to serve the asserted [compelling] interest.' "[27] In this case, the Court found that the ordinance was not "necessary" to serve the interest:

> An ordinance not limited to the favored topics, for example, would have precisely the same beneficial effect. In fact the only interest distinctively served by the content limitation is that of displaying the city council's special hostility towards the particular biases thus singled out. That is precisely what the First Amendment forbids. The politicians of St. Paul are entitled to express that hostility — but not through the means of imposing unique limitations upon speakers who (however benightedly) disagree.[28]

Justice White, joined by justices Blackmun and O'Connor and partially joined by Justice Stevens, concurred in the judgment. He agreed that the ordinance was unconstitutional, but he would have decided the case on overbreadth grounds because the ordinance applied only to displays that one knows or should know will create "anger, alarm or resentment based on racial, ethnic, gender or religious bias."

Justice Blackmun also concurred in the judgment. He would have upheld an ordinance that prohibited fighting words, but he believed that this ordinance went beyond "fighting words to speech protected by the First Amendment."[29] Justice Stevens, joined by justices White and Blackmun, also concurred. He found that the law was overbroad, but he rejected the Court's discussion of "content based" restrictions:

> "[O]ur entire First Amendment jurisprudence creates a regime based on the content of speech. The scope of the First Amendment is determined by the content of expressive [activity]. Whether a magazine is obscene, a gesture a fighting word, or a photograph child pornography is determined, in part, by its content. Even within categories of protected expression, the First Amendment status of speech is fixed by its content."[30]

He viewed the ordinance as not involving content based or viewpoint based restrictions, but as regulating "on the basis of the *harm* the speech causes."[31] "[T]he ordinance regulates only a subcategory of expression that causes *injuries based on* "race, color, creed, religion or gender," not a subcategory that involves *discussions* that concern those characteristics."[32] As a result, he would have upheld the law.

---

[27] *Id.* at 395.

[28] *Id.* at 396.

[29] *Id.* at 416.

[30] *Id.* at 421.

[31] *Id.* at 431.

[32] *Id.* at 433.

[C] Sentence Enhancement

R.A.V. was followed by the holding in *Dawson v. Delaware*.[33] In that case, a capital sentencing proceeding, the state sought to introduce evidence that the defendant was a member of an organization called the Aryan Brotherhood. The trial court admitted the evidence despite Dawson's objection that the evidence was inflammatory and irrelevant, and that its admission would violate his rights under the First and Fourteenth Amendments. After a jury concluded that the aggravating evidence outweighed the mitigating evidence, and recommended that Dawson be sentenced to death, the trial court imposed the death penalty.

The Court reversed on the basis that admission of the evidence violated defendant's right of association. Even if Dawson belonged to a racist group, "those beliefs, so far as we can determine, had no relevance to the sentencing proceeding in this case."[34] The murder victim was white and there was no linkage between racial hatred and the killing. The Court went on to note that this type of evidence might be relevant in some cases, but the relevance was not shown in this case:

> Associational evidence might serve a legitimate purpose in showing that a defendant represents a future danger to society. A defendant's membership in an organization that endorses the killing of any identifiable group, for example, might be relevant to a jury's inquiry into whether the defendant will be dangerous in the future. Other evidence concerning a defendant's associations might be relevant in proving other aggravating circumstances. But the inference which the jury was invited to draw in this case tended to prove nothing more than the abstract beliefs of the Delaware chapter. [O]n the present record one is left with the feeling that the Aryan Brotherhood evidence was employed simply because the jury would find these beliefs morally reprehensible. . . .[35]

Justice Thomas dissented, arguing that Delaware law allows a jury to consider "all relevant evidence in aggravation or mitigation" relating to either the crime or the "character and propensities" of the defendant. He found that the evidence made it clear "that the Aryan Brotherhood does not exist merely to facilitate formulation of abstract racist thoughts, but to 'respon[d]' to gangs of racial minorities.[36] The evidence thus tends to establish that Dawson has not been 'a well-behaved and well-adjusted prisoner' which itself is an indication of future dangerousness."[37]

Dawson was followed and qualified by the holding in *Wisconsin v. Mitchell*.[38] Mitchell's sentence for aggravated battery was enhanced because he intentionally selected his victim because of the victim's race. The facts showed that Mitchell gathered with a group of young black men and boys at an apartment complex, and discussed a scene from the motion picture "Mississippi Burning," in which a white

---

[33] 503 U.S. 159 (1992).

[34] *Id.* at 166.

[35] *Id.* at 167.

[36] *Id.* at 173.

[37] *Id.* at 173–74.

[38] 508 U.S. 476 (1993).

man beat a young black boy who was praying. Mitchell then asked the group: "Do you all feel hyped up to move on some white people?" When a young white boy passed by on the other side of the street, Mitchell said: "You all want to fuck somebody up? There goes a white boy; go get him." Mitchell counted to three and pointed in the boy's direction. The group beat the boy severely and stole his tennis shoes leaving him unconscious and in a coma.

Mitchell was convicted of aggravated battery, an offense that normally carries with it a maximum sentence of two years' imprisonment. However, because the jury found that Mitchell had intentionally selected his victim because of the boy's race, the maximum sentence was increased to seven years under § 939.645. That section provided for enhancement of the maximum penalty for an offense whenever the defendant "[i]ntentionally selects the person against whom the crime [is] is committed [because] of the race, religion, color, disability, sexual orientation, national origin or ancestry of that person." § 939.645(1)(b). The Circuit Court sentenced Mitchell to four years' imprisonment for the aggravated battery.

In an opinion by Chief Justice Rehnquist, the Court upheld the penalty enhancement. The Court emphasized that sentencing judges have historically considered "a wide variety of factors in addition to evidence bearing on guilt in determining what sentence to impose on a convicted defendant. [Thus,] in many States the commission of a murder, or other capital offense, for pecuniary gain is a separate aggravating circumstance under the capital sentencing statute."[39] Although the Court expressed concern about letting a sentencing judge consider a defendant's abstract beliefs, the Court held that *R.A.V.* did not preclude the penalty enhancement:

> [T]he Wisconsin statute singles out for enhancement bias-inspired conduct because this conduct is thought to inflict greater individual and societal harm. For example[,] bias-motivated crimes are more likely to provoke retaliatory crimes, inflict distinct emotional harms on their victims, and incite community unrest. The State's desire to redress these perceived harms provides an adequate explanation for its penalty-enhancement provision over and above mere disagreement with offenders' beliefs or biases. As Blackstone said long ago, "it is but reasonable that among crimes of different natures those should be most severely punished, which are the most destructive of the public safety and happiness." 4 W. BLACKSTONE, COMMENTARIES *16.[40]

The Court rejected allegations that the Wisconsin statute was unconstitutionally overbroad: "The sort of chill envisioned here is far more attenuated and unlikely than that contemplated in traditional 'overbreadth' cases. We must conjure up a vision of a Wisconsin citizen suppressing his unpopular bigoted opinions for fear that if he later commits an offense covered by the statute, these opinions will be offered at trial to establish that he selected his victim on account of the victim's protected status, thus qualifying him for penalty enhancement."[41] The Court also

---

[39] *Id.* at 485.

[40] *Id.*

[41] *Id.* at 488–89.

held that the "evidentiary use of speech" was permissible in a case like this to "establish the elements of a crime or to prove motive or intent."[42]

[D]   Campus Speech Codes

Many colleges and universities toward the end of the 20th Century enacted speech codes designed to prohibit so-called "hate speech." In general, these codes have been struck down as unconstitutional. For example, in *Doe v. University of Michigan*,[43] the court struck down the University of Michigan's anti-harassment code as vague and overbroad. Likewise, in *UMW Post, Inc. v. Board of Regents of University of Wisconsin*,[44] the court struck down the University of Wisconsin's prohibition against discriminatory epithets on similar grounds.

In general, these codes suffer from the same types of problems found with the Minneapolis ordinance involved in *R.A.V.*, including vagueness and overbreadth. In addition, they often impose "content-based" or "viewpoint-based" restrictions on speech. For example, suppose that a law school decides to adopt the following policy:

> The law faculty is unanimously committed to creating and maintaining a non-hostile, non-threatening learning environment for all students. The faculty unanimously urges all members of the law school faculty to take special care to avoid offensive statements or behavior which reasonably can be perceived as negative stereotyping or as racial, religious, sexual or other harassment. Any such statements or conduct would be unprofessional and inconsistent with the fundamental values of our law school.

In looking at the policy, one might ask whether the policy is "aspirational" or "enforceable" by sanctions. If it is intended to be enforceable, the policy is probably unconstitutional. Not only is the policy vague (*i.e.*, what do the words "non-hostile" and "non-threatening" mean, and what about the words "reasonably can be perceived as negative stereotyping?) and overbroad (does the state really have the power to prohibit negative stereotyping?), it contains content-based and viewpoint-based restrictions on speech. One can "positively" stereotype on the basis of race or sex, but cannot "negatively" stereotype.

In addition, many of these "codes" make very little sense. For example, the "code" referred to in the prior paragraph would require the teacher to respond to all of the following statements made in a constitutional law class in a discussion about affirmative action:

  – A black student states that whites have historically repressed blacks;

  – A female student states that men have historically repressed women;

  – A caucasian, male student states that a woman's place is in the home.

Although the drafters of the ordinance might not have intended to apply it to classroom discussions, the code applies by its terms to such discussions and

---

[42] *Id.* at 489.

[43] 721 F. Supp. 852 (E.D. Mich. 1989).

[44] 774 F. Supp. 1163 (E.D. Wis. 1991).

requires the teacher to take action. But all of these statements are relevant to a discussion of affirmative action, and some are highly relevant and worthwhile by any standard. The black student's statement and the woman's statement make important statements about societal history (even though they involve "negative stereotyping"). Moreover, even if the teacher views the Caucasian male's student as objectionable, it is far preferable to allow students to say what they think, and to let other students respond to offensive statementsthanto attempt to suppress the statements. In the final analysis, not only is the code unconstitutional, it is bad policy.

POINTS TO REMEMBER

- Despite the Court's earlier holding in *Beauharnais*, even "hate speech" may be protected under the First Amendment.

- Government may not engage in "viewpoint-based" or "content-based" discrimination against ideas that it finds repugnant.

- A defendant's sentence may not be enhanced when he holds repugnant views that are unrelated to the crime and the harm caused.

---

§ 7.03 CAMPAIGN FINANCE LAWS

First Amendment doctrine regarding political campaign financing has been the function of intense debate and unpredictable outcomes. Although political speech historically has been most valued under the First Amendment, significant concerns exist regarding the influence of money upon the political process. Case law has attempted to reconcile the tension between money as the enabler of electioneering and the corrupter of electoral integrity.

[A] Contribution and Expenditure Limitations.

The seminal decision is *Buckley v. Valeo*,[45] a per curiam opinion. That case involved a challenge to the Federal Election Campaign Act of 1971 (Act), and related provisions of the Internal Revenue Code of 1954, all as amended in 1974. The Act contained a number of different provisions including the following:

- a prohibition that prevented any person from giving more than $1,000 to any single candidate for an election campaign;

- a prohibition that prevented individuals from contributing more than $25,000 in a single year;

- a provision (Section 608(b)(2)) which allowed "political committees," to contribute no more than $5,000 to any candidate with respect to any election for federal office;

- A provision that excluded from the definition of contribution "the value of services provided without compensation by individuals who

---

[45] 424 U.S. 1 (1976).

volunteer a portion or all of their time on behalf of a candidate or political committee." Certain expenses incurred by persons in providing volunteer services to a candidate are exempt from the $1,000 ceiling only to the extent that they do not exceed $500. These expenses were expressly limited to (1) "the use of real or personal property and the cost of invitations, food, and beverages, voluntarily provided by an individual to a candidate in rendering voluntary personal services on the individual's residential premises for candidate-related activities"; (2) "the sale of any food or beverage by a vendor for use in a candidate's campaign at a charge (at least equal to cost but) less than the normal comparable charge"; and (3) "any unreimbursed payment for travel expenses made by an individual who on his own behalf volunteers his personal services to a candidate."

- An overall $25,000 limitation on total contributions by an individual during any calendar year.

- A provision (Section 608(e)(1)) that "[n]o person may make any expenditure [relative] to a clearly identified candidate during a calendar year which, when added to all other expenditures made by such person during the year advocating the election or defeat of such candidate, exceeds $1,000."

- Limits on expenditures by a candidate "from his personal funds, or the personal funds of his immediate family, in connection with his campaigns during any calendar year." § 608(a)(1). These ceilings varied from $50,000 for Presidential or Vice Presidential candidates to $35,000 for senatorial candidates, and $25,000 for most candidates for the House of Representatives.

- A limitation (Section 608(c)) on overall campaign expenditures by candidates seeking nomination for election and election to federal office. Presidential candidates could spend $10,000,000 in seeking nomination for office and an additional $20,000,000 in the general election campaign. The ceiling on senatorial campaigns was pegged to the size of the voting-age population of the State with minimum dollar amounts applicable to campaigns in States with small populations. In senatorial primary elections, the limit was the greater of eight cents multiplied by the voting-age population or $100,000, and in the general election the limit was increased to 12 cents multiplied by the voting-age population or $150,000. The Act imposed blanket $70,000 limitations on both primary campaigns and general election campaigns for the House of Representatives with the exception that the senatorial ceiling applied to campaigns in States entitled to only one Representative. These ceilings were to be adjusted upwards at the beginning of each calendar year by the average percentage rise in the consumer price index for the 12 preceding months.

- Section 434(e) required "[e]very person (other than a political committee or candidate) who makes contributions or expenditures" aggregating over $100 in a calendar year "other than by contribution to a political committee or candidate" to file a statement with the Commission.

The Court quickly held that campaign finance laws implicate First Amendment interests because they involve discussions regarding public issues and the qualifications of candidates, and the Court held that such discussions are essential in a free society: "In a republic where the people are sovereign, the ability of the citizenry to make informed choices among candidates for office is essential, for the identities of those who are elected will inevitably shape the course that we follow as a nation."[46] In addition, the Court reiterated the fundamental idea that the " First Amendment protects political association as well as political expression."[47]

The Court then rejected the argument that the Act's contribution and expenditure provisions should be treated as regulations of "conduct" rather than "speech." The Court found that "the giving and spending of money" produces communication that sometimes involves speech alone, sometimes involves conduct, and sometimes involves a combination of the two.[48] Moreover, the Court found that, even if such activities involved conduct rather than speech, the *O'Brien* test could not be satisfied because campaign finance laws suppress communication. "[I]t is beyond dispute that the interest in regulating the alleged 'conduct' of giving or spending money 'arises in some measure because the communication allegedly integral to the conduct is itself thought to be harmful.' "[49]

The Court also rejected the argument that the Act's contribution and expenditure limitations should be treated as valid time, place, and manner restrictions. The Court noted that modern communication methods require the expenditure of large amounts of money, and that a restriction on expenditures "necessarily reduces the quantity of expression by restricting the number of issues discussed, the depth of their exploration, or the size of the audience reached."[50]

The Court then focused separately on the "contribution" limitations and the "expenditure" limitations. The Court found that the expenditure limitations involved "substantial rather than merely theoretical restraints" on political speech. The Court noted that the $1,000 ceiling on spending "relative to a clearly identified candidate," would exclude virtually all citizens and groups (except candidates, political parties, and the institutional press) "from any significant use of the most effective modes of communication." The Court was concerned even about the limitations on expenditures by campaign organizations and political parties, noting that they would have restricted the scope of a number of congressional and Presidential campaigns and would have constrained candidates who raised sums in excess of the spending ceiling.

The Court viewed the "contribution" limitations as having a more limited impact on free expression. Although a contribution "serves as a general expression of

---

[46] *Id.* at 14.

[47] *Id.* at 15.

[48] *Id.*

[49] *Id.* at 17.

[50] *Id.* at 19.

support for [a] candidate and his views," it "does not communicate the underlying basis for the support."[51] The Court noted that the "quantity of communication by the contributor does not increase perceptibly with the size of his contribution, since the expression rests solely on the undifferentiated, symbolic act of contributing. At most, the size of the contribution provides a very rough index of the intensity of the contributor's support for the candidate."[52] In addition, in order for contributions to become speech, they require communication by someone else (the candidate or the candidate's campaign). As a result, the Court concluded that a limitation on the amount of money a person may give to a candidate or campaign organization involves less direct restraint on political communication because it permits the symbolic expression of support and does not otherwise infringe the contributor's right to publicly discuss candidates and issues.

Nevertheless, the Court recognized that contributions play an "important role" in "financing political campaigns" and that "contribution restrictions can have a severe impact on political dialogue if the limitations prevented candidates and political committees from amassing the resources necessary for effective advocacy."[53] However, the Court found that the Act's contribution limitations did not have a "dramatic adverse effect on the funding of campaigns and political associations."[54] If the size of contributions was restricted, candidates and political committees would simply be forced to raise funds from a greater number of persons. Those who wanted to exceed the limits could make direct expenditures on behalf of the candidate (as opposed to contributions).

The Court expressed greater concerns about the contribution limitations and their impact on associational freedoms. The Court found that making "a contribution, like joining a political party, serves to affiliate a person with a candidate. In addition, it enables like-minded persons to pool their resources in furtherance of common political goals."[55] However, the Court found that the Act's $1,000 limitation on independent expenditures was so low as to prevent most candidates "from effectively amplifying the voice of their adherents." As a result, the Court found that the expenditure ceilings were more troubling than the expenditure limitations.

In analyzing the contribution limitations, the court noted that both the right to associate and the right to participate in political activities are not absolute, and that interferences with those rights can be sustained "if the State demonstrates a sufficiently important interest and employs means closely drawn to avoid unnecessary abridgment of associational freedoms."[56] The Court found a "sufficiently important interest" in the desire to limit the actuality and appearance of corruption. "To the extent that large contributions are given to secure a political *quid pro quo* from current and potential office holders, the integrity of our system

---

[51] *Id.* at 22.

[52] *Id.* at 21.

[53] *Id.*

[54] *Id.*

[55] *Id.* at 23.

[56] *Id.* at 25.

of representative democracy is undermined. [Of] almost equal concern [is] the appearance of corruption stemming from public awareness of the opportunities for abuse inherent in a regime of large individual financial contributions."[57] The Court rejected the argument that bribery laws and narrowly drawn disclosure requirements constituted a less restrictive means of dealing with *quid pro quo* arrangements. The Court concluded that such laws deal with only the most blatant corruption and that the Act's contribution limits focus more precisely on the problem.

After outlining its approach to expenditure and contribution limitations, the Court then considered the individual sections of the law beginning with Section 608(b)(2) which allowed "political committees" to contribute up to $5,000 to any candidate with respect to any election for federal office. The Court upheld the provision noting that, rather than undermining freedom of association, the "provision enhances the opportunity of bona fide groups to participate in the election process, and the registration, contribution, and candidate conditions serve the permissible purpose of preventing individuals from evading the applicable contribution limitations by labeling themselves committees."[58]

The Court then upheld the statutory provision relating to volunteers' incidental expenses. Although the Act excluded from the definition of contribution "the value of services provided without compensation by individuals who volunteer a portion or all of their time on behalf of a candidate or political committee," it included expenditures made to host a private fundraising event on a candidate's behalf. Given that the Court upheld limits on the amounts that could be contributed to political campaigns, the Court found these provisions to be a "constitutionally acceptable accommodation of Congress' valid interest in encouraging citizen participation in political campaigns while continuing to guard against the corrupting potential of large financial contributions to candidates. [I]n-kind assistance in the form of food or beverages to be resold to raise funds or consumed by the participants in such an event provides material financial assistance to a candidate."[59]

The Court also upheld the overall $25,000 limitation on total contributions by an individual during any calendar year. The Court found that the provision was "quite modest" and that it prevented "evasion of the $1,000 contribution limitation by a person who might otherwise contribute massive amounts of money to a particular candidate through the use of unearmarked contributions to political committees likely to contribute to that candidate, or huge contributions to the candidate's political party."[60] The Court found that any imposition on associational freedoms was "limited" and "no more than a corollary of the basic individual contribution limitation that we have found to be constitutionally valid."[61]

---

[57]　*Id.* at 26.

[58]　*Id.* at 35.

[59]　*Id.* at 36.

[60]　*Id.* at 38.

[61]　*Id.*

The Court then struck down Section 608(e)(1) which provided that "[n]o person may make any expenditure [relative] to a clearly identified candidate during a calendar year which, when added to all other expenditures made by such person during the year advocating the election or defeat of such candidate, exceeds $1,000." Given the cost of advertising, the Court found that this section made it a federal crime "to place a single one-quarter page advertisement 'relative to a clearly identified candidate' in a major metropolitan newspaper." The Court held that the governmental interest in preventing corruption and the appearance of corruption was "inadequate" to justify this provision. "The absence of prearrangement and coordination of an expenditure with the candidate or his agent not only undermines the value of the expenditure to the candidate, but also alleviates the danger that expenditures will be given as a *quid pro quo* for improper commitments from the candidate."[62]

The Court also rejected the argument that the government had the right to equalize the resources of individuals and groups and "the relative ability of individuals and groups to influence the outcome of elections." The Court found that the "concept that government may restrict the speech of some elements of our society in order to enhance the relative voice of others is wholly foreign to the First Amendment. [The] First Amendment's protection against governmental abridgment of free expression cannot properly be made to depend on a person's financial ability to engage in public discussion."[63]

The Court also struck down the limitation on expenditures by candidates from personal or family resources. The Court concluded that this restriction imposed a substantial restraint on candidates, and that a candidate has the right "vigorously and tirelessly to advocate his own election and the election of other candidates. Indeed, it is of particular importance that candidates have the unfettered opportunity to make their views known so that the electorate may intelligently evaluate the candidates' personal qualities and their positions on vital public issues before choosing among them on election day."[64] The Court noted that the interest in preventing actual and apparent corruption was insufficient to justify this restriction. By relying on personal funds, candidates reduce their reliance on "outside contributions and thereby [counteract] the coercive pressures and attendant risks of abuse to which the Act's contribution limitations are directed."[65] In addition, the asserted interest of equalizing the relative financial resources of candidates competing for elective office could not justify the provision.

The Court also struck down the limitation on overall campaign expenditures by candidates seeking nomination for election and election to federal office. The Court found that the governmental interest in alleviating the corrupting influence of large contributions was valid, and that it had already sustained limitations on the amount of contributions by a single donor, but concluded that the "the financial resources available to a candidate's campaign, like the number of volunteers recruited, will

---

[62] *Id.* at 47.

[63] *Id.* at 49.

[64] *Id.* at 52.

[65] *Id.*

normally vary with the size and intensity of the candidate's support. There is nothing invidious, improper, or unhealthy in permitting such funds to be spent to carry the candidate's message to the electorate."[66] The Court rejected the argument that the government had an interest in "reducing the allegedly skyrocketing costs of political campaigns." "The First Amendment denies government the power to determine that spending to promote one's political views is wasteful, excessive, or unwise."[67]

The Court then upheld the reporting and disclosure requirements. Relying on *NAACP v. Alabama*, the Court found that the requirements must pass "exacting scrutiny." and that there must be a "substantial relation" between the governmental interest and the information required to be disclosed. The Court did express concern that the disclosure requirements might have a "deterrent effect on the exercise of First Amendment rights." "The right to join together 'for the advancement of beliefs and ideas,' is diluted if it does not include the right to pool money through contributions, for funds are often essential if 'advocacy' is to be truly or optimally 'effective.' "[68] In addition, the Court expressed concern that "the invasion of privacy of belief" can be as significant when information regarding the giving and spending of money is disclosed as when it concerns the joining of organizations, for "[f]inancial transactions can reveal much about a person's activities, associations, and beliefs."[69] The Court concluded that its past decisions have not drawn fine lines between contributors and members but have treated them interchangeably. Nevertheless, the Court found that the governmental interests were sufficient to outweigh the possibility of infringement:

> The governmental interests sought to be vindicated by the disclosure requirements are [of] magnitude. They fall into three categories. First, disclosure provides the electorate with information "as to where political campaign money comes from and how it is spent by the candidate" in order to aid the voters in evaluating those who seek federal office. [The] sources of a candidate's financial support also alert the voter to the interests to which a candidate is most likely to be responsive and thus facilitate predictions of future performance in office. Second, disclosure requirements deter actual corruption and avoid the appearance of corruption by exposing large contributions and expenditures to the light of publicity. [A] public armed with information about a candidate's most generous supporters is better able to detect any post-election special favors that may be given in return. Third, and not least significant, recordkeeping, reporting, and disclosure requirements are an essential means of gathering the data necessary to detect violations of the contribution limitations described above.[70]

---

[66] *Id.* at 56.

[67] *Id.* at 57.

[68] *Id.* at 65.

[69] *Id.* at 66.

[70] *Id.* at 66-69.

Finding "substantial governmental interests" supporting the disclosure requirements, the Court then balanced those interests against the "burden" that disclosure requirements impose on individual rights. The Court recognized that, by requiring public disclosure of contributions to candidates and political parties, the Act would deter some individuals from contributing for fear of harassment or retaliation. Nevertheless, the Court found that the disclosure provisions constituted "the least restrictive means of curbing the evils of campaign ignorance and corruption that Congress found to exist."[71] The Court upheld the restrictions even as applied to minor parties and independent candidates. The Court found that the governmental interest in disclosure was lower for minor parties because they had little chance of winning elections, and they usually had "definite and publicized viewpoints" so that there was "less need to inform the voters of the interests that specific candidates represent."[72] Nevertheless, the Court found that a minor party could "play a significant role in an election. Even when a minor-party candidate has little or no chance of winning, he may be encouraged by major-party interests to divert votes from other major-party contenders."[73] In addition, the Court found that the disclosure provisions increase "the fund of information concerning those who support the candidates" and that "informational interest can be as strong as it is in coordinated spending, for disclosure helps voters to define more of the candidates' constituencies."[74]

The Court did express concern about whether the disclosure provisions were overbroad since they swept in contributions as low as $10, and the Court feared that contributors of relatively small amounts may be "especially sensitive to recording or disclosure of their political preferences." Nevertheless, although the "strict requirements may well discourage participation by some citizens in the political process," the Court held that it would not "require Congress to establish that it has chosen the highest reasonable threshold.[75] The line is necessarily a judgmental decision, best left in the context of this complex legislation to congressional discretion."[76]

The Court also upheld the provisions providing for public financing of presidential election campaigns. Section 9006 established a Presidential Election Campaign Fund (Fund), financed from general revenues based on designations by individual taxpayers, to finance (1) party nominating conventions, (2) general election campaigns, and (3) primary campaigns. The law distinguished between "major," "minor," and "new" parties. A major party was defined as a party whose candidate for President in the most recent election received 25% or more of the popular vote. A minor party was defined as a party whose candidate received at least 5% but less than 25% of the vote at the most recent election. All other parties were new parties, including both newly created parties and those receiving less than 5% of the vote in the last election.

---

[71] *Id.* at 68.

[72] *Id.* at 70.

[73] *Id.*

[74] *Id.* at 81.

[75] *Id.* at 83.

[76] *Id.*

Major parties were entitled to $2,000,000 to defray their national committee Presidential nominating convention expenses, but were required to limit total expenditures to that amount, and could not use any of this money to benefit a particular candidate or delegate. A minor party received a portion of the major-party entitlement determined by the ratio of the votes received by the party's candidate in the last election to the average of the votes received by the major parties' candidates. The amounts given to the parties and the expenditure limit were adjusted for inflation, using 1974 as the base year. No financing was provided to new parties, nor was there any express provision for financing independent candidates or parties not holding a convention.

For general election campaign expenses, § 9004(a)(1) gave each major-party candidate $20 million, an amount that was adjusted for inflation. Those receiving funds were required to promise not to incur additional expenses (beyond the $20 million) and not to accept private contributions except to the extent that the fund was insufficient to provide the full $20 million. Minor-party candidates were also entitled to funding, again based on the ratio of the vote received by the party's candidate in the preceding election to the average of the major-party candidates. Minor-party candidates were also required to promise that they would not incur additional campaign expenses and that they would only accept private contributions as needed to make up any deficiency in the public funding grant. New-party candidates received no money prior to the general election, but any candidate who polled 5% or more of the popular vote in an election was entitled to post-election payments according to the formula applicable to minor-party candidates. Similarly, minor-party candidates were entitled to post-election funds if they received a greater percentage of the average major-party vote than their party's candidate did in the preceding election.

The law also established a third account, the Presidential Primary Matching Payment Account. This funding was intended to aid campaigns by candidates seeking Presidential nomination "by a political party" in "primary elections." The law required that the candidate raise at least $5,000 in each of 20 States, counting only the first $250 from each person contributing to the candidate. In addition, the candidate was required to abide by specified spending limits. Funding was provided according to a matching formula: each qualified candidate was entitled to a sum equal to the total private contributions received, disregarding contributions from any person to the extent that total contributions to the candidate by that person exceed $250. Payments to any candidate under this provision 96 could not exceed 50% of the overall expenditure ceiling accepted by the candidate.

The Court upheld the public financing provisions finding that public financing provides a "means of eliminating the improper influence of large private contributions" and therefore furthers a "significant governmental interest." In addition, the Court found that Congress could permissibly choose to relieve "major-party Presidential candidates from the rigors of soliciting private contributions." In regard to the claim that the law discriminated against candidates nominated by "minor" parties, the Court found that "Congress' interest in not funding hopeless candidacies with large sums of public money, necessarily justifies the withholding of public assistance from candidates without significant public support. Thus, Congress may legitimately require 'some preliminary showing of a significant modicum of support,' as an eligibility requirement for public funds." The Court also found that there was a governmental interest "against providing artificial incentives to 'splintered parties and unrestrained factionalism.'"

Chief Justice Burger concurred in part and dissented in part. He disagreed with the Court's holding regarding the disclosure of small contributions. In general, he regarded "disclosure" provisions as a "salutary and constitutional remedy" for the "ills" about which Congress was concerned, and he regarded disclosure of contributions by individuals and by entities particularly corporations and labor unions as "an effective means of revealing the type of political support that is sometimes coupled with expectations of special favors or rewards." But he expressed concern about the exceptionally low limits ($10) contained in the law. "Rank-and-file union members or rising junior executives may now think twice before making even modest contributions to a candidate who is disfavored by the union or management hierarchy. Similarly, potential contributors may well decline to take the obvious risks entailed in making a reportable contribution to the opponent of a well-entrenched incumbent." He concluded that the public's right to know was not "absolute when its exercise reveals private political convictions. [N]o legitimate public interest has been shown in forcing the disclosure of modest contributions that are the prime support of new, unpopular, or unfashionable political causes. There is no realistic possibility that such modest donations will have a corrupting influence especially on parties that enjoy only 'minor' status."

Chief Justice Burger also rejected the Court's distinction between the "communication inherent in political contributions from the speech aspects of political expenditures." He believed that candidates and contributors "spend money on political activity because they wish to communicate ideas, and their constitutional interest in doing so is precisely the same whether they or someone else utters the words." He argued that "freedom of association and freedom of expression were two peas from the same pod," and that the contribution restrictions were "hardly incidental" because they "foreclose some candidacies" and "alter the nature of some electoral contests drastically." He argued that contribution limitations can only be justified by "the very strongest of state interests" and he believed that other alternatives should be adequate.

He also would have struck down the system of matching grants arguing that it makes "a candidate's ability to amass private funds the sole criterion for eligibility for public funds." He believed that such an arrangement "can put at serious disadvantage a candidate with a potentially large, widely diffused but poor constituency. The ability of a candidate's supporters to help pay for his campaign cannot be equated with their willingness to cast a ballot for him."

Chief Justice Burger also expressed concern about the fact that the remaining (valid) provisions of the Act caused inequity.

> A candidate with substantial personal resources is now given by the Court a clear advantage over his less affluent opponents, who are constrained by law in fundraising, because the Court holds that the ' First Amendment cannot tolerate' any restrictions on spending. Minority parties, whose situation is difficult enough under an Act that excludes them from public funding, are prevented from accepting large single-donor contribu-

tions. At the same time the Court sustains the provision aimed at broadening the base of political support by requiring candidates to seek a greater number of small contributors, it sustains the unrealistic disclosure thresholds of $10 and $100 that I believe will deter those hoped-for small contributions. Minor parties must now compete for votes against two major parties whose expenditures will be vast.

Justice White also concurred in part and dissented in part, arguing that he would have upheld the expenditure limitations because he viewed them as "reinforcing" the contribution limits and as helping "eradicate the hazard of corruption." He argued that, without a limitation on total expenditures,

> campaign costs will inevitably and endlessly escalate. Pressure to raise funds will constantly build and with it the temptation to resort in 'emergencies' to those sources of large sums, who, history shows, are sufficiently confident of not being caught to risk flouting contribution limits. [S]uccessful candidates will also be saved from large, overhanging campaign debts which must be paid off with money raised while holding public office and at a time when they are already preparing or thinking about the next campaign. The danger to the public interest in such situations is self-evident. [T]he corrupt use of money by candidates is as much to be feared as the corrosive influence of large contributions. [U]nlimited money tempts people to spend it on *whatever* money can buy to influence an election. [L]imiting the total that can be spent will ease the candidate's understandable obsession with fundraising, and so free him and his staff to communicate in more places and ways unconnected with the fundraising function."[77]

Justice White also took issue with the Court's decision to invalidate § 608(a) which limited the amount of money that a candidate or his family may spend on his campaign. "[By] limiting the importance of personal wealth, § 608(a) helps to assure that only individuals with a modicum of support from others will be viable candidates. This in turn would tend to discourage any notion that the outcome of elections is primarily a function of money."

[B]　Corporate Contributions and Expenditures

Should the expenditures of corporations be treated differently than the expenditures of individuals? *Austin v. Michigan Chamber of Commerce*,[78] involved the constitutionality of Section 54(1) of the Michigan Campaign Finance Act. That Act prohibited corporations from making contributions and independent expenditures in connection with state candidate elections. Under the law, an expenditure was regarded as "independent" if it was "not made at the direction of, or under the control of, another person and if the expenditure is not a contribution to a committee." The Act exempted from this general prohibition against corporate political spending any expenditure made from a segregated fund. A corporation

---

[77] *Id.* at 265.

[78] 494 U.S. 652 (1990).

could solicit contributions for its political fund only from an enumerated list of persons associated with the corporation.

The Michigan State Chamber of Commerce (Chamber), a nonprofit corporation, challenged the statute. The Chamber had more than 8,000 members, most of which were for-profit corporations. The Chamber received its money from annual member dues. The Chamber's purposes were to promote economic conditions favorable to private enterprise; to analyze, compile, and disseminate information about laws of interest to the business community and to publicize to the government the views of the business community on such matters; to train and educate its members; to foster ethical business practices; to collect data on, and investigate matters of, social, civic, and economic importance to the State; to receive contributions and to make expenditures for political purposes and to perform any other lawful political activity; and to coordinate activities with other similar organizations. During a special election to fill a vacancy in the Michigan House of Representatives, the Chamber sought to use general treasury funds to advertise on behalf of one candidate. Since the law made the expenditure punishable as a felony, the Chamber sued to prevent enforcement of the Act, arguing that the restriction on expenditures is unconstitutional under both the First and the Fourteenth Amendments.

In an opinion by Justice Marshall, the Court upheld the law. The Court began by referencing its prior decision in *FEC v. Massachusetts Citizens for Life, Inc. (MCFL)*.[79] That case held that a statute requiring corporations to make independent political expenditures only through "special segregated funds" burdens corporate freedom of expression. The Court reasoned that the "small nonprofit corporation" "would face certain organizational and financial hurdles in establishing and administering a segregated political fund," hurdles that they might not be able to bear and that created a disincentive for them to engage in political speech. The law required the corporation to appoint a treasurer for the fund, maintain records of all contributions, file a statement of organization with information about the fund, and update the statement periodically. Corporations were only allowed to solicit contributions to their segregated funds from "members" which did not include persons who merely contributed to or indicated support for the organization.

In *Austin*, the Court found that Michigan's segregated fund requirement was similar to the Massachusetts requirement considered in *MCFL*, and similarly burdened the Chamber's freedom of expression. Although the requirements did not stifle corporate speech entirely, the Court held that they must be justified by a compelling state interest. In that case, Michigan argued that "the unique legal and economic characteristics of corporations necessitate some regulation of their political expenditures to avoid corruption or the appearance of corruption." The Court noted that state law granted corporations "special advantages — such as limited liability, perpetual life, and favorable treatment of the accumulation and distribution of assets — that enhance their ability to attract capital and to deploy their resources in ways that maximize the return on their shareholders' investments. These state-created advantages not only allow corporations to play a

---

[79] 479 U.S. 238 (1986).

dominant role in the Nation's economy, but also permit them to use 'resources amassed in the economic marketplace' " to obtain "an unfair advantage in the political marketplace." Relying on *MCFL*, the Court noted that this political advantage can be unfair because:

> [t]he resources in the treasury of a business corporation [are] not an indication of popular support for the corporation's political ideas. They reflect instead the economically motivated decisions of investors and customers. The availability of these resources may make a corporation a formidable political presence, even though the power of the corporation may be no reflection of the power of its ideas.

As a result, the Court held that "the compelling governmental interest in preventing corruption support[s] the restriction of the influence of political war chests funneled through the corporate form.

Whereas in *Buckley*, the Court had focused on the danger of "financial *quid pro quo*" corruption, the *Austin* opinion focused on what it referred to as "a different type of corruption in the political arena: the corrosive and distorting effects of immense aggregations of wealth that are accumulated with the help of the corporate form and that have little or no correlation to the public's support for the corporation's political ideas." The Michigan law was not designed "to equalize the relative influence of speakers on elections," but to make sure that "expenditures reflect actual public support for the political ideas espoused by corporations." The Court held that this restriction was a sufficiently compelling rationale to support restrictions on independent expenditures by corporation. The Court also found that the restriction was "precisely targeted to eliminate the distortion caused by corporate spending while also allowing corporations to express their political views. . . . Because persons contributing to [segregated] funds understand that their money will be used solely for political purposes, the speech generated accurately reflects contributors' support for the corporation's political views."

The Court rejected the Chamber's argument that the law was "substantially overinclusive" because it swept in "closely held corporations that do not possess vast reservoirs of capital." The Court noted that, although

> some closely held corporations, just as some publicly held ones, may not have accumulated significant amounts of wealth, they receive from the State the special benefits conferred by the corporate structure and present the potential for distorting the political process. This potential for distortion justifies § 54(1)'s general applicability to all corporations. The section therefore is not substantially overbroad.

The Court then rejected the argument that, although the law could be applied to for-profit corporations, it should not be applied to a "nonprofit ideological corporation like a chamber of commerce." The Chamber relied on *MCFL* where the Court held that the nonprofit organization involved in that case had "features more akin to voluntary political associations than business firms, and therefore should not have to bear burdens on independent spending solely because of [its] incorporated status." The Court noted that the Chamber engaged in a variety of non-political purposes, including the fact that it "compiles and disseminates information relating to social, civic, and economic conditions, trains and educates its members, and promotes ethical business practices." As a result, the Court found that the Chamber's nonpolitical activities distinguish it from *MCFL*.

The Court also distinguished *MCFL* on the basis of an:

> absence of 'shareholders or other persons affiliated so as to have a claim on its assets or earnings. This difference ensured that persons connected with the organization would have no economic disincentive for disassociating with it if they disagreed with its political activity. But, although the Chamber lacked members, its members might also be reluctant to withdraw because they wanted to benefit from the Chamber's nonpolitical programs and to establish contacts with other members of the business community. Nevertheless, the Court concluded that the Chamber's political agenda was "sufficiently distinct from its educational and outreach programs that members who disagree with the former may continue to pay dues to participate in the latter."

Finally, the Court distinguished *MCFL* on the basis of that "organization's independence from the influence of business corporations." "MCFL [had] a policy of not accepting contributions from, business corporations. Thus it could not '[serve] as [a conduit] for the type of direct spending that creates a threat to the political marketplace.'" The Court noted that three-quarters of the Chamber's members were:

> business corporations, whose political contributions and expenditures can constitutionally be regulated by the State. [Business corporations] could therefore circumvent [campaign finance] restriction by funneling money through the Chamber's general treasury. Because the Chamber accepts money from for-profit corporations, it could, absent application of § 54(1), serve as a conduit for corporate political spending. In sum, the Chamber does not possess the features that would compel the State to exempt it from restriction on independent political expenditures.

The Court also rejected the Chamber's claim that the law was underinclusive because it did "not regulate the independent expenditures of unincorporated labor unions." The Court noted that unions can "amass large treasuries," but noted that:

> they do so without the significant state-conferred advantages of the corporate structure; corporations are "by far the most prominent example of entities that enjoy legal advantages enhancing their ability to accumulate wealth." The desire to counterbalance those advantages unique to the corporate form is the State's compelling interest in this case; thus, excluding from the statute's coverage unincorporated entities that also have the capacity to accumulate wealth "does not undermine its justification for regulating corporations."

In addition, the Court noted that

> "labor unions differ from corporations in that union members who disagree with a union's political activities need not give up full membership in the organization to avoid supporting its political activities" and a union may not

compel "employees to support financially 'union activities beyond those germane to collective bargaining, contract administration, and grievance adjustment.' "

Although the Court required that the restrictions "be narrowly tailored to serve a compelling governmental interest, the Court upheld them:

> [T]he State's decision to regulate only corporations is precisely tailored to serve the compelling state interest of eliminating from the political process the corrosive effect of political 'war chests' amassed with the aid of the legal advantages given to corporations.

The exemption of media corporations was also affirmed:

> [M]edia corporations differ significantly from other corporations in that their resources are devoted to the collection of information and its dissemination to the public. We have consistently recognized the unique role that the press plays in 'informing and educating the public, offering criticism, and providing a forum for discussion and debate.' The Act's definition of 'expenditure' conceivably could be interpreted to encompass election-related news stories and editorials. The Act's restriction on independent expenditures therefore might discourage incorporated news broadcasters or publishers from serving their crucial societal [role].

Justice Scalia dissented. He argued that the majority's position reflects the idea that

> too much speech is an evil that the democratic majority can proscribe. I dissent because that principle is contrary to our case law and incompatible with the absolutely central truth of the First Amendment: that government cannot be trusted to assure, through censorship, the 'fairness' of political debate.

Justice Kennedy, joined by Justices O'Connor and Scalia, made a similar argument:

> [T]he Court adopts a rule that allows Michigan to stifle the voices of some of the most respected groups in public life on subjects central to the integrity of our democratic system. Each of these schemes is repugnant to the First Amendment and contradicts its central guarantee, the freedom to speak in the electoral process. I dissent.

First National Bank of Boston v. Bellotti,[80] was the next major corporate speech case. *Bellotti* involved a criminal statute that prohibited certain expenditures by banks and business corporations for the purpose of influencing the vote on referendum proposals. Expenditures could be made on matters "materially affecting any of the property, business or assets of the corporation." A corporation that violated § 8 could receive a fine of up to $50,000, and corporate officers, directors, and agents who violate the section could receive a maximum fine of $10,000 or imprisonment for up to one year, or both. Appellants wanted to spend money to publicize their views on a proposed constitutional amendment that would have permitted the legislature to impose a graduated tax on the income of individuals.

---

[80]   435 U.S. 765 (1978).

The Court struck down the law finding that the speech was "at the heart of the First Amendment's protection." "The inherent worth of the speech in terms of its capacity for informing the public does not depend upon the identity of its source, whether corporation, association, union, or individual." In addition, the Court noted that:

> [The] press does not have a monopoly on either the First Amendment or the ability to enlighten. [In] the realm of protected speech, the legislature is constitutionally disqualified from dictating the subjects about which persons may speak and the speakers who may address a public issue. If a legislature may direct business corporations to "stick to business," it also may limit other corporations — religious, charitable, or civic — to their respective "business" when addressing the public. Such power in government to channel the expression of views is unacceptable under the First Amendment. Especially where, as here, the legislature's suppression of speech suggests an attempt to give one side of a debatable public question an advantage in expressing its views to the people, the First Amendment is plainly offended. Yet the State contends that its action is necessitated by governmental interests of the highest order. We next consider these asserted interests.

The Court found that the "risk of corruption" so inherent in candidate elections was "not present in a popular vote on a public issue." Although corporate advertising could "influence the outcome of the vote," "the fact that advocacy may persuade the electorate is hardly a reason to suppress it." The Court placed faith in the people to judge and evaluate the relative merits of the conflicting arguments, and to consider and evaluate "the source and credibility of the advocate." The Court demanded proof of a "compelling state interest" and found that such interest was lacking.

United States v. Congress of Industrial Organizations,[81] involved an indictment under the Federal Corrupt Practices Act. The government charged that the Congress of Industrial Organization's (CIO) newsletter urged all members to vote for a specific candidate for Congress. The Court construed the law as not extending to the charged conduct.

[C]   Independent Political Action Committee Expenditures.

FEC v. National Conservative Political Action Committee,[82] involved the Presidential Election Campaign Fund Act (Fund Act), 26 U.S.C. § 9001 et seq., which gave Presidential candidates of major political parties the option of receiving public financing for their general election campaigns. If a Presidential candidate accepted public financing, § 9012(f) made it a crime for independent "political committees" to spend more than $1,000 to further that candidate's election.

The National Conservative Political Action Committee (NCPAC) and Fund For A Conservative Majority (FCM) challenged the law on First Amendment grounds. NCPAC was a nonprofit, nonmembership corporation registered with the FEC as a "political committee." Its primary purpose was to attempt to influence directly or

---

[81] 335 U.S. 106 (1948).

[82] 470 U.S. 480 (1985).

indirectly the election or defeat of candidates for federal, state, and local offices by making contributions and by making its own expenditures. NCPAC's three-member board of directors was elected annually by the existing board, and made all decisions concerning which candidates to support or oppose, the strategy and methods to employ, and the amounts of money to spend. NCPAC contributors had no role in these decisions. NCPAC raised money by general and specific direct mail solicitations. It did not maintain separate accounts for the receipts from its general and specific solicitations, nor was it required by law to do so. FCM was also incorporated and was also registered with the FEC as a multicandidate political committee. In all material respects it was identical to NCPAC. Both NCPAC and FCM were ideological organizations with a conservative political philosophy, and both spent money on radio and television advertisements designed to encourage voters to elect Ronald Reagan as President. Their expenditures were "independent" of the official Reagan election campaign committee.

In an opinion by Justice Rehnquist, the Court struck down the Fund Act as applied to "political committees." The term "political committee" was defined to mean "any committee, association, or organization (whether or not incorporated) which accepts contributions or makes expenditures for the purpose of influencing, or attempting to influence, the nomination or election of one or more individuals to Federal, State, or local elective public office." The term "qualified campaign expense" meant an otherwise lawful expense by a candidate or his authorized committee "to further his election" incurred during the period between the candidate's nomination and 30 days after election day. The term "eligible candidates" meant those Presidential and Vice Presidential candidates who are qualified under the Act to receive public funding and have chosen to do so. Two of the more important qualifications are that a candidate and his authorized committees not incur campaign expenses in excess of his public funding and not accept contributions to defray campaign expenses.

The Court readily found that NCPAC and FCM were political committees, that President Reagan was a qualified candidate, and that the PACs' expenditures included "qualified campaign expense." But the Court also found that the expenditures involved "speech at the core of the First Amendment." The PACs spent substantial monies to communicate their political ideas through media advertisements." And the Court found that the Act, which allowed the PACs to present their political views but prohibited them from spending more than $1,000, was equivalent "to allowing a speaker in a public hall to express his views while denying him the use of an amplifying system." The Court re-emphasized its *Buckley* holding that:

> A restriction on the amount of money a person or group can spend on political communication during a campaign necessarily reduces the quantity of expression by restricting the number of issues discussed, the depth of their exploration, and the size of the audience reached. This is because virtually every means of communicating ideas in today's mass society requires the expenditure of money. The distribution of the humblest handbill or leaflet entails printing, paper, and circulation costs. Speeches and rallies generally necessitate hiring a hall and publicizing the event. The electorate's increasing dependence on television, radio, and other mass

media for news and information has made these expensive modes of communication indispensable instruments of effective political speech.

The Court also found that both NCPAC and FCM were entitled to First Amendment protection. Both organizations were "mechanisms by which large numbers of individuals of modest means can join together in organizations which serve to 'amplif[y] the voice of their adherents.' " The Court noted that in 1979-1980 101,000 people "contributed an average of $75 each to NCPAC and in 1980 approximately 100,000 people contributed an average of $25 each to FCM."

The Court rejected the notion that NCPAC and FCM were not engaged in "individual speech, but merely 'speech by proxy.' because the contributors do not control or decide upon the use of the funds by the PACs or the specific content of the PACs' advertisements and other speech." The Court found that these contributions were small and did not "raise the same concerns as the sizable contributions involved in *California Medical Assn.*"[83] Moreover, the Court found that "contributors obviously like the message they are hearing from these organizations and want to add their voices to that message; otherwise they would not part with their money. To say that their collective action in pooling their resources to amplify their voices is not entitled to full First Amendment protection would subordinate the voices of those of modest means as opposed to those sufficiently wealthy to be able to buy expensive media ads with their own resources."

The Court then distinguished its decision in *FEC v. National Right to Work Committee*[84] (NRWC). The Court noted that NWRC "turned on the special treatment historically accorded corporations. In return for the special advantages that the State confers on the corporate form, individuals acting jointly through corporations forgo some of the rights they have as individuals." Although both NCPAC and FCM were incorporated, the Court found that § 9012(f) applied "not just to corporations but to any "committee, association, or organization (whether or not incorporated)" that accepts contributions or makes expenditures in connection with electoral campaigns. The terms of § 9012(f)'s prohibition apply equally to an informal neighborhood group that solicits contributions and spends money on a Presidential election as to the wealthy and professionally managed PACs involved in these cases."

Having concluded NCPAC and FCM's expenditures were protected by the First Amendment, the Court then looked to see whether there was a "sufficiently strong governmental interest served by § 9012(f)'s restriction" and whether the section was "narrowly tailored to the evil that may legitimately be regulated." The Court emphasized that *Buckley* had held that preventing corruption or the appearance of corruption were the only legitimate and compelling government interests for restricting campaign finances. The Court found § 9012(f)'s limitation on independent expenditures by political committees was unconstitutional because it was not designed to prevent corruption or the appearance of corruption. The "hallmark of corruption is the financial *quid pro quo*: dollars for political favors," and the Act did not prohibit contributions to candidates but independent expenditures on their

---

[83] *Id.* at 495.

[84] 459 U.S. 197 (1982).

behalf. In addition, the amounts given to the PACs were "overwhelmingly small contributions, well under the $1,000 limit on contributions upheld in *Buckley*; and the contributions are by definition not coordinated with the campaign of the candidate." Of course, candidates could "take notice of and reward those responsible for PAC expenditures by giving official favors to the latter in exchange for the supporting messages." Nevertheless, the Court fond that

> the absence of prearrangement and coordination undermines the value of the expenditure to the candidate, and thereby alleviates the danger that expenditures will be given as a quid pro quo for improper commitments from the candidate. On this record, such an exchange of political favors for uncoordinated expenditures remains a hypothetical possibility and nothing more.

In addition, the Court found that the law was overbroad. "It is not limited to multimillion dollar war chests; its terms apply equally to informal discussion groups that solicit neighborhood contributions to publicize their views about a particular Presidential candidate." The Court went on to note that:

> [While] in *NRWC* we held that the compelling governmental interest in preventing corruption supported the restriction of the influence of political war chests funneled through the corporate form, in the present cases we do not believe that a similar finding is supportable: when the First Amendment is involved, our standard of review is "rigorous," and the effort to link either corruption or the appearance of corruption to independent expenditures by PACs, whether large or small, simply does not pass this standard of review. Even assuming that Congress could fairly conclude that large-scale PACs have a sufficient tendency to corrupt, the overbreadth of § 9012(f) in these cases is so great that the section may not be upheld. We are not quibbling over fine-tuning of prophylactic limitations, but are concerned about wholesale restriction of clearly protected conduct.

Justice White, joined by justices Brennan and Marshall, dissented. He argued that, since the Court was concerned about protecting the right of association and the "effective political speech of those of modest means," the Court appears to be "concerned with the rights of contributors [to] make contributions." However, he argued that:

> But the contributors are not engaging in speech; at least, they are not engaging in speech to any greater extent than are those who contribute directly to political campaigns. *Buckley* explicitly distinguished between, on the one hand, using one's own money to express one's views, and, on the other, giving money to someone else in the expectation that that person will use the money to express views with which one is in agreement. [The] Court strikes down § 9012(f) because it prevents PAC donors from effectively speaking by proxy. But appellees are not simply mouthpieces for their individual contributors. The PAC operates independently of its contributors. Donations go into the committee's general accounts. It can safely be assumed that each contributor does not fully support every one of the variety of activities undertaken and candidates supported by the PAC to which he contributes. It is true, as the majority points out, that in general

the contributors presumably like what they hear. However, 'this sympathy of interests alone does not convert' the PAC's speech into that of its contributors. [The] provision for exclusive public funding not only enhances the danger of real or perceived corruption posed by independent expenditures, it also gives more weight to the interest in holding down the overall cost of political campaigns. [I]n the context of the public financing scheme, the apparent congressional desire that elections should be between equally well financed candidates and not turn on the amount of money spent for one or the other is all the more compelling, and the danger of funding disparities more serious.

[D]   Toward a More Assertive First Amendment Principle

A quarter of a century after its decision in *Buckley v. Valeo*, the Court introduced a new dimension to its standard of review. At issue in *McConnell v. Federal Election Commission*, 540 U.S. 93 (2003) were provisions of the Bipartisan Campaign Reform Act of 2002 (BCRA) which prohibited corporations, unions, and non-profit organizations from (1) purchasing broadcast, cable, or satellite advertisements supporting a federal candidate within 30 days of a primary or 60 days of a general election and (2) making direct donations (soft money) to political parties. The law also banned political parties from using funds to advertise on behalf of candidates (e.g., issue advertising). Unlike "hard money," which is spent on, by, or for the candidate, "soft money" is used to fund issue advertising or "get out the vote" efforts. Issue advertising focuses upon a candidate's position, contrary to traditional campaign advertising which directly supports or opposes the candidate. The restriction on soft money reflected a concern that donations were a means of gaining special access to public office-holders.

The *McConnell* case generated a multiplicity of opinions, including three different majority opinions. The Court's general sense was that soft money contributions, which may be used to register voters, turn out the vote, or support other election activities, were further removed from First Amendment concerns than campaign expenditures that underwrite promotion of political positions or values. Because the Court concluded that less was at stake with soft money, the Court decided to apply a more relaxed standard of review. Instead of utilizing strict scrutiny, as mandated by *Buckley v. Valeo*, the Court focused upon whether the restriction is "closely drawn to advance important interests." Pursuant to this standard, it found that the restriction imposed on free speech was minimal and justified by the government's legitimate interest in preventing "both the actual corruption threatened by large financial contributions [and] the appearance of corruption" that might result from those contributions.

Because the regulations dealt mostly with soft-money contributions that were used to register voters and increase attendance at the polls, not with campaign expenditures (which are more explicitly a statement of political values and therefore deserve more protection), the Court held that the restriction on free speech was minimal. It then found that the restriction was justified by the government's legitimate interest in preventing "both the actual corruption threatened by large financial contributions [and] the appearance of corruption" that might result from those contributions.

Randall and Restrictive Contribution Limits. The Court's decision, in *Randall v. Sorrell*, 548 U.S. 230 (2006). reaffirmed the pertinence of strict scrutiny when restrictions on hard money were at issue. At issue was a Vermont statute that limited how much (1) candidates for state office could spend on their campaigns and (2) individuals, organizations, and political parties could contribute thereto. The expenditure limits controlled the total amount a candidate for state office could spend during a "two-year general election cycle" and ranged from $300,000 for the governor's office to $2,000 for a state representative in a single member district. Contributions to candidates for state-wide office were limited to $400 per election cycle and to $200 for state representatives. Excluded from these restrictions were candidate contributions to their own campaigns. The Court again spoke in multiple voices and, although no majority opinion emerged, six justices embraced the standard of strict scrutiny and invalidated both the expenditure and contribution limitations.

Justice Breyer, in an opinion joined by Chief Justice Roberts and in part by Justice Alito, reaffirmed the vitality of *Buckley* and rejected arguments to overturn that decision. The Breyer plurality, in striking down the expenditure and contribution restrictions, rejected the argument that the time demands of political fund-raising compromise the ability of office holders to perform their roles effectively. It found that the contribution limitations were "too low and too strict to survive First Amendment scrutiny." The Court noted that the restrictions were significantly more restrictive than the federal limitations reviewed in *Buckley*. For example, contributions to a gubernatorial candidate were capped at about 1/20 of what the federal law permitted for national candidates. They also were the strictest in the nation. These limitations, from the plurality's perspective, created a risk that challengers could not "mount[ ] effective campaigns against incumbent officeholders, thereby reducing democratic accountability."

Justice Thomas, in a concurring opinion joined by Justice Scalia, embraced an across the board strict scrutiny standard. He questioned the ability of the Court to make principled distinctions between permissible and impermissible contributions. In this regard, he noted there was no way to determine the amount of money that would generate corruption — actual or perceived — or "how many resources must be lost before speech is disproportionately burdened."

In a dissenting opinion, Justice Stevens advocated the abandonment of strict scrutiny for expenditure restrictions. Stevens proposed that such limitations should be permissible if they serve "legitimate and sufficiently substantial" purposes. From his perspective, there was a compelling interest in "freeing candidates from the fund-raising straitjacket."

Justice Souter, joined by Justice Ginsburg and on the contributions issue by Justice Stevens, maintained that the contribution limitations should be permitted. He was not convinced that, although highly restrictive, they would preclude effective campaigning and negate the value of contributions. Souter favored remanding the expenditure restrictions issue for further review consistent with *Buckley*.

Corporate Advertisements. In *Federal Election Commission v. Wisconsin Right to Life, Inc.*, 551 U.S. 449 (2007), the Court reviewed a state law that prohibited corporations and unions from funding advertisements on radio and television under certain circumstances. Specifically precluded were those targeting a federal candidate within 60 days of the election in his or her jurisdiction. At issue were expenditures by an advocacy group, which paid for a series of advertisements with monies that included corporate contributions. The advertisements criticized a United States Senator, who was running for reelection, for his participation in and support for filibusters of judicial nominees. Chief Justice Roberts, joined by Justice Alito, found the law constitutional only insofar as it applied to advertisements that reasonably could be interpreted as advocating a vote for or against a specific candidate. Because of the high value of political speech, he maintained that any doubt should be resolved in favor of the First Amendment. Justice Souter, joined by Justices Stevens, Ginsburg, and Breyer, dissented. Souter noted that, pursuant to the standard propounded by Chief Justice Roberts, a constitutional violation would hinge upon explicit advocacy of or against a candidate.

The "Millionaire's Amendment." The Court, in *Davis v. Federal Election Commission*, 554 U.S. 724 (2008), struck down a federal law designed to level the playing field for candidates competing against wealthy self-funded individuals. The so-called "Millionaire's Amendment" to the Bipartisan Campaign Reform Act of 2002 (BCRA) enabled a candidate for the House of Representatives to solicit individual contributions of $6,900 (and thus exceed the $2,300 otherwise imposed) when his or her opponent spent more than $350,000 of personal funds. The threshold was higher for Senate races but varied on the basis of population. The Court found a First Amendment violation pursuant to a standard of review that required a "closely drawn" statute and a "sufficiently important interest" such as preventing the reality or perception of corruption. It found that neither of these concerns was present. Consistent with its generally negative view of opportunity or rights redistribution, the Court observed that it "never had upheld the constitutionality of a law that imposes different contribution limits for candidates competing against each other." If thus noted that "if [the] contribution limits applied across the board, [there] would not have [been] any basis for challenging those limits."

Justice Stevens, joined by Justices Souter, Ginsburg, and Breyer, concurred in part and dissented in part. They viewed the amendment as a "modest, sensible, and plainly constitutional attempt by Congress to minimize the advantages enjoyed by wealthy candidates." Among the "legitimate and substantial" justifications they saw was the freeing of candidates from "the interminable burden of fundraising" and an improved quality "of the exposition of ideas." This analysis reflects a philosophy, that for many years drove fairness regulation in broadcasting, that favors regulatory intervention to manage First Amendment values.

The Citizens United *Decision.* The Court in *Citizens United v. Federal Elections Commission*, 558 U.S. 310 (2010) dismantled some key elements of its campaign finance law architecture. That case concerned the airing of a documentary that was critical of Hillary Clinton, produced and paid for by a conservative nonprofit organization, and aired during the presidential primary campaign. The gist of the decision was that government may not restrict spending by corporations and unions during the campaign process. The decision overruled *Austin v. Michigan Chamber of Commerce* and the part of *McConnell v. Federal Election Commission* that had upheld limitations on corporate or union campaign spending.

The specific provision struck down by the Court prohibited the airing of "electioneering communications" paid for from the general funds of corporations of unions 30 days before a presidential primary and 60 days before a general election. Writing for a majority of five, Justice Kennedy observed that "[i]f the First Amendment has any force, [it] prohibits Congress from fining or jailing citizens, or associations of citizens, for simply engaging in political speech." Although the law exempted broadcasters, the Court maintained that there was no effective way to differentiate media corporations from other corporations. From the majority's perspective, the law thus represented a potential threat to political expression through mainstream and other media.

Justice Stevens, joined by three other justices, authored a lengthy dissent that challenged the Court's readiness to equate corporations and unions with people for First Amendment purposes. He viewed the restrictions as reasonable, especially because corporations and unions could fund expression through political action committees or outside the time frame established by the law. Stevens believed that the concern with buying access, indicated in *McConnell*, was no less relevant in this context. As he put it, [t]he difference between selling a vote and selling access is a matter of degree, not kind. [S]elling access is not qualitatively different from giving special preference to those who spent money on one's behalf." The majority countered with the observation that "by definition, an independent expenditure is political speech presented to the electorate that is not coordinated with a candidate."

This decision did not disturb precedent that permits restrictions on direct corporate and union contributions to candidates. Indeed, the Court upheld those parts of the law that required corporations and unions to disclose their spending and include disclaimers in any paid advertisement or program.

More on Disclosure Requirements. Disclosure requirements typically faclitate an increased flow of information and thus help ensure a moer informed electorate. They may implicate other concerns, however, such as privacy and associational freedom. The Court, in *Doe v. Reed*, 130 S. Ct. 2811 (2010), determined that disclosing the identity of persons who sign petitions for a ballot referendum, pursuant to a state open records law, did not abridge the First Amendment. The case arose in the context of an initiative to place a controversial domestic partnership law on the ballot. The Court employed an "exacting strict scrutiny" standard "requiring a 'substantial relation' between the disclosure requirement and a 'sufficiently important' governmental interest." Pursuant to this criterion, it found that the interest in "preserving the integrity of the electoral process by combating fraud, detecting invalid signatures, and fostering government transparency and accountability" outweighed the First Amendment concern. The Court reserved the possibility that the First Amendment might be a bar if it was demonstrated that disclosure would cause serious harm.

POINTS TO REMEMBER

- Campaign contributions and expenditures constitute "speech" within the meaning of the First Amendment.

- Regulations on such speech will be upheld only "if the State demonstrates a sufficiently important interest and employs means closely drawn to avoid unnecessary abridgment of associational freedoms."

- A "sufficiently important interest" involves the prevention of corruption by public officials, and prevention of the appearance of corruption.

- Campaign contribution limitations have been upheld to the extent that there is the appearance or the reality of a *quid pro quo* (that money is being given in exchange for political favors).

- Government has greater authority to limit (although not prohibit) the political activities of corporations.

- Some restrictions have been upheld because corporations have special advantages (limited liability, perpetual life, and favorable treatment of the accumulation and distribution of assets) "that enhance their ability to attract capital and to deploy resources" that give corporations the ability to use "resources amassed in the economic marketplace" to obtain "an unfair advantage in the political marketplace."

Chapter 8

FREEDOM OF ASSOCIATION AND COMPELLED EXPRESSION

FOCAL POINTS FOR CHAPTER 8

- Freedom of Association as a protected constitutional right.
- The right to association as including the right to "exclude."
- The right of association as including the right to "disassociate" from repugnant ideas.
- Compelled financial support for repugnant ideas.
- Unconstitutional conditions.
- The right not to hear.

---

§ 8.01 THE RIGHT TO ASSOCIATE

Although the First Amendment does not mention the right to associate, it explicitly protects a number of activities that are associational in nature including the right to peacefully assemble. In addition, since the Constitution protects "speech" it implicitly protects association, which is more effective when people can join together and speak with a common voice.

[A] Early Precedent

The right was first recognized in *NAACP v. Alabama*.[1] That case involved an Alabama statute that required "foreign corporations" to file their corporate charters with the Secretary of State and designate a place of business and an agent to receive service of process. In 1956 the Attorney General of Alabama sued to enjoin the National Association for the Advancement of Colored People (NAACP) from conducting business within the state for violating the law. The State then sought production of the NAACP's "records and papers, including [the] names and addresses of all Alabama 'members' and 'agents' of the Association." The trial court ordered production of a substantial part of the requested records, including the membership lists. When the NAACP refused to produce the lists, the court held it in civil contempt and imposed a fine of $10,000, which increased to $100,000 for noncompliance.

Before the Court, the NAACP argued that its members' constitutional right to associate allowed it to shield the membership lists from disclosure. The Court began by recognizing the importance of association: "Effective advocacy of both public and private points of view, particularly controversial ones, is undeniably enhanced by group association, as this Court has more than once recognized by remarking upon the close nexus between the freedoms of speech and assembly." And the Court recognized that the right is grounded in the "liberty" clause of the Fourteenth Amendment's Due Process Clause which incorporates the First Amendment and its protections for freedom of speech.

After recognizing the right of association, the Court found that the Alabama order involved the likelihood of a "substantial restraint" upon the NAACP's members' right. "Inviolability of privacy in group association may in many circumstances be indispensable to preservation of freedom of association, particularly where a group espouses dissident beliefs." The Court found that, in the past, when the identity of NAACP members had been revealed, they had been subjected to "economic reprisal, loss of employment, threat of physical coercion, and other manifestations of public hostility." As a result, the Court was concerned that disclosure of the membership lists might adversely affect the NAACP's ability to pursue their collective advocacy, and may dissuade prospective members from joining "because of fear of exposure of their beliefs shown through their associations and of the consequences of this exposure."

Although the Court recognized that the interest in association was not absolute, it held that the state interest must be "compelling" to override that right. The

---

[1] 357 U.S. 449 (1958).

Court found that Alabama's asserted interest (to determine whether petitioner was conducting intrastate business in violation of the Alabama foreign corporation registration statute) was not compelling. The NAACP had already admitted that it was conducting activities in the state, had offered to comply with the state's qualification statute, and had complied with the production order, except for the membership lists, by furnishing the Attorney General with various types of information (business records, the NAACP's charter and statement of purposes, the names of all of its directors and officers, and the total number of its Alabama members and the amount of their dues). Accordingly, the Court found that the state's interest in obtaining names of ordinary members was insufficient. As a result, the Court vacated the civil contempt judgment including the $100,000 fine.

[B] The House Un-American Activities Committee

Despite the holding in the *NAACP* case, the Court rejected an associational claim the following year in *Barenblatt v. United States*.[2] In that case, petitioner was convicted of refusing to answer certain questions put to him by a Subcommittee of the House Committee on Un-American Activities during the course of an inquiry concerning alleged Communist infiltration into the field of education. The conviction was based on Barenblatt's refusal to answer the following five questions based on his privilege against self-incrimination:

"Are you now a member of the Communist Party?" (Count One.)

"Have you ever been a member of the Communist Party?" (Count Two.)

"Now, you have stated that you knew Francis Crowley. Did you know Francis Crowley as a member of the Communist Party?" (Count Three.)

"Were you ever a member of the Haldane Club of the Communist Party while at the University of Michigan?" (Count Four.)

"Were you a member while a student of the University of Michigan Council of Arts, Sciences, and Professions?" (Count Five.)

In a 5-4 decision, the Court rejected Barenblatt's associational claims. Once again, the Court sought to balance the "competing private and public interests at stake," but the Court balanced those interests in favor of the government. The Court began by finding a "valid legislative purpose": "That Congress has wide power to legislate in the field of Communist activity in this Country, and to conduct appropriate investigations in aid thereof." In addition, the Court emphasized the "close nexus" between the Communist Party and violent overthrow of government. Even though the Communist Party also engaged in peaceful activities, the Court refused to treat it as an "ordinary political party from the standpoint of national security." To do so, the Court found, would be "to ask this Court to blind itself to world affairs [since] the close of World War II." As a result, the Court was deferential to Congress: "[We] conclude that the balance between the individual and the governmental interests here at stake must be struck in favor of the latter, and that therefore the provisions of the First Amendment have not been offended."

---

[2] 360 U.S. 109 (1959).

Justice Black dissented expressing concern about the government's power to punish people for their political associations. "The First Amendment means to me [that] the only constitutional way our Government can preserve itself is to leave its people the fullest possible freedom to praise, criticize or discuss, as they see fit, all governmental policies and to suggest, if they desire, that even its most fundamental postulates are bad and should be changed." As a result, he noted that any members of the Communist party "who commit acts in violation of valid laws can be prosecuted." However, he doubted that "innocent members" should be tainted by the fact some members "had some illegal aims and because some of its members were lawbreakers." Indeed, the party's goals include both the illegal as well as "perfectly normal political and social goals [including] a drive to achieve power through the ballot, if it can be done." "History should teach us [that] in times of high emotional excitement minority parties and groups which advocate extremely unpopular social or governmental innovations will always be typed as criminal gangs and attempts will always be made to drive them out." With the passage of time, Justice Black's view has become the preferred interpretation of the First Amendment.

I.R.S. Targeting of Political Groups. In 2013, a major political controversy erupted when it was revealed that the Internal Revenue Service (IRS) was targeting certain political groups for increased scrutiny regarding their applications for tax-exempt status as "social welfare" organizations. Initial reports suggested that the I.R.S. had targeted conservative groups with the terms "Tea Party" or "Patriot" in their names. Of 296 such cases, no application had been denied, but 160 applications had been delayed, some for as long as three years. Initially, President Obama responded by firing the acting IRS Commissioner. Later revelations suggested that some liberal groups may also have been subjected to increased scrutiny.[3] If the investigation reveals that the I.R.S. targeted conservative groups for increased scrutiny, has it violated their right to freedom of association? Of course, one of the fundamental issues is the question of what constitutes a "social welfare" organization. In the wake of the *Citizens United* decision, a great deal of money has flooded the political process through such organizations.

[C] *Claiborne Hardware*

NAACP v. Claiborne Hardware Co.[4] involved an NAACP boycott of white merchants in Mississippi that was supported by speeches and non-violent picketing. Merchants sued to recover losses caused by the boycott and to enjoin future boycott activity. The state court imposed joint and several liability on the defendants under a conspiracy theory, and held that the businesses had suffered lost business earnings and lost goodwill during a 7-year period from 1966 to 1972

---

[3] *See* Stephanie Kirchgaessner, *Agency Caught in Crossfire of Attack Against White House, Financial Times* at 2 (May 18, 2013); Gregory Korte, Kevin Johnson & Aamer Madhani, Obama Sacks Tax Chief, USA TODAY A-1 (May 17–19, 2012); John D. McKinnon, *Evan Perez & Damian Paletta, Tax Scandal Fells IRS Chief: Head Ousted Over Scrutiny of Conservative Groups; Obama Pledges Safeguards.* THE WALL STREET JOURNAL A-1 (May 16, 2013); John D. McKinnon & Siobhan Hughes, *FBI Launches Probe of IRS: Treatment of Tea-Party Groups Eyed; Internal Review Blames Higher-Ups,* THE WALL STREET JOURNAL, A-1 (May 15, 2013).

[4] 458 U.S. 886 (1982).

amounting to $944,699. The Supreme Court reversed, holding that "encouragement to boycott" constitutes protected speech under the First and Fourteenth Amendments. Although the Court concluded that violent activity was not protected, and that those who engaged in violence could be held liable, it held that the state could not impose liability on non-violent protestors merely because of their association with those who engaged in violence: "For liability to be imposed by reason of association alone, it is necessary to establish that the group itself possessed unlawful goals and that the individual held a specific intent to further those illegal aims."

The Court also held that liability could not be imposed on Charles Evers, the NAACP representative, nor on the NAACP, even though Evers made several inflammatory speeches: "[Charles] Evers' speeches did not transcend the bounds of protected speech set forth in *Brandenburg*. . . . An advocate must be free to stimulate his audience with spontaneous and emotional appeals for unity and action in a common cause." Since the NAACP's liability was based on Evers' speeches, the Court concluded that they could not be used to impose liability on the association.

[D] Compelled Admission to Membership

Many modern freedom of association cases focus not on whether the government can compel an organization to disclose the names of its members (as in *NAACP v. Alabama* and *Barenblatt*), but on whether the government can force an organization to accept members that it does not want. This type of case typically arises when a state or local government passes a law prohibiting discrimination on the basis of certain criteria (*e.g.*, race, sex, religion) in places of public accommodation.

The most important case is *Roberts v. United States Jaycees*.[5] That case involved a conflict between a Minnesota law designed to eliminate gender-based discrimination and the United States Jaycees associational rights. The Jaycees, founded in 1920 as the Junior Chamber of Commerce, were set-up to pursue a number of objectives including:

> "such educational and charitable purposes as will promote and foster the growth and development of young men's civic organizations in the United States, designed to inculcate in the individual membership of such organization a spirit of genuine Americanism and civic interest, and as a supplementary education institution to provide them with opportunity for personal development and achievement and an avenue for intelligent participation by young men in the affairs of their community, state and nation, and to develop true friendship and understanding among young men of all nations."

The Jaycees' bylaws provided for seven classes of membership, including individual or regular membership, associate individual membership, and local chapters. Regular membership was limited to young men between the ages of 18 and 35, and associate membership was open to individuals or groups ineligible for

---

[5] 468 U.S. 609 (1984).

regular membership (women and older men). Although associate members paid lower dues, they were ineligible to vote, to hold local or national office, or to participate in certain leadership training and awards programs. At the time of trial, the Jaycees had 295,000 members and 11,915 associate members in 7,400 chapters affiliated with 51 state organizations. There were 11,915 associate members. Women constituted approximately two percent of the Jaycees' total membership.

In 1974 and 1975, the Minneapolis and St. Paul chapters of the Jaycees began admitting women as regular members, and had a number of women as members and local directors. When the president of the national organization indicated an intention to revoke the charters of both organizations, both chapters filed discrimination charges with the Minnesota Department of Human Rights alleging a violation of the Minnesota Human Rights Act (Act), which provided in part: "It is an unfair discriminatory practice . . . To deny any person the full and equal enjoyment of the goods, services, facilities, privileges, advantages, and accommodations of a place of public accommodation because of race, color, creed, religion, disability, national origin or sex." The term "place of public accommodation" was defined as "a business, accommodation, refreshment, entertainment, recreation, or transportation facility of any kind, whether licensed or not, whose goods, services, facilities, privileges, advantages or accommodations are extended, offered, sold, or otherwise made available to the public." § 363.01, subd. 18. A state hearing examiner concluded that the Jaycees had violated the Act and ordered them to cease and desist from discriminating against any member or applicant on the basis of sex.

In an opinion by Justice Brennan, the Court upheld the Minnesota law. He distinguished between two different types of "association." The first he referred to as "intimate human relationships" involving "highly personal relationships." He described these relationships as including

> the creation and sustenance of a family — marriage, *e.g., Zablocki v. Redhail, supra*; childbirth, *e.g., Carey v. Population Services International*, [431 U.S. 678, 684–686]; the raising and education of children, *e.g., Smith v. Organization of Foster Families*, [431 U.S. 816, 844 (1977)]; and cohabitation with one's relatives, *e.g., Moore v. East Cleveland, supra*.

He characterized these relationships as involving "deep attachments and commitments to the necessarily few other individuals with whom one shares not only a special community of thoughts, experiences, and beliefs but also distinctively personal aspects of one's life." He emphasized that such relationships are distinguished by "relative smallness, a high degree of selectivity in decisions to begin and maintain the affiliation, and seclusion from others in critical aspects of the relationship." The opinion emphasized that "only relationships with these sorts of qualities are likely to reflect the considerations that have led to an understanding of freedom of association as an intrinsic element of personal liberty." The opinion concluded that such "intimate" relationships "must be secured against undue intrusion by the State because of the role of such relationships in safeguarding the individual freedom that is central to our constitutional scheme" and which are "a fundamental element of personal liberty." The opinion contrasted these "intimate relationships" with large business enterprises: "the Constitution undoubtedly imposes constraints on the State's power to control the selection of one's spouse that would not apply to regulations affecting the choice of one's fellow employees."

In deciding the case, the Court noted that the Jaycees were "large and basically unselective groups" and therefore did not fall within the constitutional protection for "intimate relationships." Both the Minneapolis and St. Paul chapters had more than 400 members, and neither chapter applied any membership criteria other than sex and age. Indeed, they admitted new members without investigating their backgrounds. Further, although women were not allowed to be full members, they were allowed to participate in many of the association's activities including community programs, ceremonies, and recruitment.

The opinion then distinguished "intimate human relationships" from "associational relationships" designed to further speech and expression interests (which include the "right to associate for the purpose of engaging in those activities protected by the First Amendment — speech, assembly, petition for the redress of grievances, and the exercise of religion)." The Court recognized that the individual right to speak, to worship, and to petition the government for the redress of grievances "could not be vigorously protected from interference by the State unless a correlative freedom to engage in group effort toward those ends were not also guaranteed." As a result, the Court reaffirmed the idea that "implicit in the right to engage in activities protected by the First Amendment is a corresponding right to associate with others in pursuit of a wide variety of political, social, economic, educational, religious, and cultural ends."

In analyzing the Minnesota law, the Court expressed concern regarding the state's power to control the membership of an organization. Such control can interfere with "the internal organization or affairs" of the Jaycees, and affect it s ability to push its views. "There can be no clearer example of an intrusion into the internal structure or affairs of an association than a regulation that forces the group to accept members it does not desire. Such a regulation may impair the ability of the original members to express only those views that brought them together. Freedom of association therefore plainly presupposes a freedom not to associate."

Nevertheless, the Court held that the right to associate for expressive purposes was not absolute even though infringements would be subjected to strict scrutiny in the sense that they must be justified by "compelling state interests, unrelated to the suppression of ideas, that cannot be achieved through means significantly less restrictive of associational freedoms." In most cases when the court applies strict scrutiny, the Court strikes down the governmental regulation. In *Roberts*, the Court found that Minnesota's law was supported by a compelling interest in "eradicating discrimination against its female citizens" that justified the infringement of associational freedoms. The Court noted that the law did not "aim at the suppression of speech," did not "distinguish between prohibited and permitted activity on the basis of viewpoint," and did not "license enforcement authorities to administer the statute on the basis of such constitutionally impermissible criteria." Nor did the Jaycees contend that the Act was applied "for the purpose of hampering the organization's ability to express its views."

In addition, the Court found that the statute reflected "the State's strong historical commitment to eliminating discrimination and assuring its citizens equal access to publicly available goods and services." The Court viewed that goal as "compelling" and of the "highest order" and "unrelated to the suppression of expression." The Court went on to note that discrimination

> "based on archaic and overbroad assumptions about the relative needs and capacities of the sexes forces individuals to labor under stereotypical notions that often bear no relationship to their actual abilities. It thereby both deprives persons of their individual dignity and denies society the benefits of wide participation in political, economic, and cultural life."

The Court found that these concerns were "strongly implicated with respect to gender discrimination in the allocation of publicly available goods and services."

After finding that the law was supported by a compelling governmental interest, the Court had no difficulty applying it to the Jaycees. The Court found that the Jaycees were covered by Minnesota's "accommodations" law because the state had adopted a functional definition of "public accommodations" that focused on whether an organization was engaged in commercial or quasi-commercial conduct. The Court agreed with the Minnesota Supreme Court that the Jaycees local chapters were "place[s] of public accommodations" within the meaning of the Act because they offered various commercial programs and benefits to their members including leadership skills and business contacts. The Court found that there was a compelling state interest in assuring women "equal access to such goods, privileges, and advantages."

The Court concluded that Minnesota had advanced its interests through "the least restrictive means of achieving its ends" because the law did not impose "any serious burdens on the male members' freedom of expressive association." The Court agreed that the Jaycees engaged in expression, and that such expression was a "not insubstantial part" of their activities, but that there was no basis for concluding that the admission of women as full voting members would "impede the organization's ability to engage in these protected activities or to disseminate its preferred views." The Court went on to note that:

> "The Act requires no change in the Jaycees' creed of promoting the interests of young men, and it imposes no restrictions on the organization's ability to exclude individuals with ideologies or philosophies different from those of its existing members. Moreover, the Jaycees already invites women to share the group's views and philosophy and to participate in much of its training and community activities. Accordingly, any claim that admission of women as full voting members will impair a symbolic message conveyed by the very fact that women are not permitted to vote is attenuated at best."

The Court rejected the court of appeals' conclusion that the admission of women would infringe the Jaycees' associational interests. That court had found that "women members might have a different view or agenda with respect to these matters so that, if they are allowed to vote, 'some change in the Jaycees' philosophical cast can reasonably be expected.'" In addition, the court of appeals found that, since the Jaycees were organized "to promote the views of young men," the admission of women as voting members might "change the message communicated by the group's speech because of the gender-based assumptions of the audience." The Court concluded that the court of appeal's concerns were unsubstantiated noting that they were based

> on unsupported generalizations about the relative interests and perspectives of men and women. . . . In the absence of a showing far more substantial than that attempted by the Jaycees, we decline to indulge in the sexual stereotyping that underlies appellee's contention that, by allowing women to vote, application of the Minnesota Act will change the content or impact of the organization's speech.

Even if the Act did cause "some incidental abridgment of the Jaycees' protected speech," the Court found that the effect was "no greater than . . . necessary to accomplish the State's legitimate purposes." "[A]cts of invidious discrimination in the distribution of publicly available goods, services, and other advantages cause unique evils that government has a compelling interest to prevent — wholly apart from the point of view such conduct may transmit. . . . In prohibiting such practices, the Minnesota Act therefore "responds precisely to the substantive problem which legitimately concerns" the State and "abridges no more speech or associational freedom than is necessary to accomplish that purpose."

Justice O'Connor concurred arguing that an "association engaged exclusively in protected expression enjoys First Amendment protection of both the content of its message and the choice of its members," and that protection "of the association's right to define its membership derives from the recognition that the formation of an expressive association is the creation of a voice, and the selection of members is the definition of that voice." But she also recognized that many associations cannot be regarded as purely commercial or purely expressive, and argued that it "is only when the association is predominantly engaged in protected expression that state regulation of its membership will necessarily affect, change, dilute, or silence one collective voice that would otherwise be heard. An association must choose its market. Once it enters the marketplace of commerce in any substantial degree it loses the complete control over its membership that it would otherwise enjoy if it confined its affairs to the marketplace of ideas." She viewed the Jaycees as "a relatively easy case for application of the expressive-commercial dichotomy." Although she found that a "good deal of what the [Jaycees] does indisputably comes within the right of association [in] pursuance of the specific ends of speech, writing, belief, and assembly for redress of grievances," she concluded that the "Junior Chamber of Commerce — is, first and foremost, an organization that, at both the national and local levels, promotes and practices the art of solicitation and management. The organization claims that the training it offers its members gives them an advantage in business, and business firms do indeed sometimes pay the dues of individual memberships for their [employees]." "The State of Minnesota has a legitimate interest in ensuring nondiscriminatory access to the commercial opportunity presented by membership in the Jaycees. [The] Jaycees may not claim constitutional immunity from Minnesota's antidiscrimination law by seeking to exercise their First Amendment rights through this commercial organization."

Roberts was followed and strengthened by the holding in *New York State Club Association, Inc. v. City of New York.*[6] That case involved a city law that prohibited discrimination by any "place of public accommodation, resort or amusement." In enacting the law, the City Council of New York stated:

> [T]he city of New York has a compelling interest in providing [all] persons, regardless of race, creed, color, national origin or sex, [a] fair and equal opportunity to participate in the business and professional life of the city. . . . One barrier to the advancement of women and minorities in the business and professional life of the city is the discriminatory practices of certain membership organizations where business deals are often made and personal contacts valuable for business purposes, employment and professional advancement are formed. While such organizations may avowedly be organized for social, cultural, civic or educational purposes, and while many perform valuable services to the community, the commercial nature of some of the activities occurring therein and the prejudicial impact of these activities on business, professional and employment opportunities of minorities and women cannot be ignored.

The Court upheld the law noting that it did "not affect 'in any significant way" the ability of individuals to form associations that will advocate public or private viewpoints." The Court noted that the law did not "require the clubs 'to abandon or alter' any activities that are protected by the First Amendment" and that the club could exclude those "who do not share the views that the club's members wish to promote." The law simply prohibited "an association from using race, sex, and the other specified characteristics as shorthand measures in place of what the city considers to be more legitimate criteria for determining membership." The Court left open the possibility that a club could show that it was "organized for specific expressive purposes" and that it "could not advocate its desired viewpoints nearly as effectively if it cannot confine its membership to those who share the same sex, for example, or the same religion." But the court found that most of the large clubs subjected to the law were "not of this kind."

Roberts and *New York State Club Association* were limited by the holding in *Boy Scouts of America v. Dale.*[7] That case involved a private, not-for-profit organization engaged in instilling values in young people. The Boy Scouts asserted that homosexual conduct was inconsistent with the values it seeks to instill. Dale, a former Eagle Scout whose adult membership in the Boy Scouts was revoked when the Scouts learned that he was an avowed homosexual and gay rights activist, sued claiming a violation of New Jersey's public accommodations law. In a 5-4 decision, the Court held that the law could not be applied to the Boy Scouts. The Court concluded that it would defer to "to an association's view of what would impair its expression." The Court went on to find that a "state requirement that the Boy Scouts retain Dale as an assistant scoutmaster would significantly burden the organization's right to oppose or disfavor homosexual conduct. The state interests [do] not justify such a severe intrusion on the Boy Scouts' rights to freedom of

---

[6] 487 U.S. 1 (1988).

[7] 530 U.S. 640 (2000).

expressive association." Four Justices dissented including Justice Stevens who argued that "[Dale's] participation sends no cognizable message to the Scouts or to the world. Unlike GLIB, Dale did not carry a banner or a sign; [and] he expressed no intent to send any message."

[E] "Fusion" Political Candidates

Timmons v. Twin Cities Area New Party[8] involved the subject of "ballot qualification." A Minnesota law prohibited "fusion" candidates — candidates who appear on the ballot as the candidate of more than one party. A political party sued claiming an associational right to list the candidate of its choice whether or not that candidate was listed on the ballot of another party. The Court (6-3) upheld the law on the basis that the law did not prohibit the New Party from endorsing, supporting, or voting for the candidate of its choice, and did not affect the party's internal structure, governance or policy making. The Court found that the law did reduce "the universe of potential candidates who may appear on the ballot as the Party's nominee only by ruling out those few individuals who both have already agreed to be another party's candidate and also, if forced to choose, themselves prefer that other party." The Court found that this burden "though not trivial" was not "severe" and was outweighed by the state's interest "in protecting the integrity, fairness, and efficiency of their ballots and election processes as means for electing public officials." The Court also found that the states have a "strong interest in the stability of their political systems" that

> permits them to enact reasonable election regulations that may, in practice, favor the traditional two-party system, and that temper the destabilizing effects of party-splintering and excessive factionalism. The Constitution permits the Minnesota Legislature to decide that political stability is best served through a healthy two-party system.

Justice Stevens dissented arguing that a party's "choice of a candidate is the most effective way in which that party can communicate to the voters what the party represents and, thereby, attract voter interest and support." He argued that the State failed to show how the ban actually served the state's asserted interests.

[F] Political Primaries

Clingman v. Beaver,[9] involved a challenge to a semi-closed primary system, pursuant to which a political party could invite only its registered members and voters registered as independents to vote in its primary. The Court found that this restriction did not violate the First Amendment's protections for freedom of political association. It determined instead that the system imposed only a minor burden on associational rights of the state's citizenry and advanced important regulatory interests in preserving political parties as viable and identifiable interests groups (*e.g.*, it aided parties' electioneering and party-building efforts, and prevented party raiding). The court quoted the decision in *California*

---

[8] 520 U.S. 351 (1997).

[9] 544 U.S. 581 (2005).

Democratic Party v. Jones,[10] in which it stated that "the associational 'interest' in selecting the candidate of a group to which one does not belong, [falls] far short of a constitutional right, if indeed it can even be fairly characterized as an interest."

In *Washington State Grange v. Washington State Republican Party*,[11] the Court upheld a political primary process adopted in response to the invalidation of a blanket primary system in *California Democratic Party v. Jones*.[12] The Court determined that the new system could survive a facial challenge because it did not on its face "impose a severe burden on political parties' associational rights." Pursuant to this structure, (1) all candidates in the primary were required to list on the ballot a party preference or their independent status, and (2) the top two vote-getters would run in the general election. Parties could nominate candidates by whatever method they chose, but (consistent with First Amendment precedent) had no right to have their nominees designated on the ballot.

The *Washington State Grange* Court found "no basis to presume that a well-informed electorate will interpret a candidate's party preference designation to mean that the candidate is the party's chosen nominee or representative or that the party associates with or approves of the candidate." The new system thus did not resemble the blanket primary, in which voters (regardless of their party affiliation) determined a party's nominee in the general election. The Court left open the possibility that the system could be challenged in the future, if there was evidence of voter confusion sufficient to support a claim of severe burden. Justices Kennedy and Scalia dissented.

In *New York State Board of Elections v. Lopez Torres*,[13] the Court rejected a challenge to a state law governing the ballot designation of trial judge candidates. The plaintiffs in this case were candidates who failed to secure their party's nomination. Nominee status was achieved by securing the support of delegates to the party's convention. Nomination resulted in placement on the general election ballot coupled with the party's endorsement. At issues were competing claims of associational rights. The party's interest related to a candidate that reflected party priorities and preferences. The candidate's concern was with an interest in party membership, participation, and influence. The Court determined that the party's interests in the operation and outcome of its processes were paramount. From its perspective, the candidates' concerns had no grounding in the First Amendment.

§ 8.02   THE RIGHT "NOT TO SPEAK"

[A]   Overview

The development of fundamental rights, that are not enumerated by the Constitution, has a long but debated history. Economic rights doctrine during the early Twentieth Century, as a means of negating the legislature's outputs and

---

[10]   530 U.S. 567 (2000).

[11]   552 U.S. 442 (2008).

[12]   530 U.S. 567 (2000).

[13]   552 U.S. 196 (2008).

vitality, is widely discredited as an exercise in judicial overreaching. Against this backdrop, the Court typically can anticipate controversy when it announces that a right not textually specified by the Constitution is nonetheless fundamental. This phenomenon is evidenced, for instance, by the criticism and discord generated when the Court announced a right of privacy as an incident of due process.

Less controversial, although no more clearly enumerated by the Constitution itself, is a right of privacy that implicates First Amendment interests. Whether framed as the right to be let or left alone, or not to speak or be free from coercion, the relationship between privacy and the First Amendment is a close one. Like the freedom to associate, it is difficult to imagine a vibrant guarantee of expressive freedom without room for the individual to refrain from speaking or to decline identification with standard orthodoxy. The concept in the moral sense that a person belongs to himself or herself, rather than to society, has been described by one constitutional expert as "nothing less than society's limiting principle."[14] Central to the understanding of freedom of speech, as shaped by case law, is the premise that the First Amendment protects freedom of conscience and thought. This perspective is central to a line of decisions that safeguard the individual from official efforts to compel expression or publicly embrace a particular orthodoxy or conviction. In *West Virginia State Board of Education v. Barnette*,[15] the state adopted a resolution ordering that the salute to the flag become "a regular part of the program of activities in the public schools, that all teachers and pupils shall be required to participate in the salute honoring the Nation represented by the Flag; provided, however, that refusal to salute the Flag be regarded as an Act of insubordination, and shall be dealt with accordingly." In an opinion by Justice Jackson, the Court held the law unconstitutional recognizing that the "the flag salute is a form of utterance" and that the Bill of Rights protects an individual from being forced to "utter what is not in his mind."

> If there is any fixed star in our constitutional constellation, it is that no official, high or petty, can prescribe what shall be orthodox in politics, nationalism, religion, or other matters of opinion or force citizens to confess by word or act their faith therein. If there are any circumstances which permit an exception, they do not now occur to us.

A similar theme was sounded, in *Wooley v. Maynard*,[16] when the Court reviewed a state law requiring car owners to display licensing plates bearing the motto "Live Free or Die." The law was challenged by a Jehovah's Witness who argued that the state was coercing him to display a message which he found morally and religiously abhorrent. The state maintained that the motto facilitated the ability of law enforcement officers to identify state license plates and promoted appreciation of history, state pride, and individualism. Applying a strict level of review, the Court found that neither of these interests was compelling. The record demonstrated that the state license plates could be readily identified without the motto. The state's regulatory interest thus could be achieved by less drastic means. With respect to the

---

[14] Laurence H. Tribe, American Constitutional Law, Section 15-1, at 1302 (2d ed. 1988).

[15] 319 U.S. 624 (1943).

[16] 430 U.S. 705 (1977).

state's interest in fostering pride and appreciation of history, the Court found that this objective cannot out-weigh a person's First Amendment right to avoid functioning as a "courier" for the message. Consistent with the philosophy of *Barnette*, the *Wooley* decision stands for the proposition that "[t]he freedom of thought protected by the First Amendment" comprehends not only the right to speak freely but "to refrain from speaking at all":

> [F]reedom of thought [includes] both the right to speak freely and the right to refrain from speaking at all. [W]e are faced with a state measure which forces an individual, as part of his daily life indeed constantly while his automobile is in public view to be an instrument for fostering public adherence to an ideological point of view he finds unacceptable. . . . The State [contends that] officers of the law are more easily able to determine whether passenger vehicles are carrying the proper plates. However, [New Hampshire] passenger license plates normally consist of a specific configuration of letters and numbers, which makes them readily distinguishable from other types of plates, even without reference to the state motto. . . . The [State also claims an] interest [in] communicat[ing] [an] appreciation of history, state pride, and individualism. [S]uch interest cannot outweigh an individual's First Amendment right to avoid becoming the courier for such message.[17]

Justice Rehnquist, joined by Justice Blackmun, dissented noting that the State did not forced "appellees to '*say*' anything."

> "The State has simply required that all noncommercial automobiles bear license tags with the state motto. . . . There is nothing in state law which precludes appellees from displaying their disagreement with the state motto as long as the methods used do not obscure the license plates. Since any implication that they affirm the motto can be so easily displaced, I cannot agree [that] appellees are unconstitutionally forced to affirm, or profess belief in, the state motto."

A similar note was struck in *Pacific Gas & Electric Co. v. Public Utilities Commission*,[18] when the Court invalidated a requirement that utility companies include in their billing materials the publication of a consumers group. The Court found that the measure violated the First Amendment, because it forced utilities to associate with speech that they otherwise disowned. A determining factor in the right not to speak cases is government prescription of a message that "invades the sphere of intellect and spirit." In *Pruneyard Shopping Center v. Robins*,[19] the Court found this element missing. The case concerned a state law that required shopping center operators to allow speech and assembly on their premises. This regulation was challenged on grounds it violated the right not to speak. Because shopping center owners only were required to provide for public access, they could post disclaimers to avoid any association with a point of view, and government itself prescribed no message, there was no First Amendment violation. Unlike the

---

[17] *Id.* at 715.

[18] 475 U.S. 1 (1986).

[19] 447 U.S. 74 (1980).

individuals or entities in *Barnette, Wooley,* and *Pacific Gas & Electric,* the shopping center operators were not compelled to affirm a particular belief or ideology or embrace an objectionable point of view.

[B] The Solomon Amendment and Law School Placement Offices

In its decision in *Rumsfeld v. Forum for Academic and Institutional Rights, Inc.,*[20] the facts of which are summarized in the unconstitutional conditions section *supra,* the Court also rejected claims that the Solomon Amendment infringed freedom of association.

The Court rejected any suggestion that the Solomon Amendment required colleges and law schools to engage in speech in violation of the compelled speech doctrine articulated in cases such as *West Virginia Bd. of Ed. v. Barnette*[21] and *Wooley v. Maynard.*[22] The Court held that the Solomon Amendment did not require any expression by law schools other than the posting of notices that military recruiters will be on campus along with a statement of the place and time. The Court concluded that its compelled speech cases involved situations in which "the complaining speaker's own message was affected by the speech it was forced to accommodate." The Court distinguished the Solomon Amendment, noting that the military's message does not affect the law schools' speech, because the schools are not speaking when they host interviews and recruiting receptions. "A law school's recruiting services lack the expressive quality of a parade, a newsletter, or the editorial page of a newspaper; its accommodation of a military recruiter's message is not compelled speech because the accommodation does not sufficiently interfere with any message of the school."

The Court also rejected the law school's associational argument which involved the argument that, if the schools are required to give military recruiters equal access, they might be viewed as suggesting that they do not object to the military's policies. "Nothing about recruiting suggests that law schools agree with any speech by recruiters, and nothing in the Solomon Amendment restricts what the law schools may say about the military's policies. We have held that high school students can appreciate the difference between speech a school sponsors and speech the school permits because legally required to do so, pursuant to an equal access policy. Surely students have not lost that ability by the time they get to law school." The Court noted that the "expressive component" of a law school's actions are not determined "by the conduct itself but by the speech that accompanies it," and the Court doubted that the actions in this case (allowing military recruiters to have equal access) was "so inherently expressive that it warrants protection under *O'Brien.*" Faculty and students were free to express their disapproval of military policies without running afoul of the Solomon Amendment.

---

[20] 547 U.S. 47 (2006).

[21] 319 U.S. 624 (1943).

[22] 430 U.S. 705 (1977).

[C] Parade Inclusion — Exclusion

In *Hurley v. Irish-American Gay, Lesbian and Bisexual Group of Boston*,[23] the Court held that parade organizers could not be forced to include a message that they did not want to convey. The case involved a St. Patrick's day/Evacuation day (which marked the date when royal troops and loyalists "evacuated" from the city) parade held on March 17th each year. The parade was sponsored by the South Boston Allied War Veterans Council, an unincorporated association of individuals elected from various South Boston veterans groups, who annually applied and received a permit for the parade. The city allowed the Council to use the city's official seal, and provided printing services as well as direct funding.

The case arose when GLIB (gay, lesbian and bisexual descendants of the Irish immigrants) sought to march in the parade as a way to express "pride in their Irish heritage as openly gay, lesbian, and bisexual individuals, to demonstrate that there are such men and women among those so descended, and to express their solidarity with like individuals who sought to march in New York's St. Patrick's Day Parade." The Council denied the request. GLIB sued claiming, *inter alia*, violations of the State and Federal Constitutions and of the state public accommodations law, which prohibited "any distinction, discrimination or restriction on account [of] sexual orientation [relative] to the admission of any person to, or treatment in any place of public accommodation, resort or amusement." Mass. Gen. Laws § 272:98 (1992). The Court found that the law violated the First Amendment.

In ruling in favor of the parade organizers, the Court noted that parades are often organized for expressive purposes. "If there were no reason for a group of people to march from here to there except to reach a destination, they could make the trip without expressing any message beyond the fact of the march itself. Some people might call such a procession a parade, but it would not be much of one." "Hence, we use the word 'parade' to indicate marchers who are making some sort of collective point, not just to each other but to bystanders along the way. . . . Parades are thus a form of expression, not just motion, and the inherent expressiveness of marching to make a point explains our cases involving protest marches." In the case of the Boston parade, the Court noted that there were multiple messages (*e.g.*, "England get out of Ireland," "Say no to drugs"), and the Court found that the organizers did not forfeit the right to control their "message" even though they allowed "multifarious voices" to participate.

The Court concluded that the Council's right to control its message also included the right to exclude messages with which it disagreed. And the Court noted that GLIB's participation was very expressive since it celebrated "its members' identity as openly gay, lesbian, and bisexual descendants of the Irish immigrants, to show that there are such individuals in the community, and to support the like men and women who sought to march in the New York parade." The Court held that the Council could exclude GLIB from participation noting that the public accommodations law violated "the fundamental rule of protection under the First Amendment, that a speaker has the autonomy to choose the content of his own message." The Court concluded that the "Council clearly decided to exclude a

---

[23] 515 U.S. 557 (1995).

message it did not like from the communication it chose to make, and that is enough to invoke its right as a private speaker to shape its expression by speaking on one subject while remaining silent on another."

> When the law is applied to expressive activity in the way it was done here, its apparent object is simply to require speakers to modify the content of their expression to whatever extent beneficiaries of the law choose to alter it with messages of their own. But in the absence of some further, legitimate end, this object is merely to allow exactly what the general rule of speaker's autonomy forbids.

In *Agency for International Development v. Alliance for Open Society International, Inc.*,[24] the Court struck down portions of the United States Leadership Against HIV/AIDS, Tuberculosis, and Malaria Act of 2003 (Leadership Act),[25] which outlined a comprehensive strategy to combat the spread of HIV/AIDS around the world. In that Act, Congress appropriated billions of dollars to fund efforts by nongovernmental organizations to assist in the fight against HIV/AIDS. Congress expressed concern that the disease had reached pandemic proportions, endangering those infected, increasing "the potential for social and political instability and economic devastation, and posing a security issue for the entire international community." In the Act, Congress directed the President to establish a "comprehensive, integrated" strategy to combat HIV/AIDS around the world, set forth 29 different objectives the President's strategy should seek to fulfill, including plans to increase the availability of treatment for infected individuals, prevent new infections, support the care of those affected by the disease, promote training for physicians and other health care workers, and accelerate research on HIV/AIDS prevention methods, all while providing a framework for cooperation with international organizations and partner countries to further the goals of the program. However, the Act also made the reduction of HIV/AIDS behavioral risks "a priority of all prevention efforts," and required the President to move to promote abstinence, encourage monogamy, increase the availability of condoms, promote voluntary counseling and treatment for drug users, [and] "educat[e] men and boys about the risks of procuring sex commercially" as well as "promote alternative livelihoods, safety, and social reintegration strategies for commercial sex workers." Congress found that the "sex industry, the trafficking of individuals into such industry, and sexual violence" were factors in the spread of the HIV/AIDS epidemic, and decided that "it should be the policy of the United States to eradicate" prostitution and "other sexual victimization."

In the Act, Congress authorized funding to organizations "with experience in health care and HIV/AIDS counseling." However, Congress imposed two conditions on those funds. First, no funds made available to carry out the Act "may be used to promote or advocate the legalization or practice of prostitution or sex trafficking." Second, Congress prohibited making funds available to any organization that "does not have a policy explicitly opposing prostitution and sex trafficking." The U.S. Department of Health and Human Services (HHS) and the United States Agency

---

[24] 133 S. Ct. 2321 (2013).

[25] 22 U. S. C. § 7601 *et seq.*

for International Development (USAID) directed that the recipient of any funding under the Act agree in the award document that it is opposed to "prostitution and sex trafficking because of the psychological and physical risks they pose for women, men, and children." The second requirement was challenged by a group of domestic organizations engaged in combating HIV/AIDS overseas. While the appeal was pending, HHS and USAID modified their guidelines to permitt affiliated organizations not bound by the Policy Requirement to work with affiliated organizations that "engage in activities inconsistent with the recipient's opposition to the practices of prostitution and sex trafficking" as long as the recipients retain "objective integrity and independence from any affiliated organization."

In striking down the requirement that funded organizations issue a statement indicating their opposition to prostitution and sex trafficking, the Court emphasized that "freedom of speech prohibits the government from telling people what they must say." In doing so, the Court cited *West Virginia Bd. of Ed. v. Barnette*,[26] and *Wooley v. Maynard*.[27] Even though the Spending Clause of the Federal Constitution grants Congress broad spending authority, including broad discretion to impose limits on the use of appropriated funds to ensure they are used in the manner Congress intends, Congress may not deny benefits to a person on a basis that "infringes his constitutionally [protected] freedom of speech even if he has no entitlement to that benefit." In the Court's view, there is a distinction between "conditions that define the limits of the government spending program — those that specify the activities Congress wants to subsidize — and conditions that mandate that grant recipients adopt the government's preferred position on an issue. "In other words, Congress sought to compel "a grant recipient to adopt a particular belief as a condition of funding." The Court concluded that, by demanding that funding recipients "adopt [the] Government's view on an issue of public concern," the condition affects "protected conduct outside the scope of the federally funded program."

Justice Scalia, joined by Justice Thomas, dissented, noting that the requirement involved "nothing more than a means of selecting suitable agents to implement the Government's chosen strategy to eradicate HIV/AIDS. That is perfectly permissible under the Constitution." "Moreover, the government may enlist the assistance of those who believe in its ideas to carry them to fruition; and it need not enlist for that purpose those who oppose or do not support the ideas." "[The] constitutional prohibition at issue here is not a prohibition against discriminating against or injuring opposing points of view, but the First Amendment's prohibition against the coercing of speech." "[T]he views that the Government demands an applicant forswear [are] relevant to the program in question." "There is no risk that this principle will enable the Government to discriminate arbitrarily against positions it disfavors. It would not [permit] the Government to exclude from bidding on defense contracts anyone who refuses to abjure prostitution. But here a central part of the Government's HIV/AIDS strategy is the suppression of prostitution, by which HIV is transmitted." "[The] most obvious manner in which the admission to a program of an ideological opponent can frustrate the purpose of the program is by freeing up

[26] 319 U. S. 624 (1943).

[27] 430 U. S. 705, 717 (1977).

the opponent's funds for use in its ideological opposition."

[D] Compelled Financial Support for Expression

In a number of cases, the Court has been confronted by "compelled financial support" issues. The seminal decision was *Abood v. Detroit Board of Education.*[28] In *Abood*, nonunion public school teachers challenged a collective bargaining agreement that required them, as a condition of their employment, to pay a "service fee" that was equivalent to union dues and equal in amount. The teachers complained that the union used a portion of their dues to engage in political speech to which they objected, and objected on freedom of association grounds to payment of dues to the extent expended on such speech. The Court agreed and held that any objecting teacher could "prevent the Union's spending a part of their required service fees to contribute to political candidates and to express political views unrelated to its duties as exclusive bargaining representative."

Abood was followed by the holding in *Keller v. State Bar of California,*[29] in which lawyers admitted to practice in California were required to join the state bar association and to fund activities "germane" to the association's mission of "regulating the legal profession and improving the quality of legal services." The Court held that, while the state could require the lawyers to join the association as a condition of practicing law, it could not require them to fund the bar association's own political expression.

The Court's most recent decision in this area is *Board of Regents of the University of Wisconsin System v. Southworth.*[30] That case involved a University of Wisconsin student activity fee of $331.50 per year. This fund was used to support student organizations (RSOs). Students could apply for funds, or they could seek funding through a student referendum (which could also be used to deny funding to RSOs). Funding was provided on a viewpoint neutral basis. Relying on *Abood* and *Keller*, students challenged the activity fee on the basis that it required them to contribute to the speech activities of organizations with which they disagreed.

In an opinion by Justice Kennedy, the Court upheld the fee. With a nod towards *Abood* and *Keller*, the Court noted that it would be "impractical" to allow each student to list those causes which he or she will or will not support. "The restriction could be so disruptive and expensive that the program to support extracurricular speech would be ineffective. . . ." The Court then held that the University could legitimately decide to provide

> the means to engage in dynamic discussions of philosophical, religious, scientific, social, and political subjects in their extracurricular campus life outside the lecture hall. If the University reaches this conclusion, it is entitled to impose a mandatory fee to sustain an open dialogue to these ends.

---

[28] 431 U.S. 209 (1977).

[29] 496 U.S. 1 (1990).

[30] 529 U.S. 217 (2000).

However, the Court made clear that it would sustain only a "viewpoint" neutral fee. "When a university requires its students to pay fees to support the extracurricular speech of other students, all in the interest of open discussion, it may not prefer some viewpoints to others." The Court did express concern about the fact that the program provided for a referendum in which students could decide which speech to fund or to defund an organization. The Court remanded for further hearings on whether the referendum could result in discrimination against minority viewpoints. "The whole theory of viewpoint neutrality is that minority views are treated with the same respect as are majority views. Access to a public forum [does] not depend upon majoritarian consent. . . . A remand is necessary and appropriate to resolve this point."

Compelled speech doctrine also did not apply to the circumstances of *Glick-man v. Wileman Brothers & Elliott, Inc.* [31] In this case, the Court reviewed a Department of Agriculture rule that imposed generic advertising costs for California tree fruit upon the state's tree fruit growers. It found that the requirement did not compel speech in a way that implicated the First Amendment. Critical to the outcome was the Court's sense that no grower was forced to speak against his or her will or embrace an objectionable political or ideological message.

In another case concerning federally required assessments for advertising farm products, the Court distinguished *Glickman.* In *United States v. United Foods, Inc.,* [32] the Court found no marketing orders regulating production and sales, antitrust exemptions, or other limitations upon the ability of mushroom producers to make their own marketing decisions. It contrasted this circumstance with the *Glickman* scenario, where cooperative advertising was part of a broader collective enterprise in which freedom already was constrained by a general regulatory scheme. Because the assessment for promotional advertising was not ancillary to a comprehensive regulatory scheme, but the principal object of it, the Court concluded that First Amendment interests against compelled speech and association should prevail. In a dissenting opinion joined by Justices O'Connor and Ginsburg, Justice Breyer found it difficult to understand why the factor of "heavy regulation" should be a determinative factor.

The Court's most recent compelled speech decision was rendered in *Johanns v. Livestock Marking Association.* [33] That case involved the Beef Promotion and Research Act of 1985 (Act) which was designed to promote the marketing and consumption of "beef and beef products" by using funds raised through an assessment on cattle sales and importation. The statute directed the Secretary of Agriculture to implement this policy by issuing a Beef Promotion and Research Order (Order), which created an Operating Committee to administer the Act, and authorized the Secretary to impose a $1-per-head assessment (or "checkoff") on all sales or importation of cattle and a comparable assessment on imported beef products. The assessment was used to fund beef-related projects, including promotional campaigns, designed by the Operating Committee and approved by the

---

[31] 521 U.S. 457 (1997).

[32] 533 U.S. 405 (2001).

[33] 544 U.S. 550 (2005).

Secretary. The Secretary or his designee were required to approve each project and, in the case of promotional materials, the content of each communication. More than $1 billion was collected under the checkoff program, and a large percentage of that amount was spent on advertising some with the trademarked slogan "Beef. It's What's for Dinner." Some of the advertising included the notation "Funded by America's Beef Producers" or the Beef Board logo "BEEF." The Act was challenged by two associations that were subject to the checkoff who complained that the advertising promotes beef as a generic commodity whereas they were trying to promote the superiority of American beef, grain-fed beef, or certified Angus or Hereford beef.

In upholding the Act, the Court distinguished the Court's compelled speech decisions. Citing *West Virginia Board of Education v. Barnette*,[34] and *Wooley v. Maynard*,[35] the Court recognized that government could not compel individuals to engage in speech. However, in *Johanns*, the Court distinguished between "compelled support of government" and compelled speech. Although the Court had struck down laws requiring individuals to fund speech programs, the Court emphasized that all of these laws involved speech that "was, or was presumed to be, that of an entity other than the government itself," and that compelled support of a private association is different than compelled support of government. The Court concluded that individuals could not object to compelled support of government even if the governmental program involved speech to which the individual objected.[36] In *Johanns*, the Court found that the message would not be attributed to the beef producers. On the contrary, the "message set out in the beef promotions is from beginning to end the message established by the Federal Government. Congress has directed the implementation of a 'coordinated program' of promotion, 'including paid advertising, to advance the image and desirability of beef and beef products.' " "Congress and the Secretary have set out the overarching message and some of its elements, and they have left the development of the remaining details to an entity whose members are answerable to the Secretary (and in some cases appointed by him as well)." In addition, department officials review all advertisements and the Secretary exercises final approval authority. Because of the degree of governmental control, the Court saw this case as different from prior subsidy/compelled speech cases. The additional question, of whether the reference to "America's Beef Producers" in the advertisements, raised a question about whether the advertisements were attributed to respondents. The Court remanded for consideration of this issue.

Justice Thomas concurred. Although he recognized that government may not involuntarily associate individuals or organizations with an unwanted message, he found that the "payment of taxes to the government for purposes of supporting government speech is not nearly as intrusive as being forced to 'utter what is not in [one's] mind,' or to carry an unwanted message on one's property." Justice Breyer also concurred on the basis that the Act implicated economic regulation issues rather than speech. Justice Ginsburg agreed with Justice Breyer.

---

[34] 319 U.S. 624 (1943).

[35] 430 U.S. 705 (1977).

[36] *Johanns*, 544 U.S. at 558.

Justice Kennedy dissented, arguing that he would have reserved the First Amendment questions for another day. Justice Souter, joined by justices Stevens and Kennedy, also dissented, arguing that, if the

> government relies on the government-speech doctrine to compel specific groups to fund speech with targeted taxes, it must make itself politically accountable by indicating that the content actually is a government message, not just the statement of one self-interested group the government is currently willing to invest with power.

He emphasized that the advertisements in question did not indicate that they were governmental speech, and in fact the ads concealed their origins by indicating that they were "[f]unded by America's Beef Producers." He argued that "[r]eaders would most naturally think that ads urging people to have beef for dinner were placed and paid for by the beef producers who stand to profit when beef is on the table." "Unless the putative government speech appears to be coming from the government, its governmental origin cannot possibly justify the burden on the First Amendment interests of the dissenters targeted to pay for it."

Davenport v. Washington Education Association,[37] involved a State of Washington law that prohibited public sector labor unions from using the agency-shop fees of nonmembers for election-related purposes unless the nonmember affirmatively consents. The Court rejected a First Amendment challenge. While the Court noted that its prior decisions, in particular *Teachers v. Hudson*,[38] had allowed government to impose procedural requirements on public-sector collection of union fees. In addition, the Court concluded that "Washington could have gone much further, restricting public-sector agency fees to the portion of union dues devoted to collective bargaining. Indeed, it is uncontested that it would be constitutional for Washington to eliminate agency fees entirely." The Court rejected the idea that the law involved a content-based restriction on speech: "[N]o suppression of ideas is afoot, since the union remains as free as any other entity to participate in the electoral process with all available funds other than the state-coerced agency fees lacking affirmative permission."

In *Knox v. Service Employees International Union, Local 1000*,[39] the Court held that the First Amendment prohibited a public-sector union from requiring objecting nonmembers to pay a special fee for the purpose of financing the union's political and ideological activities. Although state law provided that a union bargaining unit could require all employees to pay an annual fee designed to cover the cost of union services related to collective bargaining, they could not require objecting employees to pay for union's ideological activities. However, *Knox* involved a special assessment. The union notified employees of the annual assessment, and gave them the opportunity to decide whether to pay for the union's ideological activities, but it provided no similar opportunity when it imposed a special assessment. Plaintiffs included some employees who had originally opted out of the ideological part of the assessment, and some who had not, but all of whom wished to opt out of the special

---

[37] 551 U.S. 177 (2007).

[38] 475 U.S. 292 (1986).

[39] 132 S.Ct. 2277 (2012).

assessment. The Court held that the union was required to give all employees a so-called *Hudson* notice and may not exact any funds from nonmembers without their affirmative consent. Justice Breyer, joined by Justice Kagan, dissented, arguing that the union should not be required to allow employees to opt out who failed to object during the initial notice.

In *Locke v. Karass*,[40] the Court dealt with a Maine statute that required government employees to pay a service fee to a local union that serves as their exclusive bargaining agent even if those employees disagree with, and do not belong to, the union. Relying on *Railway Employees v. Hanson*,[41] and *Abate v. Detroit Bd. of Ed.*,[42] the Court upheld the fee even though the money could be used to pay for litigation expenses incurred in large part on behalf of other local units. The Court held that the charge could be imposed provided that two conditions were satisfied:

> (1) the subject matter of the (extra-local) litigation is of a kind that would be chargeable if the litigation were local, *e.g.*, litigation appropriately related to collective bargaining rather than political activities, and (2) the litigation charge is reciprocal in nature, *i.e.*, the contributing local reasonably expects other locals to contribute similarly to the national's resources used for costs of similar litigation on behalf of the contributing local if and when it takes place.

The Court found that both conditions were satisfied and that national litigation expenses should be treated like other national expenses.

§ 8.03 UNCONSTITUTIONAL CONDITIONS

Abridgment of freedom of expression typically is manifested by regulation that forecloses or deters speech by a system of subsequent punishment for violators. Expressive liberty can be cramped not just by direct means that penalize, but by methods of encouragement or incentivization. Government's role in both the economic and information marketplace is significant. Although it is empowered to set policy, implement programs necessary to effectuate its goals, and establish conditions upon distribution of resources, government must operate within constitutional limits including those imposed by the First Amendment. Government has the right to express itself and promote policies and programs that are consistent with a particular ideology or agenda. Funding of private entities to convey a particular message, therefore, may be coupled with requirements ensuring that government's message is not undermined. Consistent with this premise, government may distribute benefits but it may not condition their receipt upon waiver of a basic right or liberty. Insofar as governmental power is used to suppress, control, or steer speech, First Amendment interests may be compromised and in need of accounting.

The framing and development of government policy typically reflects value judgments and involves choices, priorities, and standards. This reality is reflected

---

[40] 555 U.S. 207 (2009).

[41] 351 U.S. 225 (1956).

[42] 431 U.S. 209 (1977).

throughout the regulatory process. The federal tax code, for instance, distributes burdens and benefits on the basis of legislative policy considerations. In *Regan v. Taxation With Representation of Washington*,[43] the Court examined Congress' decision to make contributions to nonprofit organizations deductible if they did not engage in lobbying activities. Key to the Court's decision upholding the law was a finding that Congress had not discriminated on the basis of viewpoint. The Court determined that the law did not require lobbying organizations to forego their speech rights. Nor was government obligated to subsidize them.

The finding of an unconstitutional condition on expressive freedom was made *in League of Women Voters v. Federal Communications Commission*.[44] In this case, the Court struck down a federal law which denied federal funding to public broadcasting stations that editorialized on the air. The provision aimed to insulate public broadcasters from the possibility that their funding would be jeopardized by the airing of unpopular views. The Court determined that this restriction on expression was problematic, particularly because it ensnared political speech. Although this form of expression is highly valued under the First Amendment, and triggers strict scrutiny when subject to regulation, broadcasting is the least protected medium under this guarantee. The Court thus employed a standard of review that, although heightened, inquired into whether the law accounted for a substantial or important government interest and was narrowly tailored to achieve its purpose. The Court acknowledged government's substantial and important interest in ensuring balanced coverage of public issues, but found that an editorial ban overreached to the point that it underserved this interest.

The *League of Women Voters* scenario was distinguished in *Rust v. Sullivan*,[45] a case concerning federal rules that denied federal funds to family planning clinics that counseled abortion or made abortion referrals. In upholding the condition upon funding, the Court determined that government is free to determine what programs it will subsidize provided it does not engage in viewpoint discrimination. Government's decision to fund one program but not another was found to be more akin to the circumstances of *Rust* than *League of Women Voters*. In *Rust*, government used private speakers to transmit information pertaining to its own program. Under such circumstances, it may take reasonable steps to ensure that its message is clear and not distorted. In the *League of Women Voters* case, freedom of expression was burdened without any government program or message that required protection.

Federal arts funding also has raised the issue of possible unconstitutional conditions. In *National Endowment for the Arts v. Finley*,[46] the Court examined a federal law mandating that the National Endowment for Arts factor "decency" and "respect" for the nation's diverse values and beliefs into the awarding of grants. Although the Endowment was required to take these considerations into account, it retained discretion to make awards for contrary projects. The Court determined,

---

[43] 461 U.S. 540 (1983).

[44] 468 U.S. 364 (1984).

[45] 500 U.S. 173 (1991).

[46] 524 U.S. 569 (1998).

moreover, that the decency and respect requirements did not provide the basis for a finding of viewpoint discrimination.

The Court has indicated that, when government subsidizes private speech and does not have a program or message of its own at stake, the rationale for viewpoint discrimination abates. This point was made in *Rosenberger v. University of Virginia*,[47] when the Court determined that a university could not fund all student publications except for those of religious groups. As the Court stated, the logic for viewpoint restrictions abates when government itself does not "speak of subsidize transmittal of a message it favors but instead expends funds to encourage a diversity of views from private speakers." This premise was reaffirmed in *Legal Services Corp. v. Velazquez*,[48] a case concerning a congressional enactment prohibiting federally subsidized legal aid centers from challenging the constitutional or statutory validity of welfare laws. The Court noted that Congress was not obligated to fund legal services or the entire range of legal claims. To the extent that Congress limited theories and ideas that may be critical to effective litigation, however, the Court found that the law overreached. Congress' interest basically was in insulating government's interpretation of the Constitution from challenge. Because only private speech is concerned in the context of developing and presenting legal theories, as opposed to government expression through an agent, the Court found the government's analogy to *Rust* inapt. The funding condition thus was declared invalid to the extent it was aimed to suppress ideas considered inimical to government's interests.

The Court's most recent unconstitutional conditions decision was rendered in *Rumsfeld v. Forum for Academic and Institutional Rights, Inc.*[49] The case arose when law schools began restricting access to their campuses by military recruiters because of their disagreement with the Government's policy on homosexuals in the military (the so-called "Don't Ask, Don't Tell" policy). Congress responded by enacting the Solomon Amendment which provided that if any part of an institution of higher education denies military recruiters access equal to that provided other recruiters, the entire institution would lose certain federal funds. The Solomon Amendment mandated access that is "at least equal in quality and scope to the access to campuses and to students that is provided to any other employer." 10 U.S.C.A. 983(b) (Supp. 2005). The statute provided an exception for an institution with "a longstanding policy of pacifism based on historical religious affiliation." 983(C)(2). A law school could not comply (in other words, by excluding all recruiters who discriminate based on sexual preference) by providing military recruiters the same access provided to other recruiters, but instead were required to provide military recruiters with access equivalent to that given to any other recruiter. Law schools and other sued claiming that the Solomon Amendment infringed their First Amendment right to freedom of speech and freedom of association.

In an opinion by Chief Justice Roberts, the Court unanimously upheld the Solomon Amendment. The Court began by noting that Congress has a constitu-

---

[47] 515 U.S. 819 (1995).

[48] 531 U.S. 533 (2001).

[49] 547 U.S. 47 (2006).

tional right to provide for the common defense, which includes the power to require colleges and law schools to provide campus access to military recruiters, and the Court indicated that it was deferential to Congress' judgments in this area. The Court went on to note that Congress could obtain access either through direct legislation or through the spending power, and indeed that Congress might have even greater authority under the spending power because colleges and universities are free to decline the funding.

The Court rejected the notion that the "unconstitutional conditions" doctrine would limit Congress' authority. Even though Congress "conditioned" its aid programs on providing military recruiters with access, this condition was permissible given that Congress had the power to directly require colleges and law schools to provide access to military recruiters. Moreover, the Court noted that the Solomon Amendment left colleges and law schools free to exercise their First Amendment rights because the Amendment "neither limits what law schools may say nor requires them to say anything. Law schools remain free under the statute to express whatever views they may have on the military's congressionally mandated employment policy, all the while retaining eligibility for federal funds." In addition, the Court viewed the Solomon Amendment as a regulation of conduct rather than a regulation of speech: "As a general matter, the Solomon Amendment regulates conduct, not speech. It affects what law schools must *do*-afford equal access to military recruiters-not what they may or may not *say*."

§ 8.04   THE OTHER SIDE OF THE RIGHT TO BE LET ALONE

The right to be let alone has provided a foundation for case law that secures freedom of conscience and belief. It also has been referenced as a principle that limits a person's exposure to expressive activity. This potential to operate not just as an agent for expanding First Amendment principles, but curbing them, was demonstrated in *Packer Corporation v. Utah.*[50] At issue in this case was a law that restricted the use of billboards, street car signs, and placards. The Court, in an opinion authored by Justice Brandeis, noted that advertising through these media is a pervasive presence that are "seen without the exercise of choice or volition." Unlike newspapers, magazines, or radio that require an affirmative decision and act to access them, billboards and other signs are "thrust" upon the viewer. Because such advertising media deny the individual an opportunity to decide whether he or she wants to be exposed to the message, the Court found that it should be more susceptible to control.

The potential for the right to be let alone to work for and against First Amendment interests was evidenced further in an opinion by one of the Court's foremost champions of the First Amendment. In *Public Utilities Commission v. Pollak,*[51] the Court upheld a public transit system's provision of local radio programming on city buses. Some riders had claimed that the programming invaded their "constitutional rights of privacy." Responding to the Court's finding

---

[50]   285 U.S. 105 (1932).

[51]   343 U.S. 451 (1952).

that passengers did not have a significant right of privacy on a public vehicle, Justice Douglas stressed that "the First Amendment in its respect for the conscience of the individual honors the sanctity of thought and belief." When individuals are forced to listen to another person's speech, Douglas maintained, privacy is invaded. From his standpoint, the right of privacy comprehended the freedom to select from competing entertainment, propaganda and political philosophies. For him, the right of privacy represented a "powerful deterrent to any one who would control men's minds."

Douglas' dissent in *Pollak* reflected an understanding of privacy consistent with First Amendment interests in freedom of thought, belief and conscience. This connectivity was present too in *Stanley v. Georgia*,[52] when the Court reversed a conviction based upon possession of obscene materials. In this case, the Court emphasized that the First Amendment protects not only the right to speak but to receive information and ideas. In *Stanley*, this right doubled in force because it was coupled with the right to be free from unwanted government intrusion into a homeowner's privacy. Echoing the earlier sentiments of Justices Brandeis and Douglas, the Court observed that "[i]f the First Amendment means anything, it means that a State has no business telling a man, sitting alone in his own house, what books he may read or what films he may watch. Our whole constitutional heritage rebels at the thought of giving government the power to control men's minds."

The privacy interest in *Stanley* thus rose to a level that it was a source of protection for possession of material that otherwise is beyond the First Amendment's concern and a basis for criminal sanction. It is a safeguard, however, that did not extend beyond the perimeters of the home. In *Paris Adult Theatre I v. Slaton*,[53] the Court refused to extend the privacy principle to movie theaters that limited access to obscene films to consenting adults. The concept of privacy subscribed to in *Stanley* thus was cast as a guarantee that attaches to the home rather than to the individual wherever he or she goes.

The right to be let alone, as understood in *Stanley*, secures space for freedom to think, read, observe and satisfy one's emotional and intellectual interests. A significant track of this right, however, leads to a direct conflict with First Amendment freedom. In *Lehman v. City of Shaker Heights*,[54] the Court upheld a prohibition of political advertising inside public transit cars. Justice Blackmun, in a plurality opinion, noted how the circumstances in this case departed from the usual contexts where First Amendment concerns typically prevail. Justice Douglas, in a concurring opinion, differentiated between speech directed at a willing audience and expression that is forced upon an audience incapable of declining it.

The right to be let alone, insofar as it shapes protection from unwanted expression, varies according to place. As the *Stanley* decision indicated, privacy interests are particularly strong in the home. This factor influenced the outcome of

---

[52] 394 U.S. 557 (1969).

[53] 413 U.S. 49 (1973).

[54] 418 U.S. 298 (1974).

Federal Communications Commission v. Pacifica Foundation,[55] which upheld the federal government's power to regulate indecency in broadcasting. Among other reasons, the Court found that broadcasting's uniquely pervasive presence burdened privacy, particularly in the "home, where the individual's right to be left alone plainly outweighs the First Amendment interests of the intruder." The ability to turn off a radio or television, as the Court noted, does not avoid the harm caused by the initial unwanted exposure.

The ability to turn away or avoid undesired contact with speech has spun results in other settings differently. In *Cohen v. California*,[56] the Court thus noted that persons confronted with an offensive expression on the defendant's clothing could employ a self-help remedy. Because the exposure was in a public place, they could avoid offense "simply by averting their eyes." This ability to avoid unwanted exposure also was the basis for the Court's decision, in *Erznoznik v. City of Jacksonville*,[57] invalidating a law that prohibited drive-in movie theaters from showing nudity if the screen was visible from a public thoroughfare. As in *Cohen*, a person could protect his or her sensibilities without official action that burdened freedom of expression.

---

[55] 438 U.S. 726 (1978).

[56] 403 U.S. 15 (1971).

[57] 422 U.S. 205 (1975).

POINTS TO REMEMBER

- The right to be let alone descends from tort-based privacy concerns.

- The First Amendment protects persons from being forced to express or be associated with beliefs to which they object.

- In general, the right to associate includes the right to exclude from membership, and state action that compels expression or association will be strictly scrutinized.

- However, individuals have more rights to associate in their "intimate associations" and in associations formed to promote expression or political activity.

- As a group becomes larger, less selective, and less involved with expressive activity, it may have less right to exclude others from membership.

- Government imposes an unconstitutional condition when it makes a benefit contingent upon foregoing a person's freedom of expression.

- Government does not impose an unconstitutional condition when it has a point of view and insists that recipients of funding refrain from speech that distorts or competes with its message.

- The right to be let alone provides a person with private space for thought and conscience, interests that connect closely with freedom of speech.

- The right to be let alone also establishes a principle that may limit freedom of speech.

Chapter 9

THE GOVERNMENT AS EMPLOYER, EDUCATOR, AND SOURCE OF FUNDS

FOCAL POINTS FOR CHAPTER 9

- Government employees and the right to free speech.

- Limitations on the right of governmental employees to engage in ordinary political activities.

- Limitations on the right of governmental employees to publicly discuss their employment or other public issues.

- The right of governmental employees to engage in freedom of association.

- Limitations on the right of students to engage in expressive activities.

- The government's right to finance and control expressive activities.

- Employment by government implicates the First Amendment in a way that employment in the public sector does not, and has given rise to litigation in a wide variety of contexts.

---

§ 9.01   FIRST AMENDMENT RIGHTS OF PUBLIC EMPLOYEES

[A]   Prohibiting Electioneering

One context involves whether the government can prohibit its employees from engaging in partisan political practices. The landmark decision is *United Public Workers of America v. Mitchell*,[1] That case involved a challenge to § 9(a) of the Hatch Act which provided that, "No officer or employee in the executive branch of the Federal Government . . . shall take any active part in political management or in political campaigns." Various employees of the federal government claimed that they desired to engage in acts of political management and in political campaigns out-side their hours of employment, and questioned the Commission's right to impose disciplinary action for such conduct. One employee, Poole, had served as an executive committeeman and a worker at the polls. The employees claimed that, like every other citizen, government employees had the right to act as party officials and workers in an effort to further their own political views.

In evaluating the Hatch Act, the Court concluded that it was required to "balance the extent of the guarantees of freedom against a congressional enactment to protect a democratic society against the supposed evil of political partisanship by classified employees of government." The Court noted that the "practice of excluding classified employees from party offices and personal political activity at the polls has been in effect for several decades." The Court referenced *Ex parte Curtis*,[2] in which the Court upheld a law that "forbade employees who were not appointed by the President and confirmed by the Senate from giving or receiving money for political purposes from or to other employees of the government on penalty of discharge and criminal punishment." The Court upheld the law noting that "an actively partisan governmental personnel threatens good administration has deepened since *Curtis.* Congress recognizes danger to the service in that political rather than official effort may earn advancement and to the public in that governmental favor may be channeled through political connections."[3]

The Court found that § 9 of the Hatch Act served a similar purpose. The law was directed at "political contributions of money." "Congress and the President are responsible for an efficient public service. If, in their judgment, efficiency may be best obtained by prohibiting active participation by classified employees in politics as party officers or workers, we see no constitutional objection." The Court noted that Congress left "untouched full participation by employees in political decisions at the ballot box and forbids only the partisan activity of federal personnel deemed offensive to efficiency. With that limitation only, employees may make their contributions to public affairs or protect their own interests, as before the passage of the act."

---

[1] 330 U.S. 75 (1947).

[2] 106 U.S. 371 (1882).

[3] *United Public Workers of America*, 330 U.S. at 75.

The Court accepted the proposition that "political neutrality is not indispensable to a merit system for federal employees." Nevertheless, the Court concluded that Congress had discretion: "[B]ecause it is not indispensable does not mean that it is not desirable or permissible. Modern American politics involves organized political parties. . . . Congress [may] have considered that parties would be more truly devoted to the public welfare if public servants were not overactive politically."

The Court rejected that federal employees' right to work in political campaigns was protected by the Bill of Rights. While the Court accepted the idea that federal employees are constitutionally protected, it noted that "it does not follow that a prohibition against acting as ward leader or worker at the polls is invalid. . . . It is only partisan political activity that is interdicted. It is active participation in political management and political campaigns." Otherwise, federal employees retain their First Amendment rights: "Expressions, public or private, on public affairs, personalities and matters of public interest, not an objective of party action, are unrestricted by law so long as the Government employee does not direct his activities toward party success." The Court also rejected claims that the law was overbroad. Appellants Poole claimed, for example, that his job as a roller at the Mint called for the skills of a mechanic and did not require contact with the public. As a result, appellants argued that there was no reason to prohibit him from political activity. The Court disagreed noting that:

> if in free time he is engaged in political activity, Congress may have concluded that the activity may promote or retard his advancement. . . . Congress may have thought that Government employees are handy elements for leaders in political policy to use in building a political machine. [I]t is not necessary that the act regulated be anything more than an act reasonably deemed by Congress to interfere with the efficiency of the public service. There are hundreds of thousands of United States employees with positions no more influential upon policy determination. . . . Evidently what Congress feared was the cumulative effect on employee morale of political activity by all employees who could be induced to participate actively. It does not seem to us an unconstitutional basis for legislation.

The Court held that the scope of review was limited. "Congress may regulate the political conduct of Government employees 'within reasonable limits.'" And the Court was deferential to Congress: "The determination of the extent to which political activities of governmental employees shall be regulated lies primarily with Congress. Courts will interfere only when such regulation passes beyond the general existing conception of governmental power. [When] actions of civil servants in the judgment of Congress menace the integrity and the competency of the service, legislation to forestall such danger and adequate to maintain its usefulness is required. The Hatch Act is the answer of Congress to this need. We cannot say with such a background that these restrictions are unconstitutional."

Justice Black dissenting expressed concern that federal employees could express their views, but only at their peril. "They cannot know what particular expressions may be reported to the Commission and held by it to be a sufficient political activity to cost them their jobs. Their peril is all the greater [because employees are] accountable for political activity by persons other than themselves, including wives or husbands, if, in fact, the employees are thus accomplishing by collusion and indirection what they may not lawfully do directly and openly." As a result, he worried that families were also stripped of their political rights, and thus employees and their families were left with limited rights: "They may vote in silence; they may carefully and quietly express a political view at their peril; and they may become 'spectators' [at] campaign gatherings, though it may be highly dangerous for them to 'second a motion' or let it be known that they agree or disagree with a speaker." Justice Black felt that the Court would not have sustained a similar restriction on any other group (*i.e.*, farmers or businessmen). As a result, he would have applied the law only if it were "narrowly drawn to meet the evil [and] affect only the minimum number of people [necessary] to prevent a grave and imminent danger to the public" and he felt that the government could not satisfy this standard. "[It is hardly imperative] to muzzle millions of citizens because some of them [might] corrupt the political process."

Justice Douglas dissented in part recognizing that government had legitimate reasons for limiting the political activities of government employees, but he argued that these interests should be balanced against the employees' interest in the exercise of their constitutional rights. "Those rights are too basic and fundamental in our democratic political society to be sacrificed or qualified for anything short of a clear and present danger to the civil service system. No such showing has been made."

In *United States Civil Service Commission v. National Association of Letter Carriers, AFL-CIO*,[4] the Court reaffirmed the holding in *Mitchell*. In doing so, the Court offered several justifications for the Hatch Act:

> [Forbidding partisan political activities] will reduce the hazards to fair and effective government. [I]t is not only important that the Government and its employees in fact avoid practicing political justice, but it is also critical that they appear to the public to be avoiding it, if confidence in the system of representative Government is not to be eroded to a disastrous extent. . . . Another major concern [was that] the rapidly expanding Government work force should not be employed to build a powerful, invincible, and perhaps corrupt political machine. [A] related concern [was] the goal that employment and advancement in the Government service not depend on political performance, and [that] Government employees [sh]ould be free from pressure and from express or tacit invitation to vote in a certain way or perform political chores in order to curry favor with their superiors rather than to act out their own beliefs. [I]t is not enough merely to forbid one employee to attempt to influence or coerce another.
> . . .

United States v. National Treasury Employees Union,[5] involved a law that prohibited federal employees from accepting any compensation for making speeches or writing articles. The law applied whether or not the subject of the

---

[4] 413 U.S. 548 (1973).

[5] 513 U.S. 454 (1995).

speech or article or the person or group paying for it had any connection with the employee's official duties. Violations of the law were punishable by a fine of up to $10,000 or the amount of the honorarium. The law was challenged by various federal employees who had received compensation for writing or speaking on various topics unrelated to their employment (*e.g.*, a mail handler employed by the Postal Service who had given lectures on the Quaker religion). The Court struck down the law:

> Federal employees who write for publication [include] literary giants like Nathaniel Hawthorne and Herman Melville, who were employed by the Customs Service. . . . [Section 501(b)] imposes a significant burden on expressive activity. Publishers compensate authors because compensation provides a significant incentive toward more expression. [The] ban imposes a far more significant burden on respondents than on the relatively small group of lawmakers whose past receipt of honoraria motivated its enactment [and] will inevitably diminish their expressive output. [The] large-scale disincentive to Government employees' expression also imposes a significant burden on the public's right to read and hear what the employees would otherwise have written and said. . . . Because the vast majority of the speech at issue in this case does not involve the subject matter of Government employment and takes place outside the workplace, the Government is unable to justify § 501(b) on the grounds of immediate workplace disruption. [T]he Government has based its defense of the ban on abuses of honoraria by Members of Congress. [O]ne can envision scant harm, or appearance of harm, resulting from the same employee's accepting pay to lecture on the Quaker religion or to write dance reviews.

Chief Justice Rehnquist, joined by two other Justices, dissented:

> [Some] individuals [receive] honoraria where there is a nexus between their speech and their Government employment. [Congress] reasonably could conclude that its interests in preventing impropriety and the appearance of impropriety in the federal work force outweigh the employees' interests in receiving compensation for expression that has a nexus to their Government employment.

[B]   Other Employee Speech

Do governmental employees have free speech rights related to their jobs? As the United States Supreme Court recognized in *Connick v. Myers*,[6] for many years there were doubts about the free speech rights of governmental employees. Indeed, for most of the Twentieth Century, "the unchallenged dogma was that a public employee had no right to object to conditions placed upon the terms of employment — including those which restricted the exercise of constitutional rights." But, in the 1950s and early 1960s, the Court's attitude began to change. For example, in *Wieman v. Updegraff*,[7] the Court held that public school teachers could not be required to swear an oath of loyalty to the state and to reveal the groups with which were they associated.

---

[6]   461 U.S. 138 (1983).

[7]   344 U.S. 183 (1952).

Modern cases focus on a number of considerations. First, they focus on whether the speech relates to matters of "public concern" or is "private speech." Determining the category in which a particular statement falls is not easy. The Court focuses on the "context." If speech is more of "private" than "public" concern, the Court is likely to uphold the sanction. On the other hand, when the speech relates to matters of public concern, the Court will balance the employer's interest in regulating or controlling the speech against the speech's relationship to matters of "public" concern.

An illustrative decision is *Pickering v. Board of Education.*[8] In that case, the Court extended the scope of protections available to governmental employees. In that case, the Court held that a public employee did not relinquish their right to comment on matters of public interest simple because they were government employees. In that case, a high school teacher was dismissed for criticizing a board of education's allocation of funds between athletics and education and its methods of informing taxpayers about the need for additional revenue. The Court held that the State interest in regulating the speech of its employees was greater than its interest in regulating the speech of the citizenry in general. The Court struggled to find the balance "between the interests of the [employee], as a citizen, in commenting upon matters of public concern and the interest of the State, as an employer, in promoting the efficiency of the public services it performs through its employees." "The Court overturned Pickering's dismissal because his speech involved 'a matter of legitimate public concern' upon which 'free and open debate is vital to informed decision-making by the electorate.' "

Pickering was followed by the holding in *Connick v. Myers.*[9] In *Connick*, an assistant district attorney, who was upset about a transfer, prepared a questionnaire on "office transfer policy, office morale, the need for a grievance committee, the level of confidence in supervisors, and whether employees felt pressured to work in political campaigns." She then distributed the questionnaire to 15 fellow assistant district attorneys. When Connick (the district attorney) learned about the questionnaire, he terminated Myers for refusing to accept the transfer and for "insubordination" in distributing the questionnaire.

In an opinion by Justice White, the Court upheld the dismissal. The Court focused on whether the questionnaire could "be fairly characterized as constituting speech on a matter of public concern." If not, so that the speech could fairly be characterized as "private," the Court held that it would be "unnecessary" "to scrutinize the reasons for her discharge." When

> employee expression cannot be fairly considered as relating to any matter of political, social, or other concern to the community, government officials should enjoy wide latitude in managing their offices, without intrusive oversight by the judiciary in the name of the First Amendment.

The Court went on to hold that "ordinary dismissals" are not subject to judicial review absent a violation of tenure law or a violation of some other law.

---

[8] 391 U.S. 563 (1968).

[9] 461 U.S. 138 (1983).

In the Court's view, private speech by governmental employees did not fall outside the bounds of constitutional protection. "[We] in no sense suggest that speech on private matters falls into one of the narrow and well-defined classes of expression which carries so little social value, such as obscenity, that the state can prohibit and punish such expression by all persons in its jurisdiction." But,

> when a public employee speaks not as a citizen upon matters of public concern, but instead as an employee upon matters only of personal interest, absent the most unusual circumstances, a federal court is not the appropriate forum in which to review the wisdom of a personnel decision taken by a public agency allegedly in reaction to the employee's behavior.

The critical question in the case was whether the questionnaire involved a matter of "public concern." The answer to that question turned on the "content, form, and context of a given statement." In *Connick*, the Court rejected the argument that, because the questionnaire related to conditions in the district attorney's office, it therefore related to a matter of "public concern."

> While discipline and morale in the workplace are related to an agency's efficient performance of its duties, the focus of Myers' questions is not to evaluate the performance of the office but rather to gather ammunition for another round of controversy with her superiors. These questions reflect one employee's dissatisfaction with a transfer and an attempt to turn that displeasure into a cause celebre.

> While as a matter of good judgment, public officials should be receptive to constructive criticism offered by their employees, the First Amendment does not require a public office to be run as a roundtable for employee complaints over internal office affairs.

Nevertheless, the Court held that one of Myer's questions — which asked whether assistant district attorneys "ever feel pressured to work in political campaigns on behalf of office supported candidates" — did touch upon a matter of public concern. "[O]fficial pressure upon employees to work for political candidates not of the worker's own choice constitutes a coercion of belief in violation of fundamental constitutional rights. In addition, there is a demonstrated interest in this country that government service should depend upon meritorious performance rather than political service." As a result, "the issue of whether assistant district attorneys are pressured to work in political campaigns is a matter of interest to the community upon which it is essential that public employees be able to speak out freely without fear of retaliatory dismissal."

The Court then came to the question of whether Myers' dismissal was permissible. The Court held that the burden of justification can vary "depending upon the nature of the employee's expression." Relying on *Pickering*, the Court held that it was also required to consider "the government's interest in the effective and efficient fulfillment of its responsibilities to the public." The Court found that the questionnaire did not impede Myers' ability to perform her own duties, but that it caused a "mini-insurrection" in the office and interfered with working relationships. Because "close working relationships are essential to fulfilling public responsibilities," the Court gave deference to the employer's conclusions noting that Connick was not required to "allow events to unfold to the extent that the disruption of the office and the destruction of working relationships is manifest before taking action." However, a "stronger" showing might be required "if the employee's speech more substantially involved matters of public concern." Finally, the Court focused on the context in which the dispute arose noting that "When employee speech concerning office policy arises from an employment dispute concerning the very application of that policy to the speaker, additional weight must be given to the supervisor's view that the employee has threatened the authority of the employer to run the office." In addition, although the survey involved matters of public concern in a limited sense, the Court held the questionnaire concerned "internal office policy." "The limited First Amendment interest involved here does not require that Connick tolerate action which he reasonably believed would disrupt the office, undermine his authority, and destroy close working relationships. Myers' discharge therefore did not offend the First Amendment." In conclusion, the Court emphasized that it was seeking a balance between the "First Amendment's primary aim" which the Court regarded as "the full protection of speech upon issues of public concern" and the "practical realities involved in the administration of a government office."

Justice Brennan, joined by Justices Marshall, Blackmun, and Stevens, dissented. He viewed the speech differently than Justice White:

> [S]peech about 'the manner in which government is operated or should be operated' is an essential part of the communications necessary for self-governance the protection of which was a central purpose of the First Amendment. Because the questionnaire addressed such matters and its distribution did not adversely affect the operations of the District Attorney's Office or interfere with Myers' working relationship with her fellow employees, I dissent.

> [Myers' questionnaire] addressed matters of public concern because it discussed subjects that could reasonably be expected to be of interest to persons seeking to develop informed opinions about the manner in which the Orleans Parish District Attorney, an elected official charged with managing a vital governmental agency, discharges his responsibilities.

> [The] Court's decision today inevitably will deter public employees from making critical statements about the manner in which government agencies are operated for fear that doing so will provoke their dismissal. As a result, the public will be deprived of valuable information with which to evaluate the performance of elected officials. Because protecting the dissemination of such information is an essential function of the First Amendment, I dissent.

Pickering and *Connick* were followed by the holding in *Waters v. Churchill*.[10] *Waters* involved a nurse in an obstetrics department who was discharged for talking about "how bad things are in [obstetrics] in general," and criticizing a supervisor (Waters). The nurse denied making the statements, and claimed that she actually supported Waters, and that, rather than complaining about the obstetrics department, she complained about the hospital's "cross-training" policy (under which

---

[10] 511 U.S. 661 (1994).

nurses from one department could work in another department when their usual location was overstaffed). The Court upheld the discharge: "[I]f petitioners really did believe Perkins-Graham's and Ballew's story, and fired Churchill because of it, they must win. Their belief, based on the investigation they conducted, would have been entirely [reasonable]." Justice Stevens dissented:

> The risk that a jury may ultimately view the facts differently from even a conscientious employer is not [a] needless fetter on public employers' ability to discharge their duties. It is the normal means by which our legal system protects legal rights and encourages those in authority to act with care. [There] is nothing unfair or onerous about putting the risk of error on an employer in these circumstances.

Another important decision was *Rankin v. McPherson*.[11] In that case, McPherson was a deputy in the office of the Constable of Harris County, Texas. McPherson, a black woman, was 19 years old and had attended college for a year, studying secretarial science. Her appointment was conditional for a 90-day probationary period. Although the Constable's office performed law enforcement functions, McPherson was not a commissioned peace officer, did not wear a uniform, and was not authorized to make arrests or permitted to carry a gun. McPherson's duties were purely clerical. Her work station was a desk at which there was no telephone, in a room to which the public did not have ready access. Her job was to type data from court papers into a computer that maintained an automated record of the status of civil process in the county. Her training consisted of two days of instruction in the operation of her computer terminal. The case arose when McPherson and some fellow employees heard on an office radio that there had been an attempt to assassinate the President of the United States. Upon hearing that report, McPherson engaged a co-worker, Lawrence Jackson, who was apparently her boyfriend, in a brief conversation about the shooting in which she said: "shoot, if they go for him again, I hope they get him." McPherson was fired for the remark.

In an opinion by Justice Marshall, the Court overturned the discharge. The Court began by returning to the "balance between the interests of the [employee], as a citizen, in commenting upon matters of public concern and the interest of the State, as an employer, in promoting the efficiency of the public services it performs through its employees." The Court quickly held that McPherson's comment dealt with a "matter of public concern" because it concerned "the policies of the President's administration," and "came on the heels of a news bulletin regarding what is certainly a matter of heightened public attention: an attempt on the life of the President." The Court noted that a threat to kill the President would not have been protected, but that McPherson's comment was not of that character.

In balancing McPherson's interest in making the statement against "the interest of the State, as an employer, in promoting the efficiency of the public services it performs through its employees," the opinion placed a burden on the state to justify the discharge based on the context in which "the statement will not be considered in a vacuum; the manner, time, and place of the employee's expression are relevant,

---

[11] 483 U.S. 378 (1987).

as is the context in which the dispute arose." Analyzing these factors, the Court concluded that the dismissal was invalid.

> While McPherson's statement was made at the workplace, there is no evidence that it interfered with the efficient functioning of the office. The Constable was evidently not afraid that McPherson had disturbed or interrupted other employees. . . . In fact, Constable Rankin testified that the possibility of interference with the functions of the Constable's office had *not* been a consideration in his discharge of respondent and that he did not even inquire whether the remark had disrupted the work of the office.

> Nor was there any danger that McPherson had discredited the office by making her statement in public. McPherson's speech took place in an area to which there was ordinarily no public access; her remark was evidently made in a private conversation with another employee. . . . Nor is there any evidence that employees other than Jackson who worked in the room even heard the remark. Not only was McPherson's discharge unrelated to the functioning of the office, it was not based on any assessment by the Constable that the remark demonstrated a character trait that made respondent unfit to perform her work.

The Court also expressed concern that McPherson was discharged because of the content of her speech. The Court was concerned about the "responsibilities of the employee within the agency." McPherson's

> employment-related interaction with the Constable was apparently negligible. Her duties were purely clerical and were limited solely to the civil process function of the Constable's office. There is no indication that she would ever be in a position to further — or indeed to have any involvement with — the minimal law enforcement activity engaged in by the Constable's office. Given the function of the agency, McPherson's position in the office, and the nature of her statement, we are not persuaded that Rankin's interest in discharging her outweighed her rights under the First Amendment.

Justice Powell concurred. He emphasized that her comment was made

> during a private conversation with a co-worker who happened [to] be her boyfriend. She had no intention or expectation that it would be overheard or acted on by others. Given this, [it] is unnecessary to engage in the extensive analysis normally required by *Connick* and *Pickering*. If a statement is on a matter of public concern, [it] will be an unusual case where the employer's legitimate interests will be so great as to justify punishing an employee for this type of private speech that routinely takes place at all levels in the workplace.

Justice Scalia, joined by the Chief Justice and justices White and O'Connor, dissented. "[N]o law enforcement agency is required by the First Amendment to permit one of its employees to 'ride with the cops and cheer for the robbers.' "

> [McPherson's] statement [is] only one step removed from statements that we have previously held entitled to no First Amendment protection

even in the non-employment context — including assassination threats against the President (which are illegal under 18 U.S.C. § 871), 'fighting words,' epithets or personal abuse, and advocacy of force or violence. A statement lying so near the category of completely unprotected speech cannot fairly be viewed as lying within the 'heart' of the First Amendment's protection; it lies within that category of speech that can neither be characterized as speech on matters of public concern nor properly subject to criminal penalties. Once McPherson stopped explicitly criticizing the President's policies and expressed a desire that he be assassinated, she crossed the line.

[Statements] by the Constable's employees to the effect that 'if they go for the President again, I hope they get him' might also, to put it mildly, undermine public confidence in the Constable's office. A public employer has a strong interest in preserving its reputation with the public. We know [that] McPherson had or might have had some occasion to deal with the public while carrying out her duties.

In sum, since Constable Rankin's interest in maintaining both an esprit de corps and a public image consistent with his office's law enforcement duties outweighs any interest his employees may have in expressing on the job a desire that the President be killed, even assuming that such an expression addresses a matter of public concern it is not protected by the First Amendment from suppression.

In the Court's earlier holding in *Mt. Healthy City School District v. Doyle*,[12] a principal circulated a memo on teacher dress and appearance, to teachers. Doyle, a teacher, provided a copy of the memo to a local disc jockey who announced it as a news item. A month later, the principal recommended that Doyle not be rehired for the following year because of "a notable lack of tact in handling professional matters which leaves much doubt as to your sincerity in establishing good school relationships." The principal's recommendation was followed by references to the radio station incident and to an obscene-gesture incident. The Court held that, had the non-renewal been based on Doyle's communication with the radio station, it was actionable:

[the] burden was properly placed upon respondent to show that his conduct was constitutionally protected, and that this conduct was a 'substantial factor' [or] that it was a 'motivating factor' in the Board's decision not to rehire him. Respondent having carried that burden, [the court] should have [determined] whether the Board had shown by a preponderance of the evidence that it would have reached the same decision as to respondent's reemployment even in the absence of the protected conduct.

In *Minnesota State Board for Community Colleges v. Knight*,[13] the State of Minnesota authorized public employees to bargain collectively over the terms and conditions of their employment. Under the statute, if professional employees (*i.e.*,

---

[12] 429 U.S. 274 (1977).

[13] 465 U.S. 271 (1984).

college faculty) have formed an appropriate bargaining unit and have selected an exclusive representative for mandatory bargaining, then their employer may only exchange views on nonmandatory subjects with that exclusive representative as well. Faculty at one college challenged the restriction as a violation of their constitutional rights. The Court upheld the restriction:

> The Constitution does not grant to members of the public generally a right to be heard by public bodies making decisions of policy. . . . Appellees' speech and associational rights [have] not been infringed by Minnesota's restriction of participation in 'meet and confer' sessions to the faculty's exclusive representative. The state has in no way restrained appellees' freedom to speak on any education-related issue or their freedom to associate or not to associate with whom they please, including the exclusive representative. Nor has the state attempted to suppress any ideas.

Justice Stevens, joined by two other justices, dissented:

> [T]he First Amendment [guarantees] an open marketplace for ideas — where divergent points of view can freely compete for the attention of those in power and of those to whom the powerful must account. [T]he statute gives only one speaker a realistic opportunity to present its views to state [officials].

Brown v. Glines[14] involved a challenge to United States Air Force regulations that required members of the service to obtain approval from their commanders before circulating petitions on Air Force bases. The commander can deny permission only if he determines that distribution of the material would result in "a clear danger to the loyalty, discipline, or morale of members of the Armed Forces, or material interference with the accomplishment of a military mission. . . ." Glines, a captain in the Air Force Reserves, drafted petitions to members of Congress and the Secretary of Defense complaining about the Air Force's grooming standards. When Glines gave the petitions to a sergeant to solicit signatures, his commander punished him for violating the regulations by removing him from active duty and assigning him to the standby reserves. The Court (5-3) upheld the regulations: "The unrestricted circulation of collective petitions could imperil discipline. . . ." Mr. Justice Stewart dissented: "[It cannot] conceivably be argued that [a] regulation requiring the preclearance of the content of all petitions to be circulated by servicemen in time of peace is 'necessary to the security of the United States.'"

In *Garcetti v. Ceballos*,[15] the Court imposed an important new qualification on its precedents relating to the free speech rights of public employees. Ceballos was employed as a deputy district attorney and was expected to exercise certain supervisory responsibilities over other lawyers. When a defense attorney raised concerns about a pending criminal case, noting that there were inaccuracies in an affidavit used to obtain a search warrant, Ceballos investigated and came away with deep concerns about the affidavit. Ceballos ultimately recommended dismissal of

---

[14] 444 U.S. 348 (1980).

[15] 547 U.S. 410 (2006).

the case and became involved in a heated exchange with another official. When the prosecution ultimately went forward, Ceballos was called as a defense witness. Ceballos claims that in the aftermath of these events he was subjected to a series of retaliatory employment actions, and sued alleging violations of his First and Fourteenth Amendment rights.

Citing *Connick v. Myers*,[16] the Court reiterated the notion that "public employees do not surrender all their First Amendment rights by reason of their employment," and that they retain some right "to speak as a citizen addressing matters of public concern."[17] Nonetheless, the Court refused to hold that the First Amendment protects a government employee from discipline based on speech made pursuant to the employee's official duties. Relying on its prior decision in *Pickering v. Board of Education*,[18] the Court indicated that two questions should be considered in cases involving public employee speech.

> The first requires determining whether the employee spoke as a citizen on a matter of public concern. If the answer is no, the employee has no First Amendment cause of action based on his or her employer's reaction to the speech.[19]

> If the answer is yes, then the possibility of a First Amendment claim arises. The question becomes whether the relevant government entity had an adequate justification for treating the employee differently from any other member of the general public. This consideration reflects the importance of the relationship between the speaker's expressions and employment. A government entity has broader discretion to restrict speech when it acts in its role as employer, but the restrictions it imposes must be directed at speech that has some potential to affect the entity's operations.

Despite the fact that public employees are sometimes entitled to speak out on matters of public interest, the Court held that "[w]hen a citizen enters government service, the citizen by necessity must accept certain limitations on his or her freedom." The Court held that a government employer, like a private employer, needs "a significant degree of control over their employees' words and actions" in order to provide for the "efficient provision of public services." In addition, since public employees "often occupy trusted positions in society," their speech can "express views that contravene governmental policies or impair the proper performance of governmental functions." As a result, even though employees are speaking out on matters of public concern, "they must face only those speech restrictions that are necessary for their employers to operate efficiently and effectively." Nevertheless, employees do not have the authorization to "constitutionalize" every grievance."

In applying these principles, the Court concluded that public employees receive some protection for expressions made during and at work. "Public employees

---

[16] 461 U.S. 138 (1983).

[17] *Garcetti*, 547 U.S. at 417.

[18] 391 U.S. 563 (1968).

[19] *Garcetti*, 547 U.S. at 418.

typically are the best informed regarding their employers. As a result, 'it is essential that they be able to speak out freely on such questions without fear of retaliatory dismissal.' " Nevertheless, the Court rejected Ceballos' First Amendment claim because his expressions were made "pursuant to his duties" as a prosecutor. "We hold that when public employees make statements pursuant to their official duties, the employees are not speaking as citizens for First Amendment purposes, and the Constitution does not insulate their communications from employer discipline." "Restricting speech that owes its existence to a public employee's professional responsibilities does not infringe any liberties the employee might have enjoyed as a private citizen. It simply reflects the exercise of employer control over what the employer itself has commissioned or created."

Although the Court recognized that "employees retain the prospect of constitutional protection for their contributions to the civic discourse," it also acknowledged that its precedents afford "government employers sufficient discretion to manage their operations. Employers have heightened interests in controlling speech made by an employee in his or her professional capacity." The Court recognized that "[o]fficial communications have official consequences, creating a need for substantive consistency and clarity. Supervisors must ensure that their employees' official communications are accurate, demonstrate sound judgment, and promote the employer's mission." The Court concluded that Ceballos' memo was subject to action: "It demanded the attention of his supervisors and led to a heated meeting with employees from the sheriff's department. If Ceballos' superiors thought his memo was inflammatory or misguided, they had the authority to take proper corrective action."

Moreover, although the Court recognized the public interest in exposing corruption, the Court held that there were non-constitutional protections for such individuals, including "the powerful network of legislative enactments — such as whistle-blower protection laws and labor codes — available to those who seek to expose wrongdoing." In addition, when an attorney like Ceballos is involved, there are additional protections including rules of conduct. "These imperatives, as well as obligations arising from any other applicable constitutional provisions and mandates of the criminal and civil laws, protect employees and provide checks on supervisors who would order unlawful or otherwise inappropriate actions." As a result, the Court rejected the notion "of a constitutional cause of action behind every statement a public employee makes in the course of doing his or her job."

Justice Stevens dissented, arguing that the "notion that there is a categorical difference between speaking as a citizen and speaking in the course of one's employment is quite wrong," and he doubted that it made sense "to fashion a new rule that provides employees with an incentive to voice their concerns publicly before talking frankly to their superiors." Justice Souter, joined by justices Stevens and Ginsburg, also dissented, arguing that

> private and public interests in addressing official wrongdoing and threats to health and safety can out-weigh the government's stake in the efficient implementation of policy, and when they do public employees who speak on these matters in the course of their duties should be eligible to claim First Amendment protection.

He would have distinguished between "[o]pen speech by a private citizen on a matter of public importance" which he viewed as lying "at the heart of expression subject to protection by the First Amendment," and "a statement by a government employee complaining about nothing beyond treatment under personnel rules" which, in his view, raised "no greater claim to constitutional protection against retaliatory response than the remarks of a private employee." He regarded a public employee's speech on a significant public issue as lying between these two extremes because it "is protected from reprisal unless the statements are too damaging to the government's capacity to conduct public business to be justified by any individual or public benefit thought to flow from the statements." He emphasized the public interest in receiving the "opinions and information that a public employee may disclose," especially given that "[g]overnment employees are often in the best position to know what ails the agencies for which they work."

However, he also realized that employee speech should be "qualified" because "it can distract co-workers and supervisors from their tasks at hand and thwart the implementation of legitimate policy, the risks of which grow greater the closer the employee's speech gets to commenting on his own workplace and responsibilities." As a result, he felt that the *Pickering* balancing test was the proper approach because it recognized that a "public employee can wear a citizen's hat when speaking on subjects closely tied to the employee's own job." That test seeks to reconcile "the tension between individual and public interests in the speech, on the one hand, and the government's interest in operating efficiently without distraction or embarrassment by talkative or headline-grabbing employees." He concluded that this balancing test should be equally applicable when an employee speaks on a matter within the scope of his responsibilities. Indeed, he concluded that the "individual and public value of such speech is no less, and may well be greater, when the employee speaks pursuant to his duties in addressing a subject he knows intimately for the very reason that it falls within his duties." "As for the importance of such speech to the individual, it stands to reason that a citizen may well place a very high value on a right to speak on the public issues he decides to make the subject of his work day after day." However, when an employee speaks out on a matter related to his employment, he has "greater leverage to create office uproars and fracture the government's authority to set policy to be carried out coherently through the ranks." But, rather than concluding that the employee's speech is not protected, he felt that the Court should follow the *Pickering* test so that "when constitutionally significant interests clash," the Court should resist the demand for "winner-take-all" and "try to make adjustments that serve all of the values at stake." He worried that the Court's decision might be used to limit the academic freedom of university professors because their speech is typically within the scope of their duties.

Justice Breyer, dissenting, argued that where a government employee speaks "as an employee upon matters only of personal interest," the First Amendment does not offer protection. By contrast, when a public employee speaks "as a citizen . . . upon matters of public concern," the First Amendment offers protection "but only where the speech survives [a] test, called, in legal shorthand, '*Pickering* balancing.'" He concluded that "court s should apply the *Pickering* standard, even though the government employee speaks upon matters of public concern in the course of his ordinary duties."

He felt that the present case presented two special considerations justifying First Amendment review: the fact that the speech was that of a lawyer, and the fact that a "prosecutor has a constitutional obligation to learn of, to preserve, and to communicate with the defense about exculpatory and impeachment evidence in the government's possession[, so that] the need to protect the employee's speech is augmented, the need for broad government authority to control that speech is likely diminished, and administrable standards are quite likely available." He noted that the speech of many other public employees "deals with wrongdoing, health, safety, and honesty: for example, police officers, firefighters, environmental protection agents, building inspectors, hospital workers, bank regulators, and so on." However, he worried that the "ability of a dissatisfied employee to file a complaint, engage in discovery, and insist that the court undertake a balancing of interests [may] interfere unreasonably with both the managerial function (the ability of the employer to control the way in which an employee performs his basic job) and with the use of other grievance-resolution mechanisms, such as arbitration, civil service review boards, and whistle-blower remedies, for which employees and employers may have bargained or which legislatures may have enacted. [The] list of categories substantially overlaps areas where the law already provides nonconstitutional protection through whistle-blower statutes and the like."

In *Borough of Duryea v. Guarnieri*,[20] a police chief sought to characterize his grievance against his employer (a city) as involving the petition clause of the First Amendment ("the right of the people . . . to petition the Government for a redress of grievances"), and argued that different rules apply to a claim under that clause. The case concerned the extent of the protection, if any, that the Petition Clause grants public employees in routine disputes with government employers. The Court concluded that the Clause adds nothing to an employee's claim: "If an employee does not speak as a citizen, or does not address a matter of public concern, 'a federal court is not the appropriate forum in which to review the wisdom of a personnel decision taken by a public agency allegedly in reaction to the employee's behavior.' " Indeed, even when an employee speaks on a matter of public concern, the Court concluded that it should apply the traditional balancing test. In other words, the courts must balance the First Amendment interest of the employee against "the interest of the State, as an employer, in promoting the efficiency of the public services it performs through its employees." The Court noted that Guarnieri could have proceeded under the Free Speech Clause or the Petition Clause, but that the judicial analysis would be the same under either clause.

Public Employees and the Petition Clause. In *Borough of Duryea v. Guarnieri*,[21] a police chief sought to characterize his grievance as involving the petition clause of the First Amendment ("the right of the people . . . to petition the Government for a redress of grievances."), and argued that different rules apply to a claim under that clause than to the traditional standards the government government employee

---

[20] 131 S.Ct. 2488 (2011).

[21] 131 S. Ct. 2488 (2011).

speech. The Court therefore discussed the extent of the protection that the Petition Clause grants public employees in routine disputes with government employers. The Court concluded that the Clause adds nothing to an employee's claim:

> When a public employee sues a government employer under the First Amendment's Speech Clause, the employee must show that he or she spoke as a citizen on a matter of public concern. *Connick v. Myers*, 461 U.S. 138 (1983). If an employee does not speak as a citizen, or does not address a matter of public concern, "a federal court is not the appropriate forum in which to review the wisdom of a personnel decision taken by a public agency allegedly in reaction to the employee's behavior." *Ibid.* Even if an employee does speak as a citizen on a matter of public concern, the employee's speech is not automatically privileged. Courts balance the First Amendment interest of the employee against "the interest of the State, as an employer, in promoting the efficiency of the public services it performs through its employees." *Pickering v. Board of Ed. of Township High School Dist. 205, Will Cty.*, 391 U.S. 563, 568 (1968). . . .

> [The] Petition Clause protects the right of individuals to appeal to courts and other forums established by the government for resolution of legal disputes[.] Although this case proceeds under the Petition Clause, Guarnieri just as easily could have alleged that his employer retaliated against him for the speech. [Both] speech and petition are integral to the democratic process, although not necessarily in the same way. The right to petition allows citizens to express their ideas, hopes, and concerns to their government and their elected representatives, whereas the right to speak fosters the public exchange of ideas that is integral to deliberative democracy as well as to the whole realm of ideas and human affairs. Beyond the political sphere, both speech and petition advance personal expression, although the right to petition is generally concerned with expression directed to the government seeking redress of a grievance. . . . Courts should not presume there is always an essential equivalence in the two Clauses or that Speech Clause precedents necessarily and in every case resolve Petition Clause claims Interpretation of the Petition Clause must be guided by the objectives and aspirations that underlie the right. A petition conveys the special concerns of its author to the government and, in its usual form, requests action by the government to address those concerns. . . .

> *McDonald v. Smith*, 472 U.S. 479 (1985), has sometimes been interpreted to mean that the right to petition can extend no further than the right to speak[. C]laims of retaliation by public employees do not call for this divergence. The close connection between these rights has led [courts] to apply the public concern test developed in Speech Clause cases to Petition Clause claims by public employees. [This] approach is justified by the extensive common ground in the definition and delineation of these rights. The considerations that shape the application of the Speech Clause to public employees apply with equal force to claims by those employees under the Petition Clause.

[C] Governmental Employee Associational Rights

In a number of cases, the Court has held that public employees have associational rights. For example, in *Wieman v. Updegraff*,[22] the Court held that a State could not require its employees to recite a loyalty oath denying their past affiliation with Communists. In *Keyishian v. Board of Regents*,[23] the Court invalidated New York statutes barring employment merely on the basis of membership in "subversive" organizations. The Court struck down the law on the basis that political association alone did not constitute an adequate ground for denying public employment. *United States v. Robel*,[24] involved the Subversive Activities Control Act of 1950, which provided that, when a Communist-action organization is under a final order to register, it shall be unlawful for any member of the organization "to engage in any employment in any defense facility." The law was passed to protect security and prevent sabotage at defense facilities. In *Communist Party of the United States v. Subversive Activities Control Board*,[25] the United States Supreme Court sustained an order requiring the Communist Party of the United States to register as a Communist-action organization under the Act. The order became final in 1961. At that time the appellee in *Robel* was a member of the Communist Party and was employed as a machinist at a Seattle, Washington, shipyard that was designated as a "defense facility." Appellee was indicted under § 5(a)(1)(D) of the Act. The indictment alleged that appellee had "unlawfully and willfully engage[d] in employment" at the shipyard with knowledge of the outstanding order against the Party and with knowledge and notice of the shipyard's designation as a defense facility by the Secretary of Defense. The Court concluded that the law violated appellee's right of association: "[T]he operative fact upon which the job disability depends is the exercise of an individual's right of association, which is protected by the provisions of the First Amendment."[26] After *Robel*, how does the government protect itself against espionage and sabotage at defense facilities?

In *Elrod v. Burns*,[27] the Sheriff of Cook County, Illinois, a Republican, was replaced by Richard Elrod, a Democrat. At the time, respondents, all Republicans, were employees of the Sheriff's Office. They were non-civil-service employees and were not covered by any law protecting them from arbitrary discharge. The evidence showed that it had been the practice of the Sheriff of Cook County, when he assumes office from a Sheriff of a different political party, to replace non-civil-service employees of the Sheriffs' Office with members of his own party when the existing employees lack or fail to obtain requisite support from, or fail to affiliate with, that party. Consequently, subsequent to Sheriff Elrod's assumption of office, respondents (with the exception of one individual who was under threat of imminent discharge) were discharged from their employment solely because they

---

[22] 344 U.S. 183 (1952).

[23] 385 U.S. 589 (1967).

[24] 389 U.S. 258 (1967).

[25] 367 U.S. 1 (1961).

[26] *Robel*, 389 U.S. at 263.

[27] 427 U.S. 347 (1976).

did not support and were not members of the Democratic Party and had failed to obtain the sponsorship of one of its leaders.

In an opinion by Justice Brennan, the Court overturned the dismissals. The Court found that the practice of replacing employees of one party with employees of another was a form of political patronage because, to keep their jobs, "respondents were required to pledge their political allegiance to the Democratic Party, work for the election of other candidates of the Democratic Party, contribute a portion of their wages to the Party, or obtain the sponsorship of a member of the Party, usually at the price of one of the first three alternatives." The Court noted that employees could keep their jobs only by compromising their beliefs: "Since the average public employee is hardly in the financial position to support his party and another, or to lend his time to two parties, the individual's ability to act according to his beliefs and to associate with others of his political persuasion is constrained, and support for his party is diminished." The Court felt that more than political belief was affected. "The free functioning of the electoral process also suffers. Conditioning public employment on partisan support prevents support of competing political interests. Existing employees are deterred from such support, as well as the multitude seeking jobs. . . . Patronage thus tips the electoral process in favor of the incumbent party, and where the practice's scope is substantial relative to the size of the electorate, the impact on the process can be significant." The Court ultimately struck down the dismissals.

> [Patronage,] to the extent it compels or restrains belief and association is inimical to the process which undergirds our system of government and is 'at war with the deeper traditions of democracy embodied in the First Amendment.' As such, the practice unavoidably confronts decisions by this Court either invalidating or recognizing as invalid government action that inhibits belief and association through the conditioning of public employment on political faith.

In reaching its decision, the Court recognized that the governmental interest must be weighed against the impact on associational rights. In addition, the governmental interest must be "vital" and must be achieved by ends that have the least restrictive impact on freedom of belief and association. Cook County argued that the law was supported by the need for "effective government" and efficient governmental employees. "It is argued that employees of political persuasions not the same as that of the party in control of public office will not have the incentive to work effectively and may even be motivated to subvert the incumbent administration's efforts to govern effectively." The Court rejected this argument noting that, when large numbers of public employees are replaced each time the government changes hands, there is considerable inefficiency. Moreover, the Court questioned whether patronage replacements would be more qualified "since appointment often occurs in exchange for the delivery of votes, or other party service, not job capability." Finally, the Court questioned whether an employee's political beliefs motivate poor performance by employees of the opposite political persuasion. In any event, the Court found that there were other means for ensuring employee effectiveness and efficiency including dismissal for insubordination or poor job performance." While the Court accepted the fact that patronage gives employees of the incumbent party an incentive to perform more effectively, the

Court found merit systems have been found to be as effective, if not more effective, especially given the impact on protected interests.

Cook County also argued that political loyalty was needed to keep employees from undercutting elected officials using tactics designed to obstruct implementation administration policies. The Court rejected the argument noting that the argument makes sense as applied to policymaking officials, but could not be used to justify wholesale dismissals. "Nonpolicymaking individuals usually have only limited responsibility and are therefore not in a position to thwart the goals of the in-party." But the Court found it difficult to distinguish between "policymaking" and "nonpolicymaking" positions. "While nonpolicymaking individuals usually have limited responsibility, that is not to say that one with a number of responsibilities is necessarily in a policymaking position." Even supervisors, who "have many responsibilities," "may have only limited and well-defined objectives. An employee with responsibilities that are not well defined or are of broad scope more likely functions in a policymaking position." "In determining whether an employee occupies a policymaking position, consideration should also be given to whether the employee acts as an adviser or formulates plans for the implementation of broad goals." The Court concluded that the government bore the burden of showing "an overriding interest in order to validate an encroachment on protected interests," the Court remanded to see whether it could meet that standard.

Cook County also argued that patronage dismissals were justified by the need to preserve the democratic process. The Court found that preservation "of the democratic process is certainly an interest protection of which may in some instances justify limitations on First Amendment freedoms." But the Court doubted whether "the elimination of patronage practice or, as is specifically involved here, the interdiction of patronage dismissals, will bring about the demise of party politics. Political parties existed in the absence of active patronage practice prior to the administration of Andrew Jackson, and they have survived substantial reduction in their patronage power through the establishment of merit systems."

In the final anslysis, the Court concluded that patronage dismissals were not "the least restrictive alternative to achieving the contribution they may make to the democratic process." "The process functions as well without the practice, perhaps even better, for patronage dismissals clearly also retard that process. [T]he gain to representative government provided by the practice of patronage, if any, would be insufficient to justify its sacrifice of First Amendment rights."

Chief Justice Burger dissented.

> [The] Court strains the rational bounds of First Amendment doctrine and runs counter to longstanding practices that are part of the fabric of our democratic system to hold that the Constitution commands something it has not been thought to require for 185 years. For all that time our system has wisely left these matters to the States and, on the federal level, to the Congress.

Justice Powell, joined by Chief Justice Burger and Justice Rehnquist, also dissented.

[P]atronage practices of the sort under consideration here have a long history in America [and have] played a significant role in democratizing American politics. [The] complaining employees who apparently accepted patronage jobs knowingly and willingly, while fully familiar with the 'tenure' practices long prevailing in the Sheriff's Office. Such employees have benefited from their political beliefs and activities; they have not been penalized for them. In these circumstances, [beneficiaries] of a patronage system may not be heard to challenge it when it comes their turn to be replaced.

He also argued that elected representatives are "better equipped" to determine whether patronage practices were needed in light of local conditions. "The pressure to abandon one's beliefs and associations to obtain government employment especially employment of such uncertain duration does not seem to me to assume impermissible proportions in light of the interests to be served."

In *Branti v. Finkel*,[28] defendant, a Democrat, discharged an assistant public defender solely because he was a Republican. Defendant argued that an assistant public defender performs a "policymaking" function, and therefore plaintiff could be dismissed because of his political beliefs. The Court (6-3) overturned the dismissal:

[T]he continued employment of an assistant public defender cannot properly be conditioned upon his allegiance to the political party in control of the county government. The primary, if not the only, responsibility of an assistant public defender is to represent individual citizens in controversy with the State. [W]hatever policymaking occurs in the public defender's office must relate to the needs of individual clients and not to any partisan political [interests].

Mr. Justice Stewart dissented: "[T]he petitioner, upon his appointment as Public Defender, was not constitutionally compelled to enter such a close professional and necessarily confidential association with the respondents if he did not wish to do so."

In *Rutan v. Republican Party of Illinois*,[29] the State of Illinois imposed a hiring freeze that did not permit exceptions without the Governor's express permission. Plaintiffs claimed that they were denied promotions or transfers, denied employment, or not recalled from layoffs, because they did not work for or support the Republican Party. The Court, in a 5-4 decision that relied on *Elrod*, held that the denials were unconstitutional.

Employees who do not compromise their beliefs stand to lose the considerable increases in pay and job satisfaction attendant to promotions, the hours and maintenance expenses that are consumed by long daily commutes, and even their jobs if they are not rehired after a 'temporary' layoff.

Justice Scalia dissented: "[T]he desirability of patronage is a policy question to be decided by the people's [representatives]."

---

[28] 445 U.S. 507 (1980).

[29] 497 U.S. 62 (1990).

Finally, in *City of San Diego v. Roe*,[30] a police officer was terminated for selling videotapes depicting himself engaged in sexually explicit acts. One video showed him stripping off a police uniform (not his actual unform) and masturbating. Another video portrayed him stopping a motorist to issue a citation, and then engaging in sexual activity with the motorist. The officer's website identified him "as employed in the field of law enforcement." The police department dismissed Roe concluding that he had violated specific police department policies, including engaging in conduct unbecoming of an officer and immoral conduct. The officer challenged the dismissal, arguing that all of his alleging misconduct took place during his off-duty hours.

In reviewing the discharge, the Court began by noting that government employees do not "relinquish all First Amendment rights otherwise enjoyed by citizens just by reason of [their] employment." Nevertheless, the Court recognized that "a governmental employer may impose certain restraints on the speech of its employees, restraints that would be unconstitutional if applied to the general public." In evaluating the validity of such restraints, the Court indicated that it would balance "the interests of the [employee], as a citizen, in commenting upon matters of public concern and the interest of the State, as an employer, in promoting the efficiency of the public services it performs through its employees." However, balancing would not be required when the employee's speech could compromise the proper functioning of government offices.

Applying these principles, the Court concluded that the police department had "demonstrated legitimate and substantial interests of its own that were compromised by [Roe's] speech." Roe had linked his videos and his other products in a way that was injurious to his employer: [The] debased parody of an officer performing indecent acts while in the course of official duties brought the mission of the employer and the professionalism of its officers into serious disrepute." In addition, the Court noted that Roe's expression did not implicate the public interest because Roe was not attempting to inform the public regarding any aspect of the department's functioning or operation."

Student Web Postings. There has been considerable litigation recently regarding student posting on websites such as My Space or Facebook. The cases sometimes present difficult questions because students have a right to engage in free expression outside the school, but sometimes that expression can interfere with the school environment. Thus far, none of the cases has made it to the Court for definitive resolution, but there have been a number of lower-court decisions. In one case, high school students used Facebook and My Space to make fun of school administrators, and they described the administrators as having engaged in vulgar conduct, as well as in drug and alcohol abuse, pedophilia, and shoplifting. In *J.S. v. Blue Mountain School District*, the court gave summary judgment in favor of school administrators who disciplined the students.[31]

---

[30] 543 U.S. 77 (2004).

[31] 593 F.3d 286 (3d Cir. 2010); *see also* Layshock v. Hermitage School District, 593 F.3d 239 (3d Cir. 2010).

In another case, a high school student, who was a member of the student council, posted a blog entry when a battle of the bands concert was cancelled at the school. Although the entry was posted on a non-campus blog, it urged other students to contact the superintendent of schools to urge that the concert be rescheduled. In her e-mail, the student suggested that the concert had been "cancelled due to douchebags in the central office," and provided students with a sample letter that they could send to the superintendent to "piss her off more." The blog produced a number of contacts with the superintendent's office. Because of the blog posting, the principal declined to endorse plaintiff's candidacy for senior class secretary, thereby precluding her from running for that office. The principal based her decision on the fact that the student failed to accept the principal's counsel regarding the proper way to express and resolve disagreements, the fact that the student included vulgar and inaccurate information in her blog posting, as well as the fact that the student had urged students to contact the superintended in order to "piss her off more." The court denied the student injunctive relief.[32]

The "I ♥ Boobies" Bracelets. One case involved a situation in which two female middle school students wore bracelets which said "I ♥ Boobies! (Keep A Breast)" on Breast Cancer Awareness Day. The bracelets were distributed by a breast cancer awareness group in order to "raise awareness of breast cancer and reduce the stigma associated with openly discussing breast health." In the particular case, the school disciplined the students for violating a policy that prohibits students from wearing clothes or jewelry with "sexually suggestive" messages, and being disruptive to the school environment. However, the court enjoined the school from disciplining the students.[33]

---

[32] Doninger v. Niehoff, 527 F.3d 41 (2d Cir. 2008) (court denied injunctive relief).

[33] B.H. v. Easton Area Sch. Dist., 827 F. Supp. 2d 392 (E.D. Pa. 2011).

POINTS TO REMEMBER

- Federal employees may be prohibited from taking an active part in political campaigns.

- In reviewing governmentally imposed restrictions on the partisan activities of public employees, the Court uses a limited review standard (the question is whether it acted "within reasonable limits").

- Government employees do have the right to accept compensation for writing articles or giving speeches (assuming that the compensation is not a disguised bribe).

- Although government may restrict the rights of public employees in the workplace, there are limits.

- Government may not impose so-called "loyalty oaths" on public employees.

- Although government is less able to impose restrictions on speech that involves matters of "public concern," it is more able to impose restrictions on speech about matters of purely private concern.

- The Court tries to find a balance "between the interests of the [employee], as a citizen, in commenting upon matters of public concern and the interest of the State, as an employer, in promoting the efficiency of the public services it performs through its employees."

- Although government may prohibit public employees from engaging in partisan political activities, it cannot dismiss employees solely because of the groups with which they associate (except for employees in high level, policymaking, positions).

---

§ 9.02 THE FIRST AMENDMENT IN THE PUBLIC SCHOOLS

In recent years, there has been much litigation regarding the scope of free speech rights in the public schools, and this litigation has arisen in a variety of contexts.

In the Court's landmark decision in *Tinker v. Des Moines Independent School District*,[34] the Court recognized that high school students have a First Amendment right of expression. John Tinker and Christopher Eckhardt, 15 years old and 16 years old, respectively were high school students. John's sister, Mary Tinker, was a 13-year-old junior high school student. The three were part of a group of students who objected to the Vietnam War and showed their objections by wearing black armbands during the holiday season. Aware of the protest, the principals of the schools adopted a policy that any student wearing an armband to school would be asked to remove it. Upon refusal the student would be suspended until he or she

---

[34] 393 U.S. 503 (1969).

returned without the armband. Petitioners were aware of the regulation that the school authorities adopted. All three students wore black armbands to their schools, and all were suspended from school until they agreed to return without their armbands. They did not return to school until after the planned period for wearing armbands had expired — that is, until after New Year's Day. The students sued challenging the suspension.

In an opinion by Justice Fortas, the Court invalidated the suspensions. The Court began by recognizing that "symbolic speech," including the wearing of armbands, is protected by the First Amendment. Indeed, the Court held that the wearing of armbands is "closely akin to 'pure speech'" and "is entitled to comprehensive protection under the First Amendment." Although the Court held that teachers and students have free speech rights, it recognized that those rights are tempered by the "special characteristics of the school environment" and the needs of school officials, "consistent with fundamental constitutional safeguards, to prescribe and control conduct in the schools." However, the Court found that "school officials banned and sought to punish petitioners for a silent, passive expression of opinion, unaccompanied by any disorder or disturbance on the part of petitioners." In addition, the Court found that there was "no indication that the work of the schools or any class was disrupted. Outside the classrooms, a few students made hostile remarks to the children wearing armbands, but there were no threats or acts of violence on school premises." The mere fact that school officials "feared" the "possibility" of a disturbance was insufficient. "[I]n our system, undifferentiated fear or apprehension of disturbance is not enough to overcome the right to freedom of expression." In order to prevail, school officials were required to show that the students' conduct "materially and substantially interfere with the requirements of appropriate discipline in the operation of the school." The Court found that school officials could not meet the required burden.

The Court was also concerned about the fact that school officials engaged in content based discrimination. The Court noted that the schools allowed students to wear "buttons relating to national political campaigns, and some even wore the Iron Cross, traditionally a symbol of Nazism." But it chose to prohibit the students' black arm bands. "In our system, students may not be regarded as closed-circuit recipients of only that which the State chooses to communicate. They may not be confined to the expression of those sentiments that are officially approved. In the absence of a specific showing of constitutionally valid reasons to regulate their speech, students are entitled to freedom of expression of their views." "The principal use to which the schools are dedicated is to accommodate students during prescribed hours for the purpose of certain types of activities. Among those activities is personal intercommun ication among the students." Nevertheless, the Court held that "conduct by the student, in class or out of it, which for any reason — whether it stems from time, place, or type of behavior — materially disrupts classwork or involves substantial disorder or invasion of the rights of others is, of course, not immunized by the constitutional guarantee of freedom of speech." "[T]he record does not demonstrate any facts which might reasonably have led school authorities to forecast substantial disruption of or material interference with school activities, and no disturbances or disorders on the school premises in fact occurred."

Justice Stewart, concurred.

I cannot share the Court's uncritical assumption that, school discipline aside, the First Amendment rights of children are co-extensive with those of adults. "[A] State may permissibly determine that, at least in some precisely delineated areas, a child — like someone in a captive audience — is not possessed of that full capacity for individual choice which is the presupposition of First Amendment guarantees."

Justice Black dissented. He disputed the majority's view of the facts noting that the school could have found that the armbands caused disruption:

While the record does not show that any of these armband students shouted, used profane language, or were violent in any manner, detailed testimony by some of them shows their armbands caused comments, warnings by other students, the poking of fun at them, and a warning by an older football player that other, nonprotesting students had better let them alone. There is also evidence that a teacher of mathematics had his lesson period practically "wrecked" chiefly by disputes with Mary Beth Tinker, who wore her armband for her "demonstration." Even a casual reading of the record shows that this armband did divert students' minds from their regular lessons, and that talk, comments, etc., made John Tinker "self-conscious" in attending school with his armband. While the absence of obscene remarks or boisterous and loud disorder perhaps justifies the Court's statement that the few armband students did not actually "disrupt" the classwork, I think the record overwhelmingly shows that the armbands did exactly what the elected school officials and principals foresaw they would, that is, took the students' minds off their classwork and diverted them to thoughts about the highly emotional subject of the Vietnam [war].

Justice Harlan also dissented.

I am reluctant to believe that there is any disagreement between the majority and myself on the proposition that school officials should be accorded the widest authority in maintaining discipline and good order in their institutions. To translate that proposition into a workable constitutional rule, I would, in cases like this, cast upon those complaining the burden of showing that a particular school measure was motivated by other than legitimate school concerns — for example, a desire to prohibit the expression of an unpopular point of view, while permitting expression of the dominant opinion.

In *Board of Education v. Pico*,[35] a local school board ordered the removal of certain books from the libraries of a district high school and junior high school. Among the books were *Soul on Ice* by Eldridge Cleaver, *The Naked Ape* by Desmond Morris, and *Slaughter House Five* by Kurt Vonnegut. The board characterized the books as "anti-American, anti-Christian, anti-Semitic, and just plain filthy," and asserted that "it is our duty, our moral obligation, to protect the children in our schools from this moral danger as surely as from physical and medical dangers."

---

[35] 457 U.S. 853 (1982).

Five students sued the school district under 42 U.S.C. § 1983, alleging that the board had "ordered the removal of the books from school libraries and proscribed their use in the curriculum because particular passages in the books offended their social, political and moral tastes and not because the books, taken as a whole, were lacking in educational value." They claimed that the board's actions violated their rights under the First Amendment.

The district court granted summary judgment to the defendants, but the court of appeals reversed and remanded the action for a trial on the merits. The Supreme Court affirmed the reversal by a vote of 5 to 4, with no majority opinion. A plurality opinion by Justice Brennan, joined by Justice Marshall, Justice Stevens, and (in part) by Justice Blackmun, first asserted that "the Constitution protects the right to receive information and ideas," and that "students too are beneficiaries of this principle." The plurality then said:

> [School officials] rightly possess significant discretion to determine the content of their school libraries. But that discretion may not be exercised in a narrowly partisan or political manner. If a Democratic school board, motivated by party affiliation, ordered the removal of all books written by or in favor of Republicans, few would doubt that the order violated the constitutional rights of the students denied access to those books. The same conclusion would surely apply if an all-white school board, motivated by racial animus, decided to remove all books authored by blacks or advocating racial equality and integration. Our Constitution does not permit the official suppression of *ideas.* Thus whether petitioners' removal of books from their school libraries denied respondents their First Amendment rights depends upon the motivation behind petitioners' actions. If petitioners *intended* by their removal decision to deny respondents access to ideas with which petitioners disagreed, and if this intent was the decisive factor in petitioners' decision, then petitioners have exercised their discretion in violation of the Constitution. [In] brief, we hold that local school boards may not remove books from school library shelves simply because they dislike the ideas contained in those books and seek by their removal to "prescribe what shall be orthodox in politics, nationalism, religion, or other matters of opinion."

The plurality found that, based on the evidentiary materials submitted to the district court, the defendants were not entitled to summary judgment: the evidence "plainly [did] not foreclose the possibility that [the school board's] decision to remove the books rested decisively upon disagreement with constitutionally protected ideas in those books, or upon a desire on petitioners' part to impose upon the students of the [junior and senior high schools] a political orthodoxy to which [the school board members] and their constituents adhered."

Justice White, who provided the fifth vote for affirmance, did not join any part of the plurality opinion. On the contrary, he chastised the plurality for issuing "a dissertation on the extent to which the First Amendment limits the discretion of the school board to remove books from the school library." And in a letter to Justice Brennan while the case was under consideration, Justice White made clear that he did not endorse the plurality's standard: "I am frank to say that I scarcely know what a 'political or ideological orthodoxy' is, and it would take years to find out. The removal of any book based on its content could be challenged on this basis."[36] Nevertheless, Justice White concurred in the judgment, saying, "I am not inclined to disagree with the court of appeals" on the "fact-bound issue" of "the reason or reasons underlying the school board's removal of the books."

Tinker was qualified by the holding in *Hazelwood School District v. Kuhlmeier.*[37] In *Kuhlmeier*, a high school principal ordered students to delete two pages from the school's newspaper. The practice was for the journalism teacher to submit page proofs of each Spectrum issue to the principal for review prior to publication. The issue in question described three Hazelwood East students' experiences with pregnancy; the other discussed the impact of divorce on students at the school. Reynolds believed that there was no time to make the necessary changes in the stories before the scheduled press run and that the newspaper would not appear before the end of the school year if printing were delayed to any significant extent. He concluded that his only options under the circumstances were to publish a four-page newspaper instead of the planned six-page newspaper, eliminating the two pages on which the offending stories appeared, or to publish no newspaper at all. Accordingly, he directed Emerson to withhold from publication the two pages containing the stories on pregnancy and divorce. He informed his superiors of the decision, and they concurred. The students subsequently commenced this action in federal court asserting that their First Amendment rights had been violated.

In an opinion by Justice White, the Court upheld the school's actions. The Court began by reaffirming the basic proposition that students do not "shed their constitutional rights to freedom of speech or expression at the schoolhouse gate," but that student rights "are not automatically coextensive with the rights of adults in other settings," and must be "applied in light of the special characteristics of the school environment." In addition, a "school need not tolerate student speech that is inconsistent with its 'basic educational mission'" even if the speech could not be prohibited outside the school environment. The Court held that school officials should be given deference in determining what speech is inappropriate.

The Court first dealt with the question of whether the paper could be regarded as a forum for public expression. The Court answered this question in the negative: "School officials did not evince either 'by policy or by practice,' any intent to open the pages of Spectrum to 'indiscriminate use' by its student reporters and editors, or by the student body generally. Instead, they 'reserve[d] the forum for its intended purpos[e],' as a supervised learning experience for journalism students." As a result, the Court found that school officials were entitled to impose reasonable regulations on the contents of Spectrum. The Court concluded that the "question whether the First Amendment requires a school to tolerate particular student speech — the question that we addressed in *Tinker* — is different from the question whether the First Amendment requires a school affirmatively to promote particular student speech."

---

[36] *See* DENNIS J. HUTCHINSON, THE MAN WHO ONCE WAS WHIZZER WHITE 392 (1998).

[37] 484 U.S. 260 (1988).

The latter question concerns educators' authority over school-sponsored publications, theatrical productions, and other expressive activities that students, parents, and members of the public might reasonably perceive to bear the imprimatur of the school. These activities may fairly be characterized as part of the school curriculum, whether or not they occur in a traditional classroom setting, so long as they are supervised by faculty members and designed to impart particular knowledge or skills to student participants and audiences.

The Court found that educators are "entitled to exercise greater control over this second form of student expression to assure that participants learn whatever lessons the activity is designed to teach, that readers or listeners are not exposed to material that may be inappropriate for their level of maturity, and that the views of the individual speaker are not erroneously attributed to the school." In addition, the school can disassociate itself from speech that is "ungrammatical, poorly written, inadequately researched, biased or prejudiced, vulgar or profane, or unsuitable for immature audiences." Moreover, the school can control content "on potentially sensitive topics, which might range from the existence of Santa Claus in an elementary school setting to the particulars of teenage sexual activity in a high school setting. A school must also retain the authority to refuse to sponsor student speech that might reasonably be perceived to advocate drug or alcohol use, irresponsible sex, or conduct otherwise inconsistent with 'the shared values of a civilized social order,' or to associate the school with any position other than neutrality on matters of political controversy."

The Court concluded that administrators were entitled to exercise discretion: "[W]e hold that educators do not offend the First Amendment by exercising editorial control over the style and content of student speech in school-sponsored expressive activities so long as their actions are reasonably related to legitimate pedagogical concerns." The Court held that, only when there is no "valid educational purpose" may the courts intervene to protect students' rights.

Using these standards, the Court upheld the principal's action:

The principal concluded that the students' anonymity was not adequately protected, [given] the other identifying information in the article and the small number of pregnant students at the school. It is likely that many students at Hazelwood East would have been [successful] in identifying the girls. Reynolds therefore could reasonably have feared that the article violated whatever pledge of anonymity had been given to the pregnant students. In addition, he could reasonably have been concerned that the article was not sufficiently sensitive to the privacy interests of the students' boyfriends and parents, who were discussed in the article but who were given no opportunity to consent to its publication or to offer a response. The article did not contain graphic accounts of sexual activity. The girls did comment in the article, however, concerning their sexual histories and their use or nonuse of birth control. It was not unreasonable for the principal to have concluded that such frank talk was inappropriate in a school-sponsored publication distributed to 14-year-old freshmen and presumably taken home to be read by students' even younger brothers and sisters.

In addition, one student "who was quoted by name in the version of the divorce article seen by Principal Reynolds made comments sharply critical of her father. The principal could reasonably have concluded that an individual publicly identified as an inattentive parent — indeed, as one who chose 'playing cards with the guys' over home and family — was entitled to an opportunity to defend himself as a matter of journalistic fairness."

Justice Brennan, joined by justices Marshall and Blackmun, dissented arguing that the principal should not be allowed to censor student expression that does not disrupt classwork or invade the rights of others. He specifically rejected the argument that speech could be censored simply because of incompatability with the school's message. Otherwise, "school officials could [convert] our public schools into 'enclaves of totalitarianism,' that 'strangle the free mind at its source.'" He would have applied the *Tinker* standard (whether the student expression "materially disrupts classwork or involves substantial disorder or invasion of the rights of [others].")

Kuhlmeier relied on the Court's prior decision in *Bethel School District No. 403 v. Fraser.*[38] In *Fraser*, a high school student was disciplined for delivering a "sexually explicit" speech at a school assembly at which he nominated a fellow student for student elective office. In the speech, he stated in relevant part that:

I know a man who is firm — he's firm in his pants, he's firm in his shirt, his character is firm — but most . . . of all, his belief in you, the students of Bethel, is firm.

Jeff Kuhlman is a man who takes his point and pounds it in. If necessary, he'll take an issue and nail it to the wall. He doesn't attack things in spurts — he drives hard, pushing and pushing until finally — he succeeds.

Jeff is a man who will go to the very end — even the climax, for each and every one of you.

So vote for Jeff for A.S.B. vice-president — he'll never come between you and the best our high school can be.

In upholding the disciplinary sanction, the United States Supreme Court distinguished *Tinker*:

[T]he penalties imposed in this case were unrelated to any political viewpoint. The First Amendment does not prevent the school officials from determining that to permit a vulgar and lewd speech such as [Fraser's] would undermine the school's basic educational mission. A high school assembly or classroom is no place for a sexually explicit monologue directed towards an unsuspecting audience of teenage students. Accordingly, it was perfectly appropriate for the school to disassociate itself to make the point to the pupils that vulgar speech and lewd conduct is wholly inconsistent with the 'fundamental values' of public school education.

---

[38] 478 U.S. 675 (1986).

In *Morse v. Frederick*,[39] the Court held that a high school student could be sanctioned for displaying a large banner stating "Bong hits for Jesus." The banner was displayed at a school-supervised event (students were allowed to go outside to observe the Olympic torch pass in front of the school) that the principal perceived as suggesting a message promoting illegal drug use. Although the Court reaffirmed the idea that students do not "shed their constitutional rights to freedom of speech or expression at the schoolhouse gate," it continued to recognize that "the constitutional rights of students in public school are not automatically coextensive with the rights of adults in other settings," and that the rights of students "must be applied in light of the special characteristics of the school environment." Consistent with these principles, the Court held that schools may take steps to safeguard those entrusted to their care from speech that can reasonably be regarded as encouraging illegal drug use, and therefore that the school did not act inappropriately in confiscating the pro-drug banner and suspending the student responsible for it:

> School principals have a difficult job, and a vitally important one. When Frederick suddenly and unexpectedly unfurled his banner, Morse had to decide to act — or not act — on the spot. It was reasonable for her to conclude that the banner promoted illegal drug use — in violation of established school policy — and that failing to act would send a powerful message to the students in her charge, including Frederick, about how serious the school was about the dangers of illegal drug use. The First Amendment does not require schools to tolerate at school events student expression that contributes to those dangers."

Justice Stevens dissented in *Frederick*, arguing that the principal should not be held liable in damages for removing the banner, but that the school's interest in protecting students against illegal drug use did not justify imposing sanctions on Frederick:

> [T]he First Amendment protects student speech if the message itself neither violates a permissible rule nor expressly advocates conduct that is illegal and harmful to students. This nonsense banner does neither, and the Court does serious violence to the First Amendment in upholding — indeed, lauding — a school's decision to punish Frederick for expressing a view with which it disagreed.

---

[39] 551 U.S. 393 (2007).

POINTS TO REMEMBER

- Although secondary students have free speech rights, those rights are not co-extensive with the rights of adults.

- Schools may not prohibit "symbolic speech" — passive speech that expresses a view on a political issue — absent a showing that the speech materially disrupts classwork or involves substantial disorder or invasion of the rights of others.

- While school officials normally have the right to select books for their libraries, there may be limits on the right to remove books based solely on disagreement with the ideas contained in those books.

- Of course, school officials have the right to exclude books that are inappropriate for the childrens' ages and level of educational development.

- School officials may have greater authority to edit or control the content of school-sponsored student newspapers.

- In exercising such control, the question is whether the school's control over the style and content of the newspaper was "reasonably related to legitimate pedagogical concerns."

---

§ 9.03   GOVERNMENT FINANCED SPEECH

In some instances, the government provides financial support for private speech. Does the First Amendment prohibit the government from imposing regulations or restrictions that accompany the funding?

[A]   Overview

Rust v. Sullivan[40] involved United States Department of Health and Human Services (HHS) regulations which restricted the activities of those that received funds under Title X of the Public Health Service Act (Act), which provided federal funding for family-planning services. Section 1008 of the Act provided that "none of the funds appropriated under this subchapter shall be used in programs where abortion is a method of family planning." That restriction was intended to ensure that Title X funds would be used only to support "preventive family planning services, population research, infertility services, and other related medical, informational, and educational activities." The Secretary promulgated new regulations which attached three conditions on the grant of federal funds for Title X projects. First, a "Title X project may not provide counseling concerning the use of abortion as a method of family planning or provide referral for abortion as a method of family planning." Second, the regulations broadly prohibit a Title X project from engaging in activities that "encourage, promote or advocate abortion

---

[40] 500 U.S. 173 (1991).

as a method of family planning." Third, the regulations require that Title X projects be organized so that they are "physically and financially separate" from prohibited abortion activities. To be deemed physically and financially separate, "a Title X project must have an objective integrity and independence from prohibited activities. Mere bookkeeping separation of Title X funds from other monies is not sufficient."

The regulations were challenged by a group of Title X grantees and doctors who supervised Title X funds who claimed that the regulations violated the rights of Title X clients and the First Amendment rights of Title X health providers. The Court upheld the regulations rejecting the argument that the regulation imposed "viewpoint" based restrictions on speech by prohibiting "all discussion about abortion as a lawful option — including counseling, referral, and the provision of neutral and accurate information about ending a pregnancy — while compelling the clinic or counselor to provide information that promotes continuing a pregnancy to term." In addition, the Court rejected the argument that the regulations violated the "free speech rights of private health care organizations that receive Title X funds, of their staff, and of their patients" by impermissibly imposing "viewpoint-discriminatory conditions on government subsidies" and thus "penalize speech funded with non-Title X monies."

The Court concluded that the government was free to

> selectively fund a program to encourage certain activities it believes to be in the public interest, without at the same time funding an alternative program which seeks to deal with the problem in another way. In so doing, the Government has not discriminated on the basis of viewpoint; it has merely chosen to fund one activity to the exclusion of the other.

> The challenged regulations [are] designed to ensure that the limits of the federal program are observed. [A] doctor who wished to offer prenatal care to a project patient who became pregnant could properly be prohibited from doing so because such service is outside the scope of the federally funded program. The regulations prohibiting abortion counseling and referral are of the same ilk. [This] is not a case of the Government "suppressing a dangerous idea," but of a prohibition on a project grantee or its employees from engaging in activities outside of the project's scope.

The Court also rejected the argument that the government was precluded from conditioning Title X funding on the relinquishment of a constitutional right — the right to engage in abortion advocacy and counseling. The Court held that "the Government is not denying a benefit to anyone, but is instead simply insisting that public funds be spent for the purposes for which they were authorized. The Secretary's regulations do not force the Title X grantee to give up abortion-related speech; they merely require that the grantee keep such activities separate and distinct from Title X activities." "The Title X *grantee* can continue to perform abortions, provide abortion-related services, and engage in abortion advocacy; it simply is required to conduct those activities through programs that are separate and independent from the project that receives Title X funds."

The Court rejected claims that the regulations violated the rights of the grantee's staff. Staff were only required to abide by the restrictions on abortion counseling and referral while they were performing governmental duties. Otherwise, the employees were free to pursue abortion-related activities.

The Court found that the regulations did not significantly impinge the doctor-patient relationship. The program did not require doctors to make statements that they did not believe to be true, and the program was not so "all encompassing" as to make patients believe that they were receiving comprehensive medical advice. As the Court noted, the program did not provide post-conception medical care, and therefore a doctor's silence with regard to abortion cannot reasonably be thought to mislead a client into thinking that the doctor does not consider abortion an appropriate option for her. In any event, the doctor is free to state that abortion alternatives are beyond the program's scope.

Justice Blackmun, joined by Justice Marshall and partially joined by justices Stevens and O'Connor, dissented. He argued that the government had engaged in viewpoint-based suppression of speech, and that the government may not impose "a condition that suppresses the recipient's cherished freedom of speech based solely upon the content or viewpoint of that speech."

> By refusing to fund those family-planning projects that advocate abortion *because* they advocate abortion, the Government plainly has targeted a particular viewpoint. The majority's reliance on the fact that the regulations pertain solely to funding decisions simply begs the question. [O]ur cases make clear that ideological viewpoint is [a] repugnant ground upon which to base funding decisions.

He also rejected the argument that Title X physicians and counselors "remain free . . . to pursue abortion-related activities when they are not acting under the auspices of the Title X project." Under the majority's reasoning, the First Amendment could be read to tolerate *any* governmental restriction upon an employee's speech so long as that restriction is limited to the funded workplace. This is a dangerous proposition, and one the Court has rightly rejected in the past."

He also argued that the speaker's interest was "clear and vital" noting that, when "a client becomes pregnant, the full range of therapeutic alternatives includes the abortion option, and Title X counselors' interest in providing this information is compelling." Likewise, he rejected the government's argument that it has a right to ensure that federal funds are not spent for a purpose outside the scope of the program. He found that that justification was insufficient to justify suppression of truthful information. Moreover, the offending regulation was not narrowly tailored to serve this interest. "Finally, it is of no small significance that the speech the Secretary would suppress is truthful information regarding constitutionally protected conduct of vital importance to the listener. One can imagine no legitimate governmental interest that might be served by suppressing such information."

Rust was reinforced by the Court's later holding in *Johanns v. Livestock Marking Association*.[41] That case (discussed more fully in Section 8.02 [C]) treated

---

[41]   544 U.S. 550 (2005).

the government's beef checkoff program as governmental speech.

In *Ysura v. Pocatello Education Association*,[42] although Idaho allowed a public employee to have a portion of his salary deducted for union dues, it prohibited payroll deductions for contributions to a union's political activities. A group of unions challenged the restriction as applied to county, municipal, school district, and other local public employers. In upholding the restriction, the Court emphasized that Idaho "does not restrict political speech, but rather declines to promote that speech by allowing public employee checkoffs for political activities," and noted that Idaho is under no obligation to aid unions in their political activities. The Court went on to hold that the state has an interest in demonstrating that governmental actions are not "tainted by partisan political activity." Concluding that there was no infringement of First Amendment rights, the Court applied rational basis review to the restriction, and concluded that the governmental action was reasonable, noting that "Idaho does not suppress political speech but simply declines to promote it through public employer checkoffs for political activities." Moreover, the state did not discriminate between different types of political activities or messages because the prohibition applied "regardless of viewpoint or message," and "it does not single out any candidates or issues."

[B] The National Endowment for the Arts

National Endowment for the Arts v. Finley[43] involved the National Foundation on the Arts and Humanities Act, as amended in 1990, which requires the Chairperson of the National Endowment for the Arts (NEA) to ensure that "artistic excellence and artistic merit are the criteria by which [grant] applications are judged, taking into consideration general standards of decency and respect for the diverse beliefs and values of the American public." 20 U.S.C. § 954(d)(1). The enabling statute vested the NEA with substantial discretion to award grants; it identifies only the broadest funding priorities, including "artistic and cultural significance, giving emphasis to American creativity and cultural diversity," "professional excellence," and the encouragement of "public knowledge, education, understanding, and appreciation of the arts."

Applications for NEA funding were initially reviewed by advisory panels composed of experts in the relevant field of the arts. Under the 1990 Amendments to the enabling statute, those panels must reflect "diverse artistic and cultural points of view" and include "wide geographic, ethnic, and minority representation," as well as "lay individuals who are knowledgeable about the arts." The Chairperson had ultimate authority to award grants. As the Court recognized, most NEA grants generated no controversy, but two did attract controversy. One involved a retrospective of photographer Robert Map-plethorpe's work. The exhibit, entitled *The Perfect Moment*, included homoerotic photographs that several Members of Congress condemned as pornographic. Members also denounced artist Andres Serrano's work *Piss Christ*, a photograph of a crucifix immersed in urine. Serrano had been awarded a $15,000 grant from [an] organization that received NEA

---

[42] 555 U.S. 353 (2009).

[43] 524 U.S. 569 (1998).

support. Because of the controversy over these works, Congress amended the NEA by adding § 954(d)(1) which provided as follows:

> No payment shall be made under this section except upon application therefor which is submitted to the National Endowment for the Arts in accordance with regulations issued and procedures established by the Chairperson. In establishing such regulations and procedures, the Chairperson shall ensure that —
>
> > (1) artistic excellence and artistic merit are the criteria by which applications are judged, taking into consideration general standards of decency and respect for the diverse beliefs and values of the American public; and
> >
> > (2) applications are consistent with the purposes of this section. Such regulations and procedures shall clearly indicate that obscenity is without artistic merit, is not protected speech, and shall not be funded.

The amendment was challenged as a viewpoint-based restriction on speech.

In an opinion by Justice O'Connor, the Court upheld the law rejecting the claims of viewpoint discrimination. The Court noted that the law imposed no categorical prohibition against this type of speech. On the contrary, it simply admonishes the NEA to take "decency and respect" into consideration, and that the legislation was aimed at reforming procedures rather than precluding speech. The Court found that this distinction undercut respondents' argument that the "provision inevitably will be utilized as a tool for invidious viewpoint discrimination." The Court also rejected the argument that the criteria were sufficiently "subjective" that they could be used to engage in viewpoint discrimination.

> Any content-based considerations that may be taken into account in the grant-making process are a consequence of the nature of arts funding. The NEA has limited resources and it must deny the majority of the grant applications that it receives, including many that propose 'artistically excellent' projects. . . . [A]bsolute neutrality is simply "inconceivable."

Justice Scalia, joined by Justice Thomas, concurred. "Congress did not *abridge* the speech of those who disdain the beliefs and values of the American public, nor did it *abridge* indecent speech. Those who wish to create indecent and disrespectful art are as unconstrained now as they were before the enactment of this statute. . . ." In Justice Scalia's view, the "nub of the difference between me and the Court is that I regard the distinction between "abridging" speech and funding it as a fundamental divide, on this side of which the First Amendment is inapplicable."

Justice Souter dissented arguing that the NEA amendments imposed viewpoint-based restrictions. "The Court's conclusions that the proviso is not viewpoint-based, that it is not a regulation, and that the NEA may permissibly engage in viewpoint-based discrimination, are all patently mistaken." In his view, the controlling question was

> whether the government has adopted a regulation of speech because of disagreement with the message it conveys. . . . The answer in this case is

damning. One need do nothing more th an read the text of the statute to conclude that Congress's purpose in imposing the decency and respect criteria was to prevent the funding of art that conveys an offensive message; the decency and respect provision on its face is quintessentially viewpoint-based, and quotations from the Congressional Record merely confirm the obvious legislative purpose.

He argued that the government was acting as "patron" in these cases. But he found that, as patron, it cannot discriminate. He relied on *Rosenberger* which he construed as holding that the government may not act on viewpoint when it "does not itself speak or subsidize transmittal of a message it favors but instead expends funds to encourage a diversity of views from private speakers."

> Scarce money demands choices, of course, but choices "on some acceptable [viewpoint] neutral principle," like artistic excellence and artistic merit; "nothing in our decisions indicates that scarcity would give the State the right to exercise viewpoint discrimination that is otherwise impermissible."

[C]   Legal Services Corporation Funding

Legal Services Corp. v. Velazquez[44] involved the Legal Services Corporation Act which established a nonprofit corporation to distribute funds appropriated by Congress to eligible local grantee organizations "for the purpose of providing financial support for legal assistance in noncriminal proceedings or matters to persons financially unable to afford legal assistance." LSC grantees consisted of hundreds of local organizations governed, in the typical case, by local boards of directors. In many instances the grantees are funded by a combination of LSC funds and other public or private sources. The grantee organizations hire and supervise lawyers to provide free legal assistance to indigent clients. Each year LSC appropriates funds to grantees or recipients that hire and supervise lawyers for various professional activities, including representation of indigent clients seeking welfare benefits. In the Omnibus Consolidated Rescissions and Appropriations Act of 1996 (1996 Act), and subsequent annual appropriations, Congress prohibited LSC grantees, including those paid for by non-LSC funds, from undertaking representation designed to amend or otherwise challenge existing welfare law. As interpreted by the LSC and by the Government, the restriction prevented an attorney from arguing to a court that a state statute conflicts with a federal statute or that either a state or federal statute by its terms or in its application is violative of the United States Constitution. . . .

In an opinion by Justice Kennedy, the Court struck down the restriction. Much of the Court's focus was centered upon whether *Rust v. Sullivan* should be treated as the most applicable precedent, and on whether the prohibition should be treated as a "viewpoint" based restriction on speech. "Although the LSC program differs from the program at issue in *Rosenberger* in that its purpose is not to 'encourage a diversity of views,' the salient point is that, like the program in *Rosenberger*, the LSC program was designed to facilitate private speech, not to promote a governmental message. Congress funded LSC grantees to provide attorneys to

---

[44]   531 U.S. 533 (2001).

represent the interests of indigent clients." So,

> an LSC-funded attorney speaks on the behalf of the client in a claim against the government for welfare benefits. The lawyer is not the government's speaker. The attorney defending the decision to deny benefits will deliver the government's message in the litigation. The LSC lawyer, however, speaks on the behalf of his or her private, indigent client.

The Court expressed concern that the funding restrictions "distorts the legal system by altering the traditional role of attorneys." Government "may not design a subsidy to effect this serious and fundamental restriction on advocacy of attorneys and the functioning of the judiciary."

> An informed, independent judiciary presumes an informed, independent bar. . . . By seeking to prohibit the analysis of certain legal issues and to truncate presentation to the courts, the enactment under review prohibits speech and expression upon which courts must depend for the proper exercise of the judicial power. Congress cannot wrest the law from the Constitution which is its source.

The Court concluded that the "restriction imposed by the statute here threatens severe impairment of the judicial function." The Court found that the "restriction on speech is even more problematic because in cases where the attorney withdraws from a representation, the client is unlikely to find other counsel."

Justice Scalia, joined by Chief Justice Renquist and Justices O'Connor, and Thomas, dissented:

> The LSC Act is a federal subsidy program, not a federal regulatory program, and "there is a basic difference between [the two]." Regulations directly restrict speech; subsidies do not. Subsidies, it is true, may *indirectly* abridge speech, but only if the funding scheme is " 'manipulated' to have a 'coercive effect' " on those who do not hold the subsidized position. . . .
>
> The LSC Act, like the scheme in *Rust*, does not create a public forum. Far from encouraging a diversity of views, it has always, as the Court accurately states, "placed restrictions on its use of funds." Nor does § 504(a)(16) discriminate on the basis of viewpoint, since it funds neither challenges to nor defenses of existing welfare law. The provision simply declines to subsidize a certain class of litigation, and under *Rust* that decision "does not infringe the right" to bring such litigation. . . .
>
> This has been a very long discussion to make a point that is embarrassingly simple: The LSC subsidy neither prevents anyone from speaking nor coerces anyone to change speech, and is indistinguishable in all relevant respects from the subsidy upheld in *Rust*. There is no legitimate basis for declaring § 504(a)(16) facially unconstitutional.

POINTS TO REMEMBER

- Special rules apply when the government chooses to fund speech.
- In general, the government may have greater authority to limit or control the content of speech in this context.
- But governmental authority is not without limits even in this context.

Chapter 10

MEDIA AND THE FIRST AMENDMENT

FOCAL POINTS FOR CHAPTER 10

- Competing models for defining the free press clause and their implications.

- The case for and against a First Amendment privilege.

- The case for and against First Amendment immunity from newsroom searches.

- Access to prisons and inmates.

- Access to trials.

- Prejudicial publicity and the balancing of First Amendment freedoms and defendant rights.

- Electronic media in the courtroom.

- The nature of medium specific analysis.

- First Amendment standards for print media.

- First Amendment standards for broadcasting

- First Amendment standards for cable.

- First Amendments standards for telephone systems.

- First Amendment standards for the Internet and derivative media.

First Amendment protection of the media was established in an environment dominated by the printed word. In the ensuing centuries, new technologies have been created that have reshaped methods of communication. Harnessing of the electromagnetic spectrum gave rise to radio and television, which became the dominant media during the final half of the twentieth century. Cable and satellite technology added newer media to the mix of methodologies by which information could be disseminated. The advent of the Internet represented a convergence of technologies that presented challenges to the sustainability of traditional media such as newspapers and magazines. Using the Internet and social media, individuals can bypass or minimize the role of intermediaries and the editorial process.

With significant changes in the media landscape in the years since the First Amendment was framed and ratified, each new method of communication has been challenged on whether it merits constitutional protection. Even from an originalist perspective, as Justice Scalia has noted, "technological change [has] rarely presented serious obstacles, [because] the principles underlying free speech and free press protection [can] readily be extrapolated to new media, from early 20th century innovations such as radio to present day platforms."[1] Although First Amendment status (eventually if not immediately) was conferred upon major media, the Court has not used a one size fits all standard of review. Variances in the degree of protection, as discussed later in this chapter, reflect a sense that each medium presents "unique problems" that necessitate variances in the level of constitutional protection afforded, and resulted in a "medium specific" analysis.

§ 10.01   THE SIGNIFICANCE OF THE PRESS CLAUSE

A threshold issue regarding the media is whether it is uniquely protected by the press clause, and whether it is entitled to special protections not granted to others in society. Justice Stewart, in a 1975 law review article,[2] made the case for a structural definition of the press, and he would have afforded the media special First Amendment status and protections not extended to the general public pursuant to the speech clause. By contrast, in a concurring opinion in *First National Bank of Boston v. Bellotti*,[3] Chief Justice Burger advocated a functional definition of the press that obliterated distinctions between the speech and press clauses. Although the Court has never made a definitive statement on the subject, its jurisprudence consistently has aligned with Chief Justice Burger's premise. Media thus have no favored position under the First Amendment and possess freedoms coextensive with the public. This equivalence, as we shall see, has had significant implications in cases concerning the media's immunity from the criminal justice system and protection of the newsgathering process.

Freedom of the press is set forth textually in the First Amendment apart from freedom of speech. Despite this separation, there is a long-running debate over whether the press clause has meaning independent of the speech clause. The Court never has formally resolved this issue, but the weight of case law has aligned with the notion that the press has no rights beyond those of an ordinary citizen. Specific circumstances in which this issue has arisen include grand jury processes, newsroom searches, access to prison facilities, and access to judicial proceedings. In each of these instances, the Court has maintained that the press' First Amendment freedoms do not extend beyond those of the public. For practical purposes, whether a person functions as an individual blogger on the Internet or reporter for a mass medium, First Amendment protections are coextensive.

§ 10.02   THE NEWSGATHERING FUNCTION

[A]   Reporter's Privilege

The primary resource of the press is information, which is collected, processed, and disseminated for public consumption. In the course of covering issues of public importance, the press acquires information that may have value beyond its primary

---

[1] Jess Bravin, *Scalia Speaks Part II: A Harsh Critique of the Voting Rights Act*, THE WALL STREET JOURNAL, April 17, 2013, at

[2] Potter Stewart, *Or of the Press*, 26 HASTINGS L.J. 631, 633–34 (1975).

[3] 435 U.S. 765, 801–02 (1978) (Burger, C.J., concurring).

market. For example, journalists often acquire knowledge that may be useful to the criminal justice process. The needs and interests of reporters and prosecutors, however, are not always coextensive. When reporters obtain information pursuant to a promise that the identity of the source will be kept confidential, the public derives the benefits of information it otherwise might not access. A reporter's knowledge of criminal activity or perpetrators, however, also may be a useful resource for the criminal justice process.

When the interests of media and criminal justice system are in conflict, significant policy interests have to be balanced. Sometimes, for example, a prosecutor attempts "to 'annex' the news media as an investigative arm of government."[4] In particular, a prosecutor may subpoena a reporter to appear before a grand jury. At stake in these circumstances are First Amendment interests in maximizing the flow of information to the public and the criminal justice system's interest in effective law enforcement. In *Branzburg v. Hayes*,[5] the Court considered arguments that reporters have a First Amendment privilege that shields them from having to testify before a grand jury. The premise for this proposed First Amendment privilege was that, without the ability to maintain the confidentiality of sources, reporters would lose their sources and the flow of information to the public would diminish.

The Court rejected this proposition and determined that the press had the same responsibility as everyone else to provide testimony before a grand jury. The Court was unimpressed with the argument that confidentiality of sources is necessary for a well-informed public. It noted that reporters only had to be concerned with grand jury subpoenas to the extent a source was implicated in a crime or possessed information relevant to the grand jury process. The Court was unconvinced that a significant percentage of confidential sources fit these circumstances or would be chilled by the absence of a privilege. Because the Court believed that the press had flourished without such a privilege in the past, the Court doubted the need for protection given the costs that would be imposed upon the criminal justice process. Finding that the criminal justice system's interest in "every man's evidence" outweighed the uncertain utility of a First Amendment privilege, the Court concluded that a First Amendment privilege claim could not be "seriously entertain[ed]." The ruling does not rule out the possibility of a reporter's privilege. However, such a privilege might have to be premised on a statutory provision providing for such a rivilege (as exist in some states). In addition, consistent with the coextensive nature of the speech and press clauses, reporters like any other individual can object to a subpoena in the event of official harassment or if the prosecutor conducts a grand jury investigation in bad faith.

The *Branzburg* decision sent some confusing signals that are largely attributable to the challenge of understanding Justice Powell's position. In his concurring opinion, Justice Powell indicated that a reporter could challenge a subpoena that was brought in bad faith or in the absence of "a legitimate law enforcement need." His standard seems equivalent in significant part to the

---

[4] *Id.* at 709 (Powell, J. concurring).

[5] 408 U.S. 665 (1972).

privilege concept rejected by the majority. Under his approach, the privilege would apply when there were alternative means of obtaining the information, it was not relevant to the investigation, and it was not intrinsic to a successful prosecution. Powell's concurring opinion, combined with the opinion of four dissenting justices who favored a First Amendment privilege, cast doubt upon *Branzburg's* actual meaning. Some lower courts actually cited *Branzburg* in support of a limited First Amendment privilege. The meaning of *Branzburg* was clarified eventually in *University of Pennsylvania v. E.E.O.C.*[6] In that case, concerning a university's claim of confidentiality for a tenure file, the Court referenced *Branzburg* as a decision that rejected the claim of a First Amendment privilege.

Despite rejecting the notion of a First Amendment privilege protecting reporters from having to appear and testify before grand juries, the *Branzburg* Court indicated that states were free to establish immunities for reporters that were absolute or qualified. Many states responded to this invitation by adopting shield laws. The nature and scope of these legislated privileges vary, as do the standards of review. In some instances, courts have subordinated even seemingly absolute privileges to a defendant's right to a fair trial.

The *Branzburg* decision confirmed the risk that a reporter might not be able to honor a promise of confidentiality. For reporters who make such promise, the question is whether he or she can be held liable for any breach. This issue was confronted in *Cohen v. Cowles Media Co.*,[7] when the Court reviewed a breach of contract claim based upon a breach of confidentiality. The claimant was a political campaign aide who, based upon a promise of confidentiality, leaked embarrassing information about a rival candidate. Although noting that the First Amendment protects the right to publish lawfully acquired information, the Court found that the promise of confidentiality established an enforceable contractual obligation. The Court rejected a newsworthiness defense that was grounded in the notion that the breach of confidence provided voters with information that was particularly relevant to the decision they had to make.

The durability of a "reporter's privilege" continues to be manifested by lower court opinions. In *United States v. Treacy*, 639 F.3d 32 (2d Cir. 2011), the Court of Appeals reviewed a securities fraud conviction based upon allegations that stock options had been backdated and improperly valued. During the trial, the government subpoenaed a *Wall Street Journal* reporter to testify regarding the truth of statement attributed to the defendant in an article. The trial court refused to quash the subpoena but tightly limited the opportunity to cross-examine the reporter. The Court of Appeals determined that a reporter's privilege may be trumped when the testimony "has likely relevance to a significant issue in the case, and [that it] is not reasonably obtainable from other available sources." The Court of Appeals determined that the standard of review does not vary on the basis of whether the proceeding is civil or criminal. It agreed with the trial court's decision to compel the reporter's testimony but determined that the restriction on cross-examination was improper.

---

[6] 493 U.S. 182 (1990).

[7] 501 U.S. 663 (1991).

In *In re Grand Jury Subpoena to James Risen*, 2010 U.S. Dist. LEXIS 143340 (E.D. Va. June 28, 2011), the District Court quashed a federal subpoena in a grand jury proceeding. The case concerned the prosecution's effort to compel a *New York Times* reporter to disclose his information sources regarding a CIA program to sabotage Iran's nuclear program. The District Court determined that the government did not establish a need for the testimony and had ample circumstantial evidence. This outcome further demonstrates how courts have utilized the concurring and dissenting opinions in *Branzburg v. Hayes* to maintain the vitality of a reporter's privilege.

[B] Newsroom Searches

The competing interests of the press and criminal justice process were revisited in the search and seizure context. Like subpoenas for reporters, newsroom searches are relatively uncommon. Law enforcement officials in most instances rely upon less invasive methodologies, such as subpoenas, to obtain evidence. Search warrants for newsrooms typically are utilized in exigent circumstances, such as when human life is at stake or evidence may vanish. Knowing that the sharing of information can result in a returned favor, reporters and editors often are responsive also to informal requests for evidence. A search warrant, if issued on the basis of probable cause, provides another means for the state to obtain evidence. Although the possibility is reserved for resisting informal requests for evidence, or challenging a subpoena duces tecum, a search and seizure cannot be challenged until after the fact. Utilization of this more invasive methodology was the basis for a claim, in *Zurcher v. Stanford Daily*,[8] that the First Amendment barred newsroom searches.

Zurcher arose when police searched the editorial offices of a student newspaper pursuant to a warrant issued on the basis of probable cause. The police were seeking photographs of demonstrators who had assaulted police during a campus protest. Lawyers for the newspaper argued that the First Amendment barred searches of a newsroom, because they chill the editorial process. The contention in this regard was that searches disrupt and invade the editorial process and compromise the confidentiality of sources. Unmoved by these arguments, the Court held that newsrooms are not off-limits to search warrants, and that the state is under no obligation to use the less invasive methodology of a subpoena. Although the Court refused to treat newsrooms differently than other venues for search and seizure purposes, it noted that Fourth Amendment requirements must be satisfied with "scrupulous exactitude" when First Amendment interests are implicated.

Justice Stewart, in a dissenting opinion, voiced concern that the decision would enable police to ransack newsrooms, chill sources, and thus impair the flow of information to the public. These concerns prompted Congress to enact the Privacy Protection Act of 1980.[9] This law establishes a preference for subpoenas as a means for obtaining evidence from a news organization. The primary exceptions relate to circumstances where the information holder is suspected of a crime or the

---

[8] 436 U.S. 547 (1978).

[9] 42 U.S.C. Section 2000aa-1-2000aa-12 (1980).

exigencies of life, serious injury or loss of evidence exist. Although this protection from searches and seizures is unique to the press, it is legislatively rather than constitutionally driven.

In 2013, a major scandal erupted when it was revealed that the Justice Department had seized the phone records of Associated Press (AP) reporters and editors. Two months of phone records had been seized without notice to the AP. The seized records related to the offices of the journalists, as well as their home phones and cell phones. The suspected reason for the seizures involved the CIA's inquiry of governmental leaks.[10] In addition, governmental officials subpoenaed the e-mails of a Fox News reporter.[11]

In *Lacey v. Maricopa County*,[12] the court considered the issue of whether the late night arrest of two newspaper executives was substantially designed to deter the exercise of their First Amendment rights. The arrests took place following publication of an article highly critical of county officials, including the county attorney, sheriff, and special prosecutor (each of whom allegedly had a role in the arrests). Although many of the alleged actions were protected by absolute or qualified immunity, the Court of Appeals allowed claims to proceed against the special prosecutor. It noted that "to demonstrate a First Amendment violation, [Plaintiffs] must provide evidence showing that by his actions [the special prosecutor] deterred or chilled [Plaintiffs'] political speech and such deterrence was a substantial or motivating factor in [the special prosecutor's] conduct." The court indicated that the plaintiffs need not show their "speech was actually inhibited or suppressed." Instead, it only was necessary to demonstrate "that defendants intended to interfere with [Plaintiffs'] First Amendment rights." The court further observed, citing *Branzburg v. Hayes*, that "[t]his chilling effect is especially apparent when investigative activities are alleged to have been carried out in bad faith leading to the arrest and detention of the targets, as is alleged here. . . ."

[C]   Access to Prisons

An understanding of the Press Clause as independently significant, is the basis for arguments that the media should have special news gathering opportunities. The Court has acknowledged that freedom of the press would be reduced to substantive insignificance if it did not afford "some protection for seeking out the news."[13] The proposition of a unique right to access government facilities or information has been tested most seriously in the context of prisons. In *Pell v. Procunier*[14] and *Saxbe v. Washington Post Co.*,[15] the Court examined respectively

---

[10] *See* Mark Memmott, *Holder Isn't Sure How Often Reporters' Records Are Seized*, National Public Radio, The Two-Way (May 15, 2013); Charlie Savage & Leslie Kaufman, *Phone Records of Journalists Seized by U.S.*, THE NEW YORK TIMES A-1 (May 14, 2013).

[11] *See* Theodore J. Boustrous, Jr., *A Radical Departure on Press Freedom*, THE WALL STREET JOURNAL, A-13 (May 24, 2013).

[12] 649 F.3d 1118 (9th Cir. 2011).

[13] Branzburg v. Hayes, 408 U.S. 665 (1972).

[14] 417 U.S. 817 (1974).

state and federal prison regulations that prevented the media from interviewing certain inmates. Given the security imperatives associated with prisons, the Court typically has been less inclined to second-guess prison administrators regarding access issues even when constitutional interests are present. To the extent that the prisoners themselves assert First Amendment claims, their liberty interests normally are calibrated at a reduced level. This variable contributed to outcomes in *Pell* and *Saxbe* adverse to the prisoners themselves, who possessed what the Court viewed as reasonable and effective alternative channels of communication and had not been victims of content discrimination.

With respect to the media's claim of a right to interview the inmates of their choice, the media argued that prison officials could deny such access only upon a particularized showing of a clear and present danger to prison security. The Court rejected this contention on grounds that the media's right to access a prison or its inmates was coextensive with the public's rights. This conclusion represented another rejection of the argument that the press has special privileges that are superior to or different from those provided to ordinary citizens. Although the press may seek information, the Court refused to hold that the state has a duty to provide information to the press that is not given to the general public. From the Court's perspective, the press is free to seek information from its sources, but has no special right of access to information.

A similar right of access issue arose in *Houchins v. KQED, Inc.*[16] That case concerned denial of access to an area of a jail where a prisoner had committed suicide. A plurality affirmed that the First Amendment provides no greater right of access to the press than to the public. Justice Stewart, in a concurring opinion, agreed with this proposition. He advocated, however, standards that would accommodate the practical distinctions between the press and public. Unlike the average citizen who might visit a prison, media often rely upon sound and video recording equipment to capture information that then is shared with the public. A rigid parity between press and public, at least from Justice Stewart's perspective, ignored this special proxy function. As in cases proposing a First Amendment privilege or protection from search and seizures, the Court left any adjustment in the relationship between press and public to the political process.

[D]   Access to Judicial Proceedings

The congruity principle, as it relates to the rights of the press and public, also has governed cases in which the press seeks special access to courtroom proceedings. In *Nixon v. Warner Communications, Inc.*,[17] the Court determined that the press had no greater rights in relationship to a courtroom than the public. Recognizing that space is a scarce resource, many courts (and legislatures) provide special seating for the media, so that they can perform their special proxy requirement. The *Warner Communications* decision reaffirms that this distinction is discretionary rather than constitutionally required.

---

[15]   417 U.S. 843 (1974).

[16]   438 U.S. 1 (1978).

[17]   435 U.S. 589 (1978).

Whether the press and public have different liberty interests under the First Amendment, however, has not been the primary source of litigation on the issue of access to courts. Access to judicial proceedings, particularly in high profile cases, implicates the right to a fair trial. It is the consequent need to balance and prioritize competing interests that been the primary source of constitutional controversy in this context. The right to attend trials and other court proceedings is supported by tradition, a desire to safeguard against official abuse, and the interest of ensuring an informed public. The Sixth Amendment guarantee of a public trial reflects the fundamental idea that open proceedings therefore help facilitate fair process. Dissemination of information relating to a possible or pending case, however, can compromise a defendant's right to a fair trial. Among the options for managing the risk of prejudicial publicity, which arises when prospective jurors are exposed to information that may be inadmissible as evidence or influence their thinking, is an order that closes a trial or pretrial proceeding.

Case law development on the issue of access to judicial proceedings commences with *Gannett Company, Inc. v. DePasquale.*[18] In that case, the Court reviewed a judge's decision to close a pretrial suppression hearing to the press and public. The court order sought to minimize the risk of prejudicial publicity and was entered with the support of both the prosecutor and defendant. Because the Court determined that the Sixth Amendment guarantee of a public trial accrues to the defendant, rather than a spectator, the defendant's assent was deemed to be particularly critical. Another important factor was the court's decision to make a transcript of the proceeding available once the risk of prejudicial publicity abated.

Within the four corners of the *DePasquale* decision, there were indications that the Court might view the question of closure differently in the context of an actual trial. These intimations were acted upon a year later, in *Richmond Newspapers, Inc. v. Virginia,*[19] when the Court reviewed a lower court order closing a trial to the press and public. Although every participating justice but one agreed that the trial judge's order should be overturned, there was no majority opinion. Despite general agreement that tradition favored open trials, the *Richmond Newspapers* decision announced no clear standard of review for determining when closure was permissible.

In *Globe Newspapers, Inc. v. Superior Court,*[20] a majority coalesced in support of a rationale for open trials and a standard of review for closure decisions. At issue in that case was a state law that mandated closed proceedings when a juvenile victim of a sex offense testified. The state argued that this measure was necessary to protect minors from further harm or embarrassment, and to facilitate the juvenile to testify openly. The Court struck the law down, concluding that closure is only permitted if it advances a compelling state interest that is narrowly tailored to serve that interest. In applying this standard, the Court determined that the protection of minor sex offense victims from further pain and injury was a compelling interest. It concluded, however, that the interest did not justify

---

[18] 443 U.S. 368 (1979).

[19] 448 U.S. 555 (1980).

[20] 457 U.S. 596 (1982).

mandatory closure. A more narrowly tailored approach would require the trial judge to consider the witness' and family's wishes, his or her maturity, and the nature of the crime itself. The message of the *Globe Newspapers* decision was not that closure is impermissible altogether, but that it could not be ordered categorically and without factoring the actual risks to the victim and process.

The *Globe Newspaper* decision assigned two primary utilities to a right of access to criminal trials. First, such proceedings historically had been open to the press and public. Second, a right of access facilitates public scrutiny of an important governmental function and thus helps safeguard the integrity of the process. These rationales explain the Court's determination that trials should be open, but there is more to the judicial process than trials. In the criminal justice system, most cases are plea bargained without a trial. Preliminary proceedings in such circumstances thus may provide the only opportunity for public scrutiny.

During the 1980s, the Court extended the right of access to pretrial proceedings. In *Press-Enterprise v. Superior Court*,[21] the Court held that a court could not close the *voir dire* process absent "an overriding interest based upon findings that closure is necessary to ensure higher values and is narrowly tailored to serve that interest." The Court's decision in *Waller v. Georgia*[22] extended this test to preliminary hearings, at least when the defendant objected to closure. This decision reflected an understanding that the Sixth Amendment guarantee of a public trial extends to the pretrial process. Finally, in *Press-Enterprise Co. v. Superior Court*,[23] the Court announced that the press and public have a right of access to at least some pretrial hearings. To determine whether a pretrial hearing may be closed, the court must first consider whether the particular process has traditionally been open to the public. With respect to the particular pretrial hearing at issue, the Court found a tradition of accessibility. To the extent such a history is identified, closure may be justified only if there is a substantial probability that fair trial rights will be compromised and there are no reasonable alternatives.

[E] The Problem of Prejudicial Publicity

Access to judicial proceedings, as the foregoing discussion indicates, is both a tradition and constitutional norm. Although case law with respect to access makes no distinction between the public and press for First Amendment purposes, the media may present problems for the process owing to the nature of their presence and coverage.

Foremost among these dangers is the risk to constitutional guarantees associated with the criminal justice process. The Fifth and Fourteenth Amendment Due Process Clauses provide defendants with a constitutional right to a fair trial. The Sixth Amendment guarantees a "public trial, by an impartial jury." Media coverage of a judicial proceeding may facilitate the process of informed self-governance. It also may compromise the trial rights of defendants. When

---

[21] 464 U.S. 501 (1984).

[22] 467 U.S. 39 (1984).

[23] 478 U.S. 1 (1986).

confronted with the risk of prejudicial publicity, the responsibility of the court generally is to minimize the peril, but in a way that does not impose undue burdens upon expressive freedom.

The right to a fair and impartial trial may be affected by factors of timing, content, and context. Each of these factors was relevant in *Sheppard v. Maxwell*,[24] when the Court reviewed defendant's conviction to determine whether massive pretrial publicity and disruptive courtroom conduct had unduly impact the defendant's right to a fair trial. The *Sheppard* case concerned a murder that was heavily sensationalized by the local media. Newspaper and broadcast coverage was both inflammatory and erroneous. Banner headlines blared out judgmental characterizations of the defendant, and commentators pumped out a steady stream of incriminating information that never was introduced into evidence. Juror identities were published, giving them celebrity status, but they were not sequestered until the beginning of their deliberations. Even then, the jurors were loosely supervised and allowed to make telephone calls relatively freely. At the trial itself, reporters crowded the courtroom and moved freely even within the bar area itself. They examined and handled evidence and created enough noise so that it was difficult for testimony to be heard and for the defendant and his attorney to communicate. The trial judge, who was running for reelection, took no meaningful action to control the proceedings or to stem the flow of pretrial publicity.

Although the Court acknowledged a significant First Amendment interest in allowing the press to report on defendant's trial, it stressed the need to reconcile this concern with the fair and orderly administration of justice. Based upon the totality of circumstances, the Court concluded that the confluence of pretrial and trial activity had resulted in a denial of due process. Noting that a trial judge was not powerless to avoid this consequence, the Court suggested several means to manage future risks. Among these proposed methods were:

- rules limiting the number of media representatives that could attend and governing their decorum;

- *voir dire* to screen out jurors who might be influenced by prejudicial publicity;

- sequestration of jurors to avoid external influences upon judgment;

- change of venue or continuance; and

- gag orders directed at parties, witnesses, counsel, police, and other participants.

The primary message of the *Sheppard* decision was that a trial judge should not be a passive spectator to press excesses.

Responding to the *Sheppard* decision, many courts resorted to broad-based restrictions upon pretrial publicity. However, in doing so, these courts ran afoul of another current in *Sheppard*, to the effect that "there is nothing that proscribes the press from reporting events that transpire in the courtroom." Of course, the use of gag orders represented a resort to prior restraint, traditionally a highly

---

[24] 384 U.S. 333 (1966).

disfavored means of regulating speech. Such methods may secure the trial environment from the risk of prejudicial publicity, but there was a risk that they would impose too heavy a cost on First Amendment interests.

In *Nebraska Press Association v. Stuart*,[25] the Court examined a pretrial order that prohibited the media from publishing confessions made to police, reporting information obtained during a preliminary hearing, or disseminating any information that strongly implicated the defendant. The Court's analysis began with the premise that "prior restraints on speech and publication are the most serious and the least tolerable infringement on First Amendment rights." Prior restraints have "an immediate and irreversible sanction" and do not merely chill speech, but "freeze" it. Any system of prior restraint thus has a strong presumption against its constitutionality, and the state has a heavy burden to justify it.[26] Although the risk of prejudicial publicity in *Stuart* was demonstrable, the Court was not satisfied that the trial judge had considered less restrictive options including those suggested in *Sheppard*. The Court did not dismiss the possibility of a gag order under any circumstances. However, before using such a method, a trial judge must analyze the risks and options. First, it is necessary to demonstrate a clear and present danger that pretrial publicity will compromise the right to a fair trial. The Court on this point found only that there could be a clear and present danger. Management of this risk, however, required the trial judge to exhaust options to a gag order. Second, therefore, the trial judge must determine with record findings that alternatives to prior restraint, such as continuance or change of venue, are inadequate. Third, it is necessary to determine whether the gag order actually would be effective. This standard is particularly difficult to satisfy in high profile cases, when the court does not have jurisdiction over all media that may report on the proceeding. Fourth, reporting of information acquired in open court cannot be restrained.

When speech restrictions are imposed upon parties to a proceeding and their attorneys, the standard of review is more relaxed. In these circumstances, the Court has refrained from using a clear and present danger test. Rather, as indicated in *Gentile v. State Bar of Nevada*,[27] the Court looks to whether there is a "substantial likelihood of material prejudice."

[F] Electronic Media in the Courtroom

Even if the press and public have equal rights of access to judicial proceedings, the cases concerning prejudicial publicity attest to the different natures and risks they present to the fairness of the process. A reporter's basic task is to obtain, edit, and communicate information. A member of the public typically attends a judicial proceeding to satisfy an interest that is personal in nature. For the reporter to perform his or function, recording equipment is helpful and sometimes arguably necessary. This association between individual and instrumentality is particularly strong with respect to broadcast journalists. The use of sound and video equipment

---

[25] 427 U.S. 539 (1976).

[26] New York Times Co. v. United States, 403 U.S. 713, 713 (1971) (per curiam).

[27] 501 U.S. 1030 (1991).

in the courtroom has been the basis for concern that the media's presence alone may undermine the right to a fair trial. The circus like atmosphere of the *Sheppard* case illuminates this potential and ratified the fears of those who believed that the media, by their mere presence, could seriously distort due process.

The American Bar Association Canons of Judicial Ethics originally required judges to bar cameras from the courtroom. The rationale for this rule was that such instrumentalities undermine the dignity of judicial proceedings. Early decisions by the Court also reflected the concern that cameras in the courtroom were inimical to due process. Unease with the broadcast media was a dominant feature of early decisions that reviewed televised pretrial coverage of alleged crimes. In *Irvin v. Dowd*,[28] the Court found that television coverage was so widespread that two-thirds of the jury had formed a belief of guilt prior to the trial itself. This collective state of mind constituted a denial of due process. A due process violation also was found in *Rideau v. Louisiana*,[29] a case concerning pretrial broadcast of a defendant's confession. Publicity was pervasive in this instance, and the Court required no showing of actual prejudice.

In *Estes v. Texas*,[30] the Court examined the impact of radio and television in the courtroom itself. A plurality of justices determined that the mere presence of broadcasting equipment created such a possibility of prejudice that the proceeding inherently lacked due process. The decision reflected a common concern at the time that cameras would distract jurors, parties, witnesses, lawyers, and judges, alter behavior, and diminish the quality of legal representation. Justice Harlan, in a concurring opinion, expressed similar concerns. He noted, however, that technology might lead to equipment that was less intrusive and more compatible with the dictates of due process.

The fulfillment of this prophecy ultimately moved the Court to revisit the issue. In *Chandler v. Florida*,[31] the Court reviewed a state law that permitted broadcast coverage of criminal trials even if the defendant objected. The Court rejected arguments that the presence of cameras in the courtroom inherently constitutes a due process violation. Although not precluding the possibility of a violation, the Court imposed upon the defendant the burden of establishing actual prejudice. Such a finding is not made merely by demonstrating that jurors were aware of the presence of cameras. A defendant must show either that cameras impaired the ability of jurors to decide the case only on the basis of the evidence presented, or that their presence or the prospect of broadcast impacted a participant in a way that adversely affected the trial.

Although media have a First Amendment interest in attending trials, the ability to use video or audio equipment in the courtroom is not based upon the speech or press clauses. The necessary inquiry thus relates not to what First Amendment freedom the media has, but whether utilization of their instrumentalities of coverage violates due process.

---

[28] 366 U.S. 717 (1961).

[29] 373 U.S. 723 (1963).

[30] 381 U.S. 532 (1965).

[31] 449 U.S. 560 (1981).

§ 10.03   MEDIA TECHNOLOGY AND FIRST AMENDMENT STANDARDS

When the First Amendment was framed and ratified, newspapers and pamphlets were the primary means available for disseminating information. By the early Twentieth Century, new technologies were emerging that permitted the massive and multidimensional distribution of information. The advent of photojournalism, and consequent ability to produce images in conjunction with text, broadened the appeal and impact of newspapers and magazines. The processes of industrialization and mass production, and chain ownership, enabled publishers to expand their audiences. Development of the electronic spectrum led to a broadcasting industry that, over the course of the Twentieth Century, became the nation's dominant medium. The evolution of cable television and satellite technology has provided additional (and sometimes alternative) avenues for routing data and images directly and quickly to users.

Although these technologies did not exist (and were not even envisiioned) when the First Amendment was framed, each of these media has been afforded First Amendment protection. This process has not been without complication. In considering the status of motion pictures early in the Twentieth Century, the Court in *Mutual Film Corporation v. Industrial Commission of Ohio*[32] found that they are not part of the press. Although acknowledging that movies had value in propagating opinion and thought, the Court expressed concern with their "capab[ility] for evil." These perils, attributed to the medium's manner and attractiveness of exhibition, included an appeal to prurient interest, corrupting influence, and impact upon children. Rather than balancing these potential harms, the Court chose to place motion pictures outside the First Amendment's ambit. Not until the middle of the Twentieth Century were motion pictures acknowledged to be part of the press and worthy of First Amendment protection.[33]

Content regulation in any context raises First Amendment issues. The constitutional inquiry is more layered, however, when media are involved. Regulation that burdens expression in a newspaper, radio or television broadcast, cablecast or other media setting must be analyzed on two grounds. The first consideration is the nature of the speech. The higher the value of the speech, the more protection the speech should receive. The second factor is the nature of the medium. For each medium, the standard of First Amendment review has historically varied by the nature of the medium. The print medium has traditionally received the highest level of First Amendment protection, and broadcasting has received the least protection. Thus, as they have evolved, constitutional protection of different technologies has evolved in a medium-specific direction. The consequence of this analytical framework is that the same expression published without constitutional constraint in print may be a basis for liability in broadcasting.

---

[32] 236 U.S. 230 (1915).

[33] Joseph Burstyn, Inc. v. Wilson, 343 U.S. 495 (1952); United States v. Paramount Pictures, Inc., 334 U.S. 131 (1948).

The origins of medium-specific analysis are rooted in a concurring opinion by Justice Jackson near the turn of the Twentieth Century. In *Kovacs v. Cooper*,[34] a case that upheld a noise ordinance regulating sound trucks, Justice Jackson introduced an idea that eventually became a First Amendment premise. As Justice Jackson explained it, "[t]he moving picture screen, the radio, the newspaper, the handbill, the sound truck and the street orator have differing natures, values, abuses, and dangers. Each, in my view, is a law unto itself." This framework for analyzing First Amendment questions relating to media initially was used in evaluating censorship of motion pictures. As the Court noted, in *Joseph Burstyn, Inc. v. Wilson*,[35] "each [medium] tends to present its own peculiar problems." This same premise has been the starting point for calibrating the level of protection for electronic media, including radio, television, and cable.

Medium specific analysis generates a First Amendment pecking order that hinges upon the nature of the technology rather than upon the speech itself. An example of this phenomenon is the publication of a George Carlin monologue in United States Supreme Court Reports,[36] and available in other publications, on cable, or as a sound recording, that was found in violation of federal standards governing indecent broadcasting. The rationale for these diverging outcomes is that each medium has a unique nature and presents uniqueproblems that warrant, in Justice Jackson's words, "a law unto itself." Consistent with standards that are medium specific in nature, the balance of this chapter will examine the character-istics attributed to various media and the consequent variability of First Amend-ment rules.

[A]   Print

Content regulation in the print media is subject to the most rigorous standard of judicial scrutiny. This exacting criterion for regulation burdening the most established mass medium reflects print's long tradition of editorial freedom. Content regulation in the print context has mainfested itself in the form of regulation that respectively prohibits or compels expression. An example of a case concerning content restriction is *Pittsburgh Press Co. v. Pittsburgh Commission on Human Relations*.[37] In that case, the Court reviewed a local ordinance that prohibited gender-based designations in classified advertising. Finding that gender discrimination itself was unlawful, the Court upheld this intrusion into editorial freedom. The *Pittsburgh Press* decision, as noted in Chapter 3, is a seminal case in the development of modern commercial speech doctrine. It reflects the premise that commercial speech relating to an unlawful activity is not protected by the First Amendment. The lesson of the *Pittsburgh Press* decision from a medium specific standpoint is that, when print media are concerned, the nature of the medium is not a factor in the analysis. Within the print context, the relevant case

---

[34] 336 U.S. 77 (1949).

[35] 343 U.S. 495 (1952).

[36] Federal Communications Commission v. Pacifica Foundation, 438 U.S. 726 (1978) (Appendix).

[37] 413 U.S. 376 (1973).

law seems to suggest that it is only the speech and not the medium that counts for purposes of First Amendment analysis.

This premise is underscored by the Court's review of a state law aimed at managing and balancing newspaper content as it relates to coverage of political candidates. In *Miami Herald Publishing Co. v. Tornillo*,[38] the Court reviewed an enactment law requiring newspapers to provide equal space for political candidates whose qualifications or record it had attacked editorially. Several factors inspired this legislation, which aimed to ensure fair and balanced coverage of candidates for public office. The basic concern was that newspapers had become scarce and their ownership had been concentrated in the hands of a relatively few media conglomerates. Within this framework of a mass media culture, characterized by one-way information flow and distorted and slanted reporting, the state maintained that the individual had lost the opportunity to participate meaningfully in the information marketplace. The state's argument thus was reducible to the proposition that traditional First Amendment principles of editorial freedom needed to give way to First Amendment values of expressive pluralism.

Although acknowledging the problems attributable to the economics of the newspaper industry, the Court struck down the equal space law as an unacceptable "intrusion into the function of editors." The decision reflects the Court's sense that, although editorial balance and responsibility may be desirable objectives, the First Amendment mandates neither. Effectuation of these interests requires an enforcement context that necessitates government control. Compelling editors to publish a particular story either imposes costs or deprives them of space for another story. As the Court noted, newspaper composition constitutes the exercise of editorial judgment and control. Official management of this function, at least in the print context, abridges this freedom. It was this invasion of editorial autonomy that the Court could not reconcile with the " First Amendment guarantees of a free press as they have evolved to this time."

[B] Broadcasting

Although the Court found redistribution of speech opportunities constitutionally inimical in the print context, it already had embraced this premise with respect to broadcasting. Four years prior to the *Tornillo* decision, the Court upheld federal regulation designed to achieve fair and balanced broadcast coverage of public issues. The different outcomes for print and broadcasting are a primary source of illumination for the nature, consequences, and challenges of medium-specific analysis.

[1] Fairness Regulation

Unlike its emphasis upon editorial freedom in *Tornillo*, the Court elevated different priorities in calibrating the First Amendment protection of broadcasters. In *Red Lion Broadcasting Co. v. Federal Communications Commission*,[39] the

---

[38] 418 U.S. 241 (1974).

[39] 395 U.S. 367 (1969).

Court reviewed a set of regulations similar to what was struck down in *Tornillo*. At issue were requirements for balanced programming of controversial issues of public importance and a personal attack rule and political editorial rules requiring free reply time. Collectively, these regulations were referred to as the fairness doctrine. Broadcasters challenged the rules, which were functionally equivalent to the law struck down in *Tornillo*, on grounds they invaded their freedom to determine the editorial composition of their programs.

Contrary to the outcome for fairness legislation relating to the print media, the Court upheld the broadcasting regulations. Central to its reasoning and the result was the Court's sense that there is no unabridgeable right to broadcast comparable to the right to publish. The starting point for the Court's analysis was that the unique characteristics of each medium justify different First Amendment standards for different media. This recitation of the premise underlying medium-specific analysis was followed by a discussion of problems that are unique to broadcasting and relevant to the medium's level of First Amendment protection. This special characteristic is spectrum scarcity, a condition denoted by fewer broadcast frequencies than there are individuals wanting to broadcast. Within this context, the Court found it "idle to posit" the same degree of First Amendment protection for broadcasters that is extended to publishers.

The *Red Lion* decision is notable for its departure from traditional standards of First Amendment review. Instead of framing criteria in terms of strict scrutiny or intermediate or rational basis review, the Court inverted the editorial rights of broadcasters to the viewing and listening rights of the public. It thus established a First Amendment right to have the medium function consistently with the ends and purposes of the First Amendment, specifically to secure the public's right "to receive suitable access to social, political, esthetic, moral, and other ideas." The rights of viewers and listeners not only were established, therefore, but made "paramount" to the editorial freedom of broadcasters. Put simply, the Court viewed fairness regulation as a means of achieving First Amendment goals of diverse expression by subtracting First Amendment rights from broadcasters and transferring them to the public.

The different outcomes in *Tornillo* and *Red Lion* have provided the basis for extensive commentary, much of it critical. An argument can be made that the problem of scarcity is not unique to broadcasting and is even greater in connection with newspapers. Because radio and television stations outnumber daily newspapers both nationally and locally, this contention is true if scarcity is understood in numerical terms. As used in *Red Lion*, however, scarcity is a term of art. In theory, anyone can enter the newspaper industry. Scarcity therefore is a function of economic factors that make it difficult for new competition to gain a foothold in the market, or for more than one newspaper to succeed in a given community. The opportunity to become a broadcaster is conditioned, however, by the physical limitations of the broadcast spectrum. It is this notion of allocational scarcity that the Court references in distinguishing broadcasting from print. The need to have a rational allocation scheme for a scarce resource is a well-established basis for a comprehensive system of licensing broadcasters. Particularly because the capital costs of broadcasting would preclude most persons from owning a radio or television station, even in the absence of scarcity, the differences between print and broadcasting on this front may be less than what the Court has stated.

The "unusual order" of rights announced in *Red Lion*, as the Court put it in *Columbia Broadcasting System, Inc. v. Democratic National Committee*,[40] is the basis for broadcasting's diminished First Amendment status. The assignment of First Amendment rights to viewers and listeners, however, does not necessarily mean that editorial freedom will be trumped. This reality was evidenced in the *Columbia Broadcasting System* case, when the Court examined a claim that the public had the right to access broadcasting time for speech purposes. The issue was raised by an organization that attempted to purchase time to air an antiwar message. From their perspective, a right of public access was the logical extension of the paramount right of viewers and listeners.

The Court rejected any further narrowing of editorial autonomy on grounds that a right of access would reduce broadcasters to the status of common carriers. Although reaffirming that broadcasters have the obligation to provide fair and balanced programming on important public issues, the Court emphasized that they retained discretion to determine the means of coverage. Because broadcasters under federal law operate as public trustees, the Court held that an unlimited right of access would account inadequately for the public interest that radio and television station owners by statutes must serve. A system of self-appointed editorial commentators would have no responsibility or accountability in this regard. The Court also was concerned that a system of public access would be heavily weighted in favor of the wealthy and underserve First Amendment goals of expressive diversity. The Court also introduced a new premise for broadcast regulation-the notion that viewers and listeners constitute a captive audience. Although this understanding was not dispositive in the *Columbia Broadcasting System* case, it previewed growing concern with what the Court later referenced as broadcasting's pervasive nature.[41]

The Court's reasoning drew criticism from Justice Brennan, who maintained that the Court undervalued the public interest in receiving views from advocates and partisans. Unlike fairness regulation which guarantees only a right of exposure to diversity, rather than individual participation in public debate, access would reclaim a soap box model for a mass media society. He also expressed dissatisfaction with managed diversity to the extent it actually discourages diversity. As Brennan noted, broadcasters are profit-oriented and shy away from controversy out of fear that they will antagonize viewers or listeners and thus lose sponsors.

The constitutional debate over fairness and access, at least as a basis for significant case law, has been largely dormant for the past two decades. In *C.B.S., Inc. v. Federal Communications Commission*,[42] the Court announced that any right of public access is limited rather than general and only justified when the public's interest outweighs the editorial interests of broadcasters. Exemplifying the type of limited access right that may be established, and which the Court upheld,

---

[40] 412 U.S. 94 (1973).

[41] *Federal Communications Commission*, 438 U.S. at 748.

[42] 453 U.S. 367 (1981).

was a federal law giving qualified political candidates reasonable access to the airwaves.

The *Columbia Broadcasting System* decision indicates that, although editorial discretion is more defeasible in the broadcasting context, it is not to be abridged lightly. Using language reminiscent of *Tornillo*, the Court noted that "[f]or better or for worse, editing is what editors are for."[43] Like the *Red Lion* decision, the ruling in the *Columbia Broadcasting System* case announced no clear standard of review. This need was accounted for in *Federal Communications Commission v. League of Women Voters.*[44] In striking down a law that prohibited public broadcasters from editorializing or endorsing political candidates, the Court established a new standard of review for broadcasting. Although regulation of broadcasting content will not be strictly scrutinized, it still must advance an important government interest and be narrowly tailored toward that end. The Court identified an important interest insofar as the law was designed to shield public broadcasters from funding cutbacks as a means of political retaliation against them for their expressed views. It also determined that there were less speech restrictive means of achieving this goal, such as providing opportunities for competing viewpoints. The standard of review, which fell short of strict scrutiny, indicated that broadcasting retained its constitutionally diminished status. The Court, however, indicated that Congress could abandon fairness regulation if it no longer served First Amendment interests. It also expressed its readiness to reconsider the scarcity rationale for purposes of determining whether it had outlived its utility.

Soon thereafter, the Federal Communications Commission (FCC) followed the Court's signal and abandoned the fairness doctrine. In its findings, the FCC found that fairness regulation actually chilled diversity because broadcasters were loathe to present an issue that would require more coverage to achieve balance. The agency also asserted that broadcasters should have the same First Amendment status as their print counterparts. The Court has yet to embrace this proposition, nor has it formally abandoned the scarcity premise.

[2]   Regulation of Indecent Programming

Regulation that aimed toward fair and balanced programming was aligned with First Amendment values, insofar as it attempted to facilitate the First Amendment values of expressive pluralism. Although this type of regulation largely has been abandoned in broadcasting, more traditional models of speech control survive. Sexually explicit but non-obscene expression is protected speech under the First Amendment. In broadcasting, however, indecent programming is more vulnerable to regulation than in other media contexts. This condition is consistent with the premise, set forth in *Federal Communications Commission v. Pacifica Foundation*,[45] that "of all forms of communication, it is broadcasting that has received the most limited First Amendment protection."

---

[43] Columbia Broadcasting System, Inc. v. Democratic National Committee, 418 U.S. at 124-25.

[44] 468 U.S. 364 (1984).

[45] 438 U.S. 726.

At issue in *Pacifica* was the mid-afternoon broadcast of a well-known humorist's monologue "Filthy Words." The broadcast was aired by a station with a pointed ideology, appealing to a discrete audience, and was preceded by warnings that it might offend some viewers. A motorist, who happened to be involved in an anti-indecency organization, came across the program while traveling with his son. He filed a complaint with the FCC, which did not impose formal sanctions but indicated the possibility of regulatory action in the event of future complaints. Despite arguments that the agency's action should be viewed as censorship, because violations theoretically could lead to revocation of a broadcaster's license, the Court refused to identify a prior restraint issue.

In reviewing the FCC's determination, the Court found that the agency had not violated the First Amendment. This case did not implicate the scarcity rationale, which operates in response to a presumed demand for broadcast frequencies that exceeds the supply. Although noting that the scarcity rationale was not implicated in this case, the Court identified two other aspects of broadcasting that "present[ed] special First Amendment problems." These factors were identified as broadcasting's "uniquely pervasive presence in the lives of all Americans" and the medium's being "uniquely accessible to children, even those too young to read." Reference to the medium's pervasiveness reflected a privacy concern, particularly insofar as the Court highlighted the interest of individuals in avoiding exposure to unwanted expression in their homes or in public. This concern contrasts with case law in contexts other than broadcasting, where the Court prioritizes self-help remedies such as "avert[ing] one's eyes."[46] Even if a viewer or listener can turn off a radio or television or switch stations, the Court found that this recourse does not undo the harm that already has been done. The proper analogy, from the Court's perspective, was to sound trucks whose noise levels may be regulated to prevent unwanted intrusions into the living space of unwilling listeners.

Accounting for the impressionability and vulnerability of children was referenced to government's well-established interest in protecting youth and supporting parental authority. Unlike the literacy requirement that conditions access to print, broadcasting presents no such barriers to young children who may be exposed to its content. The Court also pointed to obscenity law in support of the proposition that government's interest in the well-being of youth and supporting parental authority justified regulation of otherwise protected expression.

In determining whether broadcast programming is indecent, context is critical. Content that is appropriate for a newscast, for instance, may be unfit in another setting. *Pacifica* noted that the case concerned neither "a two-way radio conversation between a cab driver and a dispatcher, or a telecast of an Elizabethan comedy." This distinction provoked a sharp dissent by Justice Brennan, who maintained that the ruling revealed "a depressing inability to appreciate that in our land of cultural pluralism, there are many who think, act, and talk differently from the Members of this Court." Viewing the monologue as the work of a serious artist and social critic (George Carlin), he noted that the Court's rationale could be extended to a myriad of literary works including those of "Shakespeare, Joyce, Hemingway [and] Chaucer" and could support suppression of much political speech. Brennan

---

[46] *E.g.*, Cohen v. California, 403 U.S. 15 (1971).

maintained that the Court suffered from "an acute ethnocentric myopia" that disabled it from appreciating how perceptions of what is offensive may vary with socio-economic background. Brennan further argued that the privacy interests at stake were not significant, insofar as the owner of a radio or television set controls its operation and ownership. Regulation to protect children, from his viewpoint, eroded the "time-honored" right of parents to raise their children as they see fit. By upholding the FCC's action, as Brennan viewed it, the decision's greatest impact would be upon broadcasters and audiences interested in programming that goes beyond mainstream norms. In sum, Brennan viewed the decision as "another of the dominant culture's inevitable efforts to force those groups who do no share its mores to conform to its way of thinking, acting, and speaking."

The development of standards governing indecent programming consumed substantial regulatory and judicial attention over the final two decades of the Twentieth Century. After a series of failed efforts to limit or ban it altogether, the FCC adopted rules that permit indecent broadcasts from 10 p.m. to 6 a.m. Creation of this safe harbor was premised upon the sense that viewers or listeners would be forewarned sufficiently and the number of children in the audience would be relatively small.

The relative ease of access by children continues to be a basis for differentiating broadcasting from other media with respect to regulating sexually explicit expression. The Court, in *FCC v. Fox TV Stations, Inc*,[47] referenced this concern in refusing to exempt fleeting expletives from its indecency ban. The case arose from two incidents of unscripted expletives during music award shows on Fox Television and the showing of a woman's "nude buttocks" (for approximately seven seconds) and momentary display of the side of her breast on a popular crime program. The offending words in the awards programs were "fuck 'em," "fucking," and "cow shit" as "intensifiers rather than a literal descriptor." The Court upheld the Commission's finding that "the broadcasts were patently offensive under community standards for the medium." A key factor was the airing of the program during prime time, when it could be expected that many children would be in the audience. The Court determined that the FCC "could reasonably conclude that the pervasiveness of foul language, and the coarsening of public entertainment in other media such as cable, justify more stringent regulation of broadcast programs so as to give conscientious parents a relatively safe haven for their children." The Court rested its decision on grounds the Commission's policy was within its statutory power and its action was neither arbitrary nor capricious. Although avoiding the constitutional question, it observed that any chilling effect with respect to "excretory and sexual material 'surely lie at the periphery of First Amendment concern.' "

The Court remanded the case to the Court of Appeals for purposes of addressing the broadcasters' First Amendment challenges. The appellate court determined that the Commission's policy was unconstitutionally vague and vacated it in its entirety.[48] The Court, In *Fox II*, determined that the policy was vague as applied to

---

[47] 556 U.S. 502 (2009).

[48] FCC v. Fox Television Stations, Inc., 613 F.2d 317 (2d Cir. 2010).

the particular parties.[49] In this regard, it noted that policy in effect at the time of the broadcasts focused upon "whether the material dwell[ed] on or repeate[ed] at length the offending description or depiction." Finding that the FCC had failed to give the broadcasters fair notice that fleeting expletives and momentary nudity could be actionably indecent, it vacated only the Commission's order. Insofar as the case was resolved on due process grounds, the Court concluded that it "need not address the First Amendment implications of the Commission's indecency policy" and left it standing. Justice Ginsburg, in a concurring opinion, contended that *Pacifica* "was wrong when it issued [and that] [t]ime, technological advances, and the Commission's untenable rulings [show] why *Pacifica* bears reconsideration."

[C] Cable

Cable television emerged as a significant medium during the mid-Twentieth Century, initially as a means of retransmitting broadcast signals to areas where distance or terrain precluded the ability to receive over the air transmissions. A defining characteristic of cable is channel multiplicity and extensive programming options. Although the carriage of local broadcast signals attracts most of a system's viewers, cable originates some of its own programming and acquires other content from independent distributors. For approximately two-thirds of the nation, cable is the means by which broadcast signals are received by viewers. The difference between broadcasting and cable relates to technology and structure. Broadcast signals are radiated over the air, while cable signals travel over coaxial cable or fiber optic lines. Broadcasters are licensed by the FCC to serve the public interest. Cable operators are awarded franchises by local government.

A threshold question for the cable industry was whether it was entitled to First Amendment protection. In *City of Los Angeles v. Preferred Communications, Inc.*,[50] the Court answered that question in the affirmative. The Court was unwilling to indicate, however, whether cable should be treated like print or broadcasting for First Amendment purposes. Perhaps indicating its own uncertainty with respect to an appropriate standard of review, the Court noted that cable "partakes of some of the aspects of speech and the communication of ideas as do the traditional enterprises of newspaper and book publishers, public speakers, and pamphleteers." Had the Court stopped with this observation, cable would seem to have been equated with print for purposes of establishing a First Amendment standard of review. It went on to relate, however, that cable also appeared "to implicate First Amendment interests as do the activities of wireless broadcasters."

[1] Must Carriage

Redistribution of speaking opportunities, which was a primary issue in the print and broadcasting context, also became a focal point in the context of cable. In *Turner Broadcasting System, Inc. v. Federal Communications Commission*,[51] the Court reviewed federal rules that required cable operators to carry the signals of

---

[49] FCC v. Fox Television Stations, Inc., 132 S. Ct. 2037 (2012).

[50] 476 U.S. 488 (1984).

[51] 512 U.S. 622 (1994).

local broadcasters. Cable operators challenged the regulations on grounds they interfered with their editorial discretion. Their argument was that the must-carry rules were functionally indistinguishable from the right to reply statute that provided certain individuals with access to newspaper space. Based upon this analogy, the cable industry advocated a ruling to the effect that the must carry rules were irreconcilable with the basic meaning of freedom of the press.

The Court, however, did not view the problem as an invasion of editorial freedom. From its perspective, the must carry rules were not content-oriented or based. Rather, they managed an interest unrelated to speech. It thus drew upon constitutional principles that apply to content-neutral regulation and impose a reduced standard of review. Citing to *United States v. O'Brien*,[52] the Court applied a three-part test that asks whether the government interest is important or substantial, this interest is unrelated to suppression of expression, and restricts speech no more extensively than necessary to further its interest.

The Court referenced three interests in support of the first prong of the *O'Brien* test. These included preservation of free local broadcasting, preservation of diverse information sources, and maintenance of fair competition in television programming. Resolution of whether the rules met the second prong was deferred pending remand to a lower court for more evidence. The Court, in a follow-up decision,[53] found that the must carry rules directly advanced the government's interests. This determination reflected concern that the cable industry had an inherent interest in minimizing broadcasting's status as a competitor. The narrowly tailored requirement was satisfied on grounds the number of broadcast signals being carried did not exceed the number of cable channels that were displaced. This result contrasts with the Court's determination in *Tornillo* that, forcing editors to publish what they otherwise would not was fundamentally at odds with the First Amendment. In *Tornillo*, the invasion of editorial discretion as a function of redistributed speaking opportunities was "the issue." The Court in *Turner* concluded that, despite the similar impact of must carriage, abridgment of editorial freedom was not the issue.

Although it did not have to announce a standard of review for content-based cable regulation, since it reviewed the must carry rules as content-neutral, the Court indicated that the spectrum scarcity problem of broadcasting was not a factor in cable. Cable television franchises typically have been granted by local government authorities, however, pursuant to a competitive process. Most communities are served by a single cable operator. An argument thus might be constructed to the effect that scarcity is a function of government franchising and the cable operator's role as the sole gatekeeper of content. Competing against this view would be the point that this type of scarcity is not caused by less defeasible limitations of physical science.

---

[52] 391 U.S. 367 (1968).

[53] Turner Broadcasting System, Inc. v. Federal Communications Commission, 520 U.S. 180 (1997).

[2] Regulation of Indecent Programming

As in broadcasting, the Court has been called upon to review regulations aimed at indecent cable programming. Congress in 1992 enacted legislation requiring the FCC to implement indecency controls for leased access channels and public access channels. Under this law, cable television operators were (1) allowed to prohibit patently offensive programming from leased access channels; (2) required to segregate such programming on a single channel and block it or unblock it upon the subscriber's written request; and (3) allowed to prohibit patently offensive programming from public, educational, and government access channels. In *Denver Area Educational Telecommunications Consortium, Inc. v. Federal Communications Commission,*[54] the Court upheld the authority of cable operators to prohibit patently offensive programming on leased channels but struck down the block and segregate provisions and the prohibition on public, educational, and government access channels.

The Court's reasoning was fragmented. A plurality of four justices, applying a standard of strict scrutiny, concluded that the content restrictions for leased access channels were supported by a compelling state interest in protecting children and were narrowly tailored toward that end. The plurality also identified a history, albeit broken, indicating that cable operators had exercised editorial control over leased access channels. A majority struck down the segregate and block requirement on grounds it did not satisfy the least restrictive alternative requirement of strict scrutiny. The blocking and unblocking of programming required a 30-day notice from subscribers. From the Court's perspective this imposed a heavy planning burden upon subscribers and exposed them to potential embarrassment if their names were disclosed. As the Court noted, it imposed significant planning burdens on subscribers and overlooked the availability of blocking devices that would account for the government's interest in protecting children without excessively burdening speech. With respect to the public access provision, the Court was not satisfied that it represented the least restrictive alternative. Among other things, a three-justice plurality concluded that public access channels typically are subject to more extensive self-policing controls. Unlike leased access channels, that draw programming from a multiplicity of sources, public access channels typically are overseen by a government unit or entity that have mainstream orientations. The plurality also determined that the public access provision, unlike the leased access provision, did not restore to cable operators any editorial rights they had possessed.

The *Denver Area Educational Telecommunications Consortium* decision reflected significant disunity among the justices with respect to the standard of review for cable. Three justices, Thomas, Rehnquist, and Scalia, have analogized cable to the print media and thus would apply strict scrutiny. Based upon prior decisions, Justice Thomas stated that a majority of the justices have expressed support for a strict scrutiny standard of review. Justice Kennedy, who has advocated strict scrutiny, also criticized the Court for its failure to announce formally a clear standard of review in the cable context. Four other justices have indicated resistance to a wholesale analogy to print and a consequent strict scrutiny standard

---

[54] 518 U.S. 727 (1996).

in all instances. Justice Breyer, supported by Justices O'Connor, Souter, and Stevens, thus argued against "a rigid single standard" that limits the Court's ability to address problems in a"a new and changing environment."

The Court has yet to announce formally, therefore, a majority standard for analyzing content-based regulation in cable. Congress has continued to generate content-based regulation, however, particularly with respect to indecency. Consistent with this pattern, it enacted legislation requiring cable and direct broadcast satellite operators to scramble audio and video signals carrying indecent programming on any channel dedicated to sexually explicit programs. The purpose of this law was to shield persons who did not subscribe to the programming from being exposed to it through signal bleed onto an adjacent channel. Cable and direct broadcast satellite operators who did not scramble their signals were restricted to distributing such programming between 10 p.m. and 6 a.m. As it did successfully in *Pacifica*, government argued that the regulation was necessary to protect children. Opponents of the legislation argued that the unique problems of broadcasting did not extend to cable and broadcast satellite transmissions. They maintained that the scrambling requirement imposed unreasonable costs and, for practical purposes, a prohibition of indecent programming.

In *United States v. Playboy Entertainment Group*,[55] the Court invalidated the law. Unlike its approach to indecency regulation in broadcasting, the Court applied strict scrutiny. Finding that the regulation was content-based, the Court searched for a compelling state interest and found that protection of children met this standard. It found, however, insufficient evidence in support of a significant exposure risk. Moreover, the Court found that the ability of parents to block certain channels provided a less restrictive alternative.

[D] Telephony

[1] Common Carrier Status

Telephone communication is among the oldest electronic media. As a common carrier, it occupies a unique position in relationship to the First Amendment. Users of telephone service, like broadcast or cable programmers, are protected by the First Amendment. Providers of telephone service, unlike broadcasters or cable operators, are not. This distinction owes to the unique obligations of a common carrier, which must provide access to users on a nondiscriminatory basis. Editorial discretion in this context, therefore, is superseded by the obligation to provide access to anyone who can pay the tariff for the service.

Telephone companies, following the break up of the American Telephone and Telegraph Company (AT&T) in 1982,[56] have diversified into business lines beyond their traditional common carrier services. AT&T and some of its former subsidiaries, for instance, have ventured into cable television and other telecommunications

---

[55] 529 U.S. 803 (2000).

[56] United States v. American Telephone and Telegraph Co., 552 F. Supp. 131 (D.D.C. 1982), *aff'd*, 460 U.S. 1001 (1983).

services. These activities implicate the same First Amendment protection afforded other cable operators.

[2] Indecency Regulation

Telephone communications, like broadcasting and cable, have attracted regulatory interest in sexually explicit content. In *Sable Broadcasting, Inc. v. Federal Communications Commission*,[57] the Court reviewed a law that banned obscene communications and indecent dial-a-porn services. The government advanced the *Pacifica* decision as the relevant model for resolving the case. The Court, however, found that the risks posed by indecent telephone communications differed significantly from those of broadcasting. Telephone communications do not have the uniquely pervasive nature of broadcasting, insofar as they require affirmative steps to access the service and are confined to discrete and individualized interaction. Technology also provides a means for controlling access to telephones more effectively than is the case with broadcasting. In support of this point, the Court noted the need to use credit cards and access codes to access dial-a-porn services. Scrambling requirements also limited the exposure risk. The Court in *Sable* adopted a standard of strict scrutiny. Pursuant to this criterion, it found that government's interest in protecting children was compelling. Because more affirmative steps are needed to access content than in broadcasting, and technology also creates medium specific barriers, the Court determined that there were less restrictive alternatives than a ban on indecent communications.

[E] Internet

The emergence of the Internet poses significant challenges to the traditional model of medium specific analysis. The Internet represents the confluence of several technologies and intersects both print and electronic media. It has arisen against the general backdrop of media convergence, a phenomenon characterized by shared media characteristics and capabilities. Many newspapers and magazines utilize over-the-air signals, telephone lines, and satellite transmissions to transport content from editorial rooms to printing and distribution centers. Broadcasting is retransmitted on cable and satellite systems, which not only can reproduce printed words and graphics but have recording and downloading capabilities. These developments raise significant questions about the long-term viability of medium-specific analysis.

[1] Blogs, Email, and Social Media

Notable incidents of the Internet are the blogosphere and social media such as Facebook and Twitter. These tools facilitate not only networking opportunities but also the role of citizen journalists. Seminal First Amendment case law is reminiscent of the battles that motion pictures and broadcasting faced in securing constitutional protection. In *Too Much Media, LLC v. Hale*,[58] a federal district court determined that comments on an online message board do not have the same

---

[57] 492 U.S. 115 (1989).

[58] A.3d 364 (N.J. 2011).

First Amendment safeguards as those afforded to traditional journalists. This result would appear to vie against the Court's decisions that make no differentiation between the institutional press and individual speakers. The district court nonetheless concluded that the postings had "none of the recognized qualities or characteristics (i.e., gathering and processing information) traditionally associated with the news process." A contrary view of online speech was expressed by a federal district court in *Fodor v. Doe.*[59]

Social media have played a key role in the political process, ranging from the dissemination of information by political candidates to organizing and advancing movements for political change in other countries. If assessed pursuant to medium specific standards, which focus upon the "unique problems" that a communications methodology presents, social media might be singled out for the immediacy of their impact and multiplicity of their retransmission. Among other things, the nature of social media raises the potential for conflicts with the laws of other nations. The potential for "libel tourism" is highlighted by United Kingdom law, which aims to protect privacy by prohibiting reporting of certain injunctions. A case in point is that of an English soccer player who secured an injunction barring reporting of an extramarital affair. When the information was disclosed in Parliament, where speech was privileged, thousands of Twitter users retransmitted it.[60] The soccer player responded by suing Twitter and its users for disclosing his identify and violating the super injunction.[61]

Email in the latter part of the twentieth social media in the early part of the twenty-first century emerged as a primary communications methodology. Key characteristics of these media are the ability to transmit information immediately. They also have disrupted the communications marketplace by displacing or competing with traditional methodologies such as the postal service, overnight carriers, and fax machines. In *University of Illinois v. Micron Technology, Inc.,*[62] the district court denied a motion for a preliminary injunction that would have prohibited "harassing" communications from a corporation to university employee. The particular corporation was party to an infringement suit barring future harassing communications from Micron to any University employee. The corporation was a defendant in a patent infringement suit brought by the university. As grounds for refusing to grant the preliminary injunction, the court determined that the term "harassing" was vague and the requested prior restraint would likely violate the company's First Amendment rights.

---

[59] 2011 U.S. Dist. LEXIS 49672 (D. Nev. 2011).

[60] *Twitter account naming super-injunction celebrities attracts 34,000 followers,* THE TELEGRAPH, July 10, 2011.

[61] Adam Taylor, *What Is a Super-Injunction, and Why Does a UK Football Star Want to Sue Twitter?,* BUS. INSIDER, May 23, 2011.

[62] No. 11-2288 (C.D. Ill 2013).

[2] Regulation of Indecency

Consistent with its concern with the impact of electronic media upon children, Congress in 1996 passed the Communications Decency Act of 1996 (CDA). This legislation prohibited knowing dissemination of indecent messages to persons under the age of 18 and knowing dissemination of "patently offensive" messages that would be available to persons under this age. In *Reno v. American Civil Liberties Union*,[63] the Court found the statute deficient on multiple grounds. First, it determined that the "patently offensive" term was vague. The Court prefaced its analysis with an inquiry into what, if any, unique problems the Internet presented that might justify special regulatory attention. With no history of government regulation, scarcity, or intrusiveness (as in broadcasting) associated with the Internet, the Court determined that the reasons for a diminished standard of review did not apply to it. Using strict scrutiny as its standard of review, the Court acknowledged that protecting children from exposure to indecent material constituted a compelling interest. Because the CDA could not be enforced against foreign sites and age is difficult to verify, the Court determined that the regulatory means were deficient in achieving their purpose. The burden on adult users, moreover, unduly compromised their right to receive information. The Court also identified less constitutionally restrictive means, including blocking or filtering software, for achieving Congress' objectives. Justice O'Connor would have upheld provisions of the legislation that prohibited knowing transmission, such as emails, of indecent materials to minors.

Following the CDA's invalidation, Congress enacted new legislation aimed at limiting content on the web The Child On Line Pornography Act (COPA) prohibited knowing communication for commercial purposes of any material that is harmful to minors. At issue was whether the use of "community standards," as the basis for determining whether material was harmful, created a problem of substantial overbreadth. The Court concluded that, because the COPA applies to significantly less material than the CDA and defines harmful-to-minors by reference to well-established obscenity standards, the community standards provision was not overbroad. The Court did not rule on whether the COPA might be substantially overbroad on other grounds, unconstitutionally vague, or whether it would survive strict scrutiny as the district court predicted once adjudication is complete.

In *Ashcroft v. American Civil Liberties Union*,[64] the Court reviewed a preliminary injunction against the COPA's enforcement. The law was constructed so as to regulate material on the web that was obscene for children and require proof of age to access it. The basis for the lower court's ruling was that there were less restrictive alternatives to enforcement than the use of credit cards required by the law. Finding that minors could evade these and other means mandated by the statute, it identified blocking or filtering technology as a less restrictive alternative. In upholding the preliminary injunction, the Court noted that the government would have adequate opportunity at trial to demonstrate that the district court's findings were incorrect. Justice Breyer, joined by Chief Justice Rehnquist and

---

[63] 521 U.S. 844 (1997).

[64] 542 U.S. 656 (2004).

Justice O'Connor, maintained that Congress could not have achieved its objective in less restrictive ways. Justice Scalia would have upheld the law on grounds the material was not constitutionally protected.

The Court, in *Ashcroft v. Free Speech Coalition*,[65] reviewed the question of whether digitally created child pornography can be prohibited. The Child Pornography Prevention Act (CPPA) targeted any visual depiction, including computer or computer-generated images, of a minor engaged in sexually explicit conduct. The law had no prurient interest or patent offensive requirement and prohibited speech even if it had serious literary, artistic, political, or scientific value. The government argued that the law was necessary because pedophiles might use virtual child pornography to seduce children. The Court observed that there are many innocent materials that can be used for immoral purposes, including candy, video games, and cartoons, but they are not prohibited. Regulation instead should be aimed at those who provide unsuitable materials to children or engage in unlawful solicitation. Rejecting the proposition that virtual child pornography whets the appetites of pedophiles and steers them toward illegal conduct, the Court emphasized that speech cannot be banned merely for its bad tendency. Nor can speech within the rights of adults be silenced totally in an effort to protect children. The Court also rejected the argument that, because of production quality, allowing virtual child pornography makes it difficult to prosecute persons who use real children. It found that this argument "turned the First Amendment upside down" insofar as it would suppress lawful speech as a means of regulating unlawful speech.

Congress responded to the decision by enacting legislation prohibiting the distribution and possession of material marketed as child pornography. In *United States v. Williams*, 553 U.S. 285 (2008), the Court determined that such pandering could be criminalized regardless of whether it depicted actual or digital images. It rejected challenges that it was impermissibly overbroad or vague. Justices Souter and Ginsburg maintained that promoters of child pornography who do not trade in actual depictions of children should not be subject to prosecution.

[F]   Video Games

The use of video games on computers and dedicated systems such as X Box, Wii, and Playstation have opened another First Amendment frontier. Video games, which are accessible in the form of software or via the Internet, have been the target of regulation that reflects concern with exposure to sexual or violent content. In *Brown v. Entertainment Merchants Association*,[66] the Court reviewed a state law that prohibited the selling of violent video games to minors. The enactment extended to games that depicted "killing, maiming, dismembering or sexually assaulting an image of a human being" in a "patently offensive way." Violation of the law was established by showing that the content appealed to a buyer's "deviant or morbid interests" and was bereft of "serious literary, artistic, political, or scientific value."

---

[65]   535 U.S. 234 (2002).

[66]   131 S. Ct. 2729 (2011).

The law thus drew upon the standard governing obscenity (*Miller v. California*) and the less rigorous criterion for minors (*Ginsberg v. New York*). The Court declined to expand the boundaries of obscenity so as to include violence or to equate sex and violence. Justice Scalia, writing for the majority, observed that depictions of violence never have been the target of government regulation. Responding to studies purporting to establish a link between violence and anti-social behavior, the Court determined that the research failed to establish a compelling state interest. It thus noted that:

> [p]sychological studies purporting to show a connection between exposure to violent video games and harmful effects on children do not prove that such exposure causes minors to act aggressively. Any demonstrated effects are both small and indistinguishable from effects produced by other media. Since California has declined to restrict these other media, [its] video game regulation is wildly underinclusive, raising serious doubts about whether the State is pursuing the interest it invokes or is instead disfavoring a particular speaker or viewpoint.

In a concurring opinion, Justice Alito joined by Chief Justice Roberts warned against curbing legislative efforts to address what some view as "a significant and developing social problem." They favored striking down the law because of a perceived failure by the state to define "violent" more precisely.

[G]　Social Media

The First Amendment was incubated in an environment that was sensitive to the need for protecting the editorial function. The rise of mass media, particularly over the course of the 20th Century, heightened the importance of this role. Especially as broadcasting became the nation's dominant medium, journalistic discretion was reserved for a relative handful and the citizenry was consigned to the role of reader, listener, or viewer.

The Internet, in a virtual sense, has reinvigorated the role and extended the reach of the speaker in public discourse. This phenomenon has been enhanced further by the introduction of social media platforms such as Facebook, Twitter, and You Tube. The Court has yet to review any cases concerning social media. Like any other communication methodology and barring any reformulation of standards of review, however, social media would be assessed pursuant to the understanding that "each [medium] tends to present its own peculiar problems."

Distinguishing characteristics of social media include their interactivity, immediacy, and accessibility without editorial filters. Unlike traditional outlets, which more often use journalistic processes to ensure accuracy, social media tend to be traded upon spontaneously and information is less susceptible to verifiability. Access is open rather than selective (i.e., not controlled by an editor), and the medium itself creates a forum of potentially limitless reach. Minus the editorial function, and but for the virtual nature and boundlessness of the forum, social media largely create an environment akin to what existed at the time of the First Amendment's framing.

Unlike traditional media, problems associated with social media may focus less upon the medium's structural nature or incidents and more upon how it influences the consequences of speech. Social media have been identified as catalysts for and accelerators of violence and even revolution.[67] A British court in 2011 thus sentenced two men to four years in prison on grounds they violated the nation's Serious Crime Act by using Facebook to incite a riot.[68] Social media also present challenges to controlling prohibited forms of speech, such as obscenity, and may help balance the influence of money in election campaigns. The pervasive nature of social media, to the extent they replicate many of the conditions that preceded mass media, at least may invite an understanding of the First Amendment that is concerned less with the medium and more with the message.

POINTS TO REMEMBER

- Case law generally reflects an understanding that media have not greater rights under the First Amendment than an individual.

- There is no First Amendment privilege that shields reporters from having to testify in a grand jury proceeding.

- The First Amendment establishes no barrier to a newsroom search pursuant to a valid search warrant.

- Prisoners have no right of access to the media, so long as they have reasonable alternative channels of communication and are not subject to content discrimination.

- The press has no right of access to prisons beyond what the public has.

- Criminal trials typically may be closed to the public only if there is a compelling state interest and the means for achieving this interest are narrowly tailored.

- A pretrial proceeding may be closed if there is no history of openness and a substantial probability that the right to a fair trial would be compromised.

- Media coverage of the criminal justice system may implicate the right to an impartial jury and fair trial.

- It is the responsibility of the trial judge to ensure that the rights of the media and a defendant are reconciled.

- An order barring the media from publishing lawfully acquired information constitutes a prior restraint and thus is presumed to be unconstitutional and subject to a heavy burden of justification.

---

[67] Amatava Kumar, 'Revolution 2.0', How Social Media Toppled a Dictator, http://www.npr.org/2012/02/08/145470844/revolution-2-0-how-social-media-toppled-a-dictator (Feb. 8, 2012)

[68] Jeremy Kirk, Two UK Men Jailed for Inciting Violence on Facebook, IDG News Service, http://www.pcworld.com/article/238244/two_uk_men_jailed_for_inciting_violence_on_facebook.html (Aug. 16, 2011)

- A court may not prevent media from publishing lawfully acquired information unless there is a clear and present danger to the right to a fair trial, less restrictive methods would be ineffective, finding are made that a gag order would be effective, and it does not apply to information obtained in court.

- The permissibility of instrumentalities of electronic media is determined by whether it prejudices the right to a fair trial.

- Content-based regulation of media is subject to First Amendment standards of review that vary with the medium.

- Regulation that invades the editorial discretion of publishers is subject to strict scrutiny.

- Broadcasting is the least protected medium, and invasion of editorial discretion is subject to an intermediate standard of review.

- The First Amendment standard of review for cable, at least insofar as content regulation is concerned, is strict scrutiny.

- Telephone service providers are common carriers and thus have no First Amendment interests.

- Content regulation of the Internet is subject to strict scrutiny.

Chapter 11

THE ESTABLISHMENT CLAUSE

FOCAL POINTS FOR CHAPTER 11

- The constitutional prohibition against "established" religions.
- The difficulty of defining the concept of "establishment."
- The permissibility of providing financial support or other assistance to religious schools.
- The permissibility of prayer and moments of silence in legislative bodies and public schools.
- The permissibility of the Ten Commandments in public places.
- The permissibility of holiday displays.
- Religious access to governmental buildings and funding.

The Establishment Clause is simply stated: "Congress shall make no law respecting an establishment of religion." While the Clause applies, by its own terms, only to the federal government, the Supreme Court held in the 1940s that the Fourteenth Amendment incorporated the Clause binding, and made it binding on the states.[1] As a result, neither the federal government, nor the states, are allowed to "establish" a religion.

The Establishment Clause clearly prohibits certain types of governmental activities that were common in Europe:

- the establishment of a national (or, for that matter, a state) church;
- laws requiring individuals to go to church against their will;
- laws forcing individuals to profess a belief or disbelief in any religion.

The difficulty is that few establishment clause cases involve any of these prohibited types of conduct. Throughout U.S. history, there has been no attempt to declare an "official" national religion. As a result, Establishment Clause litigation focuses on whether certain lesser acts (*i.e.*, school prayer, financial aid to religious

---

[1] *See* Cantwell v. Connecticut, 310 U.S. 296 (1940) (incorporating the Free Exercise Clause); Everson v. Board of Education, 330 U.S. 1 (1947).

organizations, the posting of the Ten Commandments in public places) constitute an "establishment" of religion. Because these "lesser" acts do not clearly violate the First Amendment, the courts have struggled to define the term "establishment," and give effect to its intended purpose. The U.S. Supreme Court's consideration of Establishment Clause issues has therefore been done on a case-by-case and category-by-category basis.

§ 11.01   FINANCIAL AID TO RELIGION

A frequent source of establishment clause litigation involves governmental attempts to provide financial benefits to religion or religious organizations. The question is whether, by providing such benefits, the government transgresses the line into an establishment of religion.

[A]   Early Cases

In its early financial aid decisions, the Court has tried to avoid exhibiting hostility towards religion while at the same time avoiding entangling relationships between the state and religion. For example, in one early decision, *Bradfield v. Roberts*,[2] the Court held that the District of Columbia could pay to construct a new building on the grounds of a religiously affiliated hospital. The Court emphasized that the secular purpose of the payment (to increase hospital facilities), and the fact that the hospital did not discriminate on the basis of religion in its operation. The Court regarded the hospital's religious affiliation as "wholly immaterial."

One of the most prominent early decisions was rendered in *Everson v. Board of Education*.[3] Pursuant to New Jersey law, a local board of education decided to reimburse parents for money spent to transport their children to school on public buses. Some of the money was used to transport children to Catholic parochial schools that gave students, in addition to a secular education, regular religious instruction conforming to the religious tenets of the Catholic Faith.

The reimbursements were challenged as an "establishment of religion." In deciding the case, the Court recognized the tensions inherent in its Establishment Clause jurisprudence. On the one hand, the Court viewed the First Amendment as prohibiting New Jersey from "contributing tax-raised funds to support an institution which teaches the tenets and faith of any church." On the other hand, the Court viewed the Amendment as requiring states to be careful not to hamper citizens in the free exercise of their religion, and not to prohibit members of any faith, *"because of their faith, or lack of it,* from receiving the benefits of public welfare legislation." The Court also recognized that it "must be careful [not to] prohibit New Jersey from extending its general State law benefits to all its citizens without regard to their religious belief." After weighing these competing interests, the Court upheld the law:

---

[2] 175 U.S. 291 (1899).

[3] 330 U.S. 1 (1947).

[W]e cannot say that the First Amendment prohibits New Jersey from spending tax raised funds to pay the bus fares of parochial school pupils as a part of a general program under which it pays the fares of pupils attending public and other schools. It is undoubtedly true that children are helped to get to church schools. There is even a possibility that [some] children might not be sent to the church schools if the parents were compelled to pay their children's bus fares out of their own pockets. . . . Similarly, parents might be reluctant to permit their children to attend schools which the state had cut off from such general government services as ordinary police and fire protection, connections for sewage disposal, public highways and sidewalks. Of course, cutting off church schools from these services [would] make it far more difficult for the schools to operate. But such is obviously not the purpose of the First Amendment.

In reaching its decision, the Court emphasized that the Establishment Clause requires governmental "neutrality" towards religion: "That Amendment requires the state to be a neutral in its relations with groups of religious believers and non-believers; it does not require the state to be their adversary. State power is no more to be used so as to handicap religions, than it is to favor them." In the Court's view, the government was acting neutrally:

This Court has said that parents may [send] their children to a religious rather than a public school if the school meets the secular educational requirements which the state has power to impose. . . . The State contributes no money to the schools. It does not support them. Its legislation [does] no more than provide a general program to help parents get their children, regardless of their religion, safely and expeditiously to and from accredited schools.

Justice Black ended with a rhetorical flourish regarding the "wall" between church and state: "The First Amendment has erected a wall between church and state. That wall must be kept high and impregnable. We could not approve the slightest breach. New Jersey has not breached it here."

Justice Jackson dissented raising two major concerns. First, he doubted whether the reimbursement had any effect on safety: "As passengers on the public busses they travel as fast and no faster, and are as safe and no safer, since their parents are reimbursed as before." In addition, he expressed concern about whether the law involved favoritism towards religion because it provided for reimbursement to students who rode buses to parochial schools, but not to students who rode buses to other schools.[4] Justice Rutledge, joined by justices Frankfurter, Jackson and Burton, also dissented: "Neither so high nor so impregnable today as yesterday is the wall raised between church and state by Virginia's great statute of religious freedom and the First Amendment." He continued: "The First Amendment's

---

[4] *Id.* at 21–23: "[The] Act prohibits [payment] to private schools operated in whole or in part for profit. [The Court ignores] the essentially religious test by which beneficiaries of this expenditure are selected. [Could] we sustain an Act that said police shall protect pupils on the way to or from public schools and Catholic schools but not while going to and coming from other schools, and firemen shall extinguish a blaze in public or Catholic school buildings but shall not put out a blaze in Protestant Church schools or private schools operated for profit? [I] should think it pretty plain that such a scheme would not be valid."

purpose was not to strike merely at the official establishment of a single sect, creed or religion. [I]t was to uproot all such relationships. [It] was to create a complete and permanent separation of the spheres of religious activity and civil authority by comprehensively forbidding every form of public aid or support for religion. . . ." He then expressed concern about the potential divisiveness of such support: "Public money devoted to payment of religious costs, educational or other, brings the quest for more. It brings too the struggle of sect against sect for the larger share or for any. . . . The end of such strife cannot be other than to destroy the cherished [liberty]."

In early decisions like *Everson*, the Court tended to focus on whether financial aid was "neutrally" offered. Some commentators, for example Professor Philip Kurland, have argued that the religion clauses should be construed under a "neutrality" standard.[5] Others have questioned the utility of a "neutrality" standard. As dissenting Justice Jackson recognized in *Everson*, a neutrality standard might justify providing broad based public support for religious schools.[6] Likewise, as Professor Douglas Laycock has argued, a neutrality standard can produce "surprising results that are inconsistent with strong intuitions." He notes that, during Prohibition, the government prohibited the sale or consumption of alcohol, but created an exemption for the sacramental use of wine. In Professor Laycock's view, under formal neutrality principles, the exemption would have been unconstitutional because it "undeniably classified on the basis of religion," and it would have been a crime to celebrate the Eucharist or the Seder, and he believed that such a result could not be reconciled with the concept of religious liberty: "If the free exercise of religion includes anything beyond bare belief, it must be the right to perform the sacred rituals of the faith." In addition, he would have found the absence of an exemption troubling because a "law enacted largely at the behest of Protestants that barred the sacred rites of Catholics and Jews, a law that changed the way these rites had been performed for millennia, could not be reconciled with any concept of religious liberty worthy of the name." He also argued that formal neutrality would produce results that many Americans would "find unacceptably favorable to religion." He offers an example in the context of financial aid to private education: "Under formal neutrality, government can give unlimited amounts of unrestricted aid to religious schools, so long as the aid goes to all schools and not to religious schools alone." Indeed, he argues that any "aid to secular private schools *must* be given to religious schools, on exactly the same terms. To exclude religious schools from the aid program, or to impose restrictions on religious uses of the money, would be to classify on the basis of religion." In his view, that result "would violate formal neutrality."

As we shall see, despite these criticisms, the "neutrality" test has regained importance in recent years.

---

[5] Philip Kurland, *Of Church and State and the Supreme Court*, 29 U. CHI. L. REV. 1, 96 (1961).

[6] *Everson*, 330 U.S. at 49:

"We are told that the New Jersey statute is valid [because] the appropriation is for a public, not a private purpose, namely, the promotion of education. . . . If the fact alone be determinative[,] then I can see no possible basis [for] the state's refusal to make full appropriation for support of private, religious schools, just as is done for public instruction."

[B] The *Lemon* Test and Doctrinal Turmoil

Since 1971, the Court has frequently analyzed Establishment Clause cases using the so-called *Lemon* test. That test, articulated *in Lemon v. Kurtzman*[7] in an opinion by then Chief Justice Burger, established a three-prong test for evaluating the validity of establishment clause issues: "First, the statute must have a secular legislative purpose; second, its principal or primary effect must be one that neither advances nor inhibits religion; finally, the statute must not foster 'an excessive government entanglement with religion.' "

The *Lemon* case involved a Rhode Island law that authorized state officials to supplement the salaries of teachers of secular subjects by paying directly to the teachers an amount not exceeding 15% of their annual salary. The Act required that teachers teach only those subjects offered in the public schools, and use only teaching materials used in the public schools. At the time, Rhode Island's nonpublic elementary schools enrolled approximately 25% of the state's pupils, and 95% of these students attended schools affiliated with the Roman Catholic church. All teachers who applied for benefits under the Act taught in Roman Catholic schools.

Also at issue in *Lemon* was Pennsylvania's Nonpublic Elementary and Secondary Education Act. It authorized direct payments to nonpublic schools for the actual cost of teachers' salaries, textbooks, and instructional materials. Schools were required to maintain procedures that separately identified the cost of the "secular educational service," and reimbursement was limited to courses actually in the curricula of the public schools, and was further limited to courses in mathematics, modern foreign languages, physical science, and physical education. State officials approved the textbooks and instructional materials, and reimbursement was not permissible for any course that had subject matter involving religious teaching, or that focused on the morals or forms of worship of any sect. Under the Act, Pennsylvania spent $5 million annually, and 96% of the benefitting pupils attended church-related schools, most affiliated with the Roman Catholic church.

The Court struck down both the Rhode Island and Pennsylvania laws. The Court began by noting that it was forced to "draw lines with reference to the three main evils against which the Establishment Clause was intended to afford protection: 'sponsorship, financial support, and active involvement of the sovereign in religious activity.' *Walz v. Tax Commission*, 397 U.S. 664, 668 (1970)." The Court then articulated and applied the three-part test. It found that the laws were supported by secular purposes: "to enhance the quality of the secular education in all schools covered by the compulsory attendance laws." The Court had no difficulty sustaining this purpose: "[A] State always has a legitimate concern for maintaining minimum standards [in] schools." Because the Court struck the law down under the third prong of the test-the entanglement prong, it found it unnecessary to decide whether the law had a secular effect.

In considering the third prong, the Court began by placing limitations and qualifications on Justice Black's "wall" between church and state metaphor: "[Our]

---

[7] 403 U.S. 602 (1971).

prior holdings do not call for total separation between church and state; total separation is not possible in an absolute sense. Some relationship between government and religious organizations is inevitable. Fire inspections, building and zoning regulations, and state requirements under compulsory school-attendance laws are examples of necessary and permissible contacts. [T]he line of separation, far from being a 'wall,' is a blurred, indistinct, and variable barrier depending on all the circumstances of a particular relationship."

The Court suggested that, in determining whether a law promotes an excessive entanglement, it is necessary to examine a number of facts including "the character and purposes of the institutions that are benefited, the nature of the aid that the State provides, and the resulting relationship between the government and the religious authority." The Court went on to hold that both the Rhode Island and Pennsylvania laws resulted in excessive entanglements:

> [T]eachers have a substantially different ideological character from books. [A] textbook's content is ascertainable, but a teacher's handling of a subject is not. We cannot ignore the danger that a teacher under religious control and discipline poses to the separation of the religious from the purely secular aspects [of] education. [We] do not assume that teachers [will] be guilty of bad faith or any conscious design to evade the limitations imposed by the statute and the First Amendment. We simply recognize that a dedicated religious person, teaching in a school affiliated with his or her faith and operated to inculcate its tenets, [will] experience great difficulty [remaining] religiously neutral. [To] ensure that no trespass occurs, the State [carefully] conditioned its aid with pervasive restrictions. [A] comprehensive, discriminating, and continuing state surveillance will inevitably be required to ensure that these restrictions are obeyed and the First Amendment otherwise respected. . . . The Pennsylvania statute [involves] an educational system that is very similar.

The Court also emphasized the tendency of both the Rhode Island and Pennsylvania programs to create "political divisiveness":

> In a community where such a large number of pupils are served by church-related schools, [p]artisans of parochial schools, understandably concerned with rising costs and sincerely dedicated to both the religious and secular educational missions of their schools, will inevitably [promote] political action to achieve their goals. Those who oppose state aid, whether for constitutional, religious, or fiscal reasons, will inevitably respond and employ all of the usual political campaign techniques to prevail. Candidates will be forced to declare and voters to choose. [M]any people confronted with issues of this kind will find their votes aligned with their faith.

While the opinion recognized that "political debate and division" are generally regarded as "normal and healthy manifestations of our democratic system of government," he believed that "political division along religious lines was one of the principal evils against which the First Amendment was intended to protect." In addition, he expressed concern that this case involved "successive and very likely permanent annual appropriations that benefit relatively few religious groups.

Political fragmentation and divisiveness on religious lines are thus likely to be intensified."

Justice Douglas, joined by Justice Black, concurred. He expressed concern that governmental funding of religious education would necessarily result in governmental meddling in parochial school affairs:

> [Public] financial support of parochial schools [necessitates] governmental suppression, surveillance, or meddling in church affairs. . . . The constitutional mandate can in part be carried out by censoring the curricula. [A] sectarian course can be marked for deletion. But the problem only starts there. Sectarian instruction [can] take place in a course on Shakespeare or in one on mathematics. [I] would think that policing these grants to detect sectarian instruction would be insufferable to religious partisans and would breed division and dissension between church and state. [If] the government closed its eyes to the manner in which these grants are actually used it would be allowing public funds to promote sectarian education. If it did not close its eyes but undertook the surveillance needed, it [would] intermeddle in parochial affairs in a way that would breed only rancor and dissension.

He also argued that parochial schools are "organic whole[s] [living] on one budget. What the taxpayers give for salaries of those who teach only the humanities or science without any trace of proselytizing enables the school to use all of its own funds for religious training. . . ."

Justice Brennan concurred:

> [These] cases [involve] direct subsidies of tax monies to the schools themselves and [the] secular education those schools provide goes hand in hand with the religious mission that is the only reason for the schools' existence. [These] statutes do violence to the principle that "government may not employ religious means to serve secular interests, however legitimate they may be, at least without [a] demonstration that nonreligious means will not suffice."

Justice White dissented: "[It] is enough for me that the States and the Federal Government are financing a separable secular function of overriding importance in order to sustain the legislation here challenged. [There] is no specific allegation [that] sectarian teaching does or would invade secular classes supported by state funds."

[C] Other Applications of the *Lemon* Test

Before and after *Lemon*, the Court rendered a number of decisions on the constitutionality of statutes providing financial aid to parochial schools. Many of these decisions seemed to draw fine distinctions that were not necessarily consistent with other decisions:

(1) *Textbooks.* In *Board of Education v. Allen,*[8] the Court held that a state could loan textbooks to parochial schools, for the teaching of secular subjects, when the books were selected by (and were the same ones used in) the public schools.

(2) *Instructional Materials.* In *Meek v. Pittenger*[9] and *Wolman v. Walter,*[10] the Court held that a state could not loan "instructional material and equipment" (*i.e.*, maps, charts, periodicals, photographs, sound recordings, films and laboratory equipment) to parochial schools. Such aid would have the impermissible effect of advancing religion by aiding "the sectarian school enterprise as a whole."

(3) *Standardized Testing.* In *Wolman,* the Court also held that a state could pay for standardized testing in parochial schools, as well as for the scoring of those tests, provided the tests were the same ones used in the public schools and that nonpublic employees were not involved in the preparation or grading of the tests. However, in *Levitt v. Committee for Public Education,*[11] the Court held that a state could not reimburse parochial schools for administering teacher-prepared tests because there were "no means to assure that the tests [were] free of religious instruction."

(4) *Auxiliary Services.* In *Meek, supra,* the Court struck down a law providing "auxiliary services" — remedial and accelerated instruction, guidance counseling and testing, speech and hearing services — directly to nonpublic schoolchildren with special needs. The Court found that excessive surveillance and entanglement would result, as well as political divisiveness. However, *Wolman* upheld a statute that provided speech and hearing diagnostic services, and diagnostic psychological services, to pupils attending nonpublic schools. The Court distinguished *Meek*: "[D]iagnostic services [have] little or no educational content and are not closely associated with the educational mission of the nonpublic school."

(5) *Remedial Services.* In *Wolman, supra,* the Court also upheld a statute that expended state funds for therapeutic, guidance, and remedial services for students who had been identified as having a need for specialized attention. The personnel were employees of the state and the services were offered at neutral sites away from the parochial schools.

(6) *State Sponsored Field Trips.* In *Wolman,* the Court struck down a statute that authorized the expenditure of state funds for student field trips "to governmental, industrial, cultural, and scientific centers designed to enrich the secular studies of students." The Court found "impermissible direct aid to sectarian education," and it expressed concern about the need for "close supervision [and] excessive entanglement. . . ."

(7) *Maintenance and Repair. Committee for Public Education and Religious Liberty v. Nyquist,*[12] involved a New York law that provided direct money grants to "qualifying" nonpublic schools for the "maintenance and repair [of] school facilities

---

[8] 392 U.S. 236 (1968).

[9] 421 U.S. 349 (1975).

[10] 443 U.S. 229 (1977).

[11] 413 U.S. 472 (1973).

[12] 413 U.S. 756 (1973).

and equipment to ensure the health, welfare and safety of enrolled pupils." The Court concluded that the statute failed the "effects" test: Payments were not restricted to facilities used exclusively for secular purposes, and therefore could have been diverted to religious buildings.

(8) *Higher Education.* The Court has decided a number of cases involving aid to higher education. *Tilton v. Richardson,*[13] involved a federal law that provided construction grants to religious colleges for buildings and facilities used for secular educational purposes. The Act excluded any facility used for sectarian purposes, and the federal government retained a 20-year interest in any building. The Court upheld the law: "[C]ollege students are less impressionable and less susceptible to religious indoctrination. [Many] church-related colleges and universities are characterized by a high degree of academic freedom and seek to evoke free and critical responses. [Since] religious indoctrination is not a substantial purpose[,] there is less likelihood [that] religion will permeate [secular] education. [T]he necessity for intensive government surveillance is diminished." The Court struck down the 20-year restriction because "restrictive obligations [cannot, expire] while the building has substantial [value]."

In Hunt v. McNair,[14] the Court upheld a statute that authorized the issuance of revenue bonds for the benefit of a Baptist college. The Court found that the program's purpose was secular (education), and that "the College [was no] more an instrument of religious indoctrination than [the colleges involved] in *Tilton.*" Likewise, in *Roemer v. Board of Public Works,*[15] the Court upheld a Maryland law that provided annual grants (15% of per pupil appropriation in the state system) to private colleges subject to the restriction that the funds not be used for "sectarian purposes." Occasional audits "[would] be 'quick and non-judgmental.' "

[D]   Criticism of *Lemon*'s Three-Part Test

The seeming inconsistency of these post-*Lemon* decisions led to criticism of the three-part test. As time passed, it became clear that a number of justices were dissatisfied with the test. For example, in a dissenting opinion in *Wallace v. Jaffree,* Justice Rehnquist argued that:

> [The *Lemon* test] has simply not provided adequate standards for deciding Establishment Clause cases. . . . For example, a State may lend [geography] textbooks that contain [maps], but the State may not lend [maps] for use in geography class. A State may lend textbooks on American colonial history, but it may not lend a film on George Washington, or a film projector to show it. . . . A State may lend classroom workbooks, but may not lend workbooks in which the parochial school children write, thus rendering them nonreusable. A State may pay for bus transportation to religious schools but may not pay for bus transportation from the parochial school to the public zoo or natural history museum. . . . A State may pay for diagnostic services conducted in the parochial school but therapeutic

---

[13] 403 U.S. 672 (1971).

[14] 413 U.S. 734 (1973).

[15] 426 U.S. 736 (1976).

services must be given in a different building; speech and hearing "services" [inside] the sectarian school are forbidden, but the State may conduct speech and hearing diagnostic testing inside the sectarian school. Exceptional parochial school students may receive counseling, but it must take place outside of the parochial school. . . . A State may give cash to a parochial school to pay for the administration of state-written tests[,] but it may not provide funds for teacher-prepared tests on secular subjects. Religious instruction may not be given in public school, but the public school may release students during the day for religion classes elsewhere, and may enforce attendance at those classes with its truancy laws.[16]

In a concurring opinion in *Lamb's Chapel v. Center Moriches Union Free School District*,[17] Justice Scalia argued that:

> Like some ghoul in a late-night horror movie that repeatedly sits up in its grave and shuffles abroad, after being repeatedly killed and buried, *Lemon* stalks our Establishment Clause jurisprudence once again. . . . [No] fewer than five of the currently sitting Justices have, in their own opinions, personally driven pencils through the creature's heart (the author of today's opinion repeatedly), and a sixth has joined an opinion doing so. The secret of the *Lemon* test's survival, I think, is that it is so easy to kill. It is there to scare us (and our audience) when we wish it to do so, but we can command it to return to the tomb at will. When we wish to strike down a practice it forbids, we invoke it, when we wish to uphold a practice it forbids, we ignore it entirely. Sometimes, we take a middle course, calling its three prongs "no more than helpful signposts." Such a docile and useful monster is worth keeping around, at least in a somnolent state; one never knows when one might need him.[18]

In her concurring opinion in *Board of Education of Kiryas Joel Village School District v. Grumet*, Justice O'Connor offered the following observations:

> It is always appealing to look for a single test, a Grand Unified Theory that would resolve all the cases that may arise under a particular Clause. There is, after all, only one Establishment Clause. [But this] may sometimes do more harm than good. . . . Shoehorning new problems into a test that does not reflect the special concerns raised by those problems tends to deform the language of the test. Relatively simple phrases like "primary effect [that] neither advances nor inhibits religion" and " 'entanglement,' " acquire more and more complicated definitions which stray ever further from their literal meaning. . . . I think it is more useful to recognize the relevant concerns in each case on their own terms, rather than trying to squeeze them into language that does not really apply to them.

> [Another danger is that] the bad test may drive out the good. Rather than taking the opportunity to derive narrower, more precise tests from the

---

[16] Wallace v. Jaffree, 472 U.S. 38, 111 (1985) (Rehnquist, J., dissenting).

[17] 508 U.S. 384 (1993).

[18] Lamb's Chapel v. Center Moriches Union Free School District, 508 U.S. 384 (1993) (Scalia, J., concurring).

case law, courts tend to continually try to patch up the broad test, making it more and more amorphous and distorted. This, I am afraid, has happened with *Lemon*. Experience proves that the Establishment Clause, like the Free Speech Clause, cannot easily be reduced to a single test. . . .[19]

[E] *Agostini, Mitchell*, and Continued Doctrinal Turmoil

As more and more justices expressed discontent with *Lemon's* three-part test, it soon became clear that the Court was searching for a new test. Nevertheless, there was disagreement regarding the content of that test. In recent decisions, the Court has struggled to reach consensus.

[1] *Agostini's* Modification of *Lemon*

In *Agostini v. Felton*,[20] in an opinion by Justice O'Connor, the Court seemed to map out a new approach to Establishment Clause issues. The petitioners in that case sought relief from the Court's prior decision in *Aguilar v. Felton*[21] on the basis that *Aguilar* was not consistent with the Court's subsequent Establishment Clause jurisprudence. Petitioners asked the Court to explicitly recognize that *Aguilar* was no longer good law. Petitioners relied on the statements of five Justices in *Board of Ed. of Kiryas Joel Village School Dist. v. Grumet*.[22] In *Agostini*, the Court agreed and seemed to chart a new direction for the Court's Establishment Clause jurisprudence.

In *Aguilar*, the Court had held that the Establishment Clause barred the City of New York from sending public school teachers to parochial schools to provide remedial education to disadvantaged children. The case involved Title I of the Elementary and Secondary Education Act of 1965 which had the purpose of providing "full educational opportunity to every child regardless of economic background." The Act channeled federal funds through the States to "local educational agencies" (LEA's) which spent funds to provide remedial education, guidance, and job counseling to eligible students. An eligible student was one (i) who resided within the attendance boundaries of a public school located in a low-income area, and (ii) who was failing, or at risk of failing, the State's student performance standards. The law required that Title I funds be made available to *all* eligible children, regardless of whether they attended public schools, and the law also required that services provided to children attending private schools be "equitable in comparison to services and other benefits for public school children."

The law also contained other restrictions. Title I services could be provided only to private school students eligible for aid, and could not be used to provide services on a "school-wide" basis. In addition, the LEA was required to maintain complete control over Title I funds; maintain title to all materials used to provide Title I

---

[19] Board of Education of Kiryas Joel Village School District v. Grumet, 512 U.S. 687, 720 (1994) (O'Connor, J., concurring).

[20] 521 U.S. 203 (1997).

[21] 473 U.S. 402 (1985).

[22] 512 U.S. 687 (1994).

services; and provide those services through public employees or other persons independent of the private school and any religious institution. The Title I services themselves were required to be "secular, neutral, and non-ideological," and must "supplement, and in no case supplant, the level of services" already provided by the private school.

The Board of Education of the City of New York (Board), an LEA, started receiving Title I funds in 1966. Ten percent of the students in the district were private school students, and 90% of the private schools were sectarian. The Board initially sent children to the public schools for after-school Title I instruction. Because the children were often tired, and parents were concerned for the safety of their children, attendance was poor. In an effort to increase attendance, the Board moved the instruction to the private school campuses during school hours. Board rules provided that only public employees could serve as Title I instructors and counselors, and teachers were assigned to private schools on a voluntary basis and without regard to the religious affiliation of the employee or the wishes of the private school. A majority of Title I teachers worked in non-public schools with religious affiliations different from their own.

The Board of Education informed its Title I employees that (i) they were employees of the Board and accountable only to their public school supervisors; (ii) they had exclusive responsibility for selecting students for the Title I program and could teach only those children who met the eligibility criteria for Title I; (iii) their materials and equipment would be used only in the Title I program; (iv) they could not engage in team-teaching or other cooperative instructional activities with private school teachers; and (v) they could not introduce any religious matter into their teaching or become involved in any way with the religious activities of the private schools. All religious symbols were to be removed from classrooms used for Title I services. Although Title I teachers could consult with a student's regular classroom teacher to assess the student's particular needs, they were required to limit these consultations to mutual professional concerns regarding the student's education. To ensure that Title I employees observed these restrictions, publicly employed field supervisors made at least one unannounced visit to each teacher's classroom every month.

In *Aguilar*, the program was challenged by six federal taxpayers. The United States Supreme Court struck down the program finding an "excessive entanglement of church and state in the administration of Title I benefits." On remand, the District Court permanently enjoined the Board "from using public funds for any plan or program under [Title I] to the extent that it requires, authorizes or permits public school teachers and guidance counselors to provide teaching and counseling services on the premises of sectarian schools." The Board then modified its Title I program to revert to its prior practice of providing instruction at public school sites, at leased sites, and in mobile instructional units (essentially vans converted into classrooms) parked near the sectarian school. The Board also offered computer-aided instruction, which could be provided "on premises" because it did not require public employees to be physically present on the premises of a religious school. In the first ten years after the case was decided, the Board spent over $100 million providing computer-aided instruction, leasing sites and mobile instructional units, and transporting students to those sites. These costs reduced the amount of money that the LEA had available for remedial education, and forced it to reduce the number of students receiving Title I benefits.

In *Agostini*, the Court also discussed its decision in *School Dist. of Grand Rapids v. Ball*,[23] which was originally decided as a companion case to *Aguilar*. *Ball* involved two programs implemented by the School District of Grand Rapids, Michigan. The "Shared Time" program provided remedial and "enrichment" classes, at public expense, to students attending nonpublic schools. The classes were taught during regular school hours by publicly employed teachers, using materials purchased with public funds, on the premises of nonpublic schools. The Shared Time courses were in subjects designed to supplement the "core curriculum" of the nonpublic schools. 40 of the 41 nonpublic schools eligible for the program were "pervasively sectarian."

In *Ball*, the Court applied the *Lemon* test to the Shared Time program and concluded that it had the impermissible effect of advancing religion. The decision was based on a number of findings:

> (i) any public employee who works on the premises of a religious school is presumed to inculcate religion in her work; (ii) the presence of public employees on private school premises creates a symbolic union between church and state; and (iii) any and all public aid that directly aids the educational function of religious schools impermissibly finances religious indoctrination, even if the aid reaches such schools as a consequence of private decisionmaking.[24]

Agostini overruled *Aguilar* and *Ball*, and held that the Court's "more recent cases" had in fact undermined the assumptions upon which *Ball* and *Aguilar* had relied. The Court stated that it would continue to apply the first prong of the *Lemon* test (the purpose prong), but the Court concluded that: "What has changed [is] our understanding of the criteria used to assess whether aid to religion has an impermissible effect." The Court then redefined the second prong of the test:

> [C]ases subsequent to *Aguilar* [have] modified [the] approach we use to assess indoctrination. First, [we] abandoned the presumption [that] the placement of public employees on parochial school grounds inevitably results in the impermissible effect of state-sponsored indoctrination or constitutes a symbolic union between government and religion. In *Zobrest v. Catalina Foothills School Dist.*, 509 U.S. 1 (1993), we examined whether the IDEA, 20 U.S.C. § 1400 et seq., was constitutional as applied to a deaf student who sought to bring his state-employed sign-language interpreter with him to his Roman Catholic high school. We held that this was permissible [and refused] to presume that a publicly employed interpreter would be pressured by the pervasively sectarian surroundings to inculcate religion. . . . [W]e assumed [that] the interpreter would dutifully discharge her responsibilities as [a] public employee and comply with the ethical guidelines of her profession by accurately translating what was said. . . .

---

[23] 473 U.S. 373 (1985).

[24] *Agostini*, 521 U.S. at 204.

Second, [we] departed from the rule [that] all government aid that directly aids the educational function of religious schools is invalid. In *Witters v. Washington Dept. of Servs. for Blind*, 474 U.S. 481 (1986), we held that the Establishment Clause did not bar a State from issuing a vocational tuition grant to a blind person who wished to use the grant to attend a Christian college and become a pastor, missionary, or youth director. Even though the grant recipient [would] use the money to obtain religious education, [the] tuition grants were " 'made available generally without regard to the sectarian-nonsectarian, or public-non-public nature of the institution benefited.' " The grants were disbursed directly to students, who then used the money to pay for tuition at the educational institution of their choice. [A]ny money that ultimately went to religious institutions did so "only as a result of the genuinely independent and private choices of" individuals. The same logic applied in *Zobrest*, where we allowed the State to provide an interpreter, even though she would be a mouthpiece for religious instruction, because the IDEA's neutral eligibility criteria ensured that the interpreter's presence in a sectarian school was a "result of the private decision of individual parents" and "[could] not be attributed to state decision-making."

Because of the Court's shift in approach, the Court refused to assume that the Shared Time program (*Ball*) and New York City's Title I program (*Aguilar*) would have the effect of advancing religion through indoctrination. The Court found that there was "no reason to presume that, simply because she enters a parochial school classroom, a full-time public employee [will] depart from her assigned duties and instructions and embark on religious indoctrination." The Court also found that, simply because Title I teachers enter parochial school classrooms, there is no reason to assume that it will "create the impression of a 'symbolic union' between church and state.'

The Court then altered its approach to the third *Lemon* prong-the "excessive entanglement" prong. In *Aguilar*, the Court based its finding of "excessive" entanglement on three irrefutable assumptions: (1) governmental officials would need to engage in "pervasive monitoring" to ensure that Title I employees did not inculcate religion; (2) governmental officials and parochial schools would be forced to engage in "administrative cooperation"; and (3) the Title I program increased the dangers of "political divisiveness." *Agostini* held that the last two factors were "insufficient by themselves to create an 'excessive' entanglement. They are present no matter where Title I services are offered." The Court went on to reject the first assumption as well: "[W]e no longer presume that public employees will inculcate religion simply because they happen to be in a sectarian environment. Since we have abandoned the assumption that properly instructed public employees will fail to discharge their duties faithfully, we must also discard the assumption that pervasive monitoring of Title I teachers is required." The Court found that unannounced monthly visits of program supervisors would be sufficient to prevent Title I employees from engaging in inculcation of religion. Not only did the Court reject the assumptions of excessive entanglement, it clarified that an excessive entanglement is one which has the impermissible effect of establishing religion. Although not stated this way by the Court, entanglement becomes excessive when there is a merger of religion and the state. Symbiotic relationships, even when intertwined, are permissible; parasitic relationships are not.

As a result, the Court overruled both *Ball* and *Aguilar:* "[O]ur Establishment Clause jurisprudence has changed significantly since we decided *Ball and Aguilar.* . . . We therefore overrule *Ball and Aguilar* to the extent those decisions are inconsistent with our current understanding of the Establishment Clause."

Justice Souter dissented in part. He would have applied the so-called "endorsement" test: "The State is forbidden to subsidize religion directly and is just as surely forbidden to act in any way that could reasonably be viewed as religious endorsement. [These] principles were violated by the programs at issue in *Aguilar* and *Ball.* . . ." In addition, he expressed concern about the potentially broad nature of the Court's ruling. If the State could provide remedial education to parochial school students, then what prevented it from providing secular subjects to all students: "[If] a State may constitutionally enter the schools to [teach, it must be] free to assume [the] entire cost of instruction [in any] secular subject in any religious [school]."

[2] *Mitchell* and Neutrality

Just as the Court seemed to be coalescing around *Agostini's* modification of the *Lemon* test, the Court decided *Mitchell v. Helms*.[25] That decision was rendered by a plurality (Justice Thomas wrote an opinion that was joined by Chief Justice Rehnquist, and justices Scalia and Kennedy) that revived the concept of "neutrality," and overruled one prior decision and part of another decision (*Meek* and *Wolman*). The case involved Chapter 2 of the Education Consolidation and Improvement Act of 1981 which provided federal funds "for the acquisition and use of instructional and educational materials, including library services and materials (including media materials), assessments, reference materials, computer software and hardware for instructional use, and other curricular materials." Participating private schools received aid based on the number of children enrolled in the school. Chapter 2 funds could "supplement," but could not supplant funds from non-Federal sources. The "services, materials, and equipment" provided to private schools must be "secular, neutral, and nonideological," and private schools could not acquire control of them.

In upholding the law, the plurality overruled *Meek* and *Wolman*, focusing on the concept of neutrality:

> [W]e have consistently turned to the principle of neutrality. [If] the religious, irreligious, and areligious are [all] eligible for governmental aid, no one would conclude that any indoctrination that any particular recipient conducts has been done at the behest of the government. [I]f the government, seeking to further some legitimate secular purpose, offers aid on the same terms, without regard to religion, to all who adequately further that purpose, then it is fair to say that any aid going to a religious recipient only has the effect of furthering that secular [purpose].

---

[25] 530 U.S. 793 (2000).

> [The] second primary criterion for determining the effect of governmental aid [focuses on] whether an aid program "define[s] its recipients by reference to religion." [W]hether the criteria for allocating the aid "creat[e] a financial incentive to undertake religious indoctrination." "This incentive is not present [where] the aid is allocated on the basis of neutral, secular criteria that neither favor nor disfavor religion, and is made available to both religious and secular beneficiaries on a nondiscriminatory [basis]." [S]imply because an aid program offers private schools, and thus religious schools, a benefit that they did not previously receive does not mean that the program, by reducing the cost of securing a religious education, creates [an] "incentive" for parents to choose such an education for their children. [A]ny aid will have some such [effect].

The plurality opinion rejected any distinction between "direct" and "indirect" aid to religion: "If aid to schools [is] neutrally available and, before reaching or benefiting any religious school, first passes through the hands (literally or figuratively) of numerous private citizens who are free to direct the aid elsewhere, the government has not provided any 'support of religion.' "

In rendering its decision, the plurality abandoned several distinctions made in prior cases. First, the plurality rejected the argument that any aid to religious schools must not be divertible to religious use: "[So] long as the governmental aid is not itself "unsuitable [because] of religious content," and "eligibility for aid is determined in a constitutionally permissible manner, any use of that aid to indoctrinate cannot be attributed to the government and is thus not of constitutional concern." Second, the Court held that a school could receive aid even though the school was "pervasively sectarian": "[T]here was a period when this factor mattered. [But] that period is one that the Court should regret. [The] pervasively sectarian recipient has not received any special favor, and it [is] bizarre that the Court would [reserve] special hostility for those who take their religion seriously."

Justice O'Connor, joined by Justice Breyer, concurring, rejected the "neutrality" test as a significant departure from precedent: "[W]e have never held that a government-aid program passes constitutional muster *solely* because of the neutral criteria it employs as a basis for distributing aid."[26] She agreed that *Meek* and *Wolman* had "created an inexplicable rift within our Establishment Clause jurisprudence concerning government aid to schools." "[C]omputers are now as necessary as were schoolbooks 30 years ago." Nevertheless, she would strike down any program in which aid "actually is, or has been, used for religious purposes."

Justice Souter, joined by Justices Stevens and Ginsburg, dissented arguing that the plurality's holding "breaks fundamentally with Establishment Clause principle." He noted that "[I]f we looked no further than evenhandedness, and failed to ask what activities the aid might support[,] religious schools could be blessed with government funding as massive as expenditures made for the benefit of their public school counterparts, and religious missions would thrive on public money." He complains that the plurality's test "appears to take evenhandedness neutrality [and] promote it to a single and sufficient test for [the] constitutionality of school [aid]."

---

[26] *Id.* at 798.

And he complained that the provided aid "was highly susceptible to unconstitutional use." "[Providing] governmental aid without effective safeguards against future diversion itself offends the Establishment Clause. [To] the plurality there is nothing wrong with aiding a school's religious mission; the only question is whether religious teaching obtains its tax support under a formally evenhanded criterion of [distribution]."

[3] *Agostini* and *Mitchell's* Impact

The decisions in *Agostini* and *Mitchell* have raised questions regarding the continuing vitality of a number of cases decided under the *Lemon* three-part test. Under *Mitchell's* "neutrality" test, and even under *Agostini's* modified three-part test, one can justify far more support to parochial schools. As a result, the following decisions have been drawn into question:

A. *Levitt v. Committee for Public Education*,[27] which struck down a New York law that provided reimbursement to church-sponsored schools for the expense of teacher-prepared testing because there were "no [means] available to assure that internally prepared tests are free of religious instruction."

B. *Wolman's* holding that a state may not pay for student field trips "to governmental, industrial, cultural, and scientific centers designed to enrich the secular studies of students" because such aid provided "impermissible direct aid to sectarian education" and created the potential for excessive entanglement.

C. *Committee for Public Education and Religious Liberty v. Nyquist*,[28] which held that New York may not provide direct money grants to nonpublic schools for the "maintenance and repair [of] school facilities and equipment to ensure the health, welfare and safety of enrolled pupils" because the law did not restrict payments to those expenditures related to the upkeep of facilities used exclusively for secular purposes.

The Court's approach to these issues can have far reaching implications. President George W. Bush has proposed to amend federal welfare laws to permit "charitable choice." This proposal would allow religious groups to receive government funds for anti-poverty initiatives such as job training, high school equivalency, English as a second language, nutrition programs, homes for unmarried mothers, and alcohol treatment. The program allows religious organizations to retain their identity by displaying religious symbols and using religious criteria in selecting employees. However, such organizations are precluded from actively proselytizing, as well as from discriminating against recipients of other faiths. Recipients who object to receiving services from a religious organization must be given the choice of receiving such services from secular providers. Under a strict interpretation of *Lemon*, this program might be viewed as unconstitutional. Under the more liberal approaches articulated in *Agostini* and *Mitchell*, a different result might obtain.

---

[27] 413 U.S. 472 (1973).

[28] 413 U.S. 756 (1973).

Because of the Court's more restrictive standing principles that the Court has applied in recent years, it has become more difficult for plaintiffs to challenge alleged establishments. In a series of recent decisions, the Court has narrowly construed the *Flast v. Cohen*[29] test which had expanded the scope of standing in religion cases. For example, in *Hein v. Freedom from Religion Foundation, Inc.*,[30] the Court rejected a challenge to President Bush's Faith-Based and Community Initiatives program that was brought on Establishment Clause grounds. The Court held that the plaintiff taxpayers could not show that their taxes would be increased by the program. Although they also tried to establish standing under *Flast*, the Court rejected the challenge because they were challenging an executive branch action rather than a congressional expenditure (as required under the *Flast* test).

Likewise, in *Arizona Christian School Tuition Organization v. Winn*,[31] the Court held that plaintiffs lacked standing to challenge an Arizona law that provided tax credits for contributions to school tuition organizations (STOs) who used these contributions to provide scholarships to students attending private schools, many of which were religious. The Court held that plaintiffs could not establish sufficient injury to allow them to challenge the law. They could not show that their taxes would increase because of the credit, and also could not establish standing under the *Flast* test because tax credits do not implicate governmental interests in sectarian activities in the same way as governmental spending: "A dissenter whose tax dollars are 'extracted and spent' knows that he has in some small measure been made to contribute to an establishment in violation of conscience." However, the Court viewed tax credits as different because a tax credit is not "tantamount to a religious tax or to a tithe and does not visit the injury identified in *Flast*."

In *Arizona Christian*, Justice Scalia, joined by Justice Thomas, concurred, arguing that: "*Flast* is an anomaly in our jurisprudence, irreconcilable with the Article III restrictions on federal judicial power that our opinions have established," and therefore should be overruled. Justice Kagan, joined by Justices Ginsburg, Breyer, and Sotomayor, also dissented, arguing that the Court has exercised jurisdiction over similar cases for more than four decades: "Today, the Court breaks from this precedent by refusing to hear taxpayers' claims that the government has unconstitutionally subsidized religion through its tax system." In addition, Justice Kagan rejected the distinction between appropriations and expenditures as essentially meaningless: "Cash grants and targeted tax breaks are means of accomplishing the same government objective — to provide financial support to select individuals or organizations." In her view, such payments are equally objectionable "whether that aid flows from the one form of subsidy or the other. Either way, the government has financed the religious activity."

In *Freedom From Religion Foundation Inc. v. Obama*,[32] the court held that plaintiffs lacked standing to challenge President Obama's decision to proclaim a National Day of Prayer.

---

[29] 392 U.S. 83 (1968).

[30] 551 U.S. 587 (2007).

[31] 131 S. Ct. 1436 (2011).

[32] 641 F.3d 803 (7th Cir. 2011).

Some have argued that many of these types of support should be permitted under the Court's Establishment Clause jurisprudence. For example, Professor Jesse Choper once argued that "governmental financial aid may be extended directly or indirectly to support parochial schools without violation of the Establishment Clause so long as such aid does not exceed the value of the secular educational service rendered by the school."[33]

§ 11.02 SCHOOL VOUCHERS

In recent years, school voucher programs have generated much litigation. Some politicians and educators argue that school choice provides a solution for dealing with problems in the nation's public schools. "School choice" is achieved by providing vouchers to the parents of students. The vouchers help enable those parents to choose where to send their children to school, be it a private, a public, or a parochial school. By introducing choice into the system, vouchers force schools to compete with each other, and hopefully lead to a better educational system.

Before finally resolving the voucher issue, the Court decided a number of cases involving tuition reimbursement schemes. For example, in *Committee for Public Education and Religious Liberty v. Nyquist*,[34] the Court struck down a New York law that provided partial tuition reimbursements and tax benefits to the parents of children attending elementary or secondary non-public schools. The Court applied the *Lemon* test, and concluded that both programs failed the "effect" test: "In the absence of an effective means of guaranteeing that the state aid derived from public funds will be used exclusively for secular, neutral, and nonideological purposes, [direct] aid in whatever form is invalid. [T]he effect of the aid is unmistakably to provide [financial] support for nonpublic, sectarian institutions." Justice Rehnquist, joined by Chief Justice Burger and Justice White, dissented: "The reimbursement and tax benefit plans [are] consistent with the principle of neutrality. [T]he impact, if any, on religious education from the aid granted is significantly diminished by the fact that the benefits go to the parents rather than to the institutions."

That same year, the Court decided *Sloan v. Lemon*.[35] Following the holding in *Lemon v. Kurtzman*, Pennsylvania enacted a new law, the "Parent Reimbursement Act for Nonpublic Education," which reimbursed parents for a portion of tuition expenses incurred at nonpublic schools. Qualifying parents were entitled to receive $75 for each dependent in an elementary school, and $150 for each dependent in a secondary school, unless that amount exceeded the amount of tuition actually paid. The legislation specifically precluded the administering authority from having any "direction, supervision or control over the policy determinations, personnel, curriculum, program of instruction [or] administration [of] any nonpublic school or schools." Nevertheless, the Court struck the law down: "[W]e find no constitutionally significant distinctions between this law and the one declared invalid [in *Nyquist*]."

---

[33] Professor Jesse H. Choper, *The Establishment Clause and Aid to Parochial Schools*, 56 CALIF. L. REV. 260, 265–66 (1968).

[34] 413 U.S. 756 (1973).

[35] 413 U.S. 825 (1973).

In 1983, in an opinion written by Justice Rehnquist, the Court decided *Mueller v. Allen*.[36] That case involved a Minnesota law that allowed taxpayers, in computing their state income tax, to deduct actual expenses incurred for the "tuition, textbooks and transportation" of dependents attending elementary or secondary schools. A deduction could not exceed $500 per dependent in grades K through six and $700 per dependent in grades seven through twelve.

In upholding the law, the Court applied *Lemon's* three-part test and relied on *Everson*. The Court emphasized that it had consistently rejected the argument that "any program which in some manner aids an institution with a religious affiliation" violates the Establishment Clause. The Court began by finding a "secular" purpose:

> [A] state's decision to defray the cost of educational expenses incurred by parents — regardless of the type of schools their children attend — evidences a purpose that is both secular and understandable. An educated populace is essential to the political and economic health of any community, and a state's efforts to assist parents in meeting the rising cost of educational expenses plainly serves this secular purpose of ensuring that the state's citizenry is [well-educated].

The Court also found that the "primary effect" of the program did not advance religion, noting that the educational deduction was "only one among many deductions — such as those for medical expenses, and charitable contributions — [and was designed to equalize] the tax burden of its citizens and [encourage] desirable expenditures for educational [purposes]." In addition, the deduction was allowed for educational expenses incurred by all parents, including those with children in public schools or non-sectarian private schools, and therefore involved "neutrally" provided state assistance to a broad spectrum of citizens. Finally, all aid to parochial schools came through individual parents, and the "numerous, private choices of individual parents of school-age children." The Court distinguished its prior decisions striking down state aid to parochial schools on the basis that they "involved the direct transmission of assistance from the state to the schools themselves." The Court found that indirect payments did not fit within the "historic purposes" of the establishment clause." In addition, the Court noted that private schools make "special contributions" to society because they provide "an educational alternative for millions of young Americans," as well as "wholesome competition" for the public schools, and "they relieve substantially the tax burden incident to the operation of public schools." As a result, the Court viewed the aid as "rough return for the benefits [provided] to the state and all taxpayers by parents sending their children to parochial schools." The Court also found that there was no "excessive entanglement" because aid was given to the church as a result of individual decisions.

Justice Marshall, joined by justices Brennan, Blackmun, and Stevens, dissented arguing that the " Establishment Clause [prohibits] a State from subsidizing religious education, whether it does so directly or indirectly," and noting that "[t]he vast majority of the taxpayers [eligible] to receive the benefit are parents whose children attend religious schools." He argued that even indirect aid is impermissible

---

[36]   463 U.S. 388 (1983).

because it does not "guarantee the separation between secular and religious educational functions [and] ensure that State financial aid supports only the former." He believed that the law provides parents with a financial "incentive to parents to send their children to sectarian schools."

In *Zelman v. Simmons-Harris*,[37] the Court directly confronted the constitutionality of Cleveland, Ohio's, school voucher program. The Cleveland City School District had 75,000 children, the majority of which qualified as low-income or minority, and the District was "among the worst performing public schools in the Nation." The district was so bad that a federal court had found a "crisis of magnitude" and placed the district under state control. The district had failed to satisfy any of 18 state standards for "minimal acceptable performance," only 1 in 10 ninth graders could pass a "basic proficiency examination," and more than two-thirds of high school students dropped out before graduation. "Of those students who managed to reach their senior year, one of every four still failed to graduate. Of those students who did graduate, few could read, write, or compute at levels comparable to their counterparts in other cities."

To deal with the situation, the State of Ohio adopted its Pilot Project Scholarship Program to provide "financial assistance to families in any Ohio school district that is or has been 'under federal court order requiring supervision and operational management of the district by the state superintendent.'" Cleveland was the only Ohio school district to meet the qualification. The program provided two basic kinds of assistance to parents of children in a covered district: tuition aid for students in kindergarten through third grade, expanding each year through eighth grade, to attend a participating public or private school of their parent's choosing; and tutorial aid for students who choose to remain enrolled in public school. The tuition aid program was designed to provide educational choices to parents who reside in a covered district. All private schools, whether religious or nonreligious, were allowed to participate in the program provided that they were located within the boundaries of a covered district and met statewide educational standards. Participating private schools were required to agree not to discriminate on the basis of race, religion, or ethnic background, or to 'advocate or foster unlawful behavior or teach hatred of any person or group on the basis of race, ethnicity, national origin, or religion.'" Public schools located in a district adjacent to a covered district were also allowed to participate in the program and could receive a $2,250 tuition grant for each student accepted in addition to the full per-pupil state funding attributable to each additional student.

Tuition aid was distributed according to financial need. Families with incomes below 200% of the poverty line were given priority and were eligible to receive 90% of private school tuition up to $2,250. For the lowest-income families, participating private schools could not charge a parental co-payment greater than $250. For all other families, the program paid 75% of tuition costs, up to $1,875, with no co-payment cap. These families received tuition aid only if the number of available scholarships exceeded the number of low-income children who chose to participate. Where tuition aid was spent depended solely parental decisions regarding where to enroll their children. If parents chose a private school, checks were made payable

---

[37] 536 U.S. 639 (2002).

to the parents who then endorsed the checks over to the chosen school. The tutorial aid portion of the program provided tutorial assistance through grants to students who chose to remain in public school. During the 1999–2000 school year, 56 private schools participated in the program, 46 (or 82%) of which had a religious affiliation. None of the public schools in districts adjacent to Cleveland elected to participate. More than 3,700 students participated in the scholarship program, most of whom (96%) enrolled in religiously affiliated schools. Sixty percent of these students were from families at or below the poverty line. In the 1998–1999 school year, approximately 1,400 Cleveland public school students received tutorial aid. The goal of the program was to enhance the educational options of Cleveland's schoolchildren.

The program included community and magnet schools. Community schools were funded by the state but were run by independent school boards with the authority to hire their own teachers and determine their own curriculum. During the 1999–2000 school year, there were 10 new community schools in Cleveland with more than 1,900 students. Community schools received state funding of $4,518 per student, twice the funding provided under the tuition assistance program. Magnet schools were public schools that emphasized a particular subject area, teaching method, or service to students. The state provided $7,746 for each student enrolled in a magnet school. In 1999, Cleveland parents were able to choose from among 23 magnet schools that enrolled more than 13,000 students in kindergarten through eighth grade. These schools provided specialized teaching methods, such as Montessori, or a particularized curriculum focus, such as foreign language, computers, or the arts.

In an opinion by Justice Rehnquist, the Court upheld the tuition assistance (voucher) program against an Establishment Clause challenge. The Court found a secular purpose behind the program: "providing educational assistance to poor children in a demonstrably failing public school system." The Court then focused on whether the program had the "forbidden 'effect' of advancing or inhibiting religion." The Court drew a clear line of distinction between "government programs that provide aid directly to religious schools and programs," on the one hand, and programs involving "true private choice" under "which government aid reaches religious schools only as a result of the genuine and independent choices of private individuals." The Court found that such private choice programs were less constitutionally objectionable because government aid reaches religious institutions only because of the "deliberate choices of numerous individual recipients." Even though the aid may help the school advance its religious mission, any "perceived endorsement of a religious message" is reasonably attributable to the individual recipient, not to the government, whose role ends with the disbursement of benefits." As a result, the Court found that the Cleveland program did not have the impermissible "effect" of advancing religion:

> [The] Ohio program is neutral in all respects toward religion. It is part of a general and multifaceted undertaking by the State of Ohio to provide educational opportunities to the children of a failed school district. It confers educational assistance directly to a broad class of individuals defined without reference to religion . . . . The program permits the participation of *all* schools within the district, religious or nonreligious. Adjacent public schools also may participate and have a financial incentive

to do so. Program benefits are available to participating families on neutral terms, with no reference to religion. The only preference stated any-where in the program is a preference for low-income families, who receive greater assistance and are given priority for admission at participating schools.

There are no "financial incentive[s]" that "ske[w]" the program toward religious schools. [Aid] is allocated on the basis of neutral, secular criteria that neither favor nor disfavor religion, and is made available to both religious and secular beneficiaries on a nondiscriminatory basis." The program [in fact] creates financial *dis* incentives for religious schools, with private schools receiving only half the government assistance given to community schools and one-third the assistance given to magnet schools. Adjacent public schools, should any choose to accept program students, are also eligible to receive two to three times the state funding of a private religious school. Families too have a financial disincentive to choose a private religious school over other schools. Parents that choose [to] enroll their children in a private school (religious or nonreligious) must copay a portion of the school's tuition. Families that choose a community school, magnet school, or traditional public school pay nothing. Although such features of the program are not necessary to its constitutionality, they clearly dispel the claim that the program "[creates] financial incentive[s] for parents to choose a sectarian school."

The Court specifically rejected the argument that the Cleveland program created a "public perception that the State is endorsing religious practices and beliefs." The Court found that "no reasonable observer" would perceive that "a neutral program of private choice, where state aid reaches religious schools solely as a result of the numerous independent decisions of private individuals, carries with it the *imprimatur* of government endorsement." In addition, the Court found that " 'the reasonable observer in the endorsement inquiry must be deemed aware' of the 'history and context' underlying a challenged program. Any objective observer familiar with the full history and context of the Ohio program would reasonably view it as one aspect of a broader undertaking to assist poor children in failed schools, not as an endorsement of religious schooling in general."

The Court placed particular emphasized that the program provided a "range" of educational choices to Cleveland children. They could remain in public schools with publicly funded tutoring aid, could obtain a scholarship and choose a religious school, obtain a scholarship and choose a nonreligious private school, enroll in a community school, or enroll in a magnet school. The Court refused to place much emphasis on the fact that 46 of the 56 private schools that participated in the program were religious schools because the state did not coerce parents into sending their children to religious schools. Even though a significant percentage of parents enrolled their children in religious schools, the Court noted that "Cleveland's preponderance of religiously affiliated private schools certainly did not arise as a result of the program," and that 81% of private schools in Ohio are religious schools. The Court refused to attribute "constitutional significance" to these facts, noting that to do so might lead to the absurd result that a neutral school-choice program might be permissible in some parts of Ohio, such as Columbus, where a lower percentage of private schools are religious schools, but not in inner-city Cleveland, where Ohio has deemed such programs most sorely needed, but where the preponderance of religious schools happens to be greater.

In addition, "an identical private choice program might be constitutional in some States, such as Maine or Utah, where less than 45% of private schools are religious schools, but not in other States, such as Nebraska or Kansas, where over 90% of private schools are religious schools."

The Court also refused to attach significance to the fact that 96% of the students enrolled in the tuition assistance program attended religious schools:

> The constitutionality of a neutral educational aid program simply does not turn on whether and why, in a particular area, at a particular time, most private schools are run by religious organizations, or most recipients choose to use the aid at a religious school. As we said in *Mueller*, "[s]uch an approach would scarcely provide the certainty that this field stands in need of, nor can we perceive principled standards by which such statistical evidence might be evaluated."

The Court went on to note that 1,900 Cleveland children enrolled in alternative community schools, 13,000 children enrolled in alternative magnet schools, and 1,400 children enrolled in traditional public schools with tutorial assistance. When the Court considered these children in the calculations, it found that "the percentage enrolled in religious schools dropped from 96% to under 20%." In fact, the proportion of students attending non-religious private schools had been higher during prior years and increased "due only to the fact that two private nonreligious schools had converted to community school status."

In the final analysis, the Court found that the Ohio program was

> entirely neutral with respect to religion. It provides benefits directly to a wide spectrum of individuals, defined only by financial need and residence in a particular school district. It permits such individuals to exercise genuine choice among options public and private, secular and religious. The program is therefore a program of true private choice. In keeping with an unbroken line of decisions rejecting challenges to similar programs, we hold that the program does not offend the Establishment Clause.

The case produced a plethora of concurring and dissenting opinions. Justice O'Connor concurred on the basis that, although the Cleveland program involved more than $8 million in public funds, "it pales in comparison to the amount of funds that federal, state, and local governments already provide religious institutions." She observed that religious organizations can qualify for tax exemptions, including income tax and property tax exemptions, and individuals who contribute to them also receive tax deductions for their contributions. In addition, many governments provide tax credits for education expenses, including expenses incurred at religious schools. Moreover, most of these funds reach religious institutions without any restrictions on how they are used. In addition, religious hospitals receive a substantial amount of federal aid through Medicaid and Medicare. As a result, she concluded that "the support that the Cleveland voucher program provides religious institutions is neither substantial nor atypical of existing government programs[, and it] places in broader perspective alarmist claims about implications of the Cleveland program and the Court's decision in these cases." She went on to emphasize that the program was "neutral" towards religion, and that financial aid reaches religious schools only "as a result of true private [choice]."

Justice Thomas also concurred, arguing that "failing urban public schools disproportionately affect minority children most in need of educational opportunity." He noted that many "blacks and other minorities now support school choice programs because they provide the greatest educational opportunities for their children in struggling communities. [If] society cannot end racial discrimination, at least it can arm minorities with the education to defend themselves from some of discrimination's [effects]."

Justice Stevens dissented.

[I] am convinced that the Court's decision is profoundly misguided. [I]n reaching that conclusion I have been influenced by my understanding of the impact of religious strife on the decisions of our forbears to migrate to this continent. [Whenever] we remove a brick from the wall that was designed to separate religion and government, we increase the risk of religious strife and weaken the foundation of our democracy.

Justice Souter also dissented arguing that, in the city of Cleveland the overwhelming proportion of large appropriations for voucher money must be spent on religious schools if it is to be spent at all, and will be spent in amounts that cover almost all of tuition. The money will thus pay for eligible students' instruction not only in secular subjects but in religion as well, in schools that can fairly be characterized as founded to teach religious doctrine and to imbue teaching in all subjects with a religious dimension.

In addition, he felt that the Court had significantly departed from prior precedent, and he raised particular concerns about the concept of "neutrality," arguing that "neutrality has never been deemed sufficient, in and of itself, to justify a program under the Establishment Clause." He believed that neutrality could be used to refer to "evenhandedness in setting eligibility as between potential religious and secular recipients of public [money]," but he viewed the Rehqnuist opinion as adopting a very different view of neutrality: "The majority looks not to the provisions for tuition vouchers, but to every provision for educational opportunity. [If] regular, public schools (which can get no voucher payments) "participate" in a voucher scheme with schools that can, and public expenditure is still predominantly on public schools, then the majority's reasoning would find neutrality in a scheme of vouchers available for private tuition in districts with no secular private schools at all."

In addition, he expressed concern that the program was "influencing choices" in a way that favored religion. He noted that 43 of the 46 private schools that accepted voucher students were religious schools, and that 96.6% of all voucher recipients attended religious schools. Moreover, nearly two-thirds of all children attended religious schools of a different religion than their own, and they had done so in order to obtain educational opportunity. He argued that the $2,500 on tuition for participating low-income pupils curtails participation of nonreligious schools who charged higher tuition, but who would not take more than a small number of voucher students.

Justice Souter also expressed other concerns that the Cleveland program involved aid on a previously unprecedented scale "both in the number of dollars and in the proportion of systemic school expenditure supported." He went on to argue that "every objective underlying the prohibition of religious establishment is betrayed by this scheme." He noted that "Madison's objection to three pence has simply been lost in the majority's formalism." He noted the program it also violated the second objective "to save religion from its own corruption." He noted that participating schools were prohibited from discriminating on the basis of religion, meaning that "the school may not give admission preferences to children who are members of the patron faith; children of a parish are generally consigned to the same admission lotteries as non-believers." It might also be prohibited from discriminating in the hiring of teachers and principals.

> [I]t is well to remember that the money has barely begun to flow. [R]eligious schools in Ohio are on the way to becoming bigger businesses with budgets enhanced to fit their new stream of tax-raised income. [When] government aid goes up, so does reliance on it; the only thing likely to go down is independence. [I]s there reason to wonder when dependence will become great enough to give the State of Ohio an effective veto over basic decisions on the content of curriculums?

He noted that the third concern is the likelihood of an increase in social conflict. "Not all taxpaying Protestant citizens, for example, will be content to underwrite the teaching of the Roman Catholic Church condemning the death penalty. Nor will all of America's Muslims acquiesce in paying for the endorsement of the religious Zionism taught in many religious Jewish schools, which combines 'a nationalistic sentiment' in support of Israel with a 'deeply religious' element. Nor will every secular taxpayer be content to support Muslim views on differential treatment of the sexes, or, for that matter, to fund the espousal of a wife's obligation of obedience to her husband, presumably taught in any schools adopting the articles of faith of the Southern Baptist Convention."

Justice Breyer, joined by justices Stevens and Souter, also dissented noting that much of the Court's Establishment Clause jurisprudence had "focused directly upon social conflict, potentially created when government becomes involved in religious education." He argued that some of the restrictions on the program could lead to governmental meddling in religious affairs, including the requirement that no participating school "advocate or foster unlawful behavior or teach hatred of any person or group on the basis of race, ethnicity, national origin, or religion." He wondered how state officials would adjudicate claims that schools had violated these provisions. "Efforts to respond to these problems not only will seriously entangle church and state, but also will promote division among religious groups, as one group or another fears (often legitimately) that it will receive unfair treatment at the hands of the government." He also expressed concern about the degree of aid being given to religious schools.

In *Bush v. Holmes*,[38] the Florida Supreme Court struck down that state's voucher system as violative of other non-establishment based provisions of the Florida Constitution. The court held that the state constitution provides for a system of free public education to be provided through public schools, as well for a uniform system of public education, and that vouchers (allowing students to attend private schools) are inconsistent with that scheme.

§ 11.03 STATE SPONSORED PRAYER

May the government sponsor or promote prayer? There has been considerable litigation regarding this issue in a variety of contexts.

[A] In Public Schools

Beginning in the 1960s, litigation focused on the permissibility of prayer in public schools. In all these cases, the Court struck down school initiated prayer. The seminal decision was *Engel v. Vitale*,[39] an opinion written by Justice Black. A local board of education, acting in its official capacity under state law, prescribed a prayer to be said aloud by each class in the presence of a teacher at the beginning of each school day: "Almighty God, we acknowledge our dependence upon Thee, and we beg Thy blessings upon us, our parents, our teachers and our Country."

The Board adopted this procedure on the recommendation of the State Board of Regents which exercised broad supervisory power over New York's public school system. These state officials composed the prayer which they recommended and published as a part of their "Statement on Moral and Spiritual Training in the Schools," saying: "We believe that this Statement will be subscribed to by all men and women of good will, and we call upon all of them to aid in giving life to our program." The parents of ten students brought suit to challenge the prayer.

In striking down the law, the Court applied *the Lemon* test and concluded that the law had both a religious purpose and religious effect:

> [I]nvocation of God's blessings as prescribed in the Regents' prayer is a religious activity. It is a solemn avowal of divine faith and supplication for the blessings of the Almighty. [T]he constitutional prohibition against laws respecting an establishment of religion must at least mean that [it] is no part of the business of government to compose official prayers for any group [of] people to recite [as] part of a religious program carried on by government.

In rendering its decision, the Court placed great emphasis on the history of the Establishment Clause, noting that this "very practice of establishing governmentally composed prayers for religious services was one of the reasons which caused many of our early colonists to leave England and seek religious freedom in America." By the time that the First Amendment was adopted, many believed that "one of the greatest dangers to the freedom of the individual to worship in his own

---

[38] 919 So. 2d 392 (Fla. 2006).

[39] 370 U.S. 421 (1962).

way lay in the Government's placing its official stamp of approval upon one particular kind of prayer or one particular form of religious services." As a result, the Court concluded that the "government [is] without power to prescribe [any] particular form of prayer [to] be used as an official prayer [in] any program of governmentally sponsored religious activity." The Court went on to note that:

> There can be no doubt that New York's state prayer program officially establishes the religious beliefs embodied in the Regents' prayer. [Neither] the fact that the prayer may be denominationally neutral nor the fact that its observance on the part of the students is voluntary can serve to free it from the limitations of the Establishment Clause. [When] the power, prestige and financial support of government is placed behind a particular religious belief, the indirect coercive pressure upon religious minorities to conform to the prevailing officially approved religion is plain.

The Court went on to note that "a union of government and religion tends to destroy government and to degrade religion." Examining the "history of governmentally established religion," the Court observed that "whenever government had allied itself with one particular form of religion, the inevitable result had been that it had incurred the hatred, disrespect and even contempt of those who held contrary beliefs," and that "Religion is too personal, too sacred, too holy, to permit its 'unhallowed perversion' by a civil magistrate." Moreover, the Court observed that "governmentally established religions and religious persecutions go hand in hand." As a result, the Court concluded that it was "in large part to get completely away [from] systematic religious persecution that the Founders brought into being [our] Bill of Rights with its prohibition against any governmental establishment of religion." The Court rejected the idea that, by prohibiting the prayer, the Court was "anti-religious": "It is neither sacrilegious nor antireligious to say that [government] should stay out of the business of writing or sanctioning official prayers and leave that purely religious function to the people themselves and to those the people choose to look to for religious guidance."

Justice Stewart dissented, rejecting the idea that this prayer constituted an establishment of religion or the creation of an "official religion." He noted that the U.S. Supreme Court, itself, begins each day by invoking the protection of God, and that both the Senate and House of Representatives begin their daily sessions with prayer. He also noted that each of our Presidents had asked the protection and help of God, the Star-Spangled Banner (our official national anthem) contains religious verses, the Pledge of Allegiance refers to God, the President annual proclaims a day of prayer, and our coins contain the words "IN GOD WE TRUST." He concluded: "Countless similar examples could be listed, but there is no need to belabor the obvious. It was all summed up by this Court just ten years ago in a single sentence: " 'We are a religious people whose institutions presuppose a Supreme Being.' *Zorach v. Clauson*, 343 U.S. 306, 313."

In *Engel's* wake, some tried to amend the Constitution to permit prayer in public schools. Recent proposals also would have authorized religious icons on government property, and the use of tax dollars to pay for parochial schools. Congressional proponents of the amendments claim that court rulings have "attacked and twisted and warped" the First Amendment, and stifled religious expression "right and left all over the country." So far, all proposals have failed to garner the two-thirds vote necessary for passage.

[B] Moment of Silence Laws

Following *Engel*, some states moved to adopt "moment of silence" laws. In *Wallace v. Jaffree*,[40] the Court confronted the validity of the Alabama law. In fact, Alabama passed three separate laws. The first, § 16-1-20, authorized a 1-minute period of silence in all public schools "for meditation." The second, § 16-1-20.1, authorized a period of silence "for meditation or voluntary prayer." The third, § 16-1-20.2, authorized teachers to lead "willing students" in a prescribed prayer to "Almighty God [the] Creator and Supreme Judge of the world." After the lower courts struck down §§ 16-1-20.2 and 16-1-20, the United States Supreme Court considered § 16-1-20.1 (the period of silence for "meditation or voluntary prayer").

The Court applied the *Lemon* test to the law and struck it down because of a religious purpose. The Court found that the law was prompted by a religious purpose because of statements made by the bill's sponsor, particularly his statement that his motive in sponsoring the law was to return voluntary prayer to the public schools. In addition, the state failed to offer any evidence of a secular purpose. The Court then compared the various laws that had been passed by the Alabama legislature and again found a religious purpose. The Court construed an earlier law authorizing students to "mediate" as permitting them to either meditate or pray. As a result, when the legislature passed a law authorizing meditation "or voluntary prayer," the Court found that the second law was enacted to convey the message that "the statute was enacted to convey a message of state endorsement and promotion of prayer." As a result, the Court concluded that the "addition of 'or voluntary prayer' indicated that the State intended to characterize prayer as a favored practice. Such an endorsement is not consistent with the established principle that the government must pursue a course of complete neutrality toward religion."

Justice O'Connor concurred, emphasizing that moment of silence statutes can be valid, and that children are free to pray during these moments. But she distinguished a state-sponsored moment of silence [from] state-sponsored vocal prayer or Bible reading: "[A] moment of silence is not inherently religious. [A] pupil who participates in a moment of silence need not compromise his or her beliefs. [A] student who objects to prayer is left to his or her own thoughts, and is not compelled to listen to the prayers or thoughts of [others]." Moreover, "a State does not necessarily endorse any activity that might occur during the period. Even if a statute specifies that a student may choose to pray silently during a quiet moment, the State has not thereby encouraged prayer over other specified alternatives." Of course, the state may endorse religion if teachers encourage children to use the time to pray. She felt that moment of silence laws should be evaluated on a case-by-case basis, considering "the history, language, and administration of a particular statute to determine whether it operates as an

---

[40] 472 U.S. 38 (1985).

endorsement of religion." She agreed that the Alabama law had a religious purpose:

> [If] we assume that the religious activity that Alabama seeks to protect is silent prayer, then it is difficult to discern any state-imposed burden on that activity that is lifted by [§ 16-1-20.1]. No law prevents a student who is so inclined from praying silently in public schools. Moreover, state law already provided a moment of silence to these appellees irrespective of § 16-1-20.1.

Chief Justice Burger dissented, noting that the Court opened its session with an invocation for Divine protection, and observing that it "makes no sense to say that Alabama has 'endorsed prayer' by merely enacting a new statute 'to specify expressly that voluntary prayer is *one* of the authorized activities during a moment of silence.' He went on to note that, rather than threatening religious liberty, the law "affirmatively furthers the values of religious freedom and tolerance that the Establishment Clause was designed to [protect]." Finally, the Chief Justice questioned whether the law was passed for religious reasons:

> [A]ll of the sponsor's statements relied upon [were] made after the legislature had passed the statute. [There] is not a shred of evidence that the legislature as a whole shared the sponsor's motive or [was] even aware of the sponsor's view of the bill when it was passed. The sole relevance of the sponsor's statements, therefore, is that they reflect the personal, subjective motives of a single legislator. No case [supports the] idea that post-enactment statements [are] relevant in determining the constitutionality of legislation.

Justice White also dissented, indicating that the Court would have upheld this moment of silence statute had there been no mention of prayer even though, had a student asked whether he could pray during that moment, "it is difficult to believe that the teacher could not answer in the affirmative." As a result, he would not have invalidated a statute that at the outset provided the legislative answer to the question "May I pray?" Justice Rehnquist also dissented arguing that the states are free to endorse prayer in the schools.

Wallace did not doom all moment of silence laws. A moment of silence law can be valid if it is enacted for a secular purpose (to solemnize the opening of the school day). The difficulty with the Alabama law was that there was evidence that the state adopted the law in question with the intent of returning prayer to the public schools. Of course, some states (those that mandated prayer in public schools prior to *Engel*) might have more difficulty establishing a secular purpose for their laws. But, even in these states, a moment of silence might be valid if it comes to the Court without the historical baggage that accompanied the Alabama law.

[C] Legislative Prayer

Engel was followed by the holding in *Marsh v. Chambers*,[41] which involved the Nebraska legislature's practice of beginning each day with a prayer led by a chaplain. The chaplain was chosen by the Executive Board of the Legislative Council and paid out of public funds. The Court upheld the practice pointing to the history of the Establishment Clause:

> [From] colonial times through the founding of the Republic and ever since, the practice of legislative prayer has coexisted with the principles of disestablishment and religious freedom. [The] Continental Congress, beginning in 1774, adopted the traditional procedure of opening its sessions with a prayer offered by a paid chaplain.

In rendering its decision, the Court recognized that "historical patterns" and practices cannot justify a concededly unconstitutional act. However, the Court viewed the historical evidence leading up to and immediately following the Constitution's adoption as shedding light on "what the draftsmen intended the Establishment Clause to mean" and "how they thought that Clause applied to the practice authorized by the First Congress." The Court concluded that it

> can hardly be thought that in the same week Members of the First Congress voted to appoint and to pay a Chaplain for each House and also voted to approve the draft of the First Amendment for submission to the States, they intended the Establishment Clause of the Amendment to forbid what they had just declared acceptable.

Mr. Justice Brennan dissented. Relying on the *Lemon* test, he argued that the " 'purpose' of legislative prayer is preeminently religious" and the " 'primary effect' of legislative prayer is also clearly religious." He went on to note that "[i]nvocations in Nebraska's legislative halls explicitly link religious belief and observance to the power and prestige of the State" and he concluded that

> [t]here can be no doubt that the practice of legislative prayer leads to excessive 'entanglement' between the State and religion. [T]he process of choosing a 'suitable' chaplain, [and] insuring that the chaplain limits himself or herself to 'suitable' prayers, involves precisely the sort of supervision that agencies of government should if at all possible avoid.

He was also concerned about the "divisive political potential."

The Court did not apply *Lemon* and subsequently it has characterized *Marsh* as an exception to *Lemon*. The extent of the exception, however, remains in doubt. The Court has not said whether *Marsh* permits prayers in all state legislatures, including the two created in the late 1950s, Hawaii and Alaska. Nor did the Court suggest whether the legislative exception applied to lesser legislative bodies such as city councils and county commissions. At least one federal circuit court has invalidated legislative prayer given by a school board.

---

[41] 463 U.S. 783 (1983).

[D]　Graduation Prayer

After *Marsh*, it was clear that the Court would uphold prayer in some contexts, but unclear whether school prayer would ever be constitutional. *Engel* made it clear that the Court would strike down state mandated prayers, especially when young, impressionable, children were involved. But what if teenagers or near adults were involved? That issue was squarely presented in *Lee v. Weisman*,[42] a case involving graduation prayer at middle schools and high schools.

In Providence, Rhode Island, public school principals were allowed to invite clergy to offer invocation and benediction prayers at middle school and high school graduation ceremonies. The prayers were supposed to be non-sectarian, and the clergy were given instructions about what not to say. In an opinion by Justice Kennedy, the Court held that the prayers ran afoul of the constitutional guarantee that "government may not coerce anyone to support or participate in religion or its exercise, or otherwise act in a way which 'establishes a [state] religion or religious faith, or tends to do so.' "

The opinion began by expressing concern about the potential for divisiveness and noted that this potential existed for a number of reasons, including the choice of the clergy member. The Court also expressed concern about the "guidelines" given to clergy: Harkening back to *Engel*, the Court noted that it is " '[no] part of the business of government to compose official prayers for any group [of] American people to recite as a part of a religious program carried on by government,' and that is what the school officials attempted to do." While the Court recognized that the guidelines constituted an effort to avoid sectarian prayers, it questioned whether the government had any business intruding in this area-even if the instructions constituted a good faith attempt to avoid sectarianism. "[The] question is not the good faith of the school in attempting to make the prayer acceptable to most persons, but the legitimacy of its undertaking that enterprise at all."

The Court rejected the notion that a "practice of nonsectarian prayer" had developed, or that it would be appropriate for the government to undertake the task of developing nonsectarian prayer:

> The First Amendment's Religion Clauses mean that religious beliefs and religious expression are too precious to [be] prescribed by the State. The design of the Constitution is that preservation and transmission of religious beliefs and worship is a responsibility and a choice committed to the private sphere, which itself is promised freedom to pursue that mission.

Indeed, the Religion Clauses were designed to "protect religion from government interference," and the Court expressed concern that this concern was particularly applicable when school officials try to monitor school prayer because their "effort to monitor prayer will be perceived by the students as inducing a participation they might otherwise reject."

The Court also rejected the idea that the prayer could be regarded as an accommodation of religion. "Psychology supports the [assumption] that adolescents

---

[42]　505 U.S. 577 (1992).

[are] susceptible to pressure from their peers towards conformity, and that the influence is strongest in matters of social convention. [T]he government may no more use social pressure to enforce orthodoxy than it may use more direct means." The Court was unpersuaded by the fact that attendance at graduation ceremonies was voluntary: "[T]o say a teenage student has a real choice not to attend her high school graduation is formalistic. [I]n our society and in our culture high school graduation is one of life's most significant occasions."

The Court distinguished *Marsh* noting that

> At a high school graduation, teachers and principals must and do retain a high degree of control over the precise contents of the program. . . . In this atmosphere the state-imposed character of an invocation and benediction by clergy selected by the school combine to make the prayer a state-sanctioned religious exercise in which the student was left with no alternative but to submit.

Justice Blackmun, joined by Justices Stevens and O'Connor, concurred:

> [W]hen the government 'compose[s] official prayers,' selects the member of the clergy to deliver the prayer, has the prayer delivered at a public school event that is planned, supervised and given by school officials, and pressures students to attend and participate in the prayer, there can be no doubt that the government is advancing and promoting religion. [I]t is not enough that the government restrain from compelling religious practices: It must not engage in them either.

Justice Souter, joined by justices Stevens and O'Connor, also concurred. He rejected the argument that the Establishment Clause should be read to prohibit "nonpreferential" state promotion of religion: "[T]he Establishment Clause forbids support for religion in general no less than support for one religion or some." "[Nor] does it solve the problem to say that the State should promote a 'diversity' of religious views; that position would necessarily compel the government and, inevitably, the courts to make wholly inappropriate judgments about the number of religions the State should sponsor and the relative frequency with which it should sponsor each."

Justice Souter also rejected the allegation that historical practices justified prayer in this context. In doing so, he was responding to the argument that, "because the early Presidents included religious messages in their inaugural and Thanksgiving Day addresses, the Framers could not have meant the Establishment Clause to forbid noncoercive state endorsement of religion." While granting that the Presidents issued religious messages, Justice Souter rejected their significance: "[T]hose practices prove, at best, that the Framers simply did not share a common understanding of the Establishment Clause, and, at worst, that they, like other politicians, could raise constitutional ideals one day and turn their backs on them the next."

Finally, Justice Souter rejected the argument that the omission of graduation prayer constituted a "burden" on the students' religious beliefs noting that they could "express their religious feelings about it before and after the ceremony. They may even organize a privately sponsored baccalaureate if they desire the company of likeminded students."

Justice Scalia, joined by three other justices (Rehnquist, White, and Thomas), dissented. He began by pointing to history: "[The] history and tradition of our Nation are replete with public ceremonies featuring prayers of thanksgiving and petition." He offered a number of examples:

> From our Nation's origin, prayer has been a prominent part of govern-mental ceremonies and proclamations. The Declaration of Independence, the document marking our birth as a separate people, "appeal[ed] to the Supreme Judge of the world for the rectitude of our intentions" and avowed "a firm reliance on the protection of divine Providence." In his first inaugural address, after swearing his oath of office on a Bible, George Washington deliberately made a prayer a part of his first official act as President. . . . Such supplications have been a characteristic feature of inaugural addresses ever since. . . .

He also noted that Thanksgiving Proclamations, which included the "religious theme of prayerful gratitude to God," have been issued "by almost every President," and that both Congress and the United States Supreme Court "have a long-established practice of prayer at public events." And he argued that there was a "specific tradition" of prayer at invocations and benedictions at public school graduation exercises.

Justice Scalia argued that students who do not wish to participate in a graduation prayer could simply sit in respectful silence: "Maintaining respect for the religious observances of others is a fundamental civic virtue that government (including the public schools) can and should cultivate." He noted that students are required to stand for the Pledge of Allegiance which includes a reference to God. He also noted that graduating high school students should be treated differently than other students: "[G]raduation [is] significant [because] it [is] associated with transition from adolescence to young adulthood. Many graduating seniors [are] old enough to vote. Why, then, does the Court treat them as though they were first-graders?" He concluded: "The narrow context of the present case involves a community's celebration of one of the milestones in its young citizens' lives, and it is a bold step for this Court to seek to banish from that occasion [the] expression of gratitude to God that a majority of the community wishes to make."

[E]   Prayer at Athletic Events

Is prayer permissible at public school athletic events? In *Santa Fe Independent School District v. Doe*,[43] a school district adopted a policy allowing non-denominational prayer at football games. Students were allowed to vote on whether to have the prayer, and to select the student who would give it. The Court struck down the policy applying the so-called "endorsement" test: "one of the relevant questions is 'whether an objective observer' [would] perceive it as a state endorsement of prayer in public schools." "[A]n objective Santa Fe High School

---

[43] 530 U.S. 290 (2000).

student will unquestionably perceive the inevitable pregame prayer as stamped with her school's seal of approval." The Court went on to note that the election system was invalid: "fundamental rights may not be submitted to vote; they depend on the outcome of no elections," and the election procedures contain insufficient safeguards for diverse student speech:

> The only type of message that is expressly endorsed in the text is an "invocation" — a term that primarily describes an appeal for divine assistance. [T]he invocation is then delivered to a large audience assembled as part of a regularly scheduled, school-sponsored function conducted on school property.

Chief Justice Rehnquist, joined by Justices Scalia and Thomas, dissented:

> [T]he policy itself has plausible secular purposes: '[T]o solemnize the event, to promote good sportsmanship and student safety, and to establish the appropriate environment for the competition.' Where a governmental body 'expresses a plausible secular purpose' for an enactment, 'courts should generally defer to that stated intent.' The Court grants no deference to — and appears openly hostile toward — the policy's stated purposes, and wastes no time in concluding that they are a [sham].

§ 11.04 CURRICULAR ISSUES

To what extent may schools include religious teachings in the public school curriculum?

[A] Bible Readings

School District of Abington Township v. Schempp[44] involved a Baltimore, Maryland, law that required the reading of a chapter in the Holy Bible and/or the use of the Lord's Prayer in public school classes. The case also involved a Pennsylvania law which required that "At least ten verses from the Holy Bible be read, without comment, at the opening of each public school on each school day." In Pennsylvania, at the Abington Senior High School, opening exercises were broadcast through a communications system, and were conducted under supervision of a teacher by students in the school's radio and television workshop. Each day, students would read ten verses of the Holy Bible followed by recitation of the Lord's Prayer. Other students were asked to stand and repeat the prayer in unison. The exercise closed with the flag salute and announcements. The students reading the Bible verses were allowed to select passages and read from any version they chose, although the school furnished only the King James version. During the program, students had actually used The King James, the Douay and the Revised Standard versions of the Bible, as well as the Jewish Holy Scriptures. The verses were not preceded by prefatory statements, no questions were asked or solicited, and no comments or explanations and no interpretations were given during the exercises. Students were allowed to absent themselves from the classroom or elect not to participate in the exercises. In schools not having an intercommunications

---

[44] 374 U.S. 203 (1963).

system the Bible reading and the recitation were conducted by the home-room teacher, who chose the verses and read them herself or had students read them.

Applying the *Lemon* test, the Court struck down both the Maryland and Pennsylvania practices. The Court began by noting the states' argument that the program had secular purposes — the promotion of moral values, the contradiction to the materialistic trends of our times, the perpetuation of our institutions and the teaching of literature — but concluded that the practice was inherently religious: "[E]ven if its purpose is not strictly religious, [the] place of the Bible as an instrument of religion cannot be gainsaid, and the State's recognition of the pervading religious character of the ceremony is evident from the rule's specific permission of the alternative use of the Catholic Douay version as well as the recent amendment permitting nonattendance at the exercises. None of these factors is consistent with the contention that the Bible [is] used either as an instrument for nonreligious moral inspiration or as a reference for the teaching of secular subjects."

An interesting aspect of the decision was the Court's discussion of the "secular humanism" issue. Over the years, some have argued that, because schools teach values and at the same time have banished prayer and religious teachings from the classrooms, that schools are essentially teaching a "religion of secular humanism." The Court rejected this argument. Although the Court recognized that "the Bible is worthy of study for its literary and historic qualities," and could be studied in a secular manner consistently with the First Amendment, it concluded that the religion clauses require "strict neutrality, neither aiding nor opposing religion." The concept of neutrality does not permit a State to require a religious exercise even with the consent of the majority of those affected.

Justice Douglas concurred: "Through the mechanism of the State, [all] people are being required to finance a religious exercise that only some of the people want and that violates the sensibilities of others." Justice Brennan also concurred. He noted that religious exercises at the beginning of the school day may produce a number of beneficial effects in that they might "[foster] harmony and tolerance among the pupils, enhancing the authority of the teacher, and inspiring better discipline." But he believed that the state could achieve these objective through non-religious means by using secular materials:

> [It] has not been shown that readings from the speeches and messages of great Americans, [or] from the documents of our heritage of liberty, daily recitation of the Pledge of Allegiance, or even the observance of a moment of reverent silence at the opening of class, may not adequately serve the solely secular purposes of the devotional activities without jeopardizing [either] religious liberties [or] the proper degree of separation [between] religion and government.

And he concluded: "[T]he State acts unconstitutionally if [it tries] to [attain] religious ends by religious means, or if it uses religious means to serve secular ends where secular means would suffice."

Justice Brennan also rejected the argument that the practices in question were unobjectionable because "they prefer no particular sect or sects at the expense of others." He believed that "any version of the Bible is inherently sectarian" and there are those "whose reverence for the Holy Scriptures demands private study or reflection and to whom public reading or recitation is sacrilegious." Finally, Justice Brennan found that exemptions from the school practice could not, themselves, validate the practice:

> [T]he availability of excusal or exemption simply has no relevance to the establishment question, if it is once found that these practices are essentially religious exercises designed at least in part to achieve religious aims through the use of public school facilities during the school day. [T]he State could not constitutionally require a student to profess publicly his disbelief as the prerequisite to the exercise of his constitutional right of abstention.

Justice Stewart dissented. He argued that the Court's holding creates a religion of "secular humanism":

> [A] compulsory state educational system so structures a child's life that if religious exercises are held to be an impermissible activity in schools, religion is placed at an artificial and state-created disadvantage. [P]ermission of such exercises for those who want them is necessary if the schools are truly to be neutral in the matter of religion. And a refusal to permit religious exercises thus is seen, not as the realization of state neutrality, but rather as the establishment of a religion of secularism, or at the least, as government support of the beliefs of those who think that religious exercises should be conducted only in private.

He also argued that the "dangers" inherent in governmental support of religion were absent given that the Bible verses were read without comment. "[Since any] teacher who does not wish to do so is free not to participate, it cannot [be] contended that some infinitesimal part of the salaries paid by the State are made contingent upon the performance of a religious function." In the final analysis, Justice Stewart viewed the practice as simply an "attempt by the State to accommodate those differences which the existence in our society of a variety of religious beliefs makes inevitable."

[B] Evolution

Whether evolution can be taught in the schools has also been a controversial issue. *Epperson v. Arkansas*,[45] involved the constitutionality of Arkansas' 1928 "anti-evolution" statute — a law that the Court described as passed during an upsurge of "fundamentalist" religious fervor of the 1920s. The statute was modeled on the famous 1925 Tennessee "monkey law" that was upheld by the Supreme Court in the celebrated Scopes case in 1927. The Arkansas law made it illegal for teachers in state-supported schools or universities "to teach the theory or doctrine that mankind ascended or descended from a lower order of animals," or "to adopt or use in any such institution a textbook that teaches" this theory. A violation of the law was punishable only as a misdemeanor, but could lead to dismissal of the

---

[45] 393 U.S. 97 (1968).

teacher. Susan Epperson, a biology teacher in Little Rock, challenged the law. Until the academic year 1965–1966, the official textbook for high school biology did not have a section on Darwinian Theory. In that year, the school adopted and prescribed a textbook which contained a chapter setting forth "the theory about the origin [of] man from a lower form of animal." The adoption of this new book presented Epperson with a dilemma. She was directed to use the textbook, and presumably to teach the "statutorily condemned chapter; but to do so would be a criminal offense and subject her to dismissal."

The Court began by recognizing that the State of Arkansas has the "undoubted right to prescribe the curriculum for its public schools," but noted that the state does not have "the right to prohibit, on pain of criminal penalty, the teaching of a scientific theory or doctrine where that prohibition is based upon reasons that violate the First Amendment." The Court found that the prohibition was religiously motivated and therefore invalid: "[T]here can be no doubt that Arkansas has sought to prevent its teachers from discussing the theory of evolution because it is contrary to the belief of some that the Book of Genesis must be the exclusive source of doctrine as to the origin of man." The Court concluded that the law was not neutral: "The law's effort was confined to an attempt to blot out a particular theory because of its supposed conflict with the Biblical account, literally read."

Mr. Justice Black concurred. He questioned whether the law was religiously motivated, and suggested that Arkansas may have thought

> it would be best to remove this controversial subject from its schools; there is no [reason why] a State [cannot] withdraw from its curriculum any subject deemed too emotional and controversial. [I]t is not for us to invalidate a statute because of our views that the 'motives' behind its passage were improper; it is simply too difficult to determine what those motives were.

Professor Jesse H. Choper, in his article, *The Religion Clauses of the First Amendment: Reconciling the Conflict*[46], has argued that the Court decided the case incorrectly. He argued that there was no evidence that religious beliefs were "coerced, compromised or influenced."

[C] Balanced Treatment of Creation Science

In *Edwards v. Aguillard*,[47] the Court was confronted by a Louisiana law that provided for the "Balanced Treatment for Creation-Science and Evolution-Science in Public School Instruction" Act ("Creationism Act" or "Act"). The Act forbade the teaching of the theory of evolution in public schools unless accompanied by instruction in "creation science." Schools were not required to teach either evolution or creation science. However, if they taught either theory, they were required to teach both. The statute defined "evolution" and "creation science" as "the scientific evidences for [creation or evolution] and inferences from those scientific evidences." The suit was brought by some parents of children attending

---

[46] 41 U. Pitt. L. Rev. 673, 687 (1980).

[47] 482 U.S. 578 (1987).

Louisiana public schools, Louisiana teachers, and religious leaders.

In striking down the law, the Court applied the *Lemon* test and emphasized that it "has been particularly vigilant in monitoring compliance with the Establishment Clause in elementary and secondary schools." The Court noted that families "entrust public schools with the education of their children" and are entitled to assume that "the classroom will not purposely be used to advance religious views that may conflict with the private beliefs of the student and his or her family." The Court went on to emphasize the "impressionable" nature of school-age children. So, the Court applied the *Lemon* test "[mindful] of the particular concerns that arise in the context of public elementary and secondary schools."

In applying that test, the Court focused on the purpose prong. The Court noted that, although it is normally deferential when a state articulates a secular purpose, the Act's stated purpose (academic freedom) was a sham. The Court understood the phrase "academic freedom" to mean that teachers could teach "what they will," and concluded that the Act "was not designed to further that goal." Indeed, the Court found that the purpose of the Act's sponsor was to "narrow the science curriculum": "During the legislative hearings, Senator Keith stated: 'My preference would be that neither [creationism nor evolution] be taught.'" And the Court found that the law did not grant teachers a freedom that they did not already have. Before the passage of the Act, there was no law that prohibited Louisiana public school teachers from teaching any scientific theory. Thus, the purpose was to restrict rather than to expand academic freedom.

The Court also found a religious purpose in that the law discriminated in favor of creation science and against evolution. The Act required that curriculum guides be developed and resource services be available for creation science, but did not require that guides or resource services for evolution. In addition, the law prohibited local school boards from discriminating against teachers who taught creation science, but provided no similar protections for teachers who taught evolution. So, the Court concluded: "If the Louisiana Legislature's purpose was solely to maximize the comprehensiveness and effectiveness of science instruction, it would have encouraged the teaching of all scientific theories about the origins of humankind. But under the Act's requirements, teachers who were once free to teach any and all facets of this subject are now unable to do so." So, the Court found that the "preeminent purpose of the Louisiana Legislature was clearly to advance the religious viewpoint that a supernatural being created humankind." The Court noted that the sponsor of the bill had emphasized his "disdain" for the theory of evolution which was contrary to his religious beliefs.

In conclusion, the Court did not rule out the possibility that a legislature could validly require "scientific critiques of prevailing scientific theories." The Court concluded that such an approach might be "validly done with the clear secular intent of enhancing the effectiveness of science instruction." But, in this case, the Court found that the same act done with a religious purpose was invalid.

Justice Scalia, joined by Chief Justice Rehnquist, dissented quarreling with the Court's treatment of the Act's purpose: "'[L]egislative purpose' [means] the 'actual' motives of those responsible for the challenged action." He noted that the "Balanced Treatment Act did not fly through the Louisiana Legislature on wings of fundamentalist religious fervor — which would be unlikely [since] only a small minority of the State's citizens belong to fundamentalist religious denominations." He noted that much support for the bill came from:

> [Senator Keith] himself and from scientists and [educators], many of whom enjoyed academic credentials that may [be] regarded as quite impressive. [T]heir testimony was devoted to lengthy, [and] seemingly expert scientific expositions on the origin of life. These scientific lectures touched [upon] biology, paleontology, genetics, astronomy, astrophysics, probability analysis, and biochemistry. The witnesses [assured] committee members that "[hundreds]" of highly respected, internationally renowned scientists believed in creation science. . . .

Indeed, the legislature showed that, although "creation science is educationally valuable and strictly scientific, it is now being censored from or misrepresented in the public schools. Teachers have been brainwashed by an entrenched scientific establishment composed almost exclusively of scientists to whom evolution is like a 'religion.' " The legislature found that the censorship resulted in two harmful effects:

> First, it deprives students of knowledge of one [scientific] explanation for the origin of life and leads them to believe that evolution is proven fact; thus, [they] are wrongly taught that science has proved their religious beliefs false. Second, it violates the Establishment Clause. The United States Supreme Court has held that secular humanism is a religion. Belief in evolution is a central tenet of that religion. Thus, by censoring creation science and instructing students that evolution is fact, public school teachers [are] advancing religion in violation of the Establishment Clause.

Justice Scalia also quarreled with the majority's determination that the stated secular purpose was a sham:

> Witness after witness urged the legislators to support the Act so that students would not be "indoctrinated" but would instead be free to decide for themselves, based upon a fair presentation of the scientific evidence, about the origin of life. [Other legislators] made only a few statements[,] but those statements cast no doubt upon the sincerity of [the] articulated purpose.

As Justice Scalia's dissent recognizes, some regard "secular humanism" as a bona fide religion, and believe that "evolution is the cornerstone of that religion." They argue that, by censoring creation science and instructing students that evolution theory is factually true, public school teachers are advancing religion in violation of the Establishment Clause. Manning, in his article *The Douglas Concept of God in Government*,[48] notes that the courts "forbid the teaching of recognized religions in our public schools and forbid a prayer which simply acknowledges the existence of God." However they also permit the "teaching of some code of ethical conduct, some system of value norms." He then asks whether, given all of these facts, "does not the system which the school then sponsors become the system of

---

[48] 39 Wash. L. Rev. 47, 63 (1964).

Secular Humanism or simply secular humanism? Do we not then prefer, in public education, one religion, Secular Humanism, over other religions which are founded upon a belief in the existence of God?"

[D] Intelligent Design

In recent years, there has been much litigation about whether public schools can incorporate "intelligent design" into their curricula. For example, *Kitzmiller v. Dover Area School District*,[49] involved a Pennsylvania school district resolution which provided that students should be "made aware of gaps/problems in Darwin's theory and of other theories of evolution, including, but not limited to, intelligent design." The resolution went on to state that students should be told the following: (1) that, while Darwin's theory of evolution is "not a fact," the Pennsylvania Academic Standards require that it be taught; (2) that a "theory is defined as a well-tested explanation that unifies a broad range of observation," and that intelligent design "is an explanation of the original of life that differs from Darwin's view"; and (3) that students should "keep an open mind" with respect to any theory and that such matters are left to the students and their families. Supporters of intelligent design argue that it is scientifically-based and can be legitimately included in public school curricular. Opponents argue that intelligent design represents nothing more than a back-door method for bringing creationism back into the public school curriculum, and is therefore religiously motivated and unconstitutional.

§ 11.05   OFFICIAL ACKNOWLEDGMENT

To what extent may government acknowledge the existence of religion in public ways?

[A]   The Ten Commandments

Stone v. Graham,[50] involved a Kentucky statute that required the posting of a copy of the Ten Commandments on the wall of each public classroom in the State. Applying the *Lemon* test, the United States Supreme Court struck down the law as religiously motivated. The Commonwealth argued that the law was supported by a secular purpose: "The secular application of the Ten Commandments is clearly seen in its adoption as the fundamental legal code of Western Civilization and the Common Law of the United States." Ky. Rev. Stat. § 158.178 (1980). The Court rejected this articulation of purpose, noting that the "pre-eminent purpose for posting the Ten Commandments on schoolroom walls is plainly religious in nature. The Ten Commandments are [a] sacred text in the Jewish and Christian faiths, and no legislative recitation of a supposed secular purpose can blind us to that fact." Moreover,

> The Commandments do not confine themselves to arguably secular mat-
> ters, such as honoring one's parents, killing or murder, adultery, stealing,

---

[49] 400 F. Supp. 2d 707 (M.D. Pa. 2005).

[50] 449 U.S. 39 (1980).

false witness, and covetousness. Rather, the first part of the Command-ments concerns the religious duties of believers: worshipping the Lord God alone, avoiding idolatry, not using the Lord's name in vain, and observing the Sabbath Day.

The fact that the posting of the Ten Commandments was financed by voluntary contributions was deemed to be irrelevant.

In dicta, the Court indicated that the Ten Commandments need not be completely barred from the public schools. On the contrary, they could be "integrated into the school curriculum, where the Bible may constitutionally be used in an appropriate study of history, civilization, ethics, comparative religion, or the like." However, the Court concluded that it was inappropriate to post the Ten Commandments in such a way as "to induce the schoolchildren to read, meditate upon, perhaps to venerate and obey, the Commandments." The Court perceived that such postings serve no educational function.

Four justices dissented including Chief Justice Burger and justices Blackmun and Stewart. Justice Rhenquist also dissented arguing that the Court should have deferred to the state's articulated secular purpose. Although he conceded that the Commandments are "a sacred text," he noted that they "have had a significant impact on the development of secular legal codes of the Western World." He found no objection to posting the Ten Commandments in public schools under the right conditions: "[The] State was permitted to conclude that a document with such secular significance should be placed before its students, with an appropriate statement of the document's secular import." He went on to argue that the Establishment Clause does not "require that the public sector be insulated from all things which may have a religious significance or origin." Indeed, religion "has been closely identified with our history and government," [and] "[t]he history of man is inseparable from the history of religion."

In recent years, there has been much additional litigation regarding the constitutionality of Ten Commandments displays. In the State of Alabama, Alabama Supreme Court Chief Justice Moore decided to have a 5,280 pound Ten Command-ments monument created and displayed at the Alabama Supreme Court. Justice Moore was religiously motivated, viewing the Ten Commandments as a primary source underlying the law. When a federal court held that the display violated the First Amendment, Chief Justice Moore defiantly refused to remove it. Faced with contempt fines of $5,000 per day for each day the display remained, the other justices overruled Chief Justice Moore and ordered the monument removed. In November, 2003, Justice Moore was removed from the Alabama Supreme Court by an ethics panel for having "placed himself above the law." After the removal, he stated that "I have absolutely no regrets."

In 2005, two cases were presented to the United States Supreme Court regarding the constitutionality of Ten Commandments displays. The first case, *Van Orden v. Perry*,[51] involved a Ten Commandments display on the grounds of the Texas State Capitol. The display was one of 17 monuments and 21 historical markers on the twenty-two acre grounds that commemorated the "people, ideals,

---

[51] 545 U.S. 677 (2005).

and events that compose Texan identity." Included among the monuments and markers were displays entitled Heroes of the Alamo, Hood's Brigade, Confederate Soldiers, Volunteer Fireman, Terry's Texas Rangers, Texas Cowboy, Spanish-American War, Texas National Guard, Tribute to Texas School Children, Texas Pioneer Woman, The Boy Scouts' Statue of Liberty Replica, Pearl Harbor Veterans, Korean War Veterans, Soldiers of World War I, Disabled Veterans, and Texas Peace Officers.

The Ten Commandments display was large (6' high and 3' wide) and was located between the Capitol building and the Supreme Court building. The display included the text of the Ten Commandments, an eagle grasping the American flag, an eye inside of a pyramid, and two small tablets with what appeared to be ancient script carved above the text of the Ten Commandments. Below the text were two Stars of David and the superimposed Greek letters Chi and Rho, which represent Christ. The bottom of the monument bore the inscription "PRESENTED TO THE PEOPLE AND YOUTH OF TEXAS BY THE FRATERNAL ORDER OF EAGLES OF TEXAS 1961" in recognition of the fact that the Fraternal Order of Eagles, a national social, civic, and patriotic organization, gave the display to the state. The State selected the site for the monument based on the recommendation of the state organization responsible for maintaining the Capitol grounds. The Eagles paid the cost of erecting the monument, the dedication of which was presided over by two state legislators.

The Texas Ten Commandments monument was challenged by Van Orden, a native Texan and a resident of Austin. Van Orden testified that he had encountered the Ten Commandments monument for years during his frequent visits to the Capitol grounds to use the law library in the Supreme Court building. Forty years after the display was erected, he brought suit challenging the display as a violation of the Establishment Clause.

In upholding the display, a plurality of the Court (Justice Rehnquist, joined by justices Scalia, Kennedy and Thomas) concluded that the Court's precedent regarding the Establishment Clause points "Janus-like" in opposite directions. One face recognizes and respects the strong role that religion and religious traditions have played in United States history. The other face recognizes that governmental intrusion into religious matters can endanger religious freedom. The plurality concluded that it was required to respect both faces of this tradition and that government must not "evince a hostility to religion by disabling the government from in some ways recognizing our religious heritage." Indeed, the plurality found that "When the state encourages religious instruction or cooperates with religious authorities by adjusting the schedule of public events to sectarian needs, it follows the best of our traditions. For it then respects the religious nature of our people and accommodates the public service to their spiritual needs. To hold that it may not would be to find in the Constitution a requirement that the government show a callous indifference to religious groups. [W]e find no constitutional requirement which makes it necessary for government to be hostile to religion and to throw its weight against efforts to widen the effective scope of religious influence."[52]

---

[52] *Id.* (*quoting* Zorach v. Clauson, 343 U.S. 306, 313–14 (1952)).

In support of its position, the plurality discussed evidence suggesting all three branches of the federal government had recognized religion from the beginning. For example, in 1789, both Houses of Congress passed resolutions urging President George Washington to issue a Thanksgiving Day Proclamation to "recommend to the people of the United States a day of public thanksgiving and prayer, to be observed by acknowledging, with grateful hearts, the many and signal favors of Almighty God." President Washington complied by issuing a proclamation which "attributed to the Supreme Being the foundations and successes of our young Nation." The plurality also recognized that the Court's own decisions had allowed a state legislature to open its daily sessions with a prayer by a state-paid chaplain on the basis that the practice of legislative prayer was "deeply embedded in the history and tradition of this country" and that "it would be incongruous to interpret [the Establishment Clause] as imposing more stringent First Amendment limits on the states than the draftsmen imposed on the Federal Government." In addition, the plurality noted that it had upheld laws prohibiting the sale of merchandise on Sunday.

In upholding the Texas display, the plurality began by taking note of the fact that such displays were common throughout the United States. Indeed, the United States Supreme Court itself contains a frieze of Moses holding two tablets that reveal portions of the Ten Commandments written in Hebrew, displayed along with other lawgivers. On the metal gates lining the courtroom, as well as on the doors, there is a representation of the decalogue. The plurality noted that there were similar depictions throughout Washington, D.C., including at the Great Reading Room and the rotunda of the Library of Congress' Jefferson Building, and that a medallion with two tablets depicting the Ten Commandments decorates the floor of the National Archives. Inside the Department of Justice, a statue entitled "The Spirit of Law" includes two tablets representing the Ten Commandments lying at its feet. Outside the federal courthouse in the District of Columbia, there is a 24-foot-tall sculpture, depicting, *inter alia*, the Ten Commandments and a cross. In addition, the Chamber of the United States House of Representatives prominently features Moses, and God is reflected in various monuments and buildings including the Washington, Jefferson, and Lincoln Memorials (with phrases such as "Laus Deo" ("Praise be to God"), and various Biblical citations). The plurality also acknowledged that its own decisions had recognized the importance of the decalogue.[53]

While the plurality acknowledged that the Ten Commandments have religious significance, it found that they have dual meaning since Moses was both a lawgiver and a religious leader. Although the plurality recognized that there are limits to the extent to which the state may display religious messages or displays, it concluded that the mere fact that a display or monument contains "religious content or [promotes] a message consistent with a religious doctrine does not run afoul of the Establishment Clause." As in *Stone v. Graham*, a display might be invalid if it has an "improper and plainly religious purpose," especially if displayed in an elementary or secondary school context where it would be viewed by impressionable children. But the plurality indicated that it would be more likely to sustain religious

---

[53] *See, e.g.,* McGowan v. Maryland, 366 U.S. at 442.

displays in legislative chambers or capitol grounds.

Applying these principles, the plurality regarded the Texas Ten Commandments display as a "far more passive use of those texts" than was the case in *Stone* where the text confronted elementary school students every day. In *Van Orden*, petitioner walked by the monument for a number of years before bringing the lawsuit. In addition, the various monuments represented various strands in the State's political and legal history, and the plurality concluded that inclusion of the Ten Commandments monument in this group had a dual significance, partaking of both religion and government.

Justice Scalia concurred in the decision, arguing that he would prefer to reach the same result "by adopting an Establishment Clause jurisprudence that is in accord with our Nation's past and present practices, and that can be consistently applied — the central relevant feature of which is that there is nothing unconstitutional in a State's favoring religion generally, honoring God through public prayer and acknowledgment, or, in a nonproselytizing manner, venerating the Ten Commandments." Justice Thomas concurred, arguing that the Establishment Clause should not be regarded as incorporated and applied to the states. Even if it is incorporated, he argued that the concept of establishment included only coercive actions (e.g., mandatory observance of religious practices or mandatory payment of taxes supporting ministers), and that the Texas monument did not compel Van Orden to do anything. Van Orden's alleged injury — that he takes offense at seeing the monument — he regarded as insufficient.

Justice Breyer's concurrence argued that the religion clauses seek to "assure the fullest possible scope of religious liberty and tolerance for all," and to "avoid that divisiveness based upon religion that promotes social conflict, sapping the strength of government and religion alike." However, he concluded that these goals require that government must "neither engage in nor compel religious practices," must "effect no favoritism among sects or between religion and nonreligion," and must deter no religious belief. Nevertheless, he concluded that the Establishment Clause does not "compel the government to purge from the public sphere all that in any way partakes of the religious, especially one like the decalogue that also conveys a secular moral message about proper standards of social conduct, and a historical message about the relationship between those standards and the law." He noted that the decalogue wad displayed in courthouses throughout the nation because of these secular messages, and concluded that the monument's 40-year history on the Texas state grounds indicates that it has had secular effect there. "The display is not on the grounds of a public school, where, given the impressionability of the young, government must exercise particular care in separating church and state." In addition, he emphasized that the display was not motivated by religious objectives.

Justice Stevens, joined by Justice Ginsburg, dissented, arguing that the Establishment Clause created a strong presumption against the display of religious symbols on public property because it risks offending non-members as well as adherents who find the display disrespectful. In his view, the Establishment Clause requires religious "neutrality" toward religion which means that government may not "constitutionally pass laws or impose requirements which aid all religions as against non-believers, and neither can aid those religions based on a belief in the existence of God as against those religions founded on different beliefs." Even though the Eagles were motivated by a desire to "inspire the youth" and curb juvenile delinquency, he felt that they were not allowed to achieve that objective through biblical teachings and thereby injecting "a religious purpose into an otherwise secular endeavor." Finally, he concluded that the Texas display was not only religious, but sectarian, because the Texas display includes a version of the decalogue adopted by one religion.

Justice O'Connor also dissented, arguing that an obviously religious display is inconsistent with the requirement of neutrality. "The monument's presentation of the Commandments with religious text emphasized and enhanced stands in contrast to any number of perfectly constitutional depictions of them, the frieze of our own Courtroom providing a good example, where the figure of Moses stands among history's great lawgivers. While Moses holds the tablets of the Commandments showing some Hebrew text, no one looking at the lines of figures in marble relief is likely to see a religious purpose behind the assemblage or take away a religious message from it." She concluded that government may recognize the historical influence of the decalogue on our legal system "so long as there is a context and that context is historical. Hence, a display of the Commandments accompanied by an exposition of how they have influenced modern law would most likely be constitutionally unobjectionable. And the Decalogue could, as *Stone* suggested, be integrated constitutionally into a course of study in public schools. Seventeen monuments with no common appearance, history, or esthetic role scattered over 22 acres is not a museum, and anyone strolling around the lawn would surely take each memorial on its own terms." "If neutrality in religion means something, any citizen should be able to visit that civic home without having to confront religious expressions clearly meant to convey an official religious position that may be at odds with his own religion, or with rejection of religion."

On the same day that *Van Orden* was decided, the Court also handed down its decision in *McCreary County v. American Civil Liberties Union of Kentucky*.[54] *McCreary County* involved Ten Commandments displays in two Kentucky courthouses. Both displays included the King James version of the Ten Commandments with a citation to the Book of Exodus. After the initial displays were challenged, the counties altered their displays, eventually posting a total of three different displays. In addition, the counties passed nearly identical resolutions attempting to establish a secular basis for the displays. The resolutions recited the fact that the Ten Commandments are "the precedent legal code upon which the civil and criminal codes [of] Kentucky are founded," and stated: that "the Ten Commandments are codified in Kentucky's civil and criminal laws"; that the Kentucky House of Representatives had in 1993 "voted unanimously [to adjourn] in remembrance and honor of Jesus Christ, the Prince of Ethics"; that the "County Judge [and] magistrates agree with the arguments set out by Judge [Roy] Moore" in defense of his "display [of] the Ten Commandments in his courtroom"; and that the "Founding Father[s] [had an] explicit understanding of the duty of elected officials to publicly acknowledge God as the source of America's strength and direction."

---

[54] 545 U.S. 844 (2005).

Although the initial display involved a large framed copy of the edited King James version of the Commandments, later displays included other documents in smaller frames with religious themes. The documents were the "endowed by their Creator" passage from the Declaration of Independence; the Preamble to the Constitution of Kentucky; the national motto, "In God We Trust"; a page from the Congressional Record proclaiming the Year of the Bible and including a statement of the Ten Commandments; a proclamation by President Abraham Lincoln designating April 30, 1863, a National Day of Prayer and Humiliation; an excerpt from President Lincoln's "Reply to Loyal Colored People of Baltimore upon Presentation of a Bible," reading that "[t]he Bible is the best gift God has ever given to man"; a proclamation by President Reagan marking 1983 the Year of the Bible; and the Mayflower Compact. Assembled with the Commandments were framed copies of the Magna Carta, the Declaration of Independence, the Bill of Rights, the lyrics of the Star Spangled Banner, the Mayflower Compact, the National Motto, the Preamble to the Kentucky Constitution, and a picture of Lady Justice.

The collection, eventually entitled "The Foundations of American Law and Government Display," came with a statement of historical and legal significance. The comment on the Ten Commandments read:

> The Ten Commandments have profoundly influenced the formation of Western legal thought and the formation of our country. That influence is clearly seen in the Declaration of Independence, which declared that 'We hold these truths to be self-evident, that all men are created equal, that they are endowed by their Creator with certain unalienable Rights, that among these are Life, Liberty, and the pursuit of Happiness.' The Ten Commandments provide the moral background of the Declaration of Independence and the foundation of our legal tradition.

The Counties offered various explanations for the new display, including a desire "to demonstrate that the Ten Commandments were part of the foundation of American Law and Government," and "to educate the citizens of the county regarding some of the documents that played a significant role in the foundation of our system of law and government."

Relying on its holding in *Stone v. Graham*, the Court distinguished *Van Orden* and struck down the displays. The Court noted that the second McCreary County display was distinguishable from the *Van Orden* display because of its "predominantly religious purpose" and lack of neutrality between religions and between religion and nonreligion. The Court felt that the display "sends [the] message [to] nonadherents that they are outsiders, not full members of the political community, and an accompanying message to adherents that they are insiders, favored [members]." The Court emphasized that the second of the county's displays had an "unstinting focus" on religious passages, and that the Ten Commandments were posted "precisely because of their sectarian content." The religious theme was reinforced by "serial religious references and the accompanying resolution's claim about the embodiment of ethics in Christ."

The Court concluded that even the third display was invalid even though it included secular documents. That display was arguably distinguishable from the prior two displays because it was titled the "Foundations of American Law and

Government" exhibit, and focused on documents thought especially significant in the historical foundation of American government. In erecting this third display the counties expressed a desire "to educate the citizens of the county regarding some of the documents that played a significant role in the foundation of our system of law and government." Although the Court accepted the proposition that a sacred text can be integrated into a constitutionally permissible governmental display on the subject of law, or American history, the Court concluded that a "reasonable observer" would not believe that the counties "had cast off the [religious] objective so unmistakable in the earlier displays." The Court distinguished the frieze displayed in the United States Supreme Court (depicting Moses along with 17 other lawgivers, most of whom are secular figures) on the basis that "there is no risk that Moses would strike an observer as evidence that the National Government was violating neutrality in religion."

Justice O'Connor concurred arguing that "the purpose behind the counties' display conveys an unmistakable message of endorsement to the reasonable observer." Justice Scalia, joined by Chief Justice Rehnquist and Justices Thomas and Kennedy, dissented, arguing that the Founding Fathers did not opt for a secular republic, but instead believed "that morality was essential to the well-being of society and that encouragement of religion was the best way to foster morality." Relying on his prior dissents, Scalia emphasized that President Washington had opened his Presidency with a prayer, that President John Adams had written to the Massachusetts Militia stating that "[o]ur Constitution was made only for a moral and religious people," that President Thomas Jefferson concluded his second inaugural address with an invitation to pray, and that President James Madison's first inaugural address expressed his confidence "in the guardianship and guidance of that Almighty Being whose power regulates the destiny of nations, whose blessings have been so conspicuously dispensed to this rising Republic, and to whom we are bound to address our devout gratitude for the past, as well as our fervent supplications and best hopes for the future." Based on this historical evidence, Justice Scalia asked how the Court could *possibly* assert that "the First Amendment mandates governmental neutrality [between] religion and nonreligion," and that "[m]anifesting a purpose to [favor] adherence to religion generally," is unconstitutional? Who says so? Surely not the words of the Constitution. Surely not the history and traditions that reflect our society's constant understanding of those words. Surely not even the current sense of our society."

Justice Scalia also argued that the Constitution permits acknowledgement of monotheism. "[I]t is entirely clear from our Nation's historical practices that the Establishment Clause permits this disregard of polytheists and believers in unconcerned deities, just as it permits the disregard of devout atheists." He noted that President George Washington's Thanksgiving Proclamation was monotheistic, and that the Court had sustained legislative prayer in the "Judeo-Christian tradition" because "there is no indication that the prayer opportunity has been exploited to proselytize or advance any one, or to disparage any other, faith or belief."

Because of this historical evidence, Justice Scalia sought to draw a distinction between the "acknowledgment of a single Creator and the establishment of a religion." And he suggested that to "any person who happened to walk down the hallway of the McCreary or Pulaski County Courthouse[,] the displays must have seemed unremarkable — if indeed they were noticed at all." He noted that the courthouse walls are filled with historical documents and other assorted portraits, that the Ten Commandments display was not particularly distinguishable from these other displays, and that the explanation for the decalogue display was not sectarian. Indeed, the explanation for the third display simply asserted that the display "contains documents that played a significant role in the foundation of our system of law and government."

Following the decisions in *Van Orden* and *McCreary County*, there was extensive litigation about Ten Commandments monuments located in other places. For example, in *Green v. Haskell County Board of Commissioners*,[55] the court concluded that a monument had the effect of endorsing religion. In that case, two of the three county commissioners who attended the unveiling made highly religious statements in support of the display (*e.g.*, "That's what we're trying to live by, that right there," "The good Lord died for me. I can stand for him. And I'm going to," "I'll stand up in front of that monument and if you bring a bulldozer up here you'll have to push me down with it."). By contrast, in *American Civil Liberties Union of Kentucky v. Grayson County*, 605 F.3d 426 (6th Cir. 2010), the court upheld a Ten Commandments display.

[B] Church Vetoes

In *Larkin v. Grendel's Den, Inc.*,[56] a Massachusetts law vested in the governing bodies of churches and schools the power to veto applications for liquor licenses within a five hundred foot radius of a church or school. The Court struck down the law. Although the Court recognized that schools and churches have an interest in being insulated from businesses that serve liquor, the Court found that the state had impermissibly delegated zoning power to a religious institution: "[T]he statute, by delegating a governmental power to religious institutions, inescapably implicates the Establishment Clause." The Court also expressed concern that the law contained a "standardless" delegation "calling for no reasons, findings, or reasoned conclusions. That power may therefore be used by churches to promote goals beyond insulating the church from undesirable neighbors; it could be employed for explicitly religious goals, for example, favoring liquor licenses for members of that congregation or adherents of that faith. [In] addition, the mere appearance of a joint exercise of legislative authority by Church and State provides a significant symbolic benefit to religion in the minds of some by reason of the power conferred." Justice Rehnquist dissented, arguing that the state does not " 'advance' religion by making provision for those who wish to engage in religious activities [to] be unmolested by activities at a neighboring bar or tavern." He felt that, should a church discriminate in favor of its own adherents, "it would then be time to decide the Establishment Clause issues. The heavy First Amendment artillery that the Court fires at this sensible and unobjectionable [statute] is both unnecessary and unavailing."

---

[55] 568 F.3d 784 (10th Cir. 2009).

[56] 459 U.S. 116 (1982).

[C] Holiday Displays

In recent years, there has been considerable litigation regarding the constitutionality of holiday displays, particularly Christmas and Chanukah displays.

Perhaps the most important recent decision was the holding in *Lynch v. Donnelly*.[57] That case involved an annual Christmas display by the City of Pawtucket, R.I. that was located in a private park in the downtown shopping district. The display included a Santa Claus house, reindeer pulling Santa's sleigh, candy-striped poles, a Christmas tree, carolers, cutout figures representing such characters as a clown, an elephant, and a teddy bear, hundreds of colored lights, a large banner that reads "SEASONS GREETINGS," and a creche. Although the display was erected on private property, the City owned it.

In a 5-to-4 decision, the Court upheld the display including the creche. The Court found that the creche did not have the impermissible effect of advancing or promoting religion. In the Court's view, the creche was "no more an advancement or endorsement of religion" than other "endorsements" the Court had previously approved. In addition, the Court regarded any benefits the government's display gave religion as "no more than 'indirect, remote, and incidental.' "

Perhaps the most important part of the *Lynch* decision was Justice O'Connor's concurrence. She argued that government is not allowed to "endorse" religion because it "sends a message to nonadherents that they are outsiders, not full members of the political community, and an accompanying message to adherents that they are insiders, favored members of the political community." Justice O'Connor argued that, in evaluating a "message" to see whether it constitutes an "endorsement," the focus should be on the message that the government's practice communicates based on the context in which it appears: "[A] typical museum setting, though not neutralizing the religious content of a religious painting, negates any message of endorsement of that content.'

In analyzing the Pawtucket display, Justice O'Connor felt that the overall display did not convey a message of endorsement. She emphasized that, in addition to the creche, the display contained "a Santa Claus house with a live Santa distributing candy; reindeer pulling Santa's sleigh; a live 40-foot Christmas tree strung with lights; statues of carolers in old-fashioned dress; candy-striped poles; a 'talking' wishing well; a large banner proclaiming 'SEASONS GREETINGS'; a miniature 'village' with several houses and a church; and various 'cut-out' figures, including those of a clown, a dancing elephant, a robot, and a teddy bear." Justice O'Connor felt that "because the creche is 'a traditional symbol' of Christmas, a holiday with strong secular elements, and because the creche was 'displayed along with purely secular symbols,' the creche's setting affected how the entire display was viewed." She found that the overall display would fairly be understood to negate "any message of endorsement" of Christian beliefs.

Four justices (Justice Brennan, joined by justices Marshall, Blackmun, and Stevens) dissented arguing that the issue was "whether Pawtucket [had endorsed]

---

[57] 465 U.S. 668 (1984).

religion through its display of the creche," and they agreed that the Court should focus on the context of the display. Thus, a majority of the Court agreed that the endorsement test should govern the Court's analysis. However, the dissenters disagreed with Justice O'Connor's application of that test. The dissenters felt that the other elements of the Pawtucket display did not negate the message of endorsement. In the dissenter's view, the creche placed "the government's imprimatur of approval on the particular religious beliefs exemplified by the creche." As a result, in their view, the effect of the display on "minority religious groups [was] to convey the message that their views are not similarly worthy of public recognition nor entitled to public support."

Lynch was followed by the holding in County of *Allegheny v. American Civil Liberties Union.*[58] Justice Blackmun delivered the opinion of the Court, parts of which were joined by justices Stevens and O'Connor. *County of Allegheny* involved two separate holiday displays. The first was a creche placed by a Roman Catholic group next to the Grand Staircase inside the county court-house. The creche was surrounded by a wooden fence which bore a plaque stating: "[Donated] by the Holy Name Society." The county government placed poinsettia plants around the fence, and a small evergreen tree, decorated with a red bow, behind each of the two endposts of the fence. The evergreen trees stood alongside the manger and were slightly shorter. At the apex of the creche display was an angel. The entire display occupied a substantial amount of space on the Grand Staircase. Unlike the Pawtucket display upheld in *Lynch*, the County of Allegheny display did not include any "secular Christmas symbols" such as Santa Claus. The county held its annual Christmas-carole program at the site of the creche. The county invited high school choirs and other musical groups to perform at the creche during weekday lunch hours. The county dedicated these musical programs to world peace and to the families of prisoners-of-war and of persons missing in action in Southeast Asia.

The second display was erected at the City-County Building about a block away from the county courthouse. The building was co-owned by City of Pittsburgh and Allegheny County. The display involved a large Christmas tree under the middle arch outside the Grant Street entrance. At the foot of the tree was a sign bearing the mayor's name and the words "Salute to Liberty." Beneath the title, the sign stated:

> "During this holiday season, the city of Pittsburgh salutes liberty. Let these festive lights remind us that we are the keepers of the flame of liberty and our legacy of freedom."

The display also included an 18-foot Chanukah menorah of an abstract tree-and-branch design. The menorah was placed next to the Christmas tree. The menorah was owned by Chabad, a Jewish group, but was stored, erected, and removed each year by the city.

The Court began by recognizing that a majority of the justices who participated in the *Lynch* case expressed support for the endorsement test. The Court noted that: "Whether the key word is 'endorsement,' 'favoritism,' or 'promotion,' the essential principle remains the same. The Establishment Clause [prohibits] gov-

---

[58] 492 U.S. 573 (1989).

ernment from appearing to take a position on questions of religious belief or from 'making adherence to a religion relevant in any way to a person's standing in the political community.' "

The Court held that the creche display violated the endorsement test: "[The] creche display [uses] words, as well as the picture of the Nativity scene, to make its religious meaning unmistakably clear. 'Glory to God in the Highest!' says the angel in the creche — Glory to God because of the birth of Jesus. This praise to God in Christian terms is indisputably religious — indeed sectarian — just as it is when said in the Gospel or in a church service."

However, the Court emphasized that the constitutionality of any display turns on the setting in which it is displayed. The Court regarded the *County of Allegheny* display as quite different than the *Lynch* display because there was nothing to detract from "the creche's religious message." Unlike *Lynch*, where the crèche was surrounded by reindeer, Frosty the Snowman, etc., "[the] creche stands alone: it is the single element of the display on the Grand Staircase." Indeed, even the floral display surrounding the crèche was deemed to be objectionable because it drew attention to the crèche and contributed to the endorsement message: "It is as if the county had allowed the Holy Name Society to display a cross on the Grand Staircase at Easter, and the county had surrounded the cross with Easter lilies." "Furthermore, the creche sits on the Grand Staircase, the "main" and "most beautiful part" of the building that is the seat of county government. No viewer could reasonably think that it occupies this location without the support and approval of the government." As a result, in the Court's view, the county sent "an unmistakable message that it supports and promotes the Christian praise to God that is the creche's religious message." "The fact that the creche bears a sign disclosing its ownership by a Roman Catholic organization does not alter this conclusion. [T]he sign simply demonstrates that the government is endorsing the religious message of that organization, rather than communicating a message of its own." The Court concluded that the "government may celebrate Christmas in some manner and form, but not in a way that endorses Christian doctrine. [Allegheny County] has transgressed this line. It has [celebrated] Christmas in a way that has the effect of endorsing a patently Christian message: Glory to God for the birth of Jesus Christ."

The Court upheld the second display (the one at the City-County building). The Court conceded that the Menorah is a religious symbol because it commemorated the miracle of the oil as described in the Talmud. But the Court also recognized that Menorah is a symbol of a holiday that, like Christmas, has both religious and secular dimensions. In upholding the display, the Court noted that:

> [T]he menorah here stands next to a Christmas tree and a sign saluting liberty. [The result is] to create an "overall holiday setting" that represents both Christmas and Chanukah. [Because] government may celebrate Christmas as a secular holiday, [government] may also acknowledge Chanukah as a secular holiday. [I]t would [involve] discrimination against Jews [to] celebrate Christmas as a cultural tradition while simultaneously disallowing the city's acknowledgment of Chanukah as [a] cultural tradition. [The] combined display [has] the effect of [recognizing] that both

Christmas and Chanukah are part of the same winter-holiday season, which has attained a secular status in our society. The] Christmas tree, unlike the menorah, is not itself a religious symbol. Although Christmas trees once carried religious connotations, today they typify the secular celebration of Christmas . . . .

The tree, moreover, is clearly the predominant element in the city's display. The 45-foot tree occupies the central position [in] front of [the] entrance to the City-County Building; the 18-foot menorah is positioned to one side. Given this configuration, it [is] sensible to interpret the [menorah] in light of the tree. . . . In the shadow of the tree, the menorah [is] understood as simply a recognition that Christmas is not the only traditional way of observing the winter-holiday season. [The] combination of the tree and the menorah communicates [a] secular celebration of Christmas coupled with an acknowledgment of Chanukah as a contemporaneous alternative tradition.

The Court emphasized that, even though the menorah is a religious symbol, it was "difficult to imagine a predominantly secular symbol of Chanukah that the city could place next to its Christmas tree." In addition, the Court concluded that the mayor's sign diminished the possibility that the tree and the menorah would be "interpreted as [an] endorsement of Christianity and Judaism." As a result, the Court concluded that it was not "sufficiently likely" that reasonable observers would "perceive the combined display of the tree, the sign, and the menorah as an 'endorsement' or 'disapproval [of] their individual religious choices.'" The Court remanded for consideration of whether the display might violate either the "purpose" or "entanglement" prongs of the *Lemon* analysis.

Justice O'Connor, joined in part by justices Brennan and Stevens, concurred in part and concurred in the judgment. She responded to the argument that such things as the opening of the Court's daily sessions, with an appeal to God, were distinguishable from establishments of religion because they serve the secular purposes of "solemnizing public occasions" and "expressing confidence in the future." She regarded such acts as nothing more than "ceremonial deism." "It is the combination of the long-standing existence of practices such as opening legislative sessions with legislative prayers or opening Court sessions with 'God save the United States and this honorable Court,' as well as their nonsectarian nature, that leads me to the conclusion that [those] practices, despite their religious roots, do not convey a message of endorsement of particular religious beliefs. Similarly, the celebration of Thanksgiving as a public holiday, despite its religious origins, is now generally understood as a celebration of patriotic values rather than particular religious beliefs."

Justice Brennan, joined by justices Marshall and Stevens, concurred in part and dissented in part, arguing that: "[T]he display of an object that 'retains a specifically Christian [or other] religious meaning,' is incompatible with the separation of church and state demanded by our Constitution. . . . The menorah is indisputably a religious symbol, used ritually in a celebration that has deep religious significance. [That] is all that need be said."

Justice Stevens, joined by justices Brennan and Marshall, concurred in part and dissented in part. He argued that the Establishment Clause creates "a strong presumption against the display of religious symbols on public property." He felt that the Court should have held that even the Chanukah menorah and the Christmas tree were unconstitutional: "The presence of the Chanukah menorah, unquestionably a religious symbol, gives religious significance to the Christmas tree. The overall display thus manifests governmental approval of the Jewish and Christian religions. Although it conceivably might be interpreted as sending 'a message of pluralism and freedom to choose one's own beliefs,' the message is not sufficiently clear."

Justice Kennedy, joined by Chief Justice Rehnquist and justices White and Scalia, accused the Court of hostility towards religion. He argued that the city and county had done no more than "celebrate the season," and "acknowledge, along with many of their citizens, the historical background and the religious, as well as secular, nature of the Chanukah and Christmas holidays." Justice Kennedy viewed this as nothing more than "government accommodation and acknowledgment of religion that has marked our history from the beginning."

Justice Kennedy rejected the idea that the government had used its power "to further the interests of Christianity or Judaism in any way." He viewed the creche and the menorah as "passive symbols of religious holidays" and noted that no one had been "compelled to observe or participate in any religious ceremony or activity." Those who disagreed with "the message conveyed by these displays are free to ignore them." In addition, in his view, there was no "realistic risk that the creche and the menorah represent[ed] an effort to proselytize or [were] otherwise the first step down the road to an establishment of religion.

Justice Kennedy rejected the endorsement test as a "most unwelcome" addition to the Court's "tangled Establishment Clause jurisprudence." In his view, the "endorsement test is flawed in its fundamentals and unworkable in practice." He viewed the test as one that would "trivialize constitutional adjudication [by embracing] a jurisprudence of minutiae": "A reviewing court must consider whether the city has included Santas, talking wishing wells, reindeer, or other secular symbols as 'a center of attention separate from the creche.' After determining whether these centers of attention are sufficiently 'separate' that each 'had their specific visual story to tell,' the court must then measure their proximity to the creche. [M]unicipal greenery must be used with [care]." He also noted that, before studying these cases, he "had not known the full history of the menorah. . . . This history [was] likely unknown to the vast majority of people of all faiths who saw the symbol displayed in Pittsburgh [and hardly] informed the observers' view of the symbol. . . ."

[D] Swearing Belief in God

In *Torcaso v. Watkins*,[59] the Court held that a State may not constitutionally require an applicant for the office of Notary Public to swear or affirm that he believes in God.

---

[59] 367 U.S. 488 (1961).

[E] Day of Rest

In *McGowan v. Maryland*,[60] the Court held that state laws compelling a uniform day of rest from worldly labor do not violate the Establishment Clause even though Sunday was chosen as the day of rest. The Court concluded that, although the Sunday Laws were first enacted for religious ends, they were continued for reasons wholly secular — to provide a universal day of rest and ensure the health and tranquillity of the community. Likewise, in *Estate of Thornton v. Caldor, Inc.*,[61] the Court upheld a law that granted employees the right not to work on their sabbaths.

§ 11.06 ESTABLISHMENT-FREE EXERCISE AND FREE SPEECH TENSION

As previously noted, the Establishment and Free Exercise Clauses conflict in some cases. How is the tension between these two clauses resolved? The Court has struggled with this issue in a number of cases.

[A] *Kiryas Joel* and Special School Districts

One of the most important recent decisions was the holding in *Board of Education of Kiryas Joel Village School District v. Grumet*.[62] The case involved the Satmaar Hasidic Jewish sect that purchased an undeveloped subdivision. When a zoning dispute arose, they turned the subdivision into a small (320 acres with 8,500 residents) village owned entirely by Satmars. The Court described the Satmars in the following way:

> The residents of Kiryas Joel are vigorously religious people who make few concessions to the modern world and go to great lengths to avoid [assimilation]. They interpret the Torah strictly; segregate the sexes outside the home; speak Yiddish as their primary language; eschew television, radio, and English-language publications; and dress in distinctive ways that include headcoverings and special garments for boys and modest dresses for girls. Children are educated in private religious schools, most boys at the United Talmudic Academy where they receive [a] grounding in the Torah and limited exposure to secular subjects, [and] girls at [an] affiliated school with a curriculum designed to prepare girls for their roles as wives and mothers.

Because the religious schools did not offer special services to handicapped children, the Monroe-Woodbury Central School District provided such services for the children of Kiryas Joel at an annex. This program was terminated following the decisions in *Aguilar v. Felton and School Dist. of Grand Rapids v. Ball*. As a result, Kiryas Joel children who needed special education (including the deaf, the mentally retarded, and others suffering from a range of physical, mental, or emotional

---

[60] 366 U.S. 420 (1961).

[61] 472 U.S. 703, 709–710 (1985).

[62] 512 U.S. 687 (1994).

disorders) were forced to attend public schools outside the village. Because the Satmars were so different, they encountered "the panic, fear and trauma [suffered] in [being] with people whose ways were so different." By 1989, only one Kiryas Joel child was attending Monroe-Woodbury's public schools. The village's other handicapped children received privately funded special services or received no education at all. The New York Legislature then enacted a statute which provided that the village of Kiryas Joel "is constituted a separate school district." 1989 N.Y. Laws, ch. 748. New York Governor Mario Cuomo stated that he viewed the bill [as] "a good faith effort to solve th[e] unique problem" of providing special education services to handicapped children in the village.

Although the statute gave the school district plenary legal authority over the elementary and secondary education of all school-aged children in the village, the district ran only a special education program for handicapped children. The village's other children attended parochial schools, and received only transportation, remedial education, and health and welfare services from the public school district. Had a non-handicapped student sought a public education, the district would have paid tuition to send the child to a nearby school district. In addition, several neighboring school districts sent their handicapped Hasidic children to the Kiryas Joel school.

In an opinion written by Justice Souter, the Court struck down the law. The opinion began by noting that the State is required to "pursue a course of 'neutrality' toward religion." Justice Souter felt that New York crossed the line because it delegated its "discretionary authority over public schools to a group defined by its character as a religious community, in [a] context that gives no assurance that governmental power has been or will be exercised neutrally." The Court noted that religious officials could not, because of their political activities, be denied the right to hold public office. But the Court regarded this delegation as unconstitutional: "[T]he difference lies in the distinction between a government's purposeful delegation on the basis of religion and a delegation on principles neutral to religion, to individuals whose religious identities are incidental to their receipt of civic authority."

The Court found a religious delegation in this case. Even though New York did not delegate power with express reference to the religious beliefs of the Satmars, the Court concluded that New York had effectively identified the recipient of governmental power "by reference to doctrinal adherence." "We find this [because] the boundary lines of the school district divide residents according to religious affiliation, under the terms of an unusual and special legislative Act." The Court emphasized that the district originated in a special act of the legislature, the only district ever created that way, and noted that "[T]hose who negotiated the village boundaries [excluded] all but Satmars, [and] the New York Legislature was well aware that the village remained exclusively Satmar [when] it adopted Chapter 748." The Court concluded that "We therefore find the legislature's Act to be substantially equivalent to defining a political subdivision and hence the qualification for its franchise by a religious test, resulting in a purposeful and forbidden 'fusion of governmental and religious functions.' "

The opinion rejected the argument that the state's decision to create the special district constituted an accommodation of religion. Although the state can "accommodate religious needs by alleviating special burdens," the Court held that "accommodation is not a principle without limits." The Court found this law invalid because the "proposed accommodation singles out a particular religious sect for special treatment." The Court suggested that it would be permissible for the district to provide bilingual and bicultural special education to Satmar children at a neutral site near one of the village's parochial schools.

The Court concluded with the following remarks:

> [We] do not disable a religiously homogeneous group from exercising political power conferred on it without regard to religion. Unlike the States of Utah and New Mexico (which were laid out according to traditional political methodologies taking account of lines of latitude and longitude and topographical features), the reference line [for] the Kiryas Joel Village School District [was] drawn to separate Satmars from non-Satmars. . . .

> [T]he statute before us fails the test of neutrality. It delegates a power this Court has said "ranks at the very apex of the function of a State," to an electorate defined by common religious belief and practice, in a manner that fails to foreclose religious favoritism. It therefore crosses the line from permissible accommodation to impermissible establishment. The judgment of the Court of Appeals of the State of New York is accordingly affirmed.

Justice Stevens, joined by justices Blackmun and Ginsburg, concurred: "[Affirmative] state action in aid of segregation of this character [is] fairly characterized as establishing, rather than merely accommodating, religion."

Justice O'Connor concurred in part and concurred in the judgment. While she viewed accommodations as permissible, "even praiseworthy," "[b]ecause this benefit was given to this group based on its religion, it seems proper to treat it as a legislatively drawn religious classification." She wondered whether the legislature was acting "without any favoritism," but worried whether another group would be given the same preference. As a result, she concluded that it was "dangerous to validate" what appears to be "a clear religious preference." Nevertheless, she felt that some accommodations were permissible:

> Our invalidation of this statute in no way means that the Satmars' needs cannot be accommodated. . . . New York [may] allow all villages to operate their own school districts. If it does not want to act so broadly, it may set forth neutral criteria that a village must meet to have a school district of its own. . . . A district created under a generally applicable scheme would be acceptable even though it coincides with a village that was consciously created by its voters as an enclave for their religious group. [T]here is one other accommodation that would be [permissible]: the [scheme] which was discontinued because of our decision in *Aguilar*. [If] the government provides this education on-site at public schools and at nonsectarian private schools, it is only fair that it provide it on-site at sectarian schools as well.

Justice Kennedy concurred. He noted that there "is more than a fine line [between] the voluntary association that leads to a political community comprised of people who share a common religious faith, and the forced separation that occurs when the government draws explicit political boundaries on the basis of peoples' faith." He concluded that New York had "crossed that line."

Justice Scalia, joined by Chief Justice Rehnquist and Justice Thomas, dissented expressing surprise at the conclusion that the Satmars had become an "established religion":

> The Court today finds that the Powers That Be, up in Albany, have conspired to effect an establishment of the Satmar Hasidim. I do not know who would be more surprised at this discovery: the Founders of our Nation or Grand Rebbe Joel Teitelbaum, founder of the Satmar. The Grand Rebbe would be astounded to learn that after escaping brutal persecution and coming to America with the modest hope of religious toleration for their ascetic form of Judaism, the Satmar had become so powerful, so closely allied with Mammon, as to have become an "establishment" of the Empire State.

Ultimately, he concluded that there was no establishment because the state provided "no public funding, however slight or indirect, to private religious schools." "Unlike the district's religious schools, which were profoundly religious and segregated by sex, the public school provided only a public secular education to handicapped students. The school did not contain religious symbols or markings. . . . While the village's private schools are profoundly religious and strictly segregated by sex, classes at the public school are co-ed and the curriculum secular." He concluded that: "The only thing distinctive about the school is that all the students share the same religion." He concluded by rejecting the majority position which he viewed as involving the "novel proposition that any group of citizens [can] be invested with political power, but not if they all belong to the same religion. Of course such disfavoring of religion is positively antagonistic to the purposes of the Religion Clauses." Ultimately, Justice Scalia viewed the district as a permissible accommodation of religion: "The handicapped children suffered sufficient emotional trauma from their predicament that their parents kept them home from school. Surely the legislature could [provide] a public education for these students." "[When] a legislature acts to accommodate religion, particularly a minority sect, 'it follows the best of our traditions.' "

[B] Prohibitions Against Discrimination

In *Corporation of Presiding Bishop v. Amos*,[63] the Court upheld Section 702 of the Civil Rights Act of 1964, which exempts religious organizations from Title VII's prohibition against discrimination in employment on the basis of religion. Although appellee worked in a non-religious job, he was discharged for not being a church member. Applying the *Lemon* test, the Court stated: "Where, as here, government acts with the proper purpose of lifting a regulation that burdens the exercise of religion, we see no reason to require that the exemption comes packaged with benefits to secular entities."

---

[63] 483 U.S. 327 (1987).

[C] Armed Forces Chaplains

The armed forces hire chaplains to enable soldiers to practice the religion of their choice. These chaplains are appointed as commissioned officers with rank and uniform but without command. In *Katcoff v. Marsh*,[64] the court upheld this practice relying on historical practice: "In providing our armed forces with a military chaplaincy Congress has perpetuated a facility that began during Revolutionary days before the adoption of our Constitution, and that has continued ever since then." The Court also noted that the provision of chaplains was justified by the unusual circumstances under which the armed forces work: "The problem of meeting the religious needs of Army personnel is compounded by the mobile, deployable nature of our armed forces, who must be ready on extremely short notice to be transported from bases (whether or not in the United States) to distant parts of the world for combat duty in fulfillment of our nation's international defense commitments. Unless there were chaplains ready to move simultaneously with the troops and to tend to their spiritual needs as they face possible death, the soldiers would be left in the lurch, religiously speaking." Finally, the Court noted that chaplains are not authorized to proselytize soldiers or their families, and questioned whether chaplains were necessary in large urban areas where civilian religious personnel are available.

Consider the following comments by Professor Jesse H. Choper, *The Religion Clauses of the First Amendment: Reconciling the Conflict*:[65] He notes that the religion clauses conflict because "the Establishment Clause forbids government action whose purpose is to aid religion, but on the other hand the Court has held that the Free Exercise Clause may require government action to accommodate religion." The difficulty he finds is that "the Court's separate tests for the Religion Clauses have provided virtually no guidance for determining when an accommodation for religion, seemingly required under the Free Exercise Clause, constitutes impermissible aid to religion under the Establishment Clause." In addition, he worries that the Court has not "adequately explained why aid to religion, seemingly violative of the Establishment Clause, is not actually required by the Free Exercise Clause." He attributes many of these difficulties to the *Lemon* test and its "secular purpose" prong: "Because this part of the Court's test flatly prohibits any government action that has a religious purpose, it would make virtually *all* accommodations for religion unconstitutional." Indeed, since the purpose of "accommodations for religion is to avoid burdening religious activity, it is plain that their purpose is to assist religion."

[D] Speech and Religion

In *Rosenberger v. Rector and Visitors of the University of Virginia*,[66] in an opinion written by Justice Kennedy, the Court held a religious publication was entitled to receive state funding. The case involved the University of Virginia's Student Activities Fund (SAF). The program provided funding to an array of

---

[64] 755 F.2d 223 (2d Cir. 1985).

[65] 41 U. Pitt. L. Rev. 673, 674–75 & 685 (1980).

[66] 515 U.S. 819 (1995).

student publications, including programs focused on "student news, information, opinion, entertainment and academic communications media groups," but specifically excluded religious publications. The University was concerned that inclusion of religious organizations would violate the Establishment Clause.

In holding that Wide Awake, an avowedly religious publication, was entitled to funding, the Court found that the funding mechanism was not created to advance or aid religion: "The object of the SAF is to open a forum for speech and to support various student enterprises, including the publication of newspapers, in recognition of the diversity and creativity of student life." The Court upheld the law:

> [The] University provides printing services to a broad spectrum of student newspapers qualified as CIOs by reason of their officers and membership. Any benefit to religion is incidental to the government's provision of secular services for secular purposes on a religion-neutral basis. . . . To obey the Establishment Clause, it was not necessary for the University to deny eligibility to student publications because of their viewpoint. . . .

Justice O'Connor, applying her endorsement test, concurred, finding an absence of endorsement. In part, she relied on the fact that the University would be "providing the same assistance to Wide Awake that it does to other publications," and therefore "the University would not be endorsing the magazine's religious perspective." The student organizations are required to remain strictly independent of the University, and all student organizations were required to include the following disclaimer in their publications:

> Although this organization has members who are University of Virginia students (faculty) (employees), the organization is independent of the corporation which is the University and which is not responsible for the organization's contracts, acts or omissions." Any reader of Wide Awake would be on notice of the publication's independence from the University.

In addition, financial assistance was "distributed in a manner that ensure[d] its use only for [the] University's purpose [of] maintaining a free and robust marketplace of ideas, from whatever perspective." Finally, the University provided support to such a range of publications as to make "improbable any perception of government endorsement of the religious message." As a result, she concluded that: "[By] withholding from Wide Awake assistance that the University provides generally to all other student publications, the University has discriminated on the basis of the magazine's religious viewpoint in violation of the Free Speech Clause."

Justice Souter, joined by justices Stevens, Ginsburg and Breyer, dissented noting that this Court "for the first time, approves direct funding of core religious activities by an arm of the State." He indicated that he would have held that "the University's refusal to support petitioners' religious activities is compelled by the Establishment Clause." "This writing is not merely a descriptive examination of religious doctrine or even of ideal Christian practice in confronting life's social and personal problems. [It] is straightforward exhortation to enter into a relationship with God as revealed in Jesus Christ, and to satisfy a series of moral obligations derived from the teachings of Jesus Christ. . . ." He concludes, arguing that using "public funds for the direct subsidization of preaching the word is categorically forbidden under the Establishment Clause, and if the Clause was meant to accomplish nothing else, it was meant to bar this use of public money." "The University exercises the power of the State to compel a student to pay [a fee], and the use of any part of it for the direct support of religious activity thus strikes at what we have repeatedly held to be the heart of the prohibition on establishment."

[E] Religious Instruction in Public Schools

In *Illinois v. McCollum*,[67] an Illinois law allowed religious teachers employed by private religious groups to enter public school buildings during the regular hours set apart for secular teaching, and substitute their religious teaching for the secular education provided under the compulsory education law. The Court struck the law down: "This is [a] utilization of the tax-established and tax-supported public school system to aid religious groups to spread their faith [which] falls squarely under the ban of the First Amendment. . . ." However, in *Zorach v. Clauson*,[68] the Court upheld an arrangement whereby students are released from public school classes so that they may attend religious classes off-site.

[F] Use of Public School Facilities

In *Widmar v. Vincent*,[69] a state university made its facilities generally available to registered student groups, but closed its facilities to groups desiring to use the facilities for religious worship and religious discussion. The Court held that the university was required to allow religious groups to use its facilities: "Having created a forum generally open to student groups, the University seeks to enforce a content-based exclusion of religious speech. Its exclusionary policy violates the fundamental principle that a state regulation of speech should be content-neutral. . . ." Justice White dissented: "[This] case involves religious worship only; the fact that that worship is accomplished through speech does not add anything to respondents' argument."

Good News Club v. Milford Central School[70] involved the same issues in the context of an elementary school. Milford Central School (Milford) enacted a community use policy governing the use of its building after school hours. The Good News Club, a private Christian organization for children ages 6 to 12, sought permission to meet in the cafeteria to recite Bible verses, pray, sings songs, and engage in games involving Bible verses. Milford rejected the Club's request because it involved "conducting religious instruction and Bible study." The Court found that Milford was operating a "limited public forum" — a forum in which the state was permitted to reserve the forum for certain groups or for the discussion of certain topics — and concluded that it had improperly excluded the Good News Club: "[Milford] engaged in viewpoint discrimination when it excluded the Club from the after school forum. [T]he Club seeks to address a subject otherwise

---

[67] 333 U.S. 203 (1948).

[68] 343 U.S. 306 (1952).

[69] 454 U.S. 263 (1981).

[70] 533 U.S. 98 (2001).

permitted under the rule, the teaching of morals and character, from a religious standpoint. . . . The only apparent difference [is] that the Club chooses to teach moral lessons from a Christian perspective through live storytelling and [prayer]." Justice Stevens dissented: "[A] school [need not open] its forum to religious proselytizing or [worship]." Justice Souter also dissented: "[Good News's] exercises blur the line between public classroom instruction and private religious indoctrination, leaving a reasonable elementary school pupil unable to appreciate that the former instruction is the business of the school while the latter evangelism is [not]."

[G]   Vocational Assistance to the Handicapped

Witters v. Washington Department of Services for the Blind[71] involved a Washington statute that authorized payments to "[p]rovide for special education and/or training in the professions, business or trades" to "assist visually handicapped persons to overcome vocational handicaps and to obtain the maximum degree of self-support and self-care." The state denied assistance to a blind person who was studying at a Christian college to become a pastor, missionary, or youth director. The Court held that Witters was entitled to assistance: "[V]ocational assistance [is] paid directly to the student, who transmits it to the educational institution of his or her choice. Any aid [that] flows to religious institutions does so only as a result of [the] independent and private choices of aid recipients." Washington's program is "made available generally without regard to the sectarian-nonsectarian, or public-nonpublic nature of the institution benefited, [and] is in no way skewed towards religion." Justice O'Connor concurred: "The aid to religion [is] the result of petitioner's private choice. No reasonable observer is likely to draw from the facts before us an inference that the State itself is endorsing a religious practice or belief."

[H]   Funding of Non-Profit Private Organizations

Bowen v. Kendrick[72] involved a federal grant program, the Adolescent Family Life Act (AFLA or Act), which provided funding to public or nonprofit private organizations addressing problems relating to pregnancy and childbirth among unmarried adolescents. The grants were intended promote "self discipline and other prudent approaches to the problem of adolescent premarital sexual relations," the promotion of adoption as an alternative for adolescent parents, the establishment of new approaches to the delivery of care services for pregnant adolescents, and the support of research and demonstration projects "concerning the societal causes and consequences of adolescent premarital sexual relations, contraceptive use, pregnancy, and child rearing."

The Act was challenged when Congress specifically amended the Act to require grant applicants to describe how they would involve religious organizations in the programs funded by the AFLA. The Court rejected the challenge, noting that the law did not require that grantees be "affiliated with any religious denomination."

---

[71]   474 U.S. 481 (1986).

[72]   487 U.S. 589 (1988).

Moreover, the services provided were not "religious in character, nor has there been any suggestion that religious institutions or organizations with religious ties are uniquely well qualified to carry out those services." In the Court's view, there "provisions of the statute reflect at most Congress' considered judgment that religious organizations can help solve the problems to which the AFLA is addressed. Nothing in our previous cases prevents Congress from making such a judgment or from recognizing the important part that religion or religious organizations may play in resolving certain secular problems." Moreover, there was no indicated that a "significant proportion" of the funds would be disbursed to "pervasively sectarian" institutions.

One important issue in the case is whether the government could authorize "teaching" by religious grant recipients on "matters [that] are fundamental elements of religious doctrine," such as the harm of premarital sex and the reasons for choosing adoption over abortion. The Court observed that the Government's secular concerns "would either coincide or conflict with those of religious institutions." However, the Court concluded that "the possibility or even the likelihood that some of the religious institutions who receive AFLA funding will agree with the message that Congress intended to deliver to adolescents through the AFLA is insufficient to warrant a finding that the statute on its face has the primary effect of advancing religion." The Court also rejected the argument that AFLA excessively entangled government with religion: "There is [no] reason to fear that the less intensive monitoring involved here will cause the Government to intrude unduly in the day-to-day operation of the religiously affiliated AFLA grantees."

Justice Blackmun, joined by Justices Brennan, Marshall, and Stevens, dissented: "Whatever Congress had in mind, [it] enacted a statute [that gave] religious groups [a] pedagogical and counseling role without imposing any restraints on the sectarian quality of the participation."

[I] College Scholarships

The tension between the Establishment and Free Exercises clauses is also revealed by the Court's recent holding in *Locke v. Davey*.[73] In that case, the Washington State Legislature created the Promise Scholarship Program (PSP) to provide renewable one year scholarships for the payment of postsecondary education expenses. The scholarships, which could be used to cover any education-related expense, including room and board, were funded through the State's general fund, and the amount varied each year depending on the amount of the annual appropriations. To be eligible, a student must graduate from a Washington public or private high school in the top 15% of his graduating class, or attain on the first attempt a cumulative score of 1,200 or better on the Scholastic Assessment Test I, or a score of 27 or better on the American College Test, and the student's family income must be below 135% of the State's median. Finally, the student must enroll "at least half time in an eligible postsecondary institution in the state of Washington," and may not pursue a degree in theology at that institution while

---

[73] 540 U.S. 712 (2004).

receiving the scholarship. Private institutions, including religiously affiliated institutions, could participate provided that they were accredited by a nationally recognized accrediting body. The statute defined a "degree in theology" by reference to the State's constitutional prohibition against providing funds to students to pursue degrees that are "devotional in nature or designed to induce religious faith." Participating institutions were required to certify that eligible students were enrolled at least half time and were not pursuing a degree in devotional theology. If the student met the enrollment requirements, the scholarship funds were sent to the institution for distribution to the student.

Davey was awarded a Promise Scholarship, and chose to attend Northwest College, a private Christian college affiliated with the Assemblies of God denomination. Although the college was eligible to participate in the PSP, Davey was ineligible because he chose to pursue a double major in pastoral ministries (which was regarded as devotional) and business management. Davey brought suit under 42 U.S.C. § 1983, arguing that the denial of his scholarship based on his decision to pursue a theology degree violated, *inter alia*, the Free Exercise, Establishment, and Free Speech Clauses of the First Amendment.

In upholding the exclusion, although the Court recognized that the Establishment Clause and the Free Exercise Clause can be in tension with each other, the Court rejected the argument that its prior decision in *Church of Lukumi Babalu Aye v. Hialeah*,[74] required invalidation of the exclusion on the basis that the PSP was not facially neutral with respect to religion. The Court noted that the State of Washington did not impose criminal or civil sanctions on any type of religious service or rite, did not deny ministers the right to participate in the political affairs, and did not require students to choose between their religious beliefs and receiving a government benefit. Instead, the State had merely chosen not to fund a distinct category of degree and the Court recognized that "majoring in devotional theology is akin to a religious calling as well as an academic pursuit." Given that the First Amendment protects free exercise, as well as prohibits establishments, the Court concluded that it might be appropriate for a court to "deal differently with religious education for the ministry than with education for other callings," and that this differential in treatment simply reflects the tension between the religion clauses rather than "hostility toward religion." Moreover, the Court emphasized that most "States that sought to avoid an establishment of religion around the time of the founding placed in their constitutions formal prohibitions against using tax funds to support the ministry." Finally, the Court concluded that the PSP "goes a long way toward including religion in its benefits. The program permits students to attend pervasively religious schools, so long as they are accredited," and also allows students to take devotional theology courses (as long as they are not pursuing a devotional degree).

Justice Scalia, joined by Justice Thomas, dissented, viewing the PSP as involving discrimination against religion. "The State of Washington [has] created a generally available public benefit, [but] has then carved out a solitary course of study for exclusion. . . . No field of study but religion is singled out for disfavor in this fashion." However, he would have upheld the scholarships had they been

---

[74] 508 U.S. 520 (1993).

"redeemable only at public universities, or only for select courses of study. Either option would replace a program that facially discriminates against religion with one that just happens not to subsidize it. The State could also simply abandon the scholarship program altogether.

POINTS TO REMEMBER

- The First Amendment prohibits both the federal government and state governments from "establishing" a religion (or religions).

- Most Establishment Clause cases focus on whether certain lesser forms of conduct (*i.e.*, financial aid to religion or school prayer) constitute an establishment of religion.

- For several decades, the Court evaluated Establishment Clause challenges under the so-called *Lemon* test.

- Under that test, a reviewing court should ask whether a law has a religious purpose, a religious effect, or fosters an excessive entanglement between government and religion.

- The *Lemon* test has been subjected to considerable criticism, and the Court has searched for a replacement test.

- In recent years, in cases involving financial aid to religion, the Court has moved to a "neutrality" test that permits greater financial support for religious schools.

- While the Court has upheld legislative prayer, it has consistently struck down state mandated or directed prayer in elementary or secondary schools.

- Laws providing for a "moment of silence" in elementary or secondary schools may be valid when passed for secular reasons.

- The Court has struck down attempts to post the Ten Commandments in public schools.

- The Court has prohibited holiday displays that a reasonable observer would view as an "endorsement of religion."

- Religious groups can not be denied access to governmental facilities insofar as those facilities are open to the public on neutral terms that do not favor religion.

Chapter 12

THE FREE EXERCISE CLAUSE

SYNOPSIS

§ 12.01   BURDENS ON RELIGION

   [A]   Early Cases

   [B]   From *Sherbert* to *Smith*

   [C]   Modern Cases

§ 12.02   DISCRIMINATION AGAINST RELIGION

FOCAL POINTS FOR CHAPTER 12

- First Amendment protections for the "exercise" of religion.
- Early decisions distinguishing between religious thought and religious conduct.
- Decisions extending "strict scrutiny" to laws that burden religion.
- Special rules applicable to "neutral, generally applicable" laws.
- Special scrutiny for laws that discriminate against religion.

Because of a history of religious persecution in both Europe and the British colonies, the American colonists insisted on constitutional protections for religious freedom. These demands ultimately led to the adoption of the Establishment Clause (discussed in the prior chapter) and the Free Exercise Clause (discussed in this chapter).[1]

Because there was such widespread agreement about the need for religious freedom, the Framers left little evidence regarding their intent. Although there is widespread agreement that the clause protects religious thought, there is uncertainty about whether (and to what extent) it protects religious conduct. Even if the clause is construed to protect "conduct," most commentators agree that the clause does not protect *all* religious conduct (*e.g.*, the state can prohibit a religion that believes in human sacrifice from actually killing people). This chapter explores the limits of the Free Exercise Clause.

---

[1] *See* Everson v. Board of Education, 330 U.S. 1 (1947).

§ 12.01 BURDENS ON RELIGION

Most free exercise cases involve laws that prohibit an individual from engaging in conduct required by religious beliefs, or require conduct prohibited by religious beliefs (*i.e.*, compulsory school attendance laws, or laws prohibiting the consumption of alcohol or illegal narcotics). In most cases, these laws are not directed at religion *per se*, but are designed to deal with some secular problem that incidentally affects religious practices. The issue is whether the individual's interest in the free exercise of religion requires that the law give way (so that the individual gains an exemption from a governmental requirement or prohibition), or whether the state's interest in universal compliance prevails over the individual religious interest.

[A] Early Cases

The United States Supreme Court has decided a number of cases involving claims for religious exemption. In one of the earliest decisions, *Reynolds v. United States*,[2] the Court upheld a federal law prohibiting polygamy as applied to a Mormon whose religion required him to engage in that practice. The Court distinguished between "belief" and "conduct," and concluded that the government had broad authority to prohibit religious conduct:

> Laws are made for the government of actions, and while they cannot interfere with mere religious beliefs and opinions, they may with practices. [Can] a man excuse his practices to the contrary because of his religious belief? To permit this would be to make the professed doctrines of religious belief superior to the law of the land, and in effect to permit every citizen to become a law unto himself. Government could exist only in name under such circumstances.

Of course, the difficulty with the *Reynolds* decision is that religious "conduct" is an integral part of the practice of many religions. Catholics go to mass and receive communion while Muslims response to the call for prayer. A Free Exercise Clause that protects only religious "beliefs" would not provide much protection for religion.

Nevertheless, in *Davis v. Beason*,[3] the Court affirmed *Reynolds*: "It was never intended or supposed that the [first] amendment could be invoked as a protection against legislation for the punishment of acts inimical to the peace, good order, and morals of society."[4]

Reynolds' "belief-conduct" distinction was partially rejected in *Cantwell v. Connecticut*.[5] Cantwell and his two sons, Jehovah's witnesses and ordained ministers, were arrested in New Haven, Connecticut, and convicted of attempting to sell religious magazines without a permit and disorderly conduct. The Court

---

[2] 98 U.S. (8 Otto) 145 (1878).

[3] 133 U.S. 333 (1890).

[4] *Id.* at 350. *See also* Jacobson v. Massachusetts, 197 U.S. 11 (1905) (upholding a law requiring compulsory vaccinations against religious objections).

[5] 310 U.S. 296 (1940).

concluded that the statute prohibiting solicitation violated Cantwell's right to freely exercise his religion:

> [The First] Amendment embraces two concepts, — freedom to believe and freedom to act. The first is absolute but, in the nature of things, the second cannot be. Conduct remains subject to regulation for the protection of society. [In] every case the power to regulate must be so exercised as not, in attaining a permissible end, unduly to infringe the protected freedom. [A] state may not, by statute, wholly deny the right to preach or to disseminate religious views. [It] is equally clear that a state may by general and non-discriminatory legislation regulate the times, the places, and the manner of soliciting upon its streets, and of holding meetings thereon; and may in other respects safeguard the peace, good order and comfort of the community, without unconstitutionally invading the liberties protected by the Fourteenth Amendment. . . .

The Court struck down the solicitation statute because it gave local officials too much discretion to grant or deny permission. *Cantwell* is also important because it extended the Free Exercise Clause's protections to the states.

Cantwell was followed by *Prince v. Commonwealth of Massachusetts*.[6] In that case, Sarah Prince was convicted of violating Massachusetts' child labor laws. Prince was the aunt and custodian of a nine year old girl, and she was alleged to have enlisted the girl in selling religious magazines (*Watchtower* and *Consolation*). Prince challenged the laws based on her free exercise rights (the right and duty to bring up the child in the tenets and practices of the family's faith), as well as the girl's free exercise rights (the girl believed that it was her religious duty to perform this work and that failure her condemnation "to everlasting destruction at Armageddon"). The Court upheld the child labor laws as applied to the girl: "[T]he power of the state to control the conduct of children reaches beyond the scope of its authority over adults, as is true in the case of other freedoms, and the rightful boundary of its power has not been crossed in this case." Mr. Justice Murphy dissented:

> Religious training and activity, whether performed by adult or child, are protected [except] insofar as they violate reasonable regulations adopted for the protection of the public health, morals and welfare. . . . The state [has] completely failed to sustain its burden of proving the existence of any grave or immediate danger to any interest which it may lawfully protect. [There] is not the slightest indication [that] children engaged in distributing literature pursuant to their religious beliefs have been or are likely to be subject to any of the harmful "diverse influences of the street."

---

[6] 321 U.S. 158 (1944).

[B]   From *Sherbert* to *Smith*

Despite its early precedent, the Court began in the 1960s to strike down laws that infringed religious beliefs. For example, in *Torcaso v. Watkins*,[7] a state constitution required declaration of a belief in God as a prerequisite to assuming public office. In striking down the law, the Court held that the government may not compel anyone to affirm or deny a religious belief.

During at least part of the next three decades, the Court applied strict scrutiny to laws burdening religion. For example, in *Sherbert v. Verner*,[8] a member of the Seventh-day Adventist Church was discharged by her South Carolina employer for refusing to work on Saturday, the Sabbath Day of her faith. Unable to obtain other employment that did not require Saturday work, she sought unemployment compensation benefits under the South Carolina Unemployment Compensation Act. The state denied the application on the basis that South Carolina law disqualified her for benefits because she failed, without good cause, to accept "suitable work when offered [by] the employment office or the [employer]."

In an opinion by Justice Brennan, the Court held that the worker was entitled to unemployment benefits. The Court began by noting that South Carolina's law burdened appellant's exercise of her religion: "The ruling forces her to choose between following the precepts of her religion and forfeiting benefits, on the one hand, and abandoning one of the precepts of her religion in order to accept work, on the other hand. Governmental imposition of such a choice puts the same kind of burden upon the free exercise of religion as would a fine imposed against appellant for her Saturday worship." And the Court flatly rejected the idea that unemployment compensation benefits are not a "right" but merely a "privilege": "It is too late in the day to doubt that the liberties of religion and expression may be infringed by the denial of or placing of conditions upon a benefit or privilege. . . ."

An important aspect of the *Sherbert* opinion was the Court's decision to apply heightened scrutiny:

> [It] is basic that no showing merely of a rational relationship to some colorable state interest would suffice in this highly sensitive constitutional area, "[o]nly the gravest abuses, endangering paramount interest, give occasion for permissible limitation."

The Court found that the standard was not met. The asserted state interest (fraudulent claims by unscrupulous claimants claiming religious objections to Saturday work) was deemed to be insufficient, and the Court concluded that "alternative forms of regulation" could combat such abuses.

In *Sherbert*, the Court distinguished *Braunfeld v. Brown*[9] in which the Court had refused to grant sabbatarians an exemption from Sunday closing laws. In that case, Orthodox Jewish merchants claimed that the closing laws made the practice of their

---

[7]   367 U.S. 488 (1961).

[8]   374 U.S. 398 (1963).

[9]   366 U.S. 599 (1961).

religion more expensive given that they were closed on one weekend day (Saturday) by choice and were precluded from opening on the other weekend day. The *Braunfield* Court found an important governmental interest — in providing a uniform day of rest for all workers — that could only be served by declaring a single day of rest (in this case, Sunday). The Court found that an exemption for Sabbatarians, while theoretically possible, would present an administrative problem of great magnitude. To grant them an exemption would create a competitive advantage for sabbatarians. *Sherbert* distinguished *Braunfield* on the basis that the state interest provided less justification than in *Sherbert*.

A common problem in cases like *Sherbert* is whether, in granting a religious exemption to a law that is applicable to everyone else, the Court fosters an "establishment" of religion. In *Sherbert*, the state argued that, if it gave unemployment benefits to Sabbatarians, but denied those same benefits to Sunday worshipers, it would effectively "establish" religion. The Court found no establishment because the exemption "reflects nothing more than the governmental obligation of neutrality in the face of religious differences, and does not represent that involvement of religious with secular institutions which is the object of the Establishment Clause to forestall."

In *Sherbert*, Justice Douglas concurred:

> This case is resolvable not in terms of what an individual can demand of government, but solely in terms of what government may not do to an individual in violation of his religious scruples. [If] appellant is otherwise qualified for unemployment benefits, payments will be made to her not as a Seventh-day Adventist, but as an unemployed worker.

Justice Harlan, joined by Justice White, dissented:

> [The] meaning of today's holding [is] that the State must furnish unemployment benefits to one who is unavailable for work if the unavailability stems from the exercise of religious convictions. The State, in other words, must single out for financial assistance those whose behavior is religiously motivated, even though it denies such assistance to others whose identical behavior (in this case, inability to work no Saturdays) is not religiously motivated.

> [Those] situations in which the Constitution may require special treatment on account of religion are, in my view, few and far between. . . . Such compulsion in the present case is particularly inappropriate in light of the indirect, remote, and insubstantial effect of the decision below on the exercise of appellant's religion and in light of the direct financial assistance to religion that today's decision requires.

Disputes about unemployment compensation have generated a great deal of free exercise litigation. In general, these cases have reached the same result as *Sherbert*.[10] One of the more interesting cases is *Thomas v. Review Board*,[11] in which

---

[10] *See* Frazee v. Illinois Department of Employment Security, 489 U.S. 829 (1989) (Frazee, who refused employment because he would have been forced to work on his sabbath (Sunday), was held entitled to unemployment benefits); Hobbie v. Unemployment Appeals Commission, 480 U.S. 136 (1987)

a Jehovah's Witness, resigned his job because his religion prohibited him from participating in the production of armaments. The Court held that Thomas was entitled to unemployment compensation. The Court accepted his religious claim even though another Jehovah's Witness had no scruples about working on tank turrets, finding such work "scripturally" acceptable: "Intrafaith differences of that kind are not uncommon among followers of a particular creed, and the judicial process is singularly ill equipped to resolve such differences in relation to the Religion Clauses."

Sherbert was followed by the holding in *Wisconsin v. Yoder*[12] which involved members of the Old Order Amish religion who refused to send their children to school after the eighth grade. In refusing, they ran afoul of Wisconsin's compulsory school-attendance law that required them to send their children to school until age 16. Respondents were convicted of violating the law and fined $5 each.

The Court easily found that Wisconsin's compulsory school attendance laws burdened the Amish in the exercise of their religion. The Amish believed that salvation requires "life in a church community separate and apart from the world and worldly influences." In addition, Amish communities were devoted to a life in harmony with nature and the soil, and to making their living by farming or closely related activities. The Amish did not object to formal schooling through the eighth grade because they believed that children needed to learn basic reading, writing, and elementary mathematics. However, they viewed formal education beyond the eighth grade as inconsistent with their central religious concepts which mandated that the high school years should be used to acquire Amish attitudes favoring manual work and self-reliance and the specific skills needed to perform the adult role of an Amish farmer or housewife. All of these traits, skills, and attitudes were best learned through example and "doing" rather than in a classroom. An expert witness testified that the Amish succeed in preparing their high school age children to be productive members of the Amish community. He described their system of learning as "ideal" and perhaps superior to ordinary high school education. The Amish had an excellent record as law-abiding and generally self-sufficient members of society.

The Amish objected to high school, in particular, because the values taught were in marked variance with Amish values and the Amish way of life, as well as because it exposed children to a "wordly" influence in conflict with Amish beliefs:

> High school emphasized intellectual and scientific accomplishments, self-distinction, competitiveness, worldly success, and social life with other students. Amish society emphasized informal learning-through-doing; a life of 'goodness,' rather than a life of intellect; wisdom, rather than technical knowledge, community welfare, rather than competition; and separation from, rather than integration with, contemporary worldly society. In addition, high school teachers were not of the Amish faith and might even

---

(Hobbie, who was discharged because she refused to work on a Friday evening or Saturday because she was a Seventh Day Adventist, was also entitled to unemployment compensation).

[11] 450 U.S. 707 (1981).

[12] 406 U.S. 205 (1972).

be hostile to it. As a result, high school attendance could not only result in great psychological harm to Amish children, because of the conflicts it would produce, but would also ultimately result in the destruction of the Old Order Amish church community.

In an opinion by Chief Justice Burger, the Court recognized that the Free Exercise Clause applied, and gave parents the right to control the upbringing of their children:

> There is no doubt as to the power of a State [to] impose reasonable regulations for the control and duration of basic education. Providing public schools ranks at the very apex of the function of a State. Yet even this paramount responsibility [must] yield to the right of parents to provide an equivalent education in a privately operated system. [In *Pierce v. Society of Sisters*, 268 U.S. 510, 534 (1925),] the Court held that Oregon's statute compelling attendance in a public school from age eight to age 16 unreasonably interfered with the interest of parents in directing the rearing of their off-spring, including their education in church-operated schools. [T]he values of parental direction of the religious upbringing and education of their children in their early and formative years have a high place in our society. Thus, a State's interest in universal education, however highly we rank it, is not totally free from a balancing process when it impinges on fundamental rights and interests, such as those specifically protected by the Free Exercise Clause of the First Amendment, and the traditional interest of parents with respect to the religious upbringing of their children so long as [they] "prepare [them] for additional obligations."

Once again, the Court required an interest of the "highest order."

An interesting aspect of the opinion was the Court's discussion of whether the "Amish way of life" qualified for protection under the Free Exercise Clause. The Court answered this question in the affirmative, noting that the "traditional way of life of the Amish is not merely a matter of personal preference, but one of deep religious conviction, shared by an organized group, and intimately related to daily living." The Court also noted that their "way of life" was based on their interpretation of the Bible, and prevaded and determined "their entire way of life, regulating it with the detail of the Talmudic diet through the strictly enforced rules of the church community."

The Court found that Wisconsin's compulsory school attendance law was neutral towards religion because it was motivated by secular concerns, applied uniformly to all citizens and was facially neutral towards religion. However, the Court found that the law was not supported by a governmental interest of the "highest order." The state argued that two interests supported its asserted need for compulsory universal education: that "some degree of education is necessary to prepare citizens to participate effectively and intelligently in our open political system if we are to preserve freedom and independence;" and "education prepares individuals to be self-reliant and self-sufficient participants in society." Although the Court accepted both of these propositions as valid, the Court found that an Amish exemption would not prevent the state from achieving its objectives:

> [T]he evidence adduced by the Amish in this case is persuasively to the effect that an additional one or two years of formal high school for Amish children in place of their long-established program of informal vocational education would do little to serve those interests. [It] is one thing to say that compulsory education [may] be necessary when its goal is the preparation of the child for life in modern society as the majority live, but it is quite another if the goal of education be viewed as the preparation of the child for life in the separated agrarian community that is the keystone of the Amish faith.

The Court emphasized that the Amish have been "highly successful," and that they prepare children for adulthood in their own way, and that it is rare for the Amish to become a burden on society.

Mr. Justice White, joined by justices Brennan and Stewart, concurred arguing that since "Amish children [acquire] the basic tools of literacy to survive in modern society by attending grades one through eight and since the deviation from the State's compulsory-education law is relatively slight, [respondents'] must prevail, largely because 'religious freedom [is] one of the highest values of our society.' " Justice Douglas dissented in part:

> [I]f an Amish child desires to attend high school, and is mature [enough], the State [may] override the parents' religiously motivated objections. [T]he children themselves have constitutionally protectible interests.

> [The] emphasis [on] the "law and order" record of this Amish group of people [is] irrelevant. [I] am not at all sure how the Catholics, Episcopalians, the Baptists, Jehovah's Witnesses, the Unitarians, and my own Presbyterians would make out if subjected to such a test. . . .

Even during this three-decade period, the Court upheld some burdens on religion. For example, in *United States v. Lee*,[13] a member of the Old Order Amish refused to pay Social Security taxes because he had religious objections to the receipt of public insurance benefits and to the payment of taxes to support public insurance funds. The Court overruled the objections:

> Because the social security system is nationwide, the governmental interest is apparent. The social security system [serves] the public interest by providing a comprehensive insurance system with a variety of benefits available to all participants, with costs shared by employers and employees. [M]andatory participation is indispensable to the fiscal vitality of the social security system. [Unlike] the situation presented in *Yoder*, it would be difficult to accommodate the comprehensive social security system with myriad exceptions flowing from a wide variety of religious beliefs. . . .

In *Jimmy Swaggart Ministries v. Board of Education*,[14] the Court held that a sales and use tax that applied to the sale of all goods and services could be applied to the sale of religious literature.

---

[13] 455 U.S. 252 (1982).

[14] 493 U.S. 378 (1990).

[C]   Modern Cases

In its early cases, the United States Supreme Court seemed to balance religious interests against the governmental interests in deciding whether to grant an exemption to a law. In a number of cases (*i.e.*, *Sherbert* and *Yoder*), the Court applied strict scrutiny. Then, in 1990, the Court decided *Employment Division v. Smith*,[15] and signaled a major shift in approach.

Smith involved an Oregon law that prohibited the knowing or intentional possession of a "controlled substance" unless the substance has been prescribed by a medical practitioner. Persons who violated the law by possessing a Schedule I controlled substance were "guilty of a Class B felony." Included on the list of "controlled substances" was the drug peyote, a hallucinogen. Respondents, who ingested peyote for sacramental purposes at a ceremony of the Native American Church (both were members) were fired from their jobs with a private drug rehabilitation organization. When they applied for unemployment compensation, respondents were deemed ineligible because they had been discharged for work-related "misconduct."

In an opinion written by Justice Scalia, the Court upheld the dismissal. The Court began by distinguishing *Sherbert v. Verner*[16] and similar cases such as *Thomas v. Review Board*[17] and *Hobbie v. Unemployment Appeals Comm'n of Florida*,[18] as cases that conditioned the availability of unemployment insurance on an individual's willingness to forgo conduct required by his religion. The Court noted that none of the claimants in those cases had engaged in conduct prohibited by law.

In deciding the case, the Court marked out the parameters of the Free Exercise Clause. The Clause clearly protected certain types of things:

> [The] free exercise of religion means, first and foremost, the right to believe and profess whatever religious doctrine one desires. [But] the "exercise of religion" often involves not only belief and profession but the performance of (or abstention from) physical acts: assembling with others for a worship service, participating in sacramental use of bread and wine, proselytizing, abstaining from certain foods or certain modes of transportation. [A] State would be "prohibiting the free exercise [of religion]" if it sought to ban such acts or abstentions only when they are engaged in for religious reasons, or only because of the religious belief that they display. It would doubtless be unconstitutional, for example, to ban the casting of "statues that are to be used for worship purposes," or to prohibit bowing down before a golden calf.

But the Court concluded that respondents sought to extend the meaning of the Free Exercise Clause "one large step further": "They contend that their religious

---

[15] 494 U.S. 872 (1990).

[16] 374 U.S. 398 (1963).

[17] 450 U.S. 707 (1981).

[18] 480 U.S. 136 (1987).

motivation for using peyote places them beyond the reach of a criminal law that is not specifically directed at their religious practice, and that is concededly constitutional as applied to those who use the drug for other reasons."

Smith distinguished laws that discriminate against religion or particular religious groups from laws that are directed at religious groups not at religion — laws that are "generally applicable and otherwise valid" that have the "incidental" effect of burdening religion. While the Court held that the former type of law should be subjected to strict scrutiny, the Court held that the First Amendment is not "offended" by the latter type of law. The Court went on to explain its reluctance to invalidate neutral generally applicable laws:

> [We] have never held that an individual's religious beliefs excuse him from compliance with an otherwise valid law prohibiting conduct that the State is free to regulate. On the contrary, the record of more than a century of our free exercise jurisprudence contradicts that proposition. [In] *Reynolds v. United States*, 98 U.S. 145 (1879), [we] rejected the claim that criminal laws against polygamy could not be constitutionally applied to those whose religion commanded the practice. . . . Subsequent decisions have consistently held that the right of free exercise does not relieve an individual of the obligation to comply with a "valid and neutral law of general applicability on the ground that the law proscribes (or prescribes) conduct that his religion prescribes (or proscribes)." *United States v. Lee*, 455 U.S. 252, 263, n.3 (1982) (Stevens, J., concurring in judgment).

The Court indicated that it would strike down a law that burdens religion in only two situations. The first, previously mentioned, is when a law is targeted at, and discriminates against, religions or religious groups. The second is when the law implicates other constitutional rights, particularly free speech rights. The Court offered the example of *Wooley v. Maynard*[19] in which the Court held that a state could not compel an individual to display a license plate containing a slogan that offended his religious beliefs. But that case involved free speech and the concept that an individual could not be forced to associate with beliefs that he found repugnant (on religious grounds or otherwise). The Court also discussed *West Virginia Bd. of Education v. Barnette*[20] in which the Court struck down a state statute requiring a flag salute. Once again, the Court relied heavily on free speech principles. In *Smith*, the Court found that the Oregon law did not discriminate against religion and did not present a combination of constitutional claims.

In deciding *Smith*, the Court specifically rejected *Sherbert's* "compelling government interest" test. The Court viewed *Sherbert* as applicable only in the unemployment compensation field, and only then when a "generally applicable criminal law" is absent: "The government's ability to enforce generally applicable prohibitions of socially harmful conduct, like its ability to carry out other aspects of public policy, 'cannot depend on measuring the effects of a governmental action on a religious objector's spiritual development.'" The Court feared that, to create exemptions under such circumstances, would be to allow a religious objector "to

---

[19] 430 U.S. 705 (1977).

[20] 319 U.S. 624 (1943).

become a law unto himself." The Court felt that the "compelling government interest" standard promotes equality when speech and race are involved, but the standard produces "a private right to ignore generally applicable laws" in the free exercise area, something that the Court referred to as "a constitutional anomaly."

In *Smith*, respondents argued that, even if the "compelling state interest" is not applied to all free exercise claims, it should apply to religious conduct that is "central" to the individual's religion. The Court rejected this argument noting that it is not the court's job to determine whether or not a particular belief is "central" to an individual's religious beliefs. In the Court's view, if the "compelling interest" test is to be applied to free exercise claims, it must be applied "across the board" to "all actions thought to be religiously commanded." The Court was unwilling to do that. The Court's position was undoubtedly influenced by that the fact that the courts have had great difficulty defining the concept of religion and have shown an unwillingness to involve themselves in attempting to determine whether an individual's religious beliefs are genuinely held. Given the court's inability to define religion, and its unwillingness to determine the genuineness of beliefs, the "compelling interest" standard threatened to create exceptions to numerous criminal laws. Justice Scalia's opinion recognized this fact:

> [M]any laws will not meet the [compelling interest] test. Any society adopting such a system would be courting anarchy, but that danger increases in direct proportion to the society's diversity of religious beliefs, and its determination to coerce or suppress none of them. [The] rule respondents favor would open the prospect of constitutionally required religious exemptions from civic obligations of almost every conceivable kind — ranging from compulsory military service, to the payment of taxes, to health and safety regulation such as manslaughter and child neglect laws, compulsory vaccination laws, drug laws, and traffic laws, to social welfare legislation such as minimum wage laws, child labor laws, animal cruelty laws, environmental protection laws, and laws providing for equality of opportunity for the races. The First Amendment's protection of religious liberty does not require this.

Justice O'Connor, joined by justices Brennan, Marshall, and Blackmun, concurred in part of the judgment. She began by arguing that the Court had departed "dramatically" from "well-settled First Amendment jurisprudence" arguing that both religious "conduct" and religious "beliefs" are protected by the Free Exercise Clause. She went on to note that, in *Yoder*, the Court expressly rejected the interpretation the Court now adopts: "[A] regulation neutral on its face may, in its application, nonetheless offend the constitutional requirement for government neutrality if it unduly burdens the free exercise of religion."

After noting the Court's departure, Justice O'Connor argued that the language of the First Amendment

> does not distinguish between religious belief and religious conduct, conduct motivated by sincere religious belief, like the belief itself, must be at least presumptively protected by the Free Exercise Clause. [A] person who is barred from engaging in religiously motivated conduct is barred from freely exercising his [religion].

She also noted that the First Amendment does not distinguish between laws that target religious practices and laws that are generally applicable: "Indeed, few States would be so naive as to enact a law directly prohibiting or burdening a religious practice as such. Our free exercise cases have all concerned generally applicable laws that had the effect of significantly burdening a religious [practice]." As a result she would have required the government to satisfy the "compelling state interest" test and to show that it has used "means narrowly tailored to achieve that interest."

Despite her disagreement with the majority's approach, Justice O'Connor would have reached the same result under her analysis. Even though she found that "Oregon's criminal prohibition of peyote places a severe burden on the ability of respondents to freely exercise their religion," she found that Oregon had "a significant interest in enforcing laws that control the possession and use of controlled substances by its citizens." As a result, she would have held that Oregon had "a compelling interest in regulating peyote use by its citizens and that accommodating respondents' religiously motivated conduct 'will unduly interfere with fulfillment of the governmental interest.' "

Justice Blackmun, dissenting, joined by justices Brennan and Marshall, argued that Oregon had not shown "any concrete interest in enforcing its drug laws against religious users of peyote" noting the absence of "evidence that the religious use of peyote has ever harmed anyone." He also noted that the Native American Church placed restrictions and supervision on its members' use of peyote, that church "doctrine forbid nonreligious use of peyote; it also generally advocates self-reliance, familial responsibility, and abstinence from [alcohol]." Finally, he argued that there is "practically no illegal traffic in peyote. [Peyote] simply is not a popular drug; its distribution for use in religious rituals has nothing to do with the vast and violent traffic in illegal narcotics that plagues this country."

Justice Blackmun also challenged the majority's claim that "granting an exception for religious peyote use would erode its interest in the uniform, fair, and certain enforcement of its drug laws," and that the exemption would create a "flood of other religious claims."[21] He noted that nearly half the states, as well as the federal government, "have maintained an exemption for religious peyote use for many years, and apparently have not found themselves overwhelmed by claims to other religious exemptions." So, he distinguished the Native American Church's limited use of peyote from the Ethiopian Zion Coptic Church's policy of smoking marijuana "continually all day."[22] He also distinguished peyote from marijuana and heroin, "in which there is significant illegal traffic, with its attendant greed and violence, so that it would be difficult to grant a religious exemption without seriously compromising law enforcement efforts."[23] As a result, he would have held that "the State might grant an exemption for religious peyote use, but deny other religious claims arising in different circumstances, [without violating] the Establishment Clause."

---

[21] *Id.* at 917.

[22] *Id.* at 918.

[23] *Id.*

The Ministerial Exception. *Smith* was qualified in *Hosanna-Tabor Evangelical Lutheran Church and School v. Equal Employment Opportunity Commission,*[24] in which the Court held that the First Amendment religion clauses exempts a church from employment discrimination laws for the termination of an employee who performs ministerial functions. The case involved a "called teacher" in a school that employed both "called" and "lay" teachers. "Called" teachers were regarded as called to their vocation by God through a congregation. They were required to satisfy academic requirements involving theological study, be endorsed by their local Synod, and pass an oral examination. "Called" teachers received the formal title of "Minister of Religion, Commissioned." "Lay" or "contract" teachers need not be trained or even Lutheran. They were appointed by the school board to one-year renewable terms. Although teachers at the school generally performed the same duties regardless of whether they were lay or called, lay teachers were hired only when called teachers were unavailable.

The case arose when a called teacher at the school became sick and went on sick leave. When she believed that she was ready to return to her work, but the school did not, she protested. The church responded by revoking her "call" and dismissing her. The teacher sued, claiming a violation of the Americans with Disabilities Act, and she sought reinstatement, backpay, compensatory and punitive damages, attorney's fees, and other injunctive relief. The Court concluded that the church's action was protected by the First Amendment's "ministerial exception." The Court began by tracing the history of governmental attempts to control church appointments and church decisions. The Court concluded that the exception is premised on both the Establishment Clause and the Free Exercise Clause: "The Establishment Clause prevents the Government from appointing ministers, and the Free Exercise Clause prevents it from interfering with the freedom of religious groups to select their own." The Court emphasized that "members of a religious group put their faith in the hands of their ministers," and that the government cannot force them "to accept or retain an unwanted minister," or punish a church for failing to do so. "Such action interferes with the internal governance of the church, depriving the church of control over the selection of those who will personify its beliefs." The Court distinguished *Employment Div., Dept. of Human Resources of Ore. v. Smith*[25] on the basis that "a church's selection of its ministers is unlike an individual's ingestion of peyote. *Smith* involved government regulation of only outward physical acts. The present case, in contrast, concerns government interference with an internal church decision that affects the faith and mission of the church itself. The contention that *Smith* forecloses recognition of a ministerial exception rooted in the Religion Clauses has no merit."

The EEOC and Perich foresaw a parade of horribles that would follow the Court's recognition of a ministerial exception to employment discrimination suits. According to the EEOC and Perich, such an exception would protect religious organizations from liability for retaliating against employees for reporting criminal misconduct or for testifying before a grand jury or in a criminal trial. They also claimed that the exception would give religious employers "unfettered discretion" to

---

[24] 132 S.Ct. 694 (2012).

[25] 494 U.S. 872 (1990).

violate employment laws by, for example, hiring children or aliens. The Court found these arguments unpersuasive, noting that the "ministerial exception has been around in the lower courts for 40 years, and has not given rise to the dire consequences predicted by the EEOC and Perich." The Court declined to hold that the exception would protect religious organization from liability against liability for retaliating against employees for reporting criminal misconduct or for testifying before a grand jury or in a criminal trial, and also declined to decide whether the exception would exempt churches from other employment laws. Noting that the exception has existed for more than four decades, and has not given rise to such claims, the Court decided to postpone consideration of those issues until they arise in an actual case.

In the aftermath of *Smith*, Congress passed the Religious Freedom Restoration Act (RFRA),[26] in an effort to expand the scope of religious exemption. In passing RFRA, Congress declared that the Framers of the Constitution viewed the free exercise of religion as an "unalienable right," as evidenced by the protections set forth in the First Amendment. Congress viewed the holding in *Smith* as having "virtually eliminated the requirement that the government justify burdens on religious exercise imposed by laws neutral toward religion," and Congress declared that the "compelling interest test" sets forth a more "workable test for striking sensible balances between religious liberty and competing prior governmental interests." RFRA provided that the government could not "substantially burden a person's exercise of religion even if the burden results from a rule of general applicability," unless it demonstrates that the burden to the person —

(1)   is in furtherance of a compelling governmental interest; and

(2)   is the least restrictive means of furthering that compelling governmental interest.

RFRA further provided that its provisions should not be construed as affecting the court's interpretation of the Establishment Clause. In *City of Boerne v. Flores*,[27] the Court struck down RFRA concluding that: "Broad as the power of Congress is under the Enforcement Clause of the Fourteenth Amendment, RFRA contradicts vital principles necessary to maintain separation of powers and the federal balance."

In *Gonzales v. O Centro Espirita Beneficente Uniao Do Vegetal*,[28] in a unanimous decision authored by Chief Justice Roberts, the Court used RFRA to strike down a federal ban on the use of sacramental tea. O Centro Espirita Beneficente Uniã do Vegetal (UDV) was a Christian Spiritist sect based in Brazil, with an American branch of approximately 130 individuals. Central to the UDV's faith is the receipt of communion through *hoasca* (pronounced "wass-ca"), a sacramental tea made from two plants unique to the Amazon region. One of the plants, *psychotria viridis*, contains dimethyltryptamine (DMT), a hallucinogen whose effects are enhanced by alkaloids from the other plant, *banisteriopsis caapi*. DMT, as well as "any material, compound, mixture, or preparation, which contains any quantity of [DMT]," is listed in Schedule I of the Controlled Substances Act. 812(c), Schedule I(C). The difficulty

---

[26]   42 U.S.C. § 2000bb, *et seq.*

[27]   521 U.S. 507 (1997).

[28]   546 U.S. 418 (2006).

for the sect was that the Controlled Substances Act, which regulates the importation, manufacture, distribution, and use of psychotropic substances, prohibited the use of *hoasca*, making it a crime to possess it "with intent to manufacture, distribute, or dispense."

The Government conceded that the religious practice was sincere, but nonetheless sought to ban the practice. The sect sued under the Religious Freedom Restoration Act of 1993 (RFRA),[29] which prohibits the Federal Government from substantially burdening a person's exercise of religion, unless the Government "demonstrates that application of the burden to the person" represents the least restrictive means of advancing a compelling interest. 42 U.S.C. § 2000bb-1(b). In deciding whether RFRA required an exemption, the Court focused on whether the federal government had a "compelling" governmental interest in the uniform application of the CSA, as well as the government's claim that it could not make an exception to the ban on use of the hallucinogen to accommodate the sect's sincere religious practice. The Court concluded that the United States was unable to carry its burden.

The Court distinguished *Employment Division v. Smith*,[30] which held that the Free Exercise Clause of the First Amendment does not prohibit governments from burdening religious practices through generally applicable laws, by noting that Congress responded to *Smith* by enacting RFRA, which adopts a statutory rule comparable to the constitutional rule rejected in *Smith*. In doing so, the Court distinguished its prior holding in *City of Boerne v. Flores*,[31] striking down portions of RFRA as beyond Congress' legislative authority under § 5 of the 14th Amendment.

In applying the compelling government interest test, the government recognized that the Act substantially burdened the sincere exercise of religion, but argued that the burden was justified because the burden was the least restrictive means of advancing three compelling governmental interests: protecting the health and safety of UDV members, preventing the diversion of *hoasca* from the church to recreational users, and complying with the 1971 United Nations Convention on Psychotropic Substances, a treaty signed by the United States and implemented by the Act. Although both parties presented evidence regarding the health effects of *hoasca*, the trial court found that the evidence was in equilibrium.

Despite the uncertainty of the health evidence, the government argued that it's refusal to create an exemption for *hoasca* was justified by the fact that Schedule I substances have "a high potential for abuse," "no currently accepted medical use in treatment in the United States," and "a lack of accepted safety for use [under] medical supervision."[32] The Government contended that the law established a "closed" system that prohibits all use of controlled substances except as authorized by the Act itself, and that the Act "cannot function with its necessary rigor and comprehensiveness if subjected to judicial exemptions." The Government went on to

---

[29]   107 Stat. 1488, as amended, 42 U.S.C. § 2000bb *et seq.*

[30]   494 U.S. 872 (1990).

[31]   521 U.S. 507 (1997).

[32]   21 U.S.C. § 812(b)(1).

argue that "there would be no way to cabin religious exceptions once recognized," and that "the public will misread" such exceptions as signaling that *hoasca* is not harmful. As a result, the government argued that there was no need to assess the particulars of the UDV's use or weigh the impact of an exemption for that specific use, because the Act serves a compelling purpose and simply admits of no exceptions.

In rejecting the government's arguments, the Court emphasized that RFRA had adopted the compelling interest test "as set forth in *Sherbert v. Verner*,[33] and *Wisconsin v. Yoder*."[34] The *Gonzales* Court concluded that, in each of those cases, the Court had "looked beyond broadly formulated interests justifying the general applicability of government mandates and scrutinized the asserted harm of granting specific exemptions to particular religious claimants." As a result, the Court concluded that the government's reliance on the general characteristics of Schedule I substances provided an insufficient basis for making an exemption. The Court noted that federal law has contained an exception for peyote use for the last 35 years, and that Congress had extended this exemption in 1994 to every recognized Indian tribe. Moreover, the Court found that all of the government's arguments regarding *hoasca* — e.g., that it "has a high potential for abuse," "has no currently accepted medical use," and has "a lack of accepted safety for use [under] medical supervision" — applied as well to the use of peyote. Given the peyote exception, the Court was reluctant to conclude that the government had a compelling interest in prohibiting *hoasca*. The Court noted that the Government could "demonstrate a compelling interest in uniform application of a particular program by offering evidence that granting the requested religious accommodations would seriously compromise its ability to administer the program." However, the Court concluded that the government had failed to satisfy this burden.

Cutter v. Wilkinson,[35] involved Section 3 of the Religious Land Use and Institutionalized Persons Act of 2000 (RLUIPA), 42 U.S.C. § 2000cc-1(a)(1)-(2), which provided in part: "No government shall impose a substantial burden on the religious exercise of a person residing in or confined to an institution," unless the burden furthers "a compelling governmental interest," and does so by "the least restrictive means." Plaintiffs were current and former inmates of the Ohio Department of Rehabilitation and Correction who asserted that they were adherents of "nonmainstream" religions (e.g., Satanist, Wicca, and Asatru religions, and the Church of Jesus Christ Christian), and who complained that prison officials violated RLUIPA by failing to accommodate their religious exercise in various ways: "retaliating and discriminating against them for exercising their nontraditional faiths, denying them access to religious literature, denying them the same opportunities for group worship that are granted to adherents of mainstream religions, forbidding them to adhere to the dress and appearance mandates of their religions, withholding religious ceremonial items that are substantially identical to those that the adherents of mainstream religions are permitted, and failing to

---

[33] 374 U.S. 398 (1963).

[34] 406 U.S. 205 (1972).

[35] 544 U.S. 709 (2005).

provide a chaplain trained in their faith." Prison officials responded by challenging RLUIPA.

The Court rejected plaintiffs' challenges against RLUIPA. First, it rejected the argument that Congress had exceeded its commerce clause power in enacting the law. The Court distinguished RFRA on the basis that the jurisdictional scope of RLUIPA was more limited. It applied only when a "substantial burden" on religious exercise is imposed by a program or activity that receives Federal financial assistance, or "the substantial burden affects, or removal of that substantial burden would affect, commerce with foreign nations, among the several States, or with Indian tribes."

The Court also rejected the argument that RLUIPA improperly advanced religion in violation of the Establishment Clause, noting that RLUIPA involved a permissible legislative accommodation of religion "because it alleviates exceptional government-created burdens on private religious exercise." "RLUIPA thus protects institutionalized persons who are unable freely to attend to their religious needs and are therefore dependent on the government's permission and accommodation for exercise of their religion," and it makes religious accommodation subordinate to "an institution's need to maintain order and safety" in applying the "compelling governmental interest standard."

In *Sossamon v. Texas*,[36] the Court held that a state which accepts federal funds does not (by virtue of the acceptance of federal funds) consent to waive its sovereign immunity to suits for money damages under the Religious Land Use and Institutionalized Persons Act of 2000 (RLUIPA).[37]

In non-RFRA, non-RLUIPA cases the Court decided *Goldman v. Weinberger.*[38] Goldman claimed that the Free Exercise Clause allowed him to wear a yarmulke in conjunction with his military uniform, despite an Air Force regulation mandating uniform dress. The Court concluded that "the military is, by necessity, a specialized society separate from civilian society" and that "[t]he essence of military service is the subordination of the desires and interests of the individual to the needs of the service." Accordingly, the Court (5–4) upheld the prohibition: "The Air Force has drawn the line essentially between religious apparel that is visible and that which is not, and we hold [the] regulations challenged here reasonably and evenhandedly regulate dress in the interest of the military's perceived need for uniformity." Justice Brennan dissented: "It cannot be seriously contended that a serviceman in a yarmulke presents so extreme, so unusual, or so faddish an image that public confidence in his ability to perform his duties will be destroyed." Justice Blackmun also dissented: "I feel that the Air Force is justified in considering not only the costs of allowing Captain Goldman to cover his head indoors, but also the cumulative costs of accommodating constitutionally indistinguishable requests for religious exemptions. [T]he Government has failed to make any meaningful showing that either set of costs is [significant]."

---

[36]   131 S. Ct. 1651 (2011).

[37]   114 Stat. 803, 42 U.S.C. § 2000cc *et seq.*

[38]   475 U.S. 503 (1986).

O'Lone v. Shabazz[39] was decided before *Smith*, but also took a more restrictive view of the Free Exercise Clause. In that case, respondents, members of the Islamic faith who were incarcerated in New Jersey's Leesburg State Prison, sought to challenge prison policies. Under the policies, prisoners who were to be transferred from maximum security to minimum security prisons were first assigned to work gangs that labored outside the prison (to give them a transitional phase and allow them to adjust to the greater freedom available in minimum security). Because these transitional prisoners were outside the building, they were unable to attend Jumu'ah, a weekly Muslim congregational service regularly held in the main prison building and in a separate prison facility. Jumu'ah is commanded by the Koran and must be held every Friday after the sun reaches its zenith and before the Asr, or afternoon prayer. Prison officials refused to allow "gang" workers to return to the prison during the day because of security risks and administrative problems. Muslim prisoners sued seeking an accommodation, which the Court held was not required:

> '[L]awful incarceration brings about the necessary withdrawal or limi-
> tation of many privileges and rights, a retraction justified by the consider-
> ations underlying our penal system.' [E]valuation of penological objectives
> is committed to the considered judgment of prison administrators. [P]rison
> officials have acted in a reasonable manner. [Prison] officials testified that
> the returns from outside work details generated congestion and delays at
> the main gate, a high risk area in any event. Return requests also placed
> pressure on guards supervising outside details, who previously were
> required to 'evaluate each reason possibly justifying a return to the
> facilities and either accept or reject that reason.' Rehabilitative concerns
> further supported the policy.

Justice Brennan, joined by three other Justices, dissented: "Jumu'ah is the central religious ceremony of Muslims. . . . Despite the plausibility of [alternatives,] officials have essentially provided mere pronouncements that such alternatives are not workable."

Although *Smith* is the most important recent decision, another significant decision is *Lyng v. Northwest Indian Cemetery Protective Association.*[40] The United States Forest Service, as part of a road building effort designed to link two California towns, decided to build a 6-mile paved segment through the Chimney Rock section of the Six Rivers National Forest. The area of the 6 mile stretch of road was "significant as an integral and indispensable part of Indian religious conceptualization and practice." Indians used specific sites for certain rituals, and "successful use of the [area] is dependent upon and facilitated by certain qualities of the physical environment, the most important of which are privacy, silence, and an undisturbed natural setting." An environmental study concluded that construct-ing a road along any of the available routes "would cause serious and irreparable damage to the sacred areas which are an integral and necessary part of the belief systems and lifeway of North-west California Indian peoples." Nevertheless, the

---

[39] 482 U.S. 342 (1987).

[40] 485 U.S. 439 (1988).

Forest Service decided to build the road "because [alternative routes] would have required the acquisition of private land, had serious soil stability problems, and would in any event have traversed areas having ritualistic value to American Indians." At about the same time, the Forest Service adopted a management plan allowing for the harvesting of significant amounts of timber in this area of the forest. The management plan provided for a one-half mile protective zone around all of the religious sites identified in the report that had been commissioned in connection with the road. Various Indians and Indian organizations challenged the proposed road and the timber-harvesting decisions on Free Exercise grounds.

In an opinion written by Justice O'Connor, the Court held that an accommodation was not required. The opinion recognized that respondents' beliefs were "sincere" and that the Government's proposed actions would have severe adverse effects on the practice of their religion. Nevertheless, the Court held that the " Free Exercise Clause simply cannot be understood to require the Government to conduct its own internal affairs in ways that comport with the religious beliefs of particular citizens." "[The] Free Exercise Clause affords an individual protection from certain forms of governmental compulsion; it does not afford an individual a right to dictate the conduct of the Government's internal procedures."

In *Lyng*, the Court was asked to distinguish the facts before it from prior cases on the basis that the infringement of religious liberty was "significantly greater," or on the basis of the "centrality" or "indispensability" of the religious practice. The Court refused to make such distinctions, or to involve itself in determinations regarding the genuineness or religious beliefs or the "centrality" or "indispensability" of those beliefs. "Without the ability to make such comparisons, we cannot say that the one form of incidental interference with an individual's spiritual activities should be subjected to a different constitutional analysis than the other."

Justice Brennan, joined by justices Marshall and Blackmun, dissented: "[R]espondents have demonstrated that the Government's proposed activities will completely prevent them from practicing their religion, and such a showing [entitles] them to the protections of the Free Exercise Clause." He went on to argue that the respondents should be required to make a showing of "centrality." If so, the Government should be required to show a "compelling" justification for its proposed action. "[T]he Court's concern that the claims of Native Americans will place "religious servitudes" upon vast tracts of federal property cannot justify its refusal to recognize the constitutional injury respondents will suffer here."

§ 12.02 DISCRIMINATION AGAINST RELIGION

Laws that explicitly discriminate against religion have always received heightened scrutiny. In *McDaniel v. Paty*,[41] the Court struck down a statute that prohibited ministers or members of religious orders from being members of state legislatures. However, overt governmental discrimination against religion is relatively rare. In *Fowler v. Rhode Island*,[42] the Court held that a municipal ordinance

---

[41] 435 U.S. 618 (1978).

[42] 345 U.S. 67 (1953).

was applied in an unconstitutional manner when interpreted to prohibit preaching in a public park by a Jehovah's Witness, but to permit preaching during the course of a Catholic mass or Protestant church service.

Smith reaffirmed the anti-discrimination principle, as did the Court's subsequent decision in *Church of the Lukumi Babalu Aye, Inc. v. City of Hialeah.*[43] That case involved the Santeria religion which originated in the 19th century when thousands of members of the Yoruba people were brought as slaves from western Africa to Cuba. The religion was unique because it integrated elements of Roman Catholicism into traditional African religion. The result was Santeria, "the way of the saints," a religion that expressed its devotion to spirits ("orishas") through the iconography of Catholic saints. The religion incorporates Catholic symbols and sacraments, but the Santeria believe that every individual has a destiny from God. The spirits ("orishas") help people fulfill their destinies. Although the orishas are regarded as "powerful," they are not "immortal" and exist on animal sacrifices. Santeria sacrifice involves chickens, pigeons, doves, ducks, guinea pigs, goats, sheep and turtles at birth, marriage, and death rituals, as well as to cure the sick and at various initiation and annual celebration rituals. Sacrifice is conducted by cutting the carotid artery in the neck. Sacrificed animals are then cooked and eaten (except in conjunction with healing and death rituals).

Historically, Santerians were persecuted and practiced their religion in secret. Following the Cuban revolution, some Santerians moved to Florida, and Church of the Lukumi Babalu Aye, Inc. (Church) announced its intention to establish a worship house, a school, a cultural center, and a museum in Hialeah, Florida, in 1987. At the time, the church announced that it would bring the Santeria faith, including its animal sacrifice ritual, into the open. Some residents of Hialeah were distressed and the city council responded with an emergency public session. At this time, the council adopted Resolution 87-66, which explicitly stated that city residents were concerned "that certain religions may propose to engage in practices which are inconsistent with public morals, peace or safety," and declared that "[t]he City reiterates its commitment to a prohibition against any and all acts of any and all religious groups which are inconsistent with public morals, peace or safety." The council then passed Ordinance 87-40, which incorporated in full, except as to penalty, Florida's animal cruelty laws. Among other things, the incorporated state law subjected to criminal punishment "[whoever] unnecessarily or cruelly [kills] any animal." After requesting advice from the attorney general of Florida, who concluded that animal sacrifice was against state law, the city council passed Resolution 87-90 which noted city residents' "great concern regarding the possibility of public ritualistic animal sacrifices." The resolution declared the city policy "to oppose the ritual sacrifices of animals" within Hialeah and announced that any person or organization practicing animal sacrifice "will be prosecuted."

In September 1987, the city council passed three more ordinances. Ordinance 87-52 defined "sacrifice" as including a situation when an individual takes action "to unnecessarily kill, torment, torture, or mutilate an animal in a public or private ritual or ceremony not for the primary purpose of food consumption." However, the ordinance also provided that the prohibition applied only to an individual or group

---

[43] 508 U.S. 520 (1993).

that "kills, slaughters or sacrifices animals for any type of ritual, regardless of whether or not the flesh or blood of the animal is to be consumed." The ordinance contained an exemption for slaughtering by "licensed establishment[s]" of animals "specifically raised for food purposes." The city council declared "that the sacrificing of animals within the city limits is contrary to the public health, safety, welfare and morals of the community," and adopted Ordinance 87-71 which provided that "[i]t shall be unlawful for any person, persons, corporations or associations to sacrifice any animal within the corporate limits of the City of Hialeah, Florida." The final Ordinance, 87-72, defined "sl aughter" as "the killing of animals for food" and prohibited slaughter outside of areas zoned for slaughterhouse use. The ordinance provided an exemption for the slaughter or processing for sale of "small numbers of hogs and/or cattle per week in accordance with an exemption provided by state law." Violations of each of the four ordinances were punishable by fines not exceeding $500 or imprisonment not exceeding 60 days, or both. The Church sought to challenge all of the ordinances as a violation of the Free Exercise Clause.

In an opinion by Justice Kennedy, the Court struck down the Hialeah ordinances. The Court recognized that animal sacrifice can constitute a religious practice, and the Court reaffirmed its holding in *Smith* to the effect that the Court will not apply strict scrutiny to a law that is "neutral and of general applicability" even if that law incidentally burdens a particular religious practice. But the Court distinguished *Smith* noting that the First Amendment "forbids an official purpose to disapprove of a particular religion or of religion in general," and noted that the Free Exercise Clause was included because of "historical instances of religious persecution and intolerance." The Court held that a law that discriminates on the basis of religion should be subject to strict scrutiny:

> Although a law targeting religious beliefs as such is never permissible, if the object of a law is to infringe upon or restrict practices because of their religious motivation, the law is not neutral, and it is invalid unless it is justified by a compelling interest and is narrowly tailored to advance that interest.

How do courts decide whether a given law discriminates against religion? The *Church of the Lukumi* Court offered the lower courts some guiding principles. The examination should begin with the text of the law: "A law lacks facial neutrality if it refers to a religious practice without a secular meaning discernable from the language or context." But facial neutrality is not enough, by itself, save a law: "Official action that targets religious conduct for distinctive treatment cannot be shielded by mere compliance with the requirement of facial neutrality." The Court emphasized that it was entitled to consider, not only the wording and function of the ordinances, but also their background.

In applying this test, the Court found that the Hialeah ordinances were facially neutral even though they used the terms "sacrifice" and "ritual" and even though the Court admitted that both words had "strong religious connotations." The Court found that both words also have secular meanings and that the ordinances defined the words in secular terms without reference to religious practices. But, as the Court moved beyond the wording of the ordinances, it quickly found that the city had purposefully discriminated. The Court noted that citizen objections to Santeria practices had led to enactment of the ordinances:

> [S]uppression of the central element of the Santeria worship service was the object of the ordinances. First, though use of the words "sacrifice" and "ritual" does not compel a finding of improper targeting of the Santeria religion, the choice of these words is support for our conclusion. There are further respects in which the text of the city council's enactments discloses the improper attempt to target Santeria. Resolution 87-66, adopted June 9, 1987, recited that "residents and citizens of the City of Hialeah [expressed] their concern that certain religions may propose to engage in practices which are inconsistent with public morals, peace or safety," and "reiterate[d]" the city's commitment to prohibit "any and all [such] acts of any and all religious groups." No one suggests [that]city officials had in mind a religion other than Santeria.

> It becomes evident that these ordinances target Santeria sacrifice when the ordinances' operation is considered. Apart from the text, the effect of a law in its real operation is strong evidence of its object. . . . The subject at hand does implicate, of course, multiple concerns unrelated to religious animosity, for example, the suffering or mistreatment visited upon the sacrificed animals and health hazards from improper disposal. But the ordinances when considered together disclose an object remote from these legitimate concerns. The design of these laws accomplishes instead a "religious gerrymander," an impermissible attempt to target petitioners and their religious practices.

> It is a necessary conclusion that almost the only conduct subject to Ordinances 87-40, 87-52, and 87-71 is the religious exercise of Santeria church members. [Ordinance 87-71] prohibits the sacrifice of animals, but defines sacrifice as "to unnecessarily kill [an] animal in a public or private ritual or ceremony not for the primary purpose of food consumption." The definition excludes almost all killings of animals except for religious sacrifice, and the primary purpose requirement narrows the proscribed category even further, in particular by exempting kosher slaughter. . . . The net result [is] that few if any killings of animals are prohibited other than Santeria sacrifice, which is proscribed because it occurs during a ritual or ceremony and its primary purpose is to make an offering to the orishas, not food consumption. Indeed, careful drafting ensured that, although Santeria sacrifice is prohibited, killings that are no more necessary or humane in almost all other circumstances are unpunished.

> Operating in similar fashion is Ordinance 87-52, which prohibits the "possess [ion], sacrifice, or slaughter" of an animal with the "inten[t] to use such animal for food purposes." This prohibition, extending to the keeping of an animal as well as the killing itself, applies if the animal is killed in "any type of ritual" and there is an intent to use the animal for food, whether or not it is in fact consumed for food. The ordinance exempts, however, "any licensed [food] establishment" with regard to "any animals which are specifically raised for food purposes," if the activity is permitted by zoning and other laws. This exception, too, seems intended to cover kosher

slaughter. Again, the burden of the ordinance, in practical terms, falls on Santeria adherents but almost no others: If the killing is — unlike most Santeria sacrifices — unaccompanied by the intent to use the animal for food, then it is not prohibited by Ordinance 87-52; if the killing is specifically for food but does not occur during the course of "any type of ritual," it again falls outside the prohibition; and if the killing is for food and occurs during the course of a ritual, it is still exempted if it occurs in a properly zoned and licensed establishment and involves animals "specifically raised for food purposes." A pattern of exemptions parallels the pattern of narrow prohibitions. Each contributes to the gerrymander.

Ordinance 87-40 incorporates the Florida animal cruelty statute. Its prohibition is broad on its face, punishing "[w]hoever [unnecessarily] kills any animal." The city claims that this ordinance is the epitome of a neutral prohibition. The problem, however, is the interpretation given to the ordinance by respondent and the Florida attorney general. Killings for religious reasons are deemed unnecessary, whereas most other killings fall outside the prohibition. The city, on what seems to be a per se basis, deems hunting, slaughter of animals for food, eradication of insects and pests, and euthanasia as necessary. There is no indication in the record that respondent has concluded that hunting or fishing for sport is unnecessary. Indeed, one of the few reported Florida cases decided under § 828.12 concludes that the use of live rabbits to train greyhounds is not unnecessary. Further, because it requires an evaluation of the particular justification for the killing, this ordinance represents a system of "individualized governmental assessment of the reasons for the relevant conduct." [I]n circumstances in which individualized exemptions from a general requirement are available, the government "may not refuse to extend that system to cases of 'religious hardship' without compelling reason." Respondent's application of the ordinance's test of necessity devalues religious reasons for killing by judging them to be of lesser import than nonreligious reasons. Thus, religious practice is being singled out for discriminatory treatment.

We also find significant evidence of the ordinances' improper targeting of Santeria sacrifice in the fact that they proscribe more religious conduct than is necessary to achieve their stated ends. It is not unreasonable to infer, at least when there are no persuasive indications to the contrary, that a law which visits "gratuitous restrictions" on religious conduct, seeks not to effectuate the stated governmental interests, but to suppress the conduct because of its religious motivation.

Of course, the mere fact that a law discriminates against religion does not require invalidation, but does require application of strict scrutiny. In order to withstand scrutiny, the law must be supported by a "compelling interest," and proof that reasonable alternatives are unavailable. In *Church of the Lukumi*, the Court found that the "legitimate governmental interests in protecting the public health and preventing cruelty to animals could be addressed by restrictions stopping far short of a flat prohibition of all Santeria sacrificial practice." For example, if the city was concerned about the proper disposal of carcasses, "the city could have imposed a general regulation on the disposal of organic garbage." The Court also found that a "narrower regulation could achieve the city's interest in preventing cruelty to animals." The regulation would not prevent the sacrifice, but would ensure that animals were killed humanely by the simultaneous and instantaneous severance of the carotid arteries.

Although the Court found that Ordinance 87-72 did not apply to non-religious conduct and was not overbroad, the Court struck that Ordinance down because of its linkage with Ordinance 87-72. Not only did the Court find that the city intended to discriminate against religion, the Court held that the ordinances were not "of general applicability." The Court reached this result after analyzing how the ordinances' functioned:

> Respondent claims that Ordinances 87-40, 87-52, and 87-71 advance two interests: protecting the public health and preventing cruelty to animals. The ordinances are underinclusive for those ends. They fail to prohibit nonreligious conduct that endangers these interests in a similar or greater degree than Santeria sacrifice does. The underinclusion is substantial, not inconsequential. Despite the city's proffered interest in preventing cruelty to animals, the ordinances . . . forbid few killings but those occasioned by religious sacrifice. Many types of animal deaths or kills for nonreligious reasons are either not prohibited or approved by express provision. For example, fishing [is] legal. Extermination of mice and rats within a home is also permitted. Florida law incorporated by Ordinance 87-40 sanctions euthanasia of "stray, neglected, abandoned, or unwanted animals"; destruction of animals judicially removed from their owners "for humanitarian reasons" or when the animal "is of no commercial value"; the infliction of pain or suffering "in the interest of medical science"; the placing of poison in one's yard or enclosure; and the use of a live animal "to pursue or take wildlife or to participate in any hunting," and "to hunt wild hogs."

> The city [asserts] that animal sacrifice is "different" from the animal killings that are permitted by law. According to the city, it is "self-evident" that killing animals for food is "important"; the eradication of insects and pests is "obviously justified"; and the euthanasia of excess animals "makes sense." These ipse dixits do not explain why religion alone must bear the burden of the ordinances, when many of these secular killings fall within the city's interest in preventing the cruel treatment of animals.

> The ordinances are also underinclusive with regard to the city's interest in public health, which is threatened by the disposal of animal carcasses in open public places and the consumption of uninspected meat. Neither interest is pursued [with] regard to conduct that is not motivated by religious conviction. [The] city does [not] prohibit hunters from bringing their kill to their houses, nor does it regulate disposal after their activity. Despite [testimony] that the same public health hazards result from improper disposal of garbage by restaurants, restaurants are outside the scope of the ordinances. [the] ordinances are underinclusive as well with regard to the health risk posed by consumption of uninspected meat. Under the city's ordinances, hunters may eat their kill and fishermen may eat their catch without undergoing governmental inspection. Likewise, state law

requires inspection of meat that is sold but exempts meat from animals raised for the use of the owner and "members of his household and nonpaying guests and employees." The asserted interest in inspected meat is not pursued in contexts similar to that of religious animal sacrifice.

Because of this analysis, the Court found that "each of Hialeah's ordinances pursues the city's governmental interests only against conduct motivated by religious belief," and therefore the ordinances " 'ha[ve] every appearance of a prohibition that society is prepared to impose upon [Santeria worshippers] but not upon itself.' This precise evil is what the requirement of general applicability is designed to prevent."

The Court ended with a flourish regarding the meaning of the Free Exercise Clause:

> The Free Exercise Clause commits government itself to religious tolerance, and upon even slight suspicion that proposals for state intervention stem from animosity to religion or distrust of its practices, all officials must pause to remember their own high duty to the Constitution and to the rights it secures. Those in office must be resolute in resisting importunate demands and must ensure that the sole reasons for imposing the burdens of law and regulation are secular. Legislators may not devise mechanisms, overt or disguised, designed to persecute or oppress a religion or its practices. The laws here in question were enacted contrary to these constitutional principles, and they are void.

POINTS TO REMEMBER

- Many of the early American settlers to this land came to escape religious persecution in Europe.

- Most free exercise cases involve governmental prohibitions on religiously mandated conduct, or that require conduct prohibited by religious beliefs.

- Early precedent protected the right to "believe" but did not protect religious conduct.

- For several decades, the Court applied strict scrutiny to laws that burden religion.

- Modern case law holds that laws that are "neutral" and "generally applicable" should be subjected to a lower standard of review.

- The Court will strike down neutral and generally applicable laws that infringe free speech interests.

- The Court will also strike down laws that discriminate against religion.

TABLE OF CASES

[References are to pages.]

[References are to pages.]

[References are to pages.]

[References are to pages.]

[References are to pages.]

[References are to pages.]

INDEX

[References are to sections.]

I-1

[References are to sections.]

[References are to sections.]

H

HATE SPEECH (See BOUNDARIES OF DOCTRINE, subhead: Hate speech)

I

ILLEGAL OR VIOLENT ACTION, ADVOCACY OF (See VIOLENT OR ILLEGAL ACTION, ADVOCACY OF)

INJUNCTIONS (See PRIOR RESTRAINTS, subhead: Injunctions)

INTERNET (See MEDIA AND FIRST AMENDMENT, subhead: Internet)

J

JUDICIAL PROCEEDINGS, ACCESS TO
Generally . . . 10.02[D]

L

LEGAL SERVICES CORPORATION FUNDING
Government financed speech . . . 9.03[C]

***LEMON* TEST**
Generally . . . 11.01[B]
Applications, other . . . 11.01[C]
Lemon's three-part test, criticism of . . . 11.01[D]

LICENSE (See PRIOR RESTRAINTS, subhead: Licensing)

M

MEDIA AND FIRST AMENDMENT
Blogs . . . 10.03[E][1]
Broadcasting
   Generally . . . 10.03[B]
   Fairness regulation . . . 10.03[B][1]
   Indecent programming, regulation of
     . . . 10.03[B][2]
Cable television
   Generally . . . 10.03[C]
   Indecent programming, regulation of
     . . . 10.03[C][2]
   Must carriage . . . 10.03[C][1]
Email . . . 10.03[E][1]
Fairness regulation . . . 10.03[B][1]
Indecent programming, regulation of
   Broadcasting . . . 10.03[B][2]
   Cable television . . . 10.03[C][2]
   Internet . . . 10.03[E][2]
   Telephony . . . 10.03[D][2]
Internet
   Blogs . . . 10.03[E][1]
   Email . . . 10.03[E][1]
   Indecency regulation . . . 10.03[E][2]
   Social media . . . 10.03[E][1]
Must carriage . . . 10.03[C][1]

MEDIA AND FIRST AMENDMENT—Cont.
Newsgathering function
   Access to judicial proceedings . . . 10.02[D]
   Access to prisons . . . 10.02[C]
   Electronic media in courtroom . . . 10.02[F]
   Judicial proceedings, access to . . . 10.02[D]
   Newsroom searches . . . 10.02[B]
   Prejudicial publicity, problem of . . . 10.02[E]
   Prisons, access to . . . 10.02[C]
   Reporter's privilege . . . 10.02[A]
Press clause, significance of . . . 10.01
Print . . . 10.03[A]
Social media
   Generally . . . 10.03[G]
   Internet . . . 10.03[E][1]
Technology
   Generally . . . 10.03
   Broadcasting (See subhead: Broadcasting)
   Cable (See subhead: Cable television)
   Internet (See subhead: Internet)
   Print . . . 10.03[A]
   Social media . . . 10.03[G]
   Telephony
     Common carrier status . . . 10.03[D][1]
     Indecency regulation . . . 10.03[D][2]
   Video games . . . 10.03[F]
Telephony
   Common carrier status . . . 10.03[D][1]
   Indecency regulation . . . 10.03[D][2]
Video games . . . 10.03[F]

N

NATIONAL ENDOWMENT FOR THE ARTS (NEA)
Government financed speech . . . 9.03[B]

NATIONAL SECURITY
Prior restraints and . . . 5.02[B][2]

NEA (See NATIONAL ENDOWMENT FOR THE ARTS (NEA))

O

OBSCENITY (See CONTENT REGULATION, subhead: Obscenity)

OFFENSIVE SPEECH
Generally . . . 4.01

OFFICIAL ACKNOWLEDGMENT
Generally . . . 11.05
Church vetoes . . . 11.05[B]
Day of rest . . . 11.05[E]
Holiday displays . . . 11.05[C]
Swearing belief in God . . . 11.05[D]
Ten Commandments . . . 11.05[A]

OVERBREADTH
Generally . . . 5.01; 5.01[A]

[References are to sections.]

P

R

S

[References are to sections.]